DISNEY MASTERS

MICKEY MOUSE:
THE PIRATES OF TABASCO BAY

by Paul Murry and Carl Fallberg

Publisher: GARY GROTH
Senior Editor: J. MICHAEL CATRON
Archival Editor: DAVID GERSTEIN
Designer: KEELI McCARTHY
Production: PAUL BARESH
Associate Publisher: ERIC REYNOLDS

Fantagraphics Books, Inc. • 7563 Lake City Way NE • Seattle WA 98115 • (800) 657-1100

Visit us at fantagraphics.com. Follow us on Twitter at @fantagraphics
and on Facebook at facebook.com/fantagraphics.

Thanks to Thomas Jensen, Ken Shue, and Anne-Marie Mersing.

First printing: June 2019
ISBN 978-1-68396-181-9
Printed in Korea
Library of Congress Control Number: 2017956971

The stories in this volume were originally published in English in the United States.
"The Lost City" in *Walt Disney's Comics and Stories* #176-178, May–July 1955 (W WDC 176-10P)
"Yesterday Ranch" in *Walt Disney's Comics and Stories* #179-181, August–October 1955 (W WDC 179-10P)
"Mickey Mouse and the Marvelous Magnet" in *Walt Disney's Comics and Stories* #182-184,
November 1955–January 1956 (W WDC 182-11P)
"The Vanishing Railroad" in *Walt Disney's Comics and Stories* #185-187, February–April 1956 (W WDC 185-08P)
"The Case of the Hungry Ghost" in *Walt Disney's Comics and Stories* #188-190, May–July 1956 (W WDC 188-09P)
"The Pirates of Tabasco Bay" in *Walt Disney's Comics and Stories* #191-193, August–October 1955 (W WDC 191-11P)
"The Great Stamp Hunt" in *Walt Disney's Comics and Stories* #194-196, November 1956–January 1957 (W WDC 194-09P)

These stories were created during an earlier time and may include cartoon violence,
historically dated content, or gags that depict smoking, drinking, gunplay, or ethnic stereotypes.
We present them here with their original flaws with a caution to the reader that they reflect a bygone era.

TITLES IN THIS SERIES

Mickey Mouse: The Delta Dimension (Romano Scarpa) (*Disney Masters* Vol. 1)
Donald Duck: Uncle Scrooge's Money Rocket (Luciano Bottaro) (*Disney Masters* Vol. 2)
Mickey Mouse: The Case of the Vanishing Bandit (Paul Murry) (*Disney Masters* Vol. 3)
Donald Duck: The Great Survival Test (Daan Jippes and Freddy Milton) (*Disney Masters* Vol. 4)
Mickey Mouse: The Phantom Blot's Double Mystery (Romano Scarpa) (*Disney Masters* Vol. 5)
Uncle Scrooge: King of The Golden River (Giovan Battista Carpi) (*Disney Masters* Vol. 6)
Mickey Mouse: The Pirates of Tabasco Bay (Paul Murry) (*Disney Masters* Vol. 7)

COMING SOON

Donald Duck: Duck Avenger Strikes Again (Romano Scarpa and Carl Barks) (*Disney Masters* Vol. 8)

ALSO AVAILABLE

Mickey Mouse: The Greatest Adventures (Floyd Gottfredson)
Walt Disney's Uncle Scrooge: "The Mines of King Solomon" (Carl Barks)
The Complete Life and Times of Scrooge McDuck Volume 1 (Don Rosa)

Walt Disney

Mickey Mouse

The Pirates of Tabasco Bay

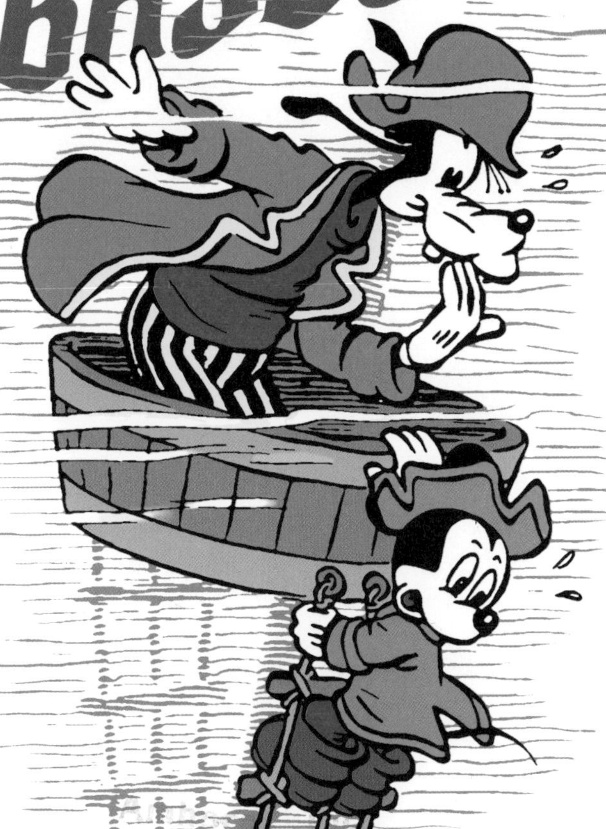

FANTAGRAPHICS BOOKS

SEATTLE

CONTENTS

All comics stories written by Carl Fallberg and illustrated by Paul Murry

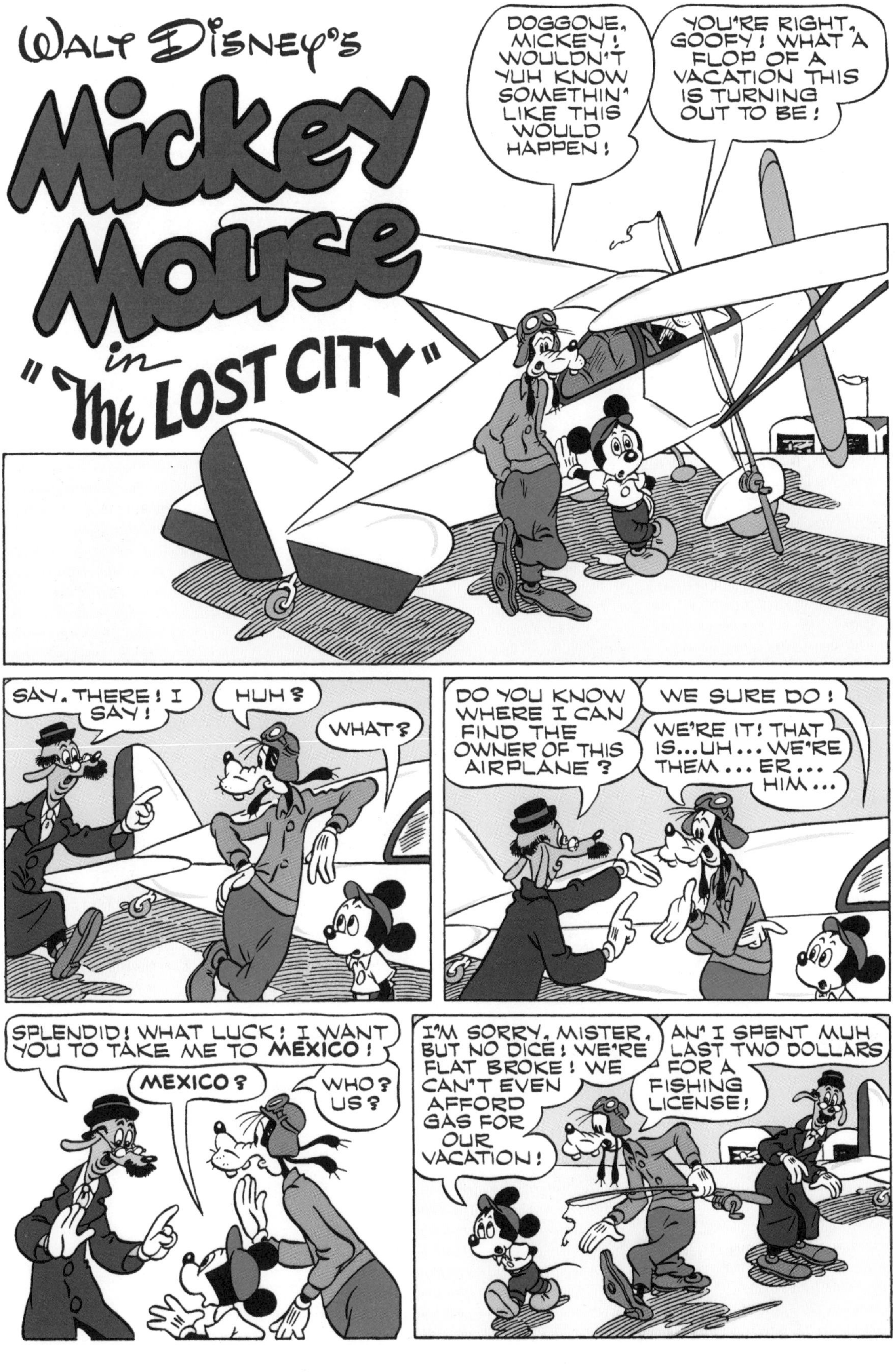
WALT DISNEY'S
Mickey Mouse
in
"The LOST CITY"
DOGGONE, MICKEY! WOULDN'T YUH KNOW SOMETHIN' LIKE THIS WOULD HAPPEN!
YOU'RE RIGHT, GOOFY! WHAT A FLOP OF A VACATION THIS IS TURNING OUT TO BE!
SAY. THERE! I SAY!
HUH?
WHAT?
DO YOU KNOW WHERE I CAN FIND THE OWNER OF THIS AIRPLANE?
WE SURE DO!
WE'RE IT! THAT IS...UH... WE'RE THEM ... ER ... HIM ...
SPLENDID! WHAT LUCK! I WANT YOU TO TAKE ME TO MEXICO!
MEXICO?
WHO? US?
I'M SORRY, MISTER, BUT NO DICE! WE'RE FLAT BROKE! WE CAN'T EVEN AFFORD GAS FOR OUR VACATION!
AN' I SPENT MUH LAST TWO DOLLARS FOR A FISHING LICENSE!

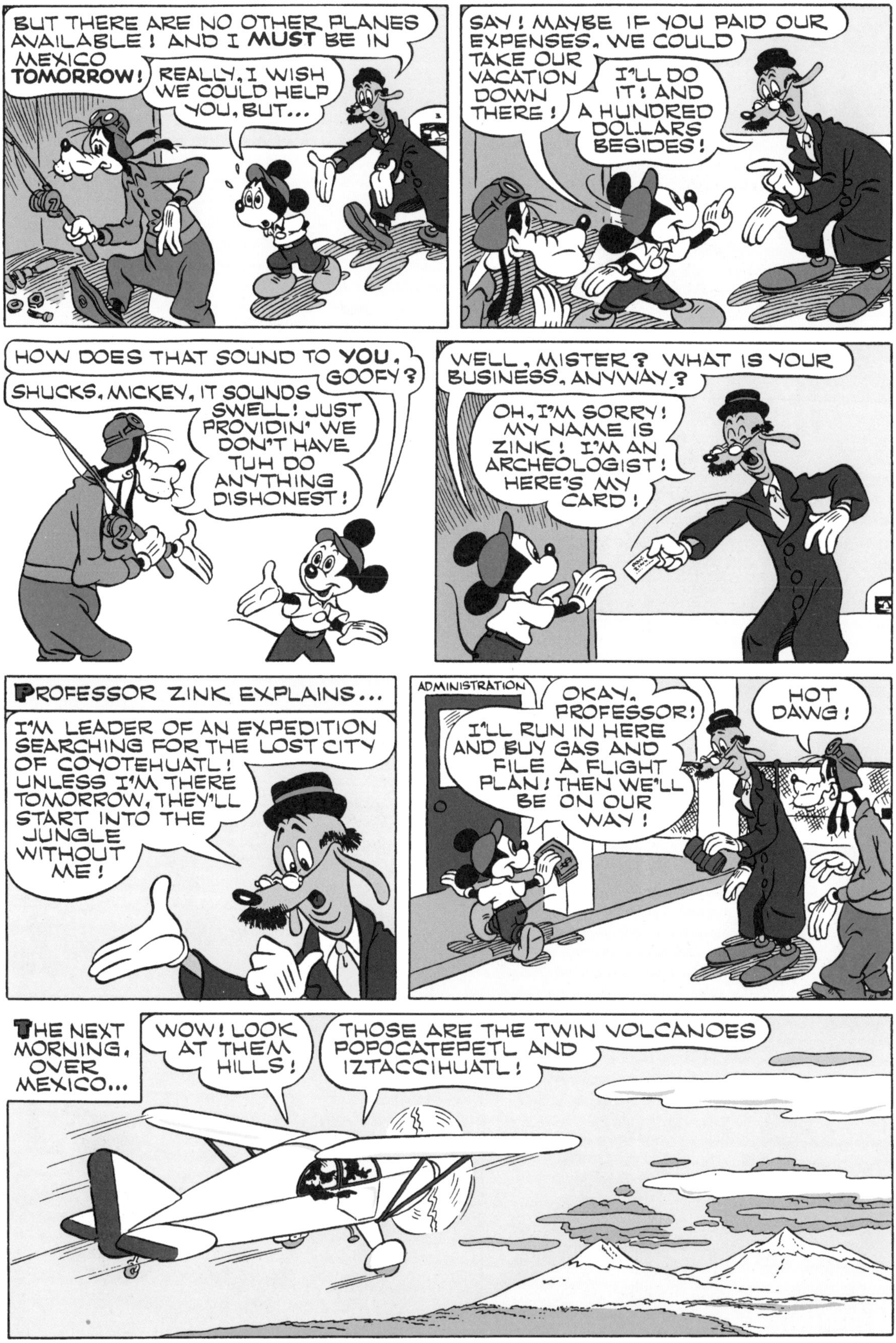
BUT THERE ARE NO OTHER PLANES AVAILABLE! AND I MUST BE IN MEXICO TOMORROW!
REALLY, I WISH WE COULD HELP YOU, BUT...
SAY! MAYBE IF YOU PAID OUR EXPENSES, WE COULD TAKE OUR VACATION DOWN THERE!
I'LL DO IT! AND A HUNDRED DOLLARS BESIDES!
HOW DOES THAT SOUND TO YOU, GOOFY?
SHUCKS, MICKEY, IT SOUNDS SWELL! JUST PROVIDIN' WE DON'T HAVE TUH DO ANYTHING DISHONEST!
WELL, MISTER? WHAT IS YOUR BUSINESS, ANYWAY?
OH, I'M SORRY! MY NAME IS ZINK! I'M AN ARCHEOLOGIST! HERE'S MY CARD!
PROFESSOR ZINK EXPLAINS...
I'M LEADER OF AN EXPEDITION SEARCHING FOR THE LOST CITY OF COYOTEHUATL! UNLESS I'M THERE TOMORROW, THEY'LL START INTO THE JUNGLE WITHOUT ME!
ADMINISTRATION
OKAY, PROFESSOR! I'LL RUN IN HERE AND BUY GAS AND FILE A FLIGHT PLAN! THEN WE'LL BE ON OUR WAY!
HOT DAWG!
THE NEXT MORNING, OVER MEXICO...
WOW! LOOK AT THEM HILLS!
THOSE ARE THE TWIN VOLCANOES POPOCATEPETL AND IZTACCIHUATL!

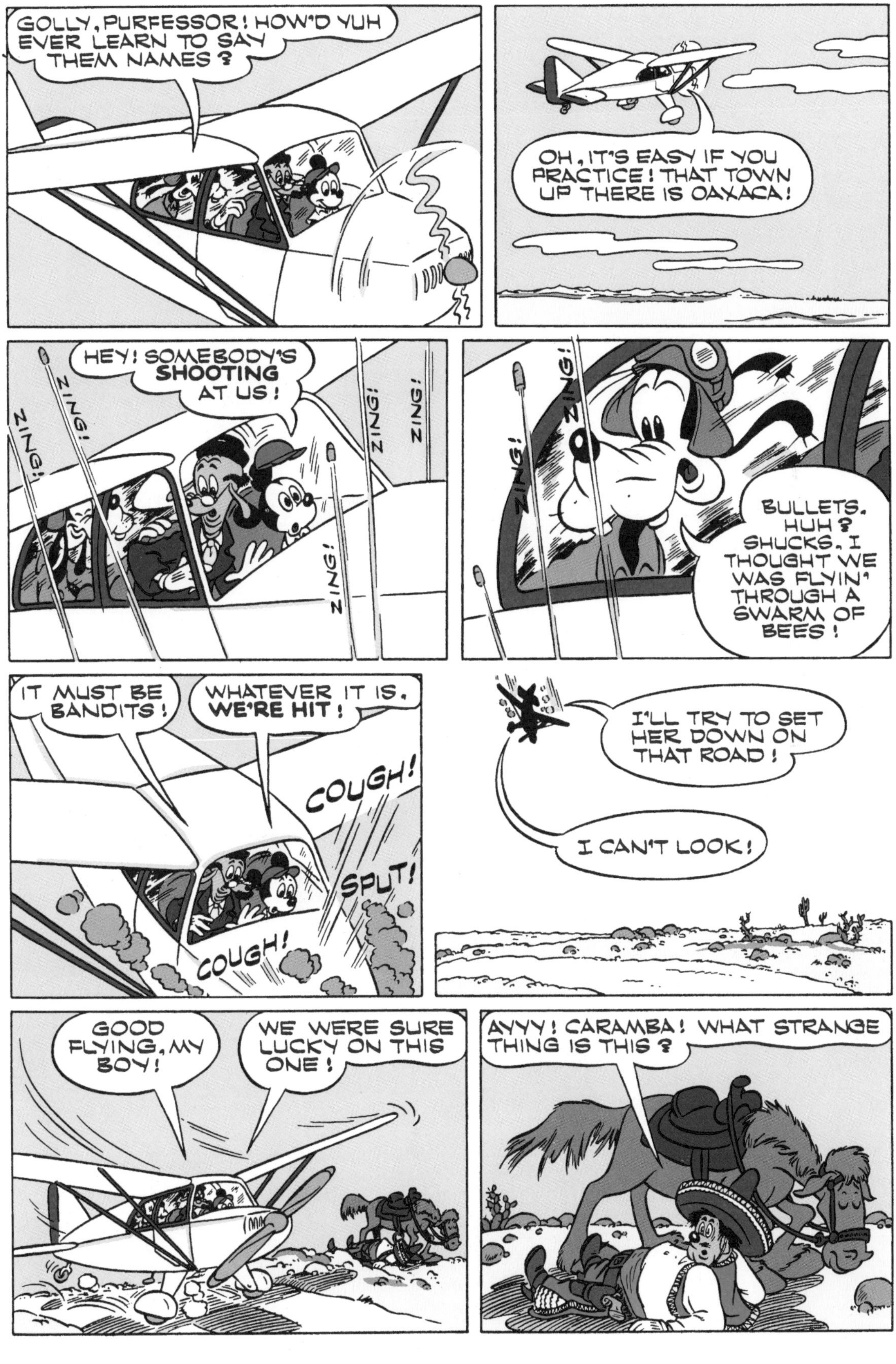
GOLLY, PURFESSOR! HOW'D YUH EVER LEARN TO SAY THEM NAMES?
OH, IT'S EASY IF YOU PRACTICE! THAT TOWN UP THERE IS OAXACA!
HEY! SOMEBODY'S **SHOOTING** AT US!
ZING!
ZING!
ZING!
ZING!
ZING!
ZING!
ZING!
BULLETS, HUH? SHUCKS, I THOUGHT WE WAS FLYIN' THROUGH A SWARM OF BEES!
IT MUST BE BANDITS!
WHATEVER IT IS, **WE'RE HIT**!
COUGH!
SPUT!
COUGH!
I'LL TRY TO SET HER DOWN ON THAT ROAD!
I CAN'T LOOK!
GOOD FLYING, MY BOY!
WE WERE SURE LUCKY ON THIS ONE!
AYYY! CARAMBA! WHAT STRANGE THING IS THIS?

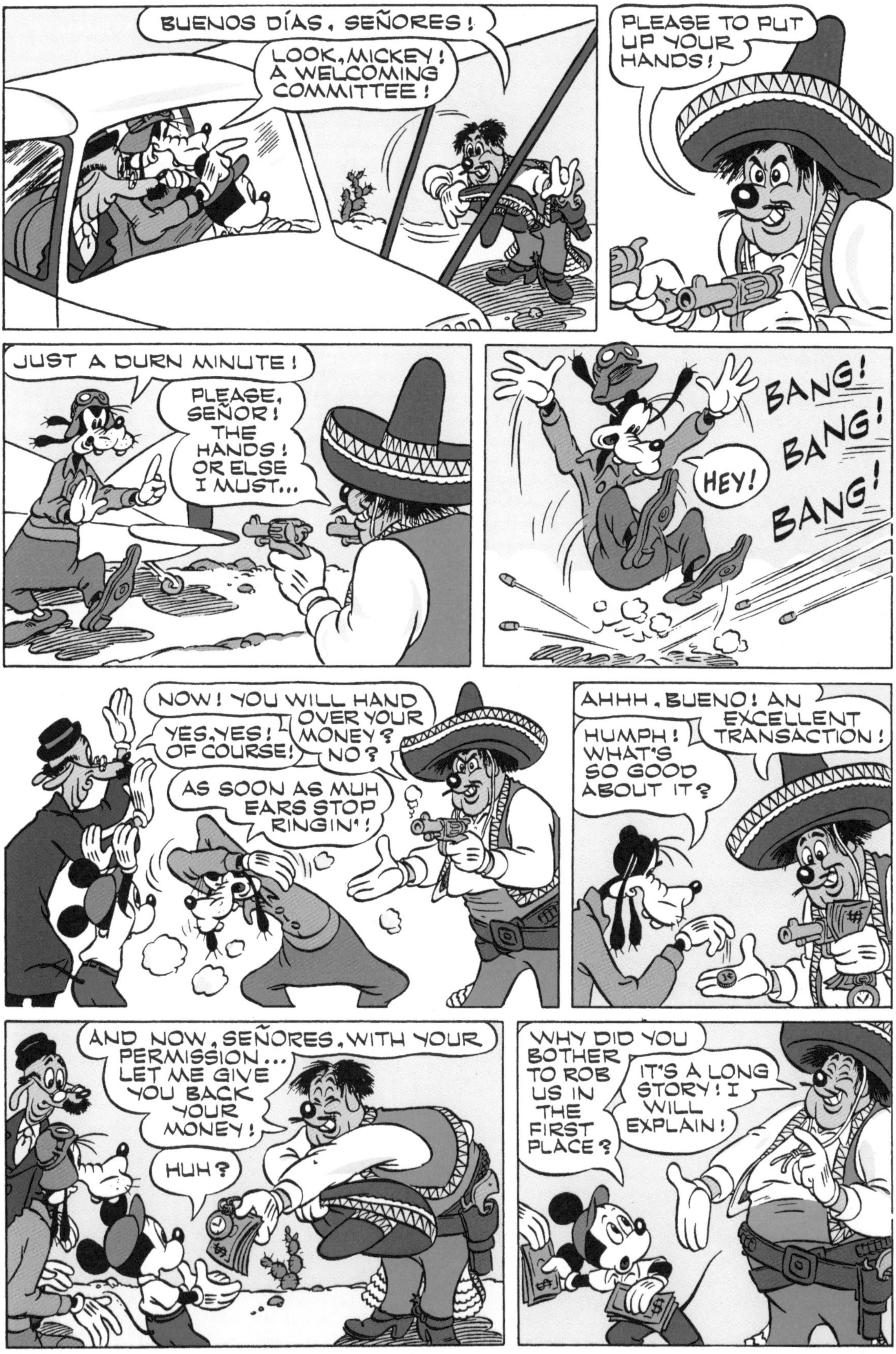
BUENOS DÍAS, SEÑORES!
LOOK, MICKEY! A WELCOMING COMMITTEE!
PLEASE TO PUT UP YOUR HANDS!
JUST A DURN MINUTE!
PLEASE, SEÑOR! THE HANDS! OR ELSE I MUST...
HEY!
BANG! BANG! BANG!
NOW! YOU WILL HAND OVER YOUR MONEY? NO?
YES, YES! OF COURSE!
AS SOON AS MUH EARS STOP RINGIN'!
AHHH, BUENO! AN EXCELLENT TRANSACTION!
HUMPH! WHAT'S SO GOOD ABOUT IT?
AND NOW, SEÑORES, WITH YOUR PERMISSION... LET ME GIVE YOU BACK YOUR MONEY!
HUH?
WHY DID YOU BOTHER TO ROB US IN THE FIRST PLACE?
IT'S A LONG STORY! I WILL EXPLAIN!

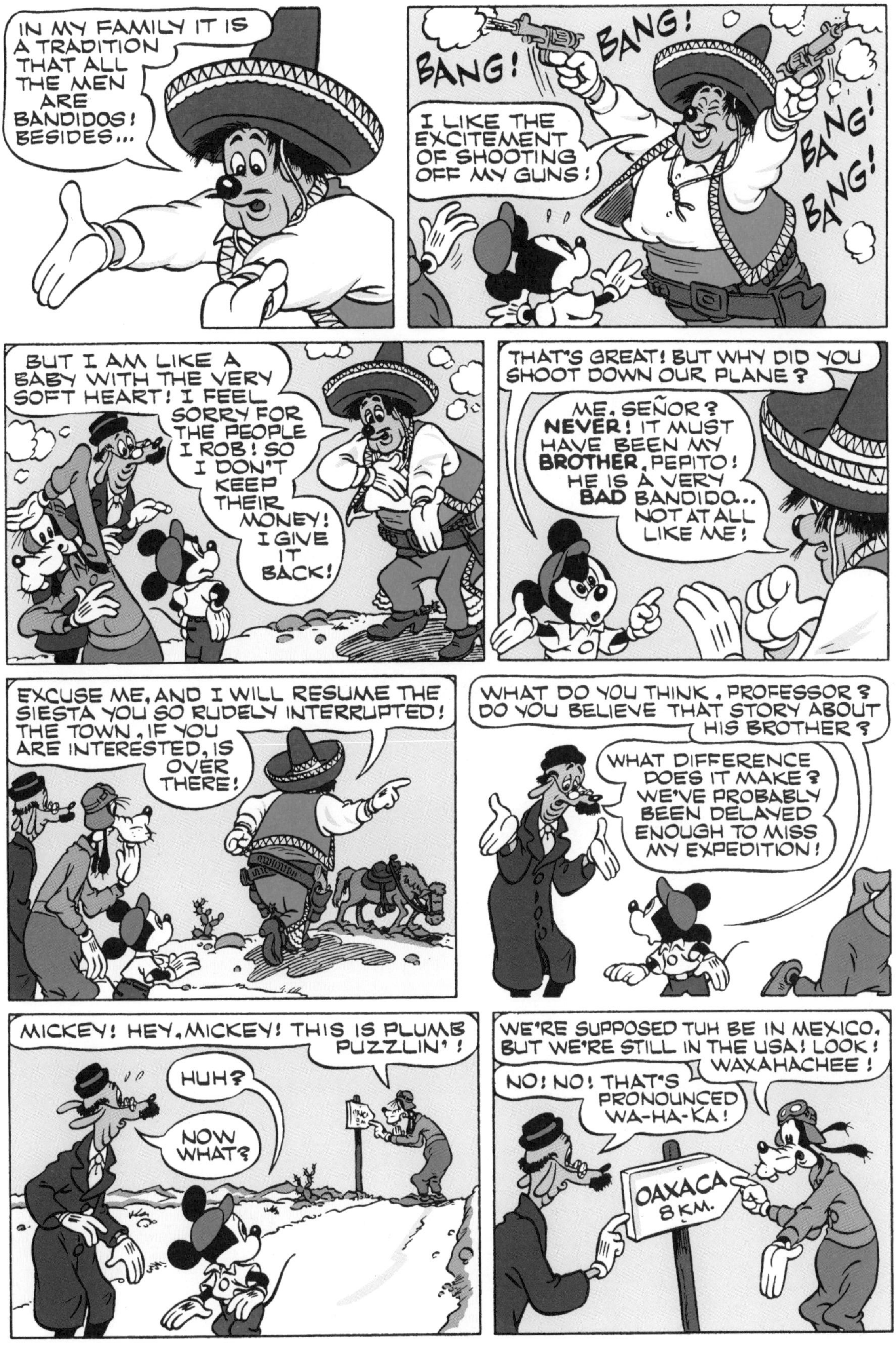

IN MY FAMILY IT IS A TRADITION THAT ALL THE MEN ARE BANDIDOS! BESIDES...
BANG!
BANG!
I LIKE THE EXCITEMENT OF SHOOTING OFF MY GUNS!
BANG!
BANG!
BUT I AM LIKE A BABY WITH THE VERY SOFT HEART! I FEEL SORRY FOR THE PEOPLE I ROB! SO I DON'T KEEP THEIR MONEY! I GIVE IT BACK!
THAT'S GREAT! BUT WHY DID YOU SHOOT DOWN OUR PLANE?
ME, SEÑOR? **NEVER**! IT MUST HAVE BEEN MY **BROTHER**, PEPITO! HE IS A VERY **BAD** BANDIDO... NOT AT ALL LIKE ME!
EXCUSE ME, AND I WILL RESUME THE SIESTA YOU SO RUDELY INTERRUPTED! THE TOWN, IF YOU ARE INTERESTED, IS OVER THERE!
WHAT DO YOU THINK, PROFESSOR? DO YOU BELIEVE THAT STORY ABOUT HIS BROTHER?
WHAT DIFFERENCE DOES IT MAKE? WE'VE PROBABLY BEEN DELAYED ENOUGH TO MISS MY EXPEDITION!
MICKEY! HEY, MICKEY! THIS IS PLUMB PUZZLIN'!
HUH?
NOW WHAT?
WE'RE SUPPOSED TUH BE IN MEXICO, BUT WE'RE STILL IN THE USA! LOOK! WAXAHACHEE!
NO! NO! THAT'S PRONOUNCED WA-HA-KA!
OAXACA 8 KM.

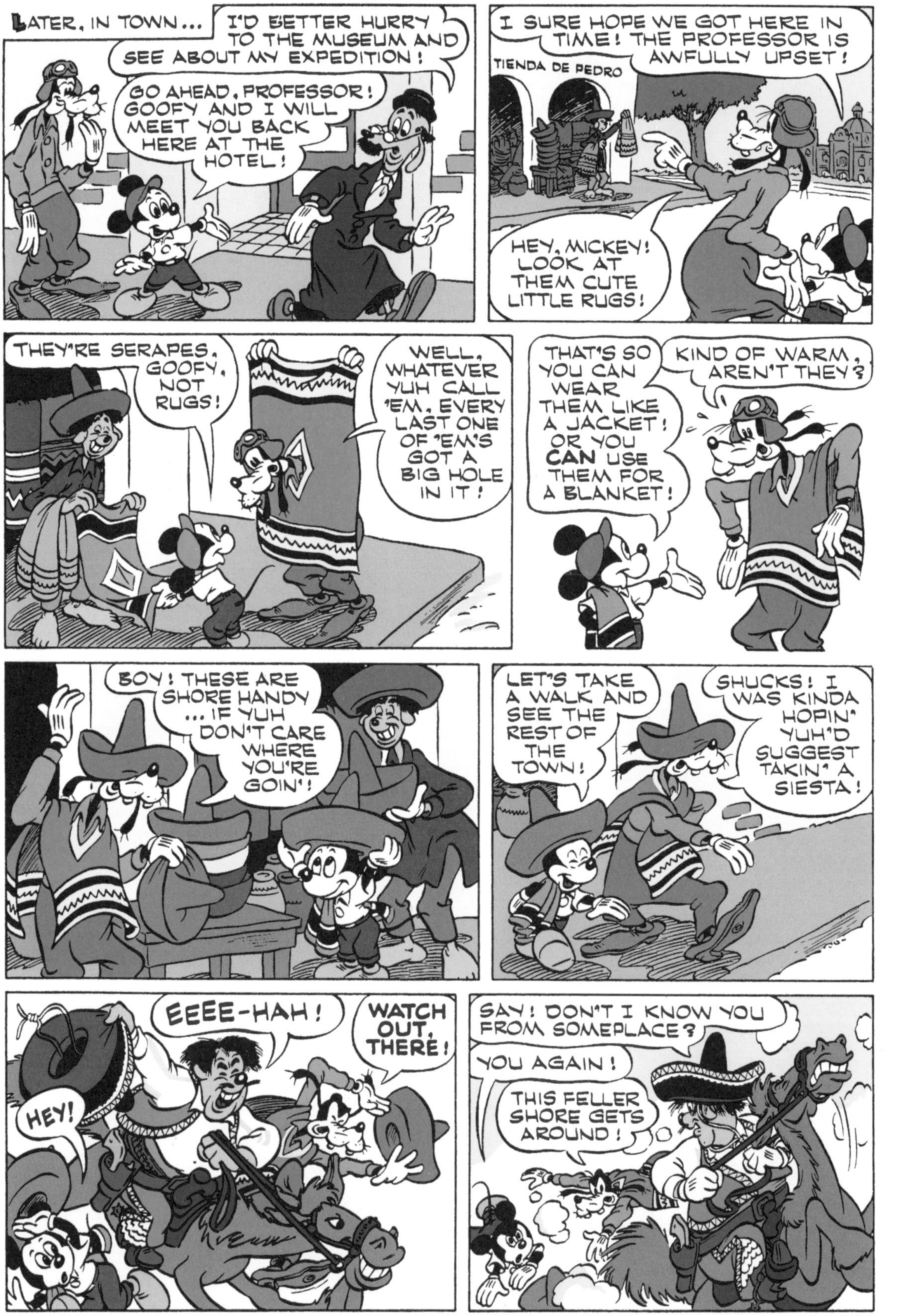
LATER, IN TOWN...
I'D BETTER HURRY TO THE MUSEUM AND SEE ABOUT MY EXPEDITION!
GO AHEAD, PROFESSOR! GOOFY AND I WILL MEET YOU BACK HERE AT THE HOTEL!
I SURE HOPE WE GOT HERE IN TIME! THE PROFESSOR IS AWFULLY UPSET!
TIENDA DE PEDRO
HEY, MICKEY! LOOK AT THEM CUTE LITTLE RUGS!
THEY'RE SERAPES, GOOFY, NOT RUGS!
WELL, WHATEVER YUH CALL 'EM, EVERY LAST ONE OF 'EM'S GOT A BIG HOLE IN IT!
KIND OF WARM, AREN'T THEY?
THAT'S SO YOU CAN WEAR THEM LIKE A JACKET! OR YOU CAN USE THEM FOR A BLANKET!
BOY! THESE ARE SHORE HANDY ... IF YUH DON'T CARE WHERE YOU'RE GOIN'!
LET'S TAKE A WALK AND SEE THE REST OF THE TOWN!
SHUCKS! I WAS KINDA HOPIN' YUH'D SUGGEST TAKIN' A SIESTA!
HEY!
EEEE-HAH!
WATCH OUT, THERE!
SAY! DON'T I KNOW YOU FROM SOMEPLACE?
YOU AGAIN!
THIS FELLER SHORE GETS AROUND!

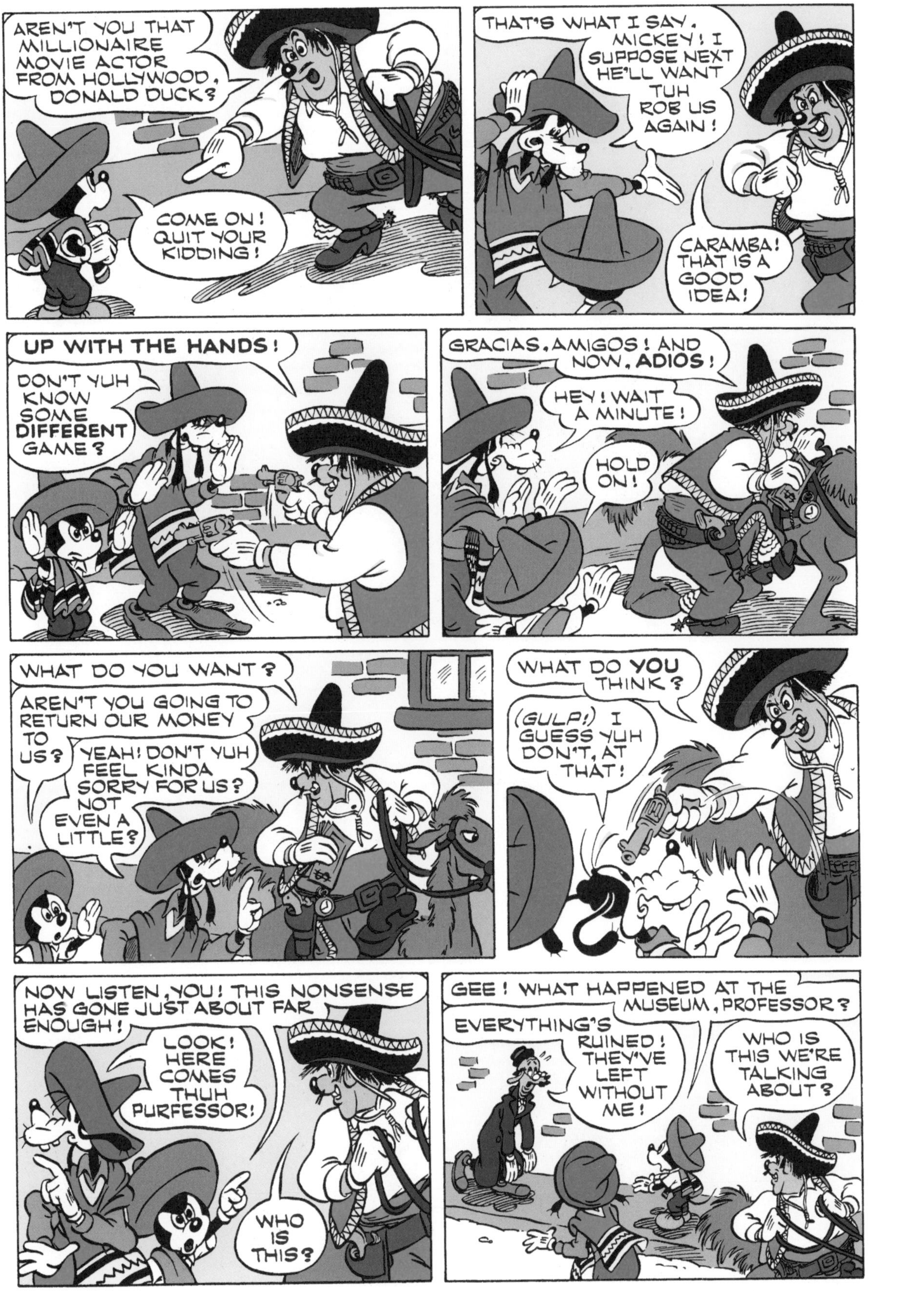

AREN'T YOU THAT MILLIONAIRE MOVIE ACTOR FROM HOLLYWOOD, DONALD DUCK?
COME ON! QUIT YOUR KIDDING!
THAT'S WHAT I SAY, MICKEY! I SUPPOSE NEXT HE'LL WANT TUH ROB US AGAIN!
CARAMBA! THAT IS A GOOD IDEA!
UP WITH THE HANDS!
DON'T YUH KNOW SOME DIFFERENT GAME?
GRACIAS, AMIGOS! AND NOW, ADIOS!
HEY! WAIT A MINUTE!
HOLD ON!
WHAT DO YOU WANT?
AREN'T YOU GOING TO RETURN OUR MONEY TO US?
YEAH! DON'T YUH FEEL KINDA SORRY FOR US? NOT EVEN A LITTLE?
WHAT DO YOU THINK?
(GULP!) I GUESS YUH DON'T, AT THAT!
NOW LISTEN, YOU! THIS NONSENSE HAS GONE JUST ABOUT FAR ENOUGH!
LOOK! HERE COMES THUH PURFESSOR!
WHO IS THIS?
GEE! WHAT HAPPENED AT THE MUSEUM, PROFESSOR?
EVERYTHING'S RUINED! THEY'VE LEFT WITHOUT ME!
WHO IS THIS WE'RE TALKING ABOUT?

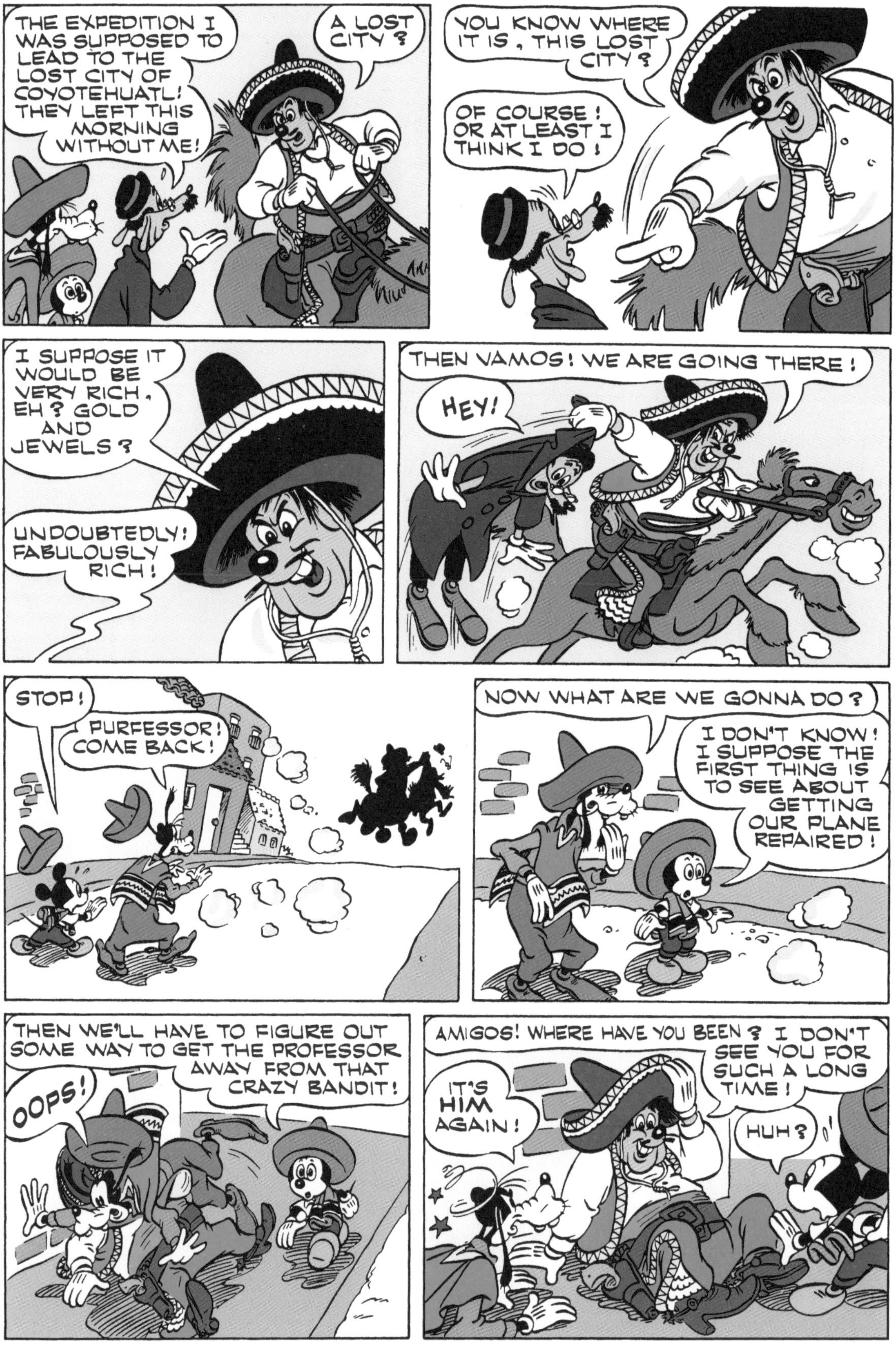
THE EXPEDITION I WAS SUPPOSED TO LEAD TO THE LOST CITY OF COYOTEHUATL! THEY LEFT THIS MORNING WITHOUT ME!
A LOST CITY ?
YOU KNOW WHERE IT IS, THIS LOST CITY ?
OF COURSE! OR AT LEAST I THINK I DO!
I SUPPOSE IT WOULD BE VERY RICH, EH ? GOLD AND JEWELS ?
UNDOUBTEDLY! FABULOUSLY RICH!
THEN VAMOS! WE ARE GOING THERE!
HEY!
STOP!
PURFESSOR! COME BACK!
NOW WHAT ARE WE GONNA DO ?
I DON'T KNOW! I SUPPOSE THE FIRST THING IS TO SEE ABOUT GETTING OUR PLANE REPAIRED!
THEN WE'LL HAVE TO FIGURE OUT SOME WAY TO GET THE PROFESSOR AWAY FROM THAT CRAZY BANDIT!
OOPS!
AMIGOS! WHERE HAVE YOU BEEN ? I DON'T SEE YOU FOR SUCH A LONG TIME!
IT'S HIM AGAIN!
HUH ?

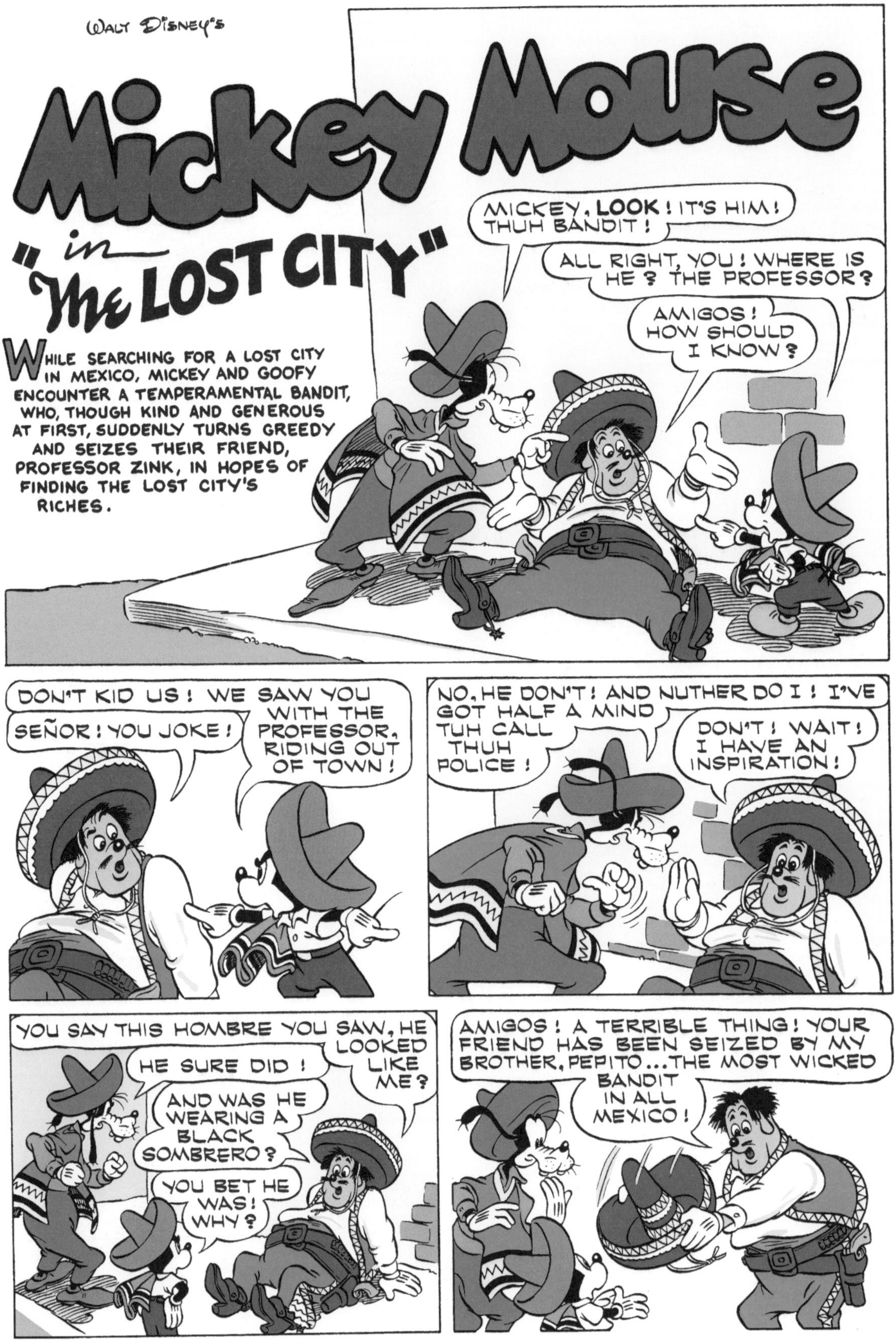
WALT DISNEY'S
MICKEY MOUSE
in "THE LOST CITY"
WHILE SEARCHING FOR A LOST CITY IN MEXICO, MICKEY AND GOOFY ENCOUNTER A TEMPERAMENTAL BANDIT, WHO, THOUGH KIND AND GENEROUS AT FIRST, SUDDENLY TURNS GREEDY AND SEIZES THEIR FRIEND, PROFESSOR ZINK, IN HOPES OF FINDING THE LOST CITY'S RICHES.
MICKEY, LOOK! IT'S HIM! THUH BANDIT!
ALL RIGHT, YOU! WHERE IS HE? THE PROFESSOR?
AMIGOS! HOW SHOULD I KNOW?
DON'T KID US! WE SAW YOU WITH THE PROFESSOR, RIDING OUT OF TOWN!
SEÑOR! YOU JOKE!
NO, HE DON'T! AND NUTHER DO I! I'VE GOT HALF A MIND TUH CALL THUH POLICE!
DON'T! WAIT! I HAVE AN INSPIRATION!
YOU SAY THIS HOMBRE YOU SAW, HE LOOKED LIKE ME?
HE SURE DID!
AND WAS HE WEARING A BLACK SOMBRERO?
YOU BET HE WAS! WHY?
AMIGOS! A TERRIBLE THING! YOUR FRIEND HAS BEEN SEIZED BY MY BROTHER, PEPITO...THE MOST WICKED BANDIT IN ALL MEXICO!

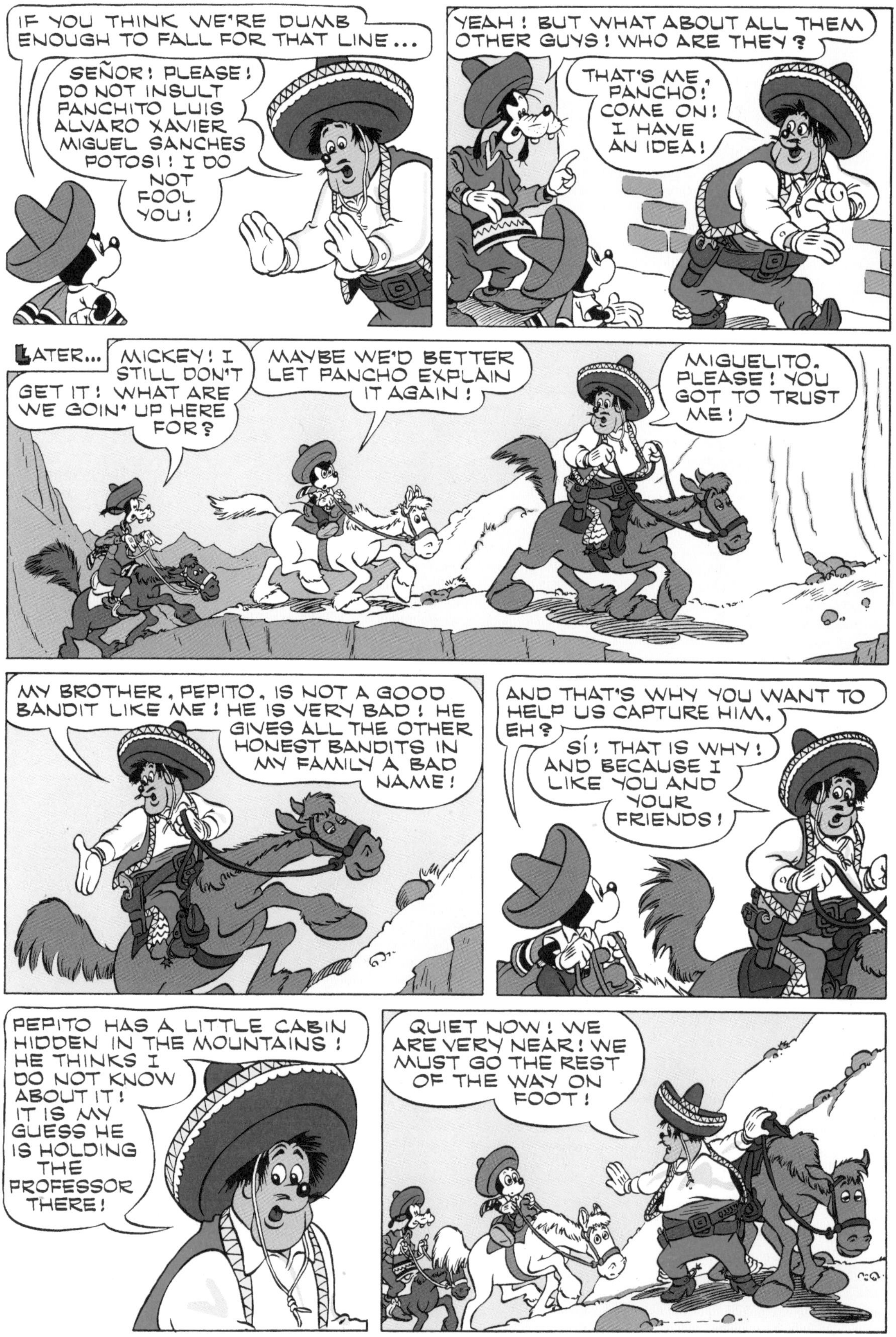
IF YOU THINK WE'RE DUMB ENOUGH TO FALL FOR THAT LINE...
SEÑOR! PLEASE! DO NOT INSULT PANCHITO LUIS ALVARO XAVIER MIGUEL SANCHES POTOSI! I DO NOT FOOL YOU!
YEAH! BUT WHAT ABOUT ALL THEM OTHER GUYS! WHO ARE THEY?
THAT'S ME, PANCHO! COME ON! I HAVE AN IDEA!
LATER...
MICKEY! I STILL DON'T GET IT! WHAT ARE WE GOIN' UP HERE FOR?
MAYBE WE'D BETTER LET PANCHO EXPLAIN IT AGAIN!
MIGUELITO, PLEASE! YOU GOT TO TRUST ME!
MY BROTHER, PEPITO, IS NOT A GOOD BANDIT LIKE ME! HE IS VERY BAD! HE GIVES ALL THE OTHER HONEST BANDITS IN MY FAMILY A BAD NAME!
AND THAT'S WHY YOU WANT TO HELP US CAPTURE HIM, EH?
SÍ! THAT IS WHY! AND BECAUSE I LIKE YOU AND YOUR FRIENDS!
PEPITO HAS A LITTLE CABIN HIDDEN IN THE MOUNTAINS! HE THINKS I DO NOT KNOW ABOUT IT! IT IS MY GUESS HE IS HOLDING THE PROFESSOR THERE!
QUIET NOW! WE ARE VERY NEAR! WE MUST GO THE REST OF THE WAY ON FOOT!

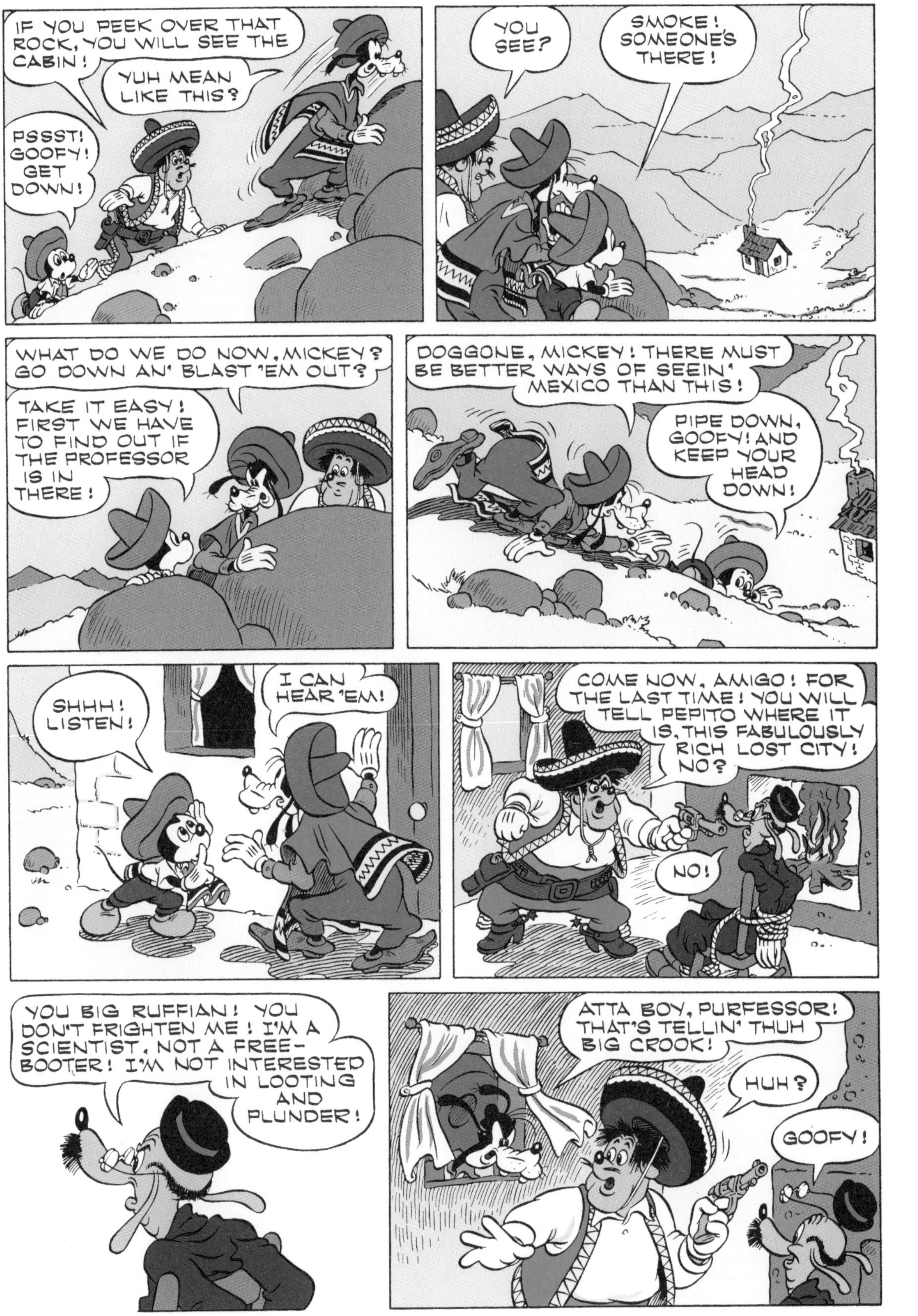
IF YOU PEEK OVER THAT ROCK, YOU WILL SEE THE CABIN!
YUH MEAN LIKE THIS?
PSSST! GOOFY! GET DOWN!
YOU SEE?
SMOKE! SOMEONE'S THERE!
WHAT DO WE DO NOW, MICKEY? GO DOWN AN' BLAST 'EM OUT?
TAKE IT EASY! FIRST WE HAVE TO FIND OUT IF THE PROFESSOR IS IN THERE!
DOGGONE, MICKEY! THERE MUST BE BETTER WAYS OF SEEIN' MEXICO THAN THIS!
PIPE DOWN, GOOFY! AND KEEP YOUR HEAD DOWN!
SHHH! LISTEN!
I CAN HEAR 'EM!
COME NOW, AMIGO! FOR THE LAST TIME! YOU WILL TELL PEPITO WHERE IT IS, THIS FABULOUSLY RICH LOST CITY! NO?
NO!
YOU BIG RUFFIAN! YOU DON'T FRIGHTEN ME! I'M A SCIENTIST, NOT A FREE-BOOTER! I'M NOT INTERESTED IN LOOTING AND PLUNDER!
ATTA BOY, PURFESSOR! THAT'S TELLIN' THUH BIG CROOK!
HUH?
GOOFY!

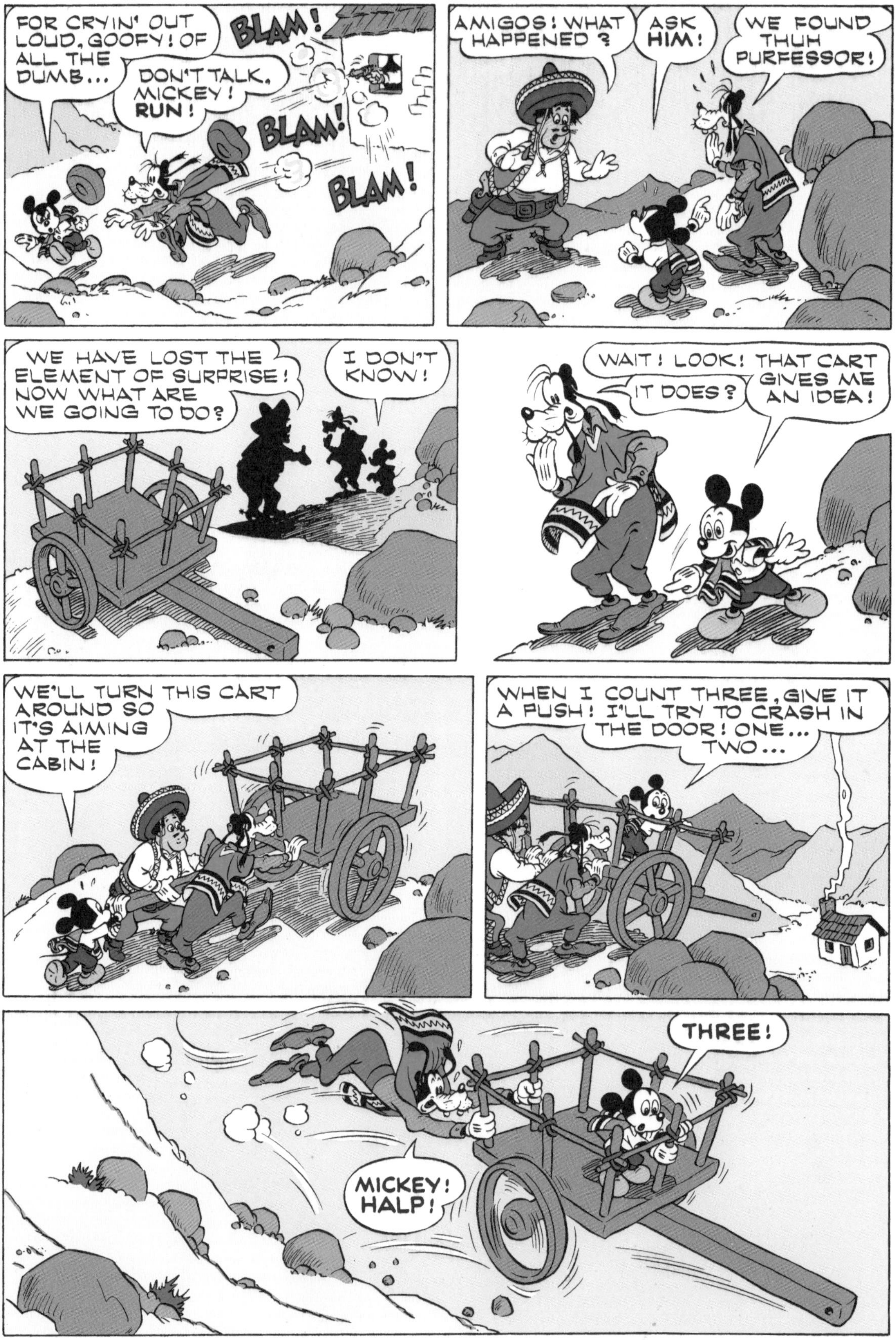
FOR CRYIN' OUT LOUD, GOOFY! OF ALL THE DUMB...
DON'T TALK, MICKEY! RUN!
BLAM!
BLAM!
BLAM!
AMIGOS! WHAT HAPPENED?
ASK HIM!
WE FOUND THUH PURFESSOR!
WE HAVE LOST THE ELEMENT OF SURPRISE! NOW WHAT ARE WE GOING TO DO?
I DON'T KNOW!
WAIT! LOOK! THAT CART GIVES ME AN IDEA!
IT DOES?
WE'LL TURN THIS CART AROUND SO IT'S AIMING AT THE CABIN!
WHEN I COUNT THREE, GIVE IT A PUSH! I'LL TRY TO CRASH IN THE DOOR! ONE... TWO...
THREE!
MICKEY! HALP!

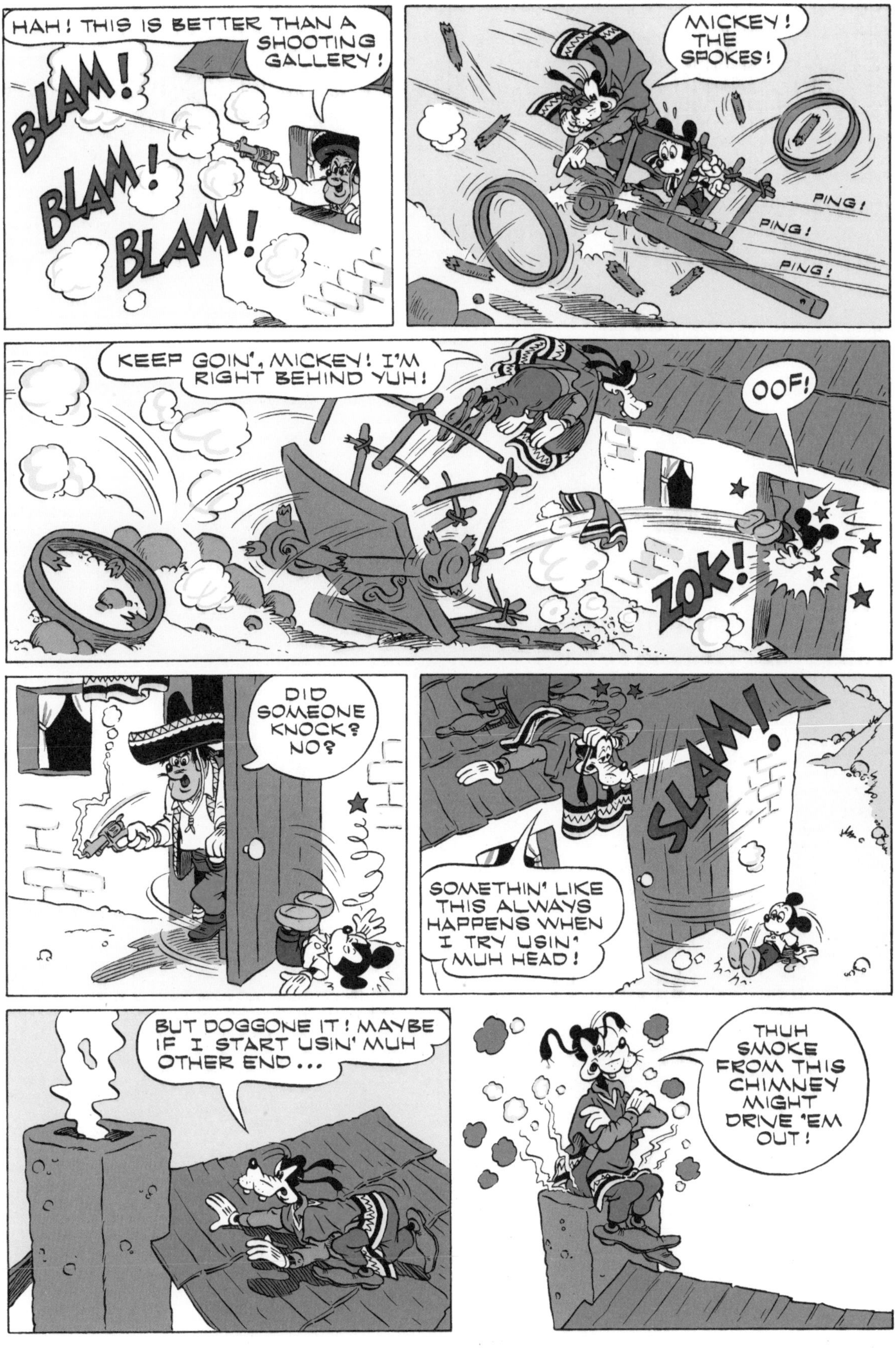
HAH! THIS IS BETTER THAN A SHOOTING GALLERY!
BLAM! BLAM! BLAM!
MICKEY! THE SPOKES!
PING! PING! PING!
KEEP GOIN', MICKEY! I'M RIGHT BEHIND YUH!
OOF!
ZOK!
DID SOMEONE KNOCK? NO?
SLAM!
SOMETHIN' LIKE THIS ALWAYS HAPPENS WHEN I TRY USIN' MUH HEAD!
BUT DOGGONE IT! MAYBE IF I START USIN' MUH OTHER END...
THUH SMOKE FROM THIS CHIMNEY MIGHT DRIVE 'EM OUT!

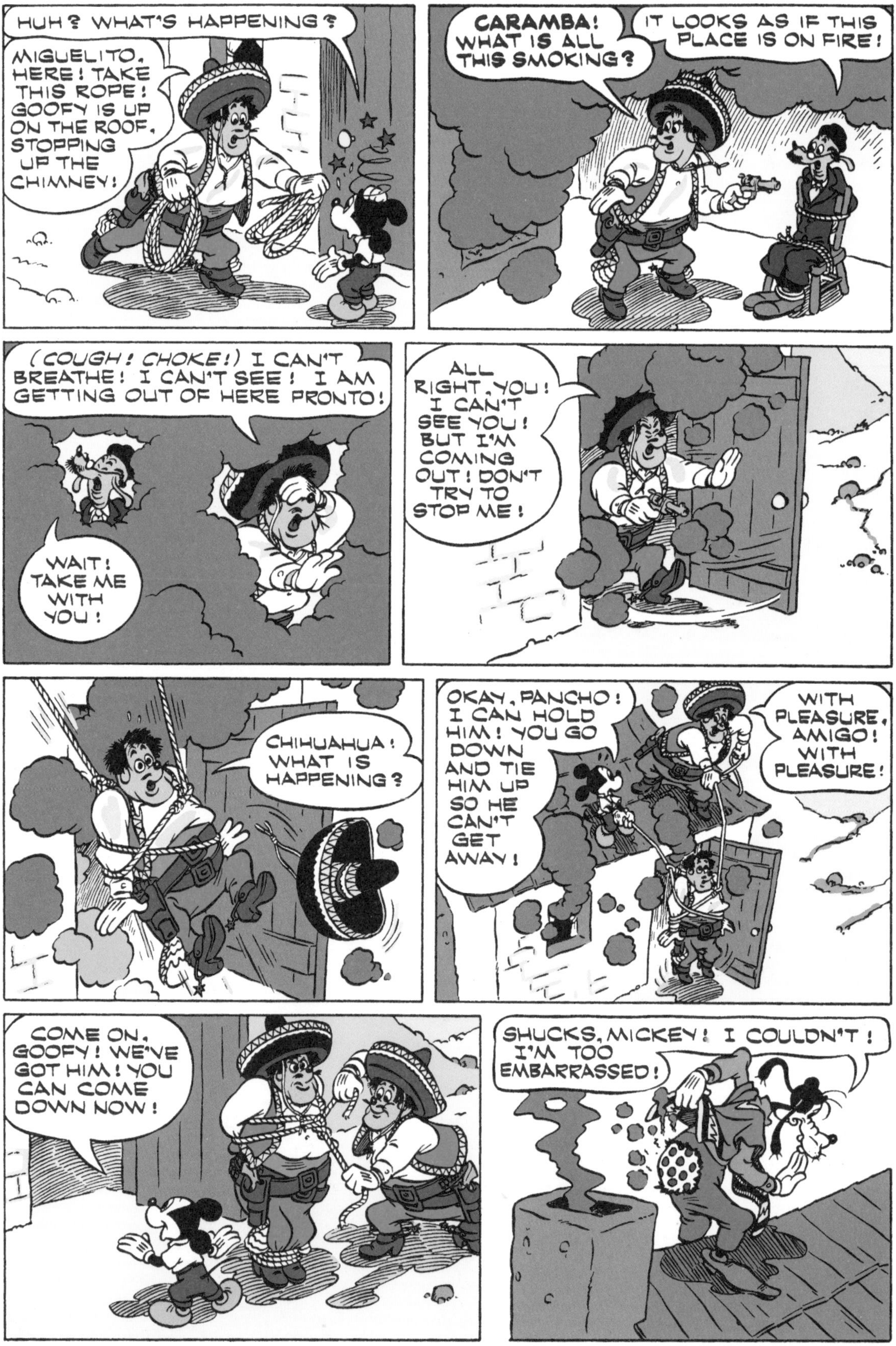

HUH? WHAT'S HAPPENING?
MIGUELITO, HERE! TAKE THIS ROPE! GOOFY IS UP ON THE ROOF, STOPPING UP THE CHIMNEY!
CARAMBA! WHAT IS ALL THIS SMOKING?
IT LOOKS AS IF THIS PLACE IS ON FIRE!
(COUGH! CHOKE!) I CAN'T BREATHE! I CAN'T SEE! I AM GETTING OUT OF HERE PRONTO!
WAIT! TAKE ME WITH YOU!
ALL RIGHT, YOU! I CAN'T SEE YOU! BUT I'M COMING OUT! DON'T TRY TO STOP ME!
CHIHUAHUA! WHAT IS HAPPENING?
OKAY, PANCHO! I CAN HOLD HIM! YOU GO DOWN AND TIE HIM UP SO HE CAN'T GET AWAY!
WITH PLEASURE, AMIGO! WITH PLEASURE!
COME ON, GOOFY! WE'VE GOT HIM! YOU CAN COME DOWN NOW!
SHUCKS, MICKEY! I COULDN'T! I'M TOO EMBARRASSED!

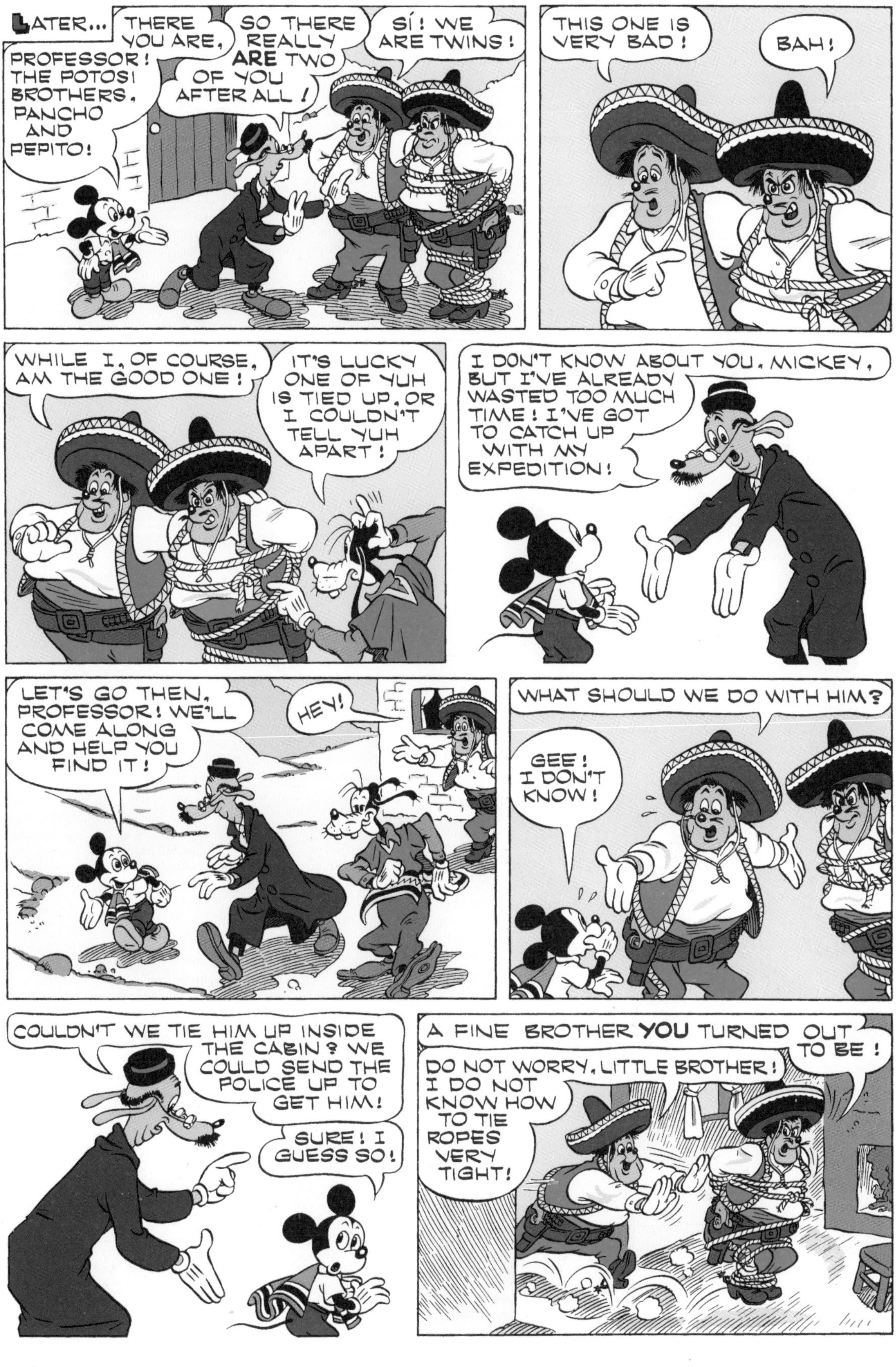
LATER...
THERE YOU ARE, PROFESSOR! THE POTOSI BROTHERS, PANCHO AND PEPITO!
SO THERE REALLY ARE TWO OF YOU AFTER ALL!
SÍ! WE ARE TWINS!
THIS ONE IS VERY BAD!
BAH!
WHILE I, OF COURSE, AM THE GOOD ONE!
IT'S LUCKY ONE OF YUH IS TIED UP, OR I COULDN'T TELL YUH APART!
I DON'T KNOW ABOUT YOU, MICKEY, BUT I'VE ALREADY WASTED TOO MUCH TIME! I'VE GOT TO CATCH UP WITH MY EXPEDITION!
LET'S GO THEN, PROFESSOR! WE'LL COME ALONG AND HELP YOU FIND IT!
HEY!
WHAT SHOULD WE DO WITH HIM?
GEE! I DON'T KNOW!
COULDN'T WE TIE HIM UP INSIDE THE CABIN? WE COULD SEND THE POLICE UP TO GET HIM!
SURE! I GUESS SO!
A FINE BROTHER YOU TURNED OUT TO BE!
DO NOT WORRY, LITTLE BROTHER! I DO NOT KNOW HOW TO TIE ROPES VERY TIGHT!

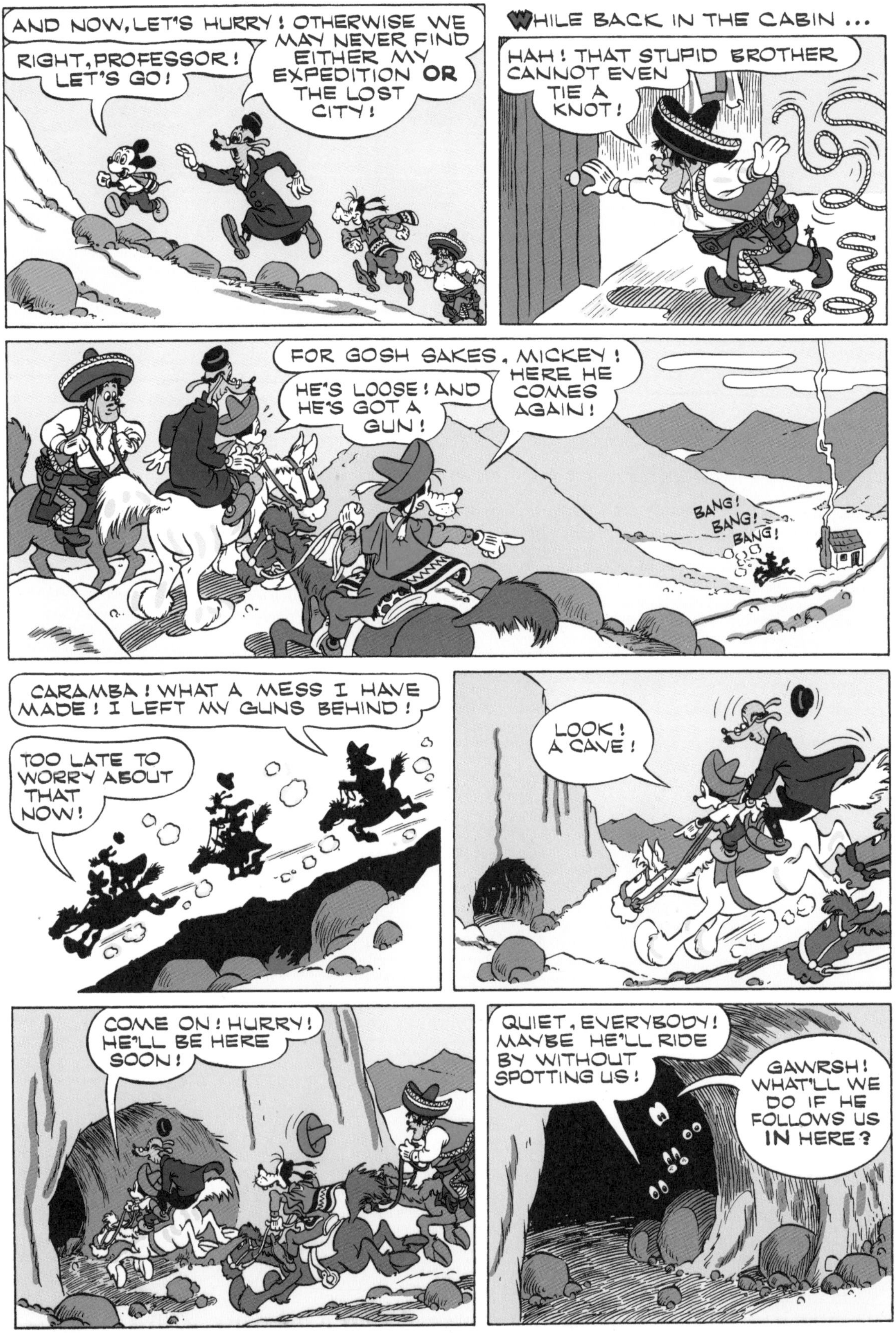
AND NOW, LET'S HURRY! OTHERWISE WE MAY NEVER FIND EITHER MY EXPEDITION OR THE LOST CITY!
RIGHT, PROFESSOR! LET'S GO!
WHILE BACK IN THE CABIN ...
HAH! THAT STUPID BROTHER CANNOT EVEN TIE A KNOT!
FOR GOSH SAKES, MICKEY! HERE HE COMES AGAIN!
HE'S LOOSE! AND HE'S GOT A GUN!
BANG! BANG! BANG!
CARAMBA! WHAT A MESS I HAVE MADE! I LEFT MY GUNS BEHIND!
TOO LATE TO WORRY ABOUT THAT NOW!
LOOK! A CAVE!
COME ON! HURRY! HE'LL BE HERE SOON!
QUIET, EVERYBODY! MAYBE HE'LL RIDE BY WITHOUT SPOTTING US!
GAWRSH! WHAT'LL WE DO IF HE FOLLOWS US IN HERE?

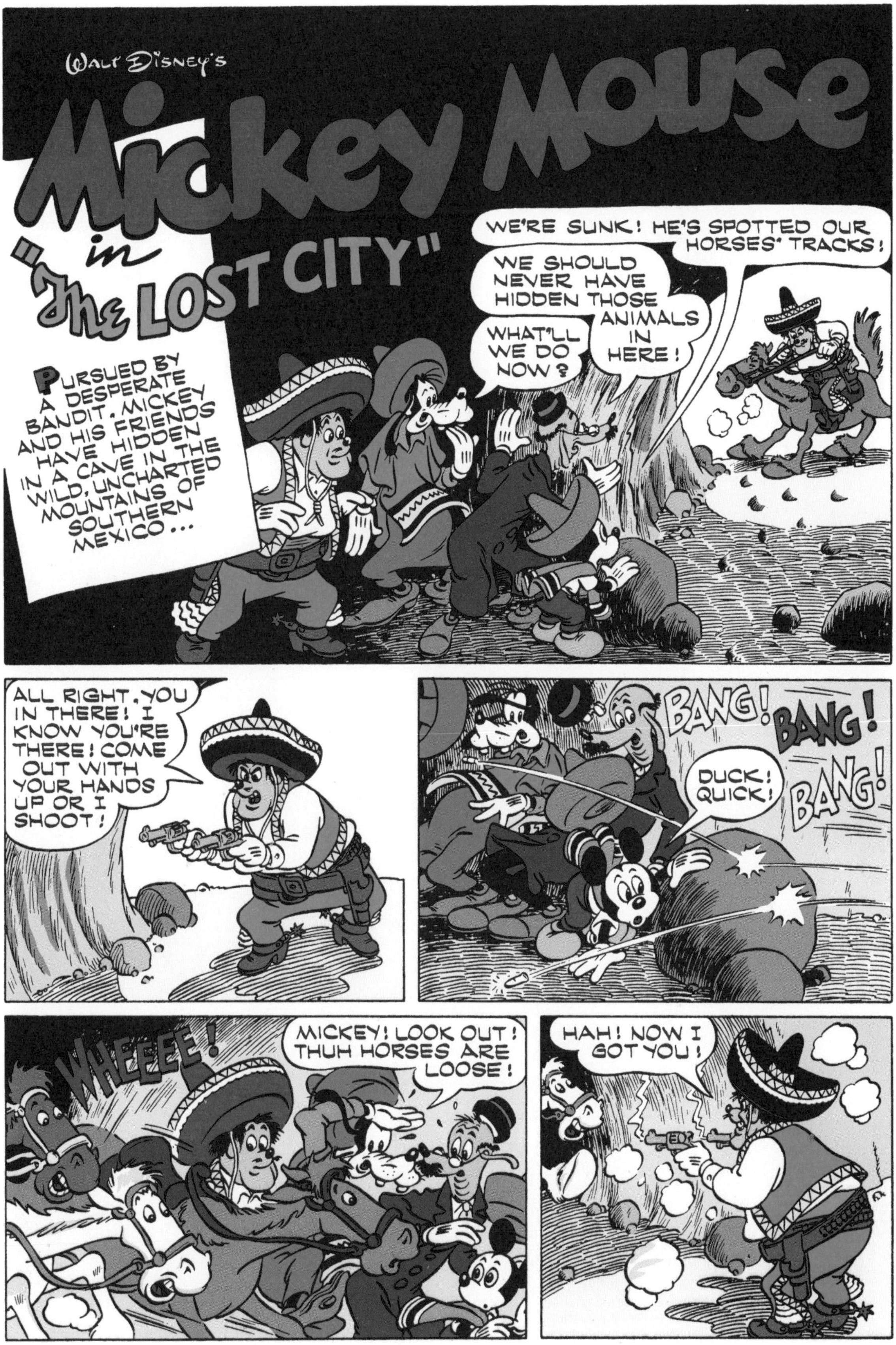
WALT DISNEY'S
Mickey Mouse
in
"The LOST CITY"
PURSUED BY A DESPERATE BANDIT, MICKEY AND HIS FRIENDS HAVE HIDDEN IN A CAVE IN THE WILD, UNCHARTED MOUNTAINS OF SOUTHERN MEXICO...
WE'RE SUNK! HE'S SPOTTED OUR HORSES' TRACKS!
WE SHOULD NEVER HAVE HIDDEN THOSE ANIMALS IN HERE!
WHAT'LL WE DO NOW?
ALL RIGHT, YOU IN THERE! I KNOW YOU'RE THERE! COME OUT WITH YOUR HANDS UP OR I SHOOT!
BANG! BANG! BANG!
DUCK! QUICK!
WHEEEE!
MICKEY! LOOK OUT! THUH HORSES ARE LOOSE!
HAH! NOW I GOT YOU!

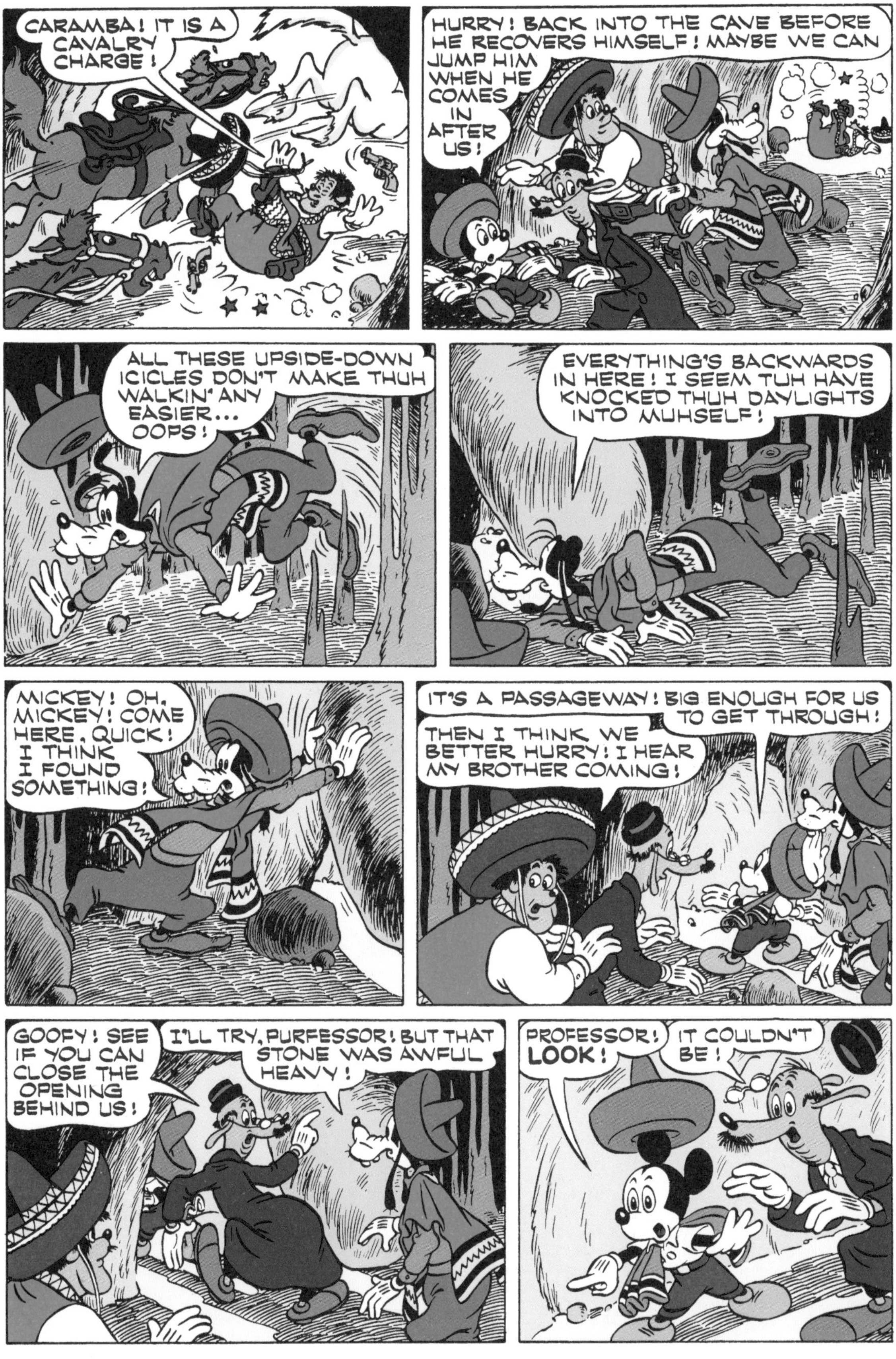

CARAMBA! IT IS A CAVALRY CHARGE!
HURRY! BACK INTO THE CAVE BEFORE HE RECOVERS HIMSELF! MAYBE WE CAN JUMP HIM WHEN HE COMES IN AFTER US!
ALL THESE UPSIDE-DOWN ICICLES DON'T MAKE THUH WALKIN' ANY EASIER... OOPS!
EVERYTHING'S BACKWARDS IN HERE! I SEEM TUH HAVE KNOCKED THUH DAYLIGHTS INTO MUHSELF!
MICKEY! OH, MICKEY! COME HERE, QUICK! I THINK I FOUND SOMETHING!
IT'S A PASSAGEWAY! BIG ENOUGH FOR US TO GET THROUGH!
THEN I THINK WE BETTER HURRY! I HEAR MY BROTHER COMING!
GOOFY! SEE IF YOU CAN CLOSE THE OPENING BEHIND US!
I'LL TRY, PURFESSOR! BUT THAT STONE WAS AWFUL HEAVY!
PROFESSOR! **LOOK!**
IT COULDN'T BE!

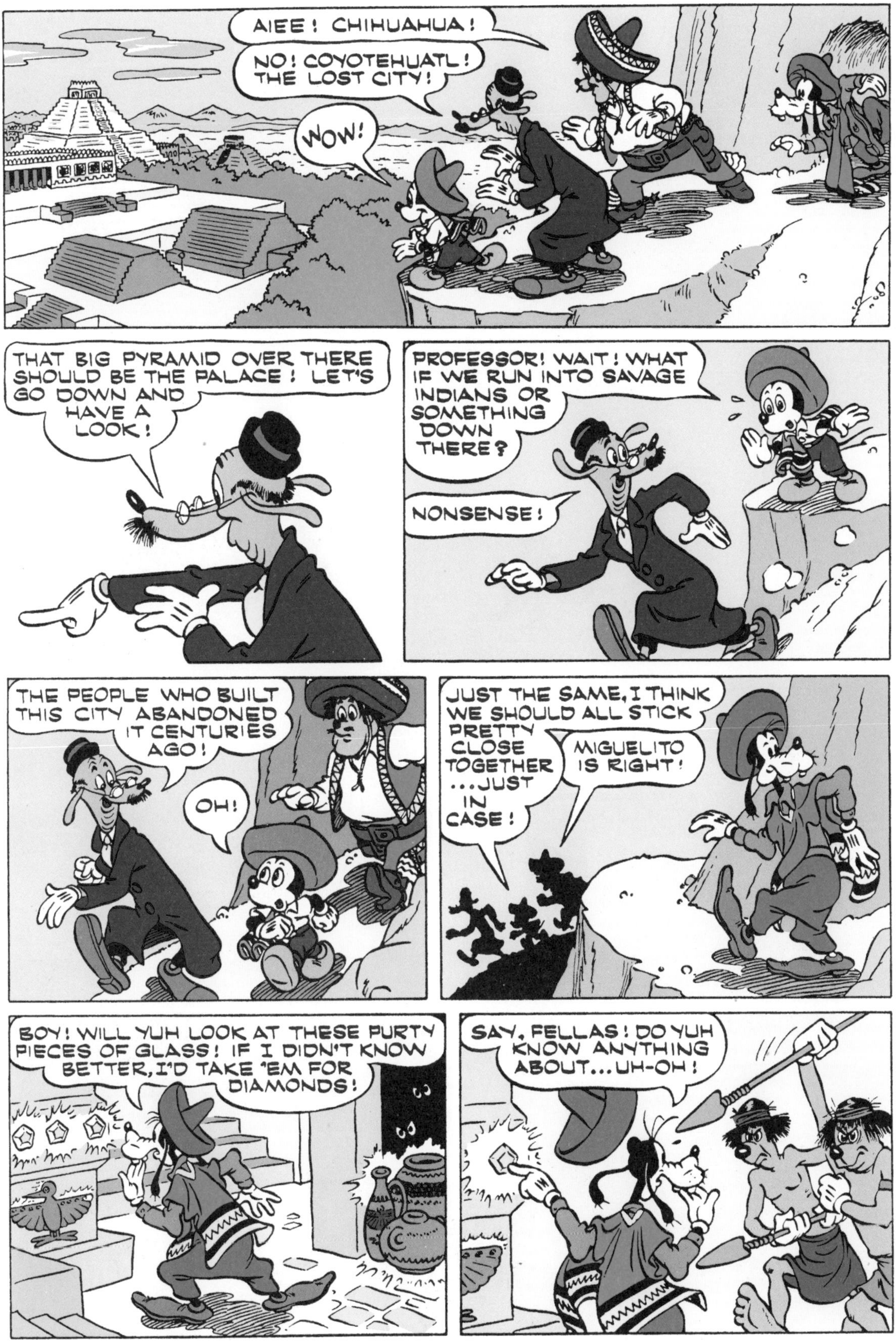

AIEE! CHIHUAHUA!
NO! COYOTEHUATL! THE LOST CITY!
WOW!
THAT BIG PYRAMID OVER THERE SHOULD BE THE PALACE! LET'S GO DOWN AND HAVE A LOOK!
PROFESSOR! WAIT! WHAT IF WE RUN INTO SAVAGE INDIANS OR SOMETHING DOWN THERE?
NONSENSE!
THE PEOPLE WHO BUILT THIS CITY ABANDONED IT CENTURIES AGO!
OH!
JUST THE SAME, I THINK WE SHOULD ALL STICK PRETTY CLOSE TOGETHER ...JUST IN CASE!
MIGUELITO IS RIGHT!
BOY! WILL YUH LOOK AT THESE PURTY PIECES OF GLASS! IF I DIDN'T KNOW BETTER, I'D TAKE 'EM FOR DIAMONDS!
SAY, FELLAS! DO YUH KNOW ANYTHING ABOUT...UH-OH!

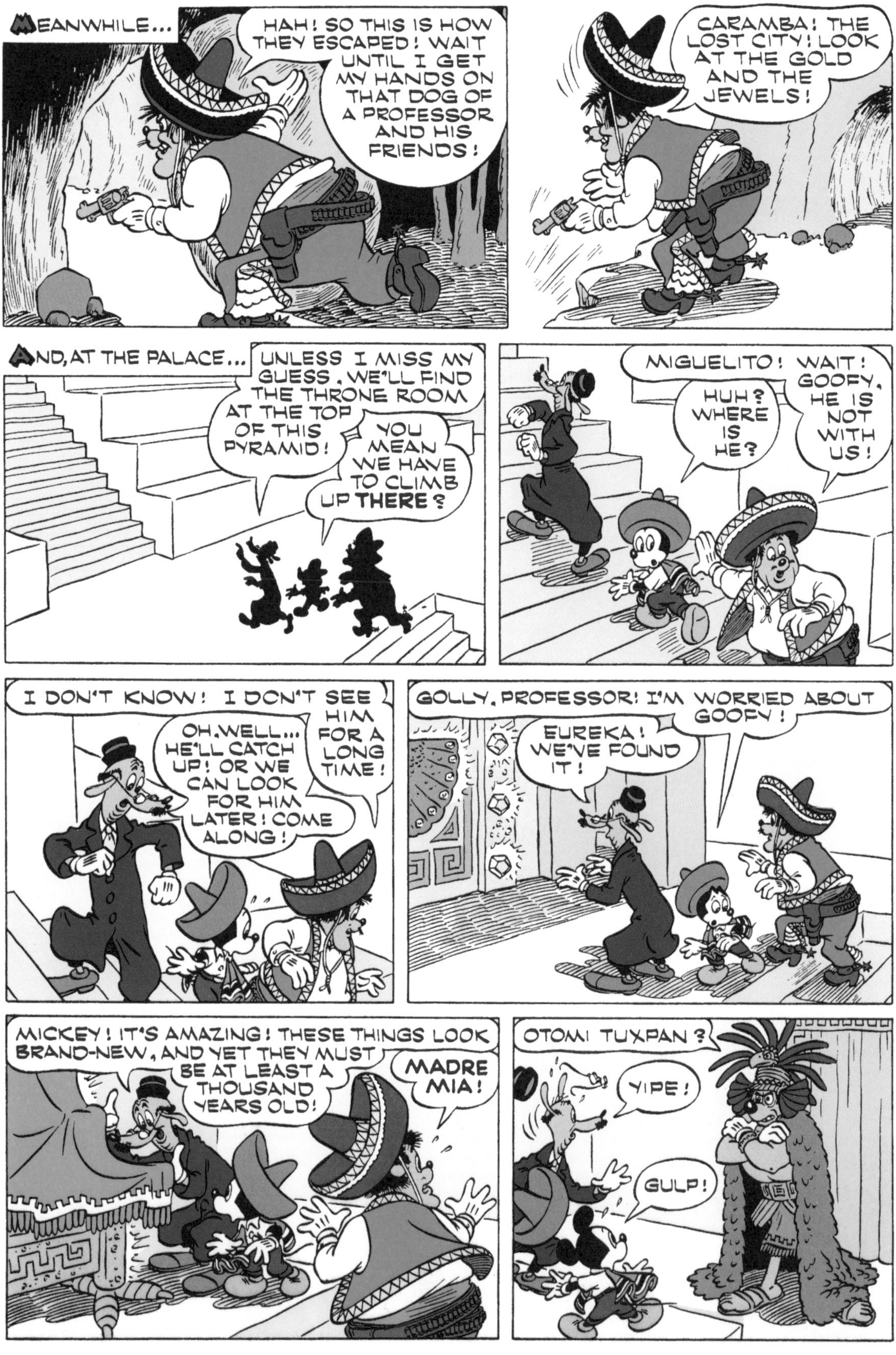
MEANWHILE...
HAH! SO THIS IS HOW THEY ESCAPED! WAIT UNTIL I GET MY HANDS ON THAT DOG OF A PROFESSOR AND HIS FRIENDS!
CARAMBA! THE LOST CITY! LOOK AT THE GOLD AND THE JEWELS!
AND, AT THE PALACE...
UNLESS I MISS MY GUESS, WE'LL FIND THE THRONE ROOM AT THE TOP OF THIS PYRAMID!
YOU MEAN WE HAVE TO CLIMB UP THERE?
MIGUELITO! WAIT!
HUH? WHERE IS HE?
GOOFY, HE IS NOT WITH US!
I DON'T KNOW! I DON'T SEE HIM FOR A LONG TIME!
OH, WELL... HE'LL CATCH UP! OR WE CAN LOOK FOR HIM LATER! COME ALONG!
GOLLY, PROFESSOR! I'M WORRIED ABOUT GOOFY!
EUREKA! WE'VE FOUND IT!
MICKEY! IT'S AMAZING! THESE THINGS LOOK BRAND-NEW, AND YET THEY MUST BE AT LEAST A THOUSAND YEARS OLD!
MADRE MIA!
OTOMI TUXPAN?
YIPE!
GULP!

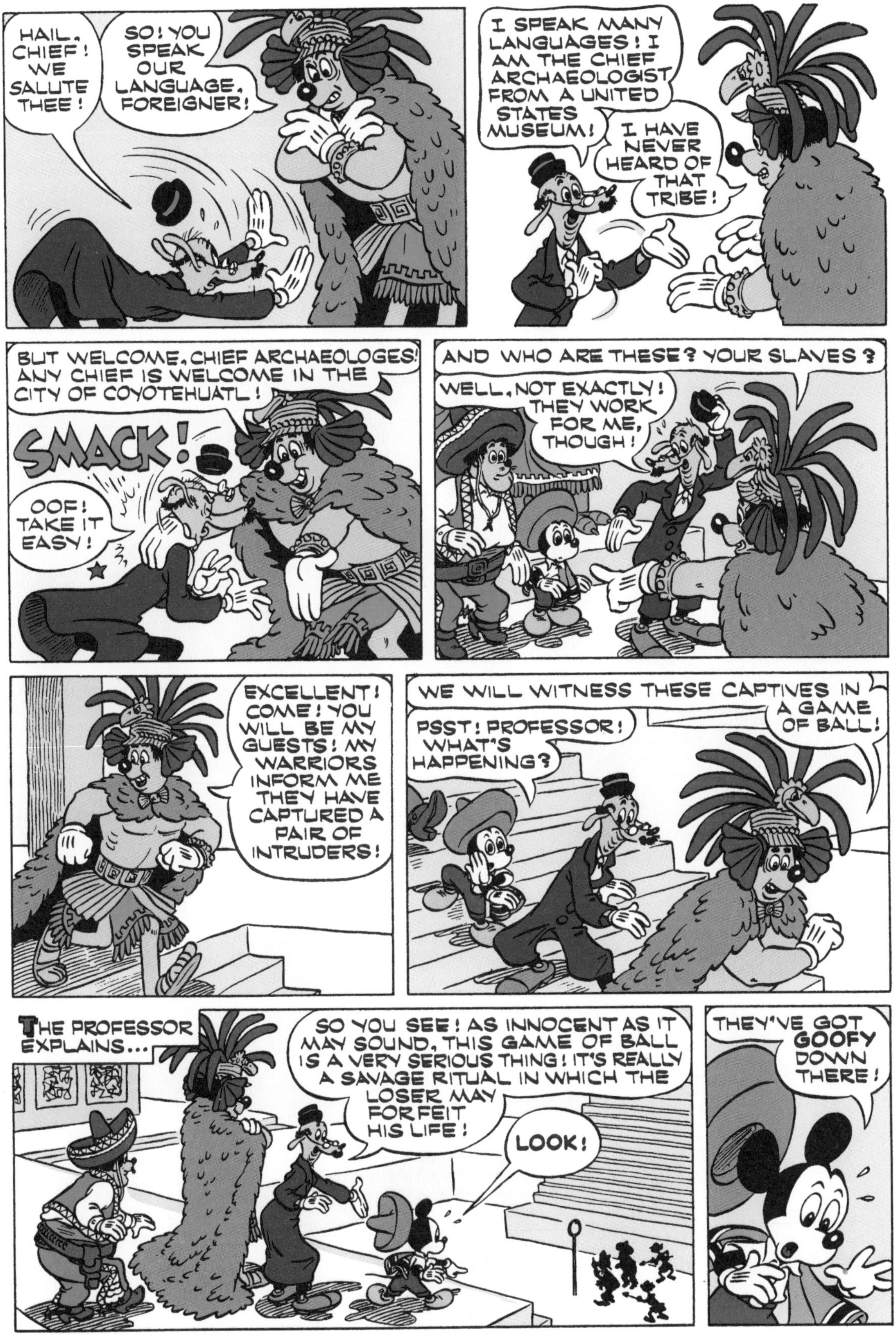

HAIL, CHIEF! WE SALUTE THEE!
SO! YOU SPEAK OUR LANGUAGE, FOREIGNER!
I SPEAK MANY LANGUAGES! I AM THE CHIEF ARCHAEOLOGIST FROM A UNITED STATES MUSEUM!
I HAVE NEVER HEARD OF THAT TRIBE!
BUT WELCOME, CHIEF ARCHAEOLOGES! ANY CHIEF IS WELCOME IN THE CITY OF COYOTEHUATL!
SMACK!
OOF! TAKE IT EASY!
AND WHO ARE THESE? YOUR SLAVES?
WELL, NOT EXACTLY! THEY WORK FOR ME, THOUGH!
EXCELLENT! COME! YOU WILL BE MY GUESTS! MY WARRIORS INFORM ME THEY HAVE CAPTURED A PAIR OF INTRUDERS!
WE WILL WITNESS THESE CAPTIVES IN A GAME OF BALL!
PSST! PROFESSOR! WHAT'S HAPPENING?
THE PROFESSOR EXPLAINS...
SO YOU SEE! AS INNOCENT AS IT MAY SOUND, THIS GAME OF BALL IS A VERY SERIOUS THING! IT'S REALLY A SAVAGE RITUAL IN WHICH THE LOSER MAY FORFEIT HIS LIFE!
LOOK!
THEY'VE GOT GOOFY DOWN THERE!

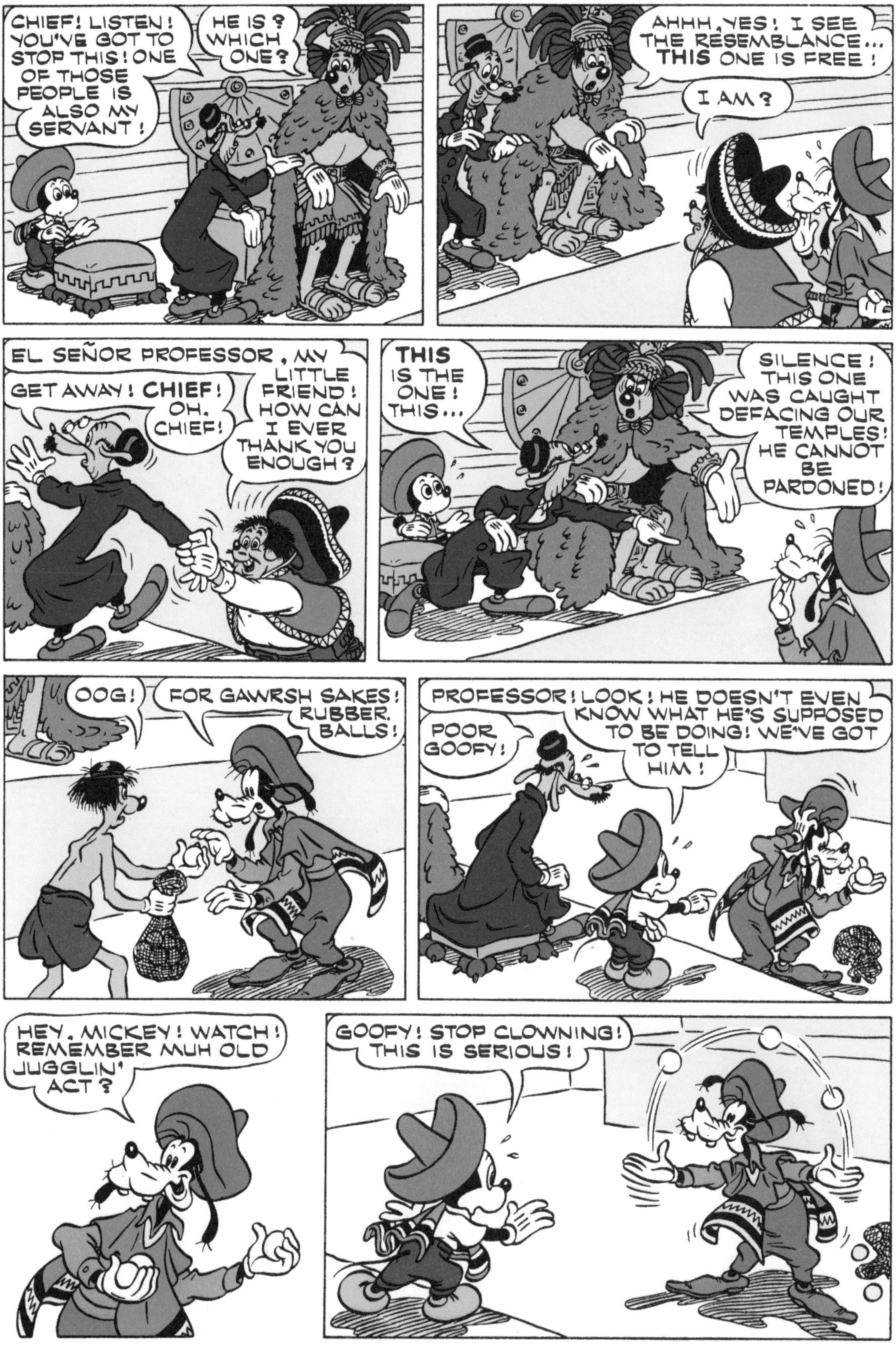
CHIEF! LISTEN! YOU'VE GOT TO STOP THIS! ONE OF THOSE PEOPLE IS ALSO MY SERVANT!
HE IS? WHICH ONE?
AHHH, YES! I SEE THE RESEMBLANCE... THIS ONE IS FREE!
I AM?
EL SEÑOR PROFESSOR, MY LITTLE FRIEND! HOW CAN I EVER THANK YOU ENOUGH?
GET AWAY! CHIEF! OH, CHIEF!
THIS IS THE ONE! THIS...
SILENCE! THIS ONE WAS CAUGHT DEFACING OUR TEMPLES! HE CANNOT BE PARDONED!
OOG!
FOR GAWRSH SAKES! RUBBER BALLS!
PROFESSOR! LOOK! HE DOESN'T EVEN KNOW WHAT HE'S SUPPOSED TO BE DOING! WE'VE GOT TO TELL HIM!
POOR GOOFY!
HEY, MICKEY! WATCH! REMEMBER MUH OLD JUGGLIN' ACT?
GOOFY! STOP CLOWNING! THIS IS SERIOUS!

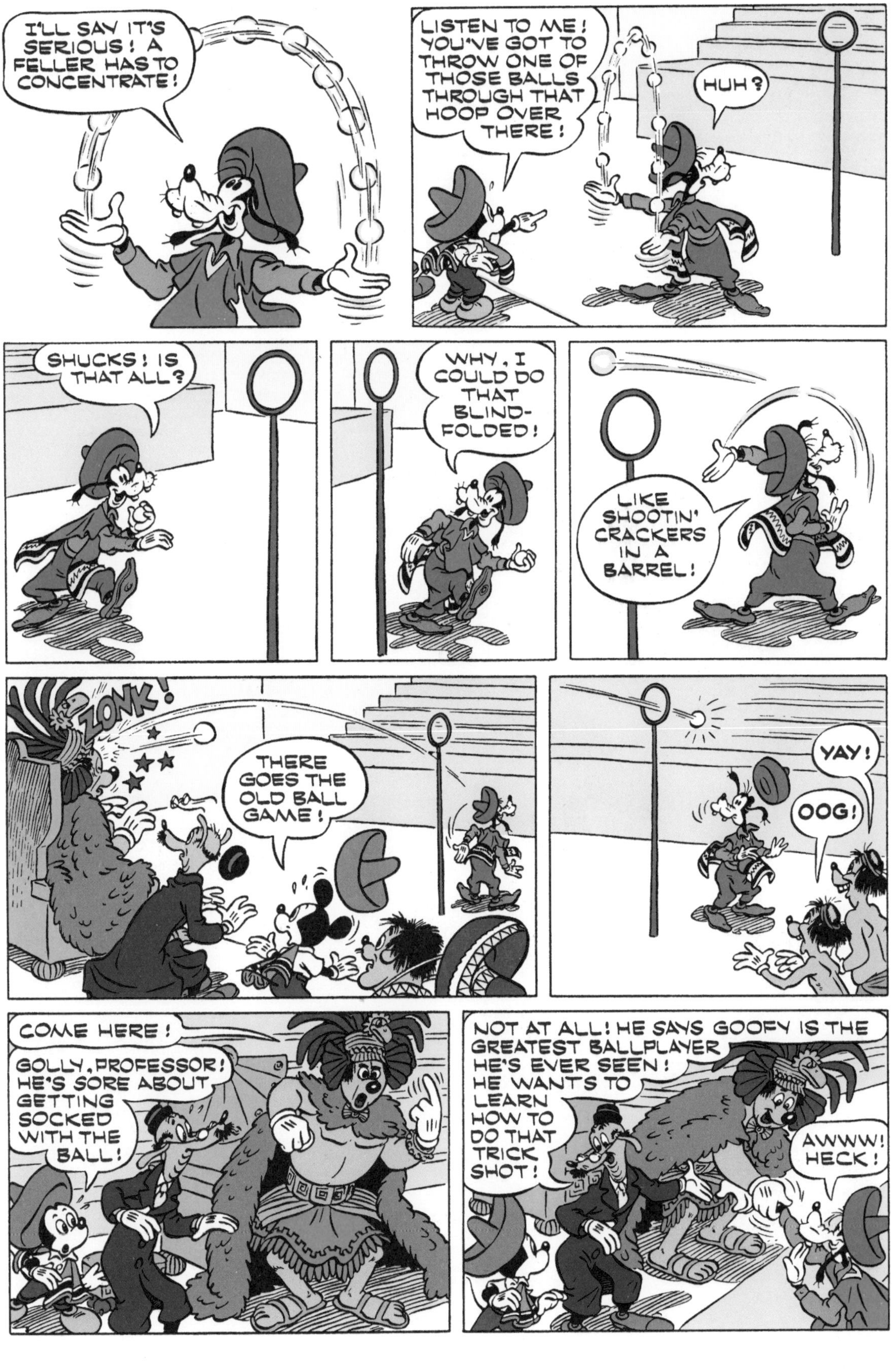

I'LL SAY IT'S SERIOUS! A FELLER HAS TO CONCENTRATE!
LISTEN TO ME! YOU'VE GOT TO THROW ONE OF THOSE BALLS THROUGH THAT HOOP OVER THERE!
HUH?
SHUCKS! IS THAT ALL?
WHY, I COULD DO THAT BLIND-FOLDED!
LIKE SHOOTIN' CRACKERS IN A BARREL!
ZONK!
THERE GOES THE OLD BALL GAME!
YAY!
OOG!
COME HERE!
GOLLY, PROFESSOR! HE'S SORE ABOUT GETTING SOCKED WITH THE BALL!
NOT AT ALL! HE SAYS GOOFY IS THE GREATEST BALLPLAYER HE'S EVER SEEN! HE WANTS TO LEARN HOW TO DO THAT TRICK SHOT!
AWWW! HECK!

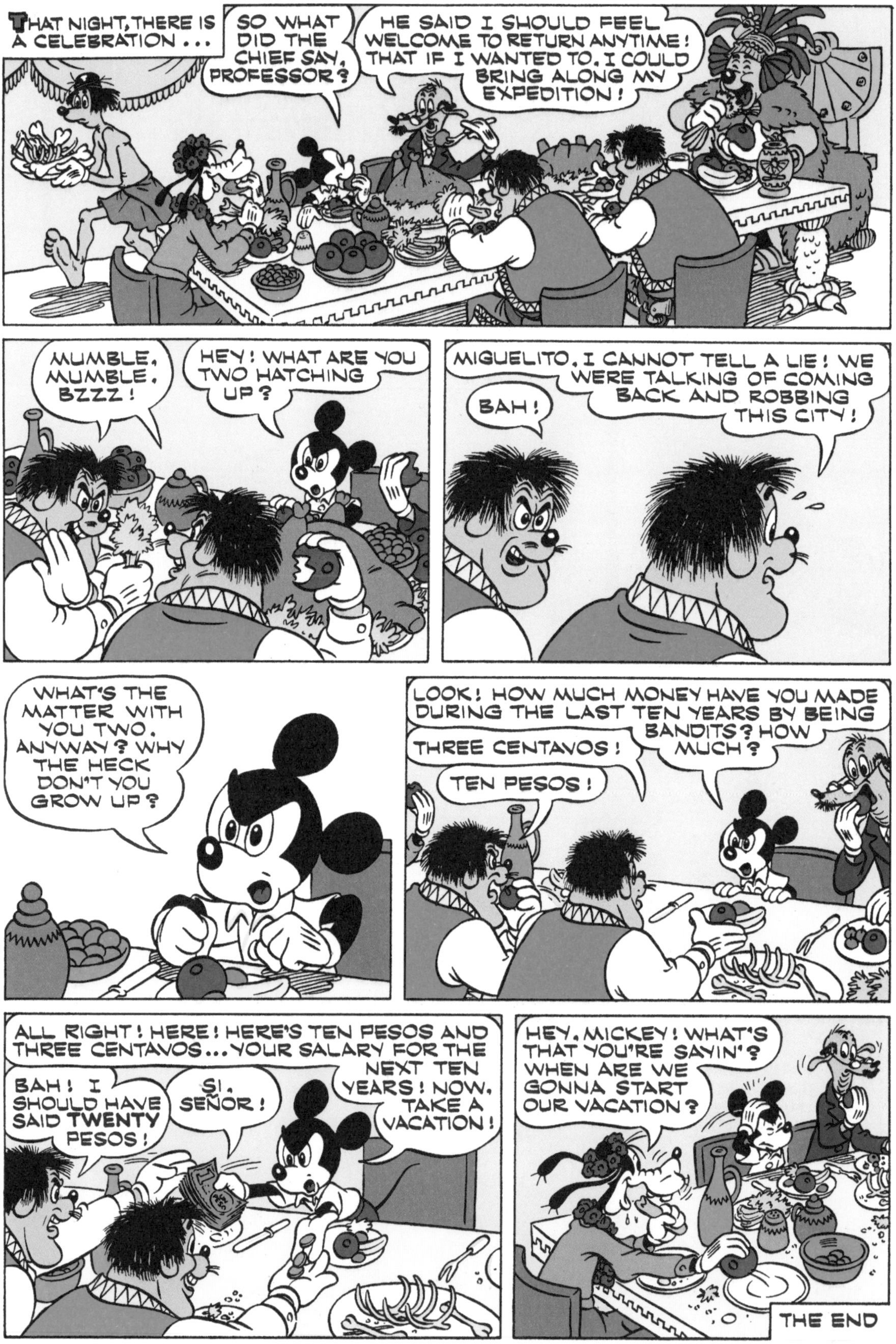
THAT NIGHT, THERE IS A CELEBRATION ...
SO WHAT DID THE CHIEF SAY, PROFESSOR?
HE SAID I SHOULD FEEL WELCOME TO RETURN ANYTIME! THAT IF I WANTED TO, I COULD BRING ALONG MY EXPEDITION!
MUMBLE, MUMBLE, BZZZ!
HEY! WHAT ARE YOU TWO HATCHING UP?
MIGUELITO, I CANNOT TELL A LIE! WE WERE TALKING OF COMING BACK AND ROBBING THIS CITY!
BAH!
WHAT'S THE MATTER WITH YOU TWO, ANYWAY? WHY THE HECK DON'T YOU GROW UP?
LOOK! HOW MUCH MONEY HAVE YOU MADE DURING THE LAST TEN YEARS BY BEING BANDITS? HOW MUCH?
THREE CENTAVOS!
TEN PESOS!
ALL RIGHT! HERE! HERE'S TEN PESOS AND THREE CENTAVOS... YOUR SALARY FOR THE NEXT TEN YEARS! NOW, TAKE A VACATION!
BAH! I SHOULD HAVE SAID TWENTY PESOS!
SI, SEÑOR!
HEY, MICKEY! WHAT'S THAT YOU'RE SAYIN'? WHEN ARE WE GONNA START OUR VACATION?
THE END

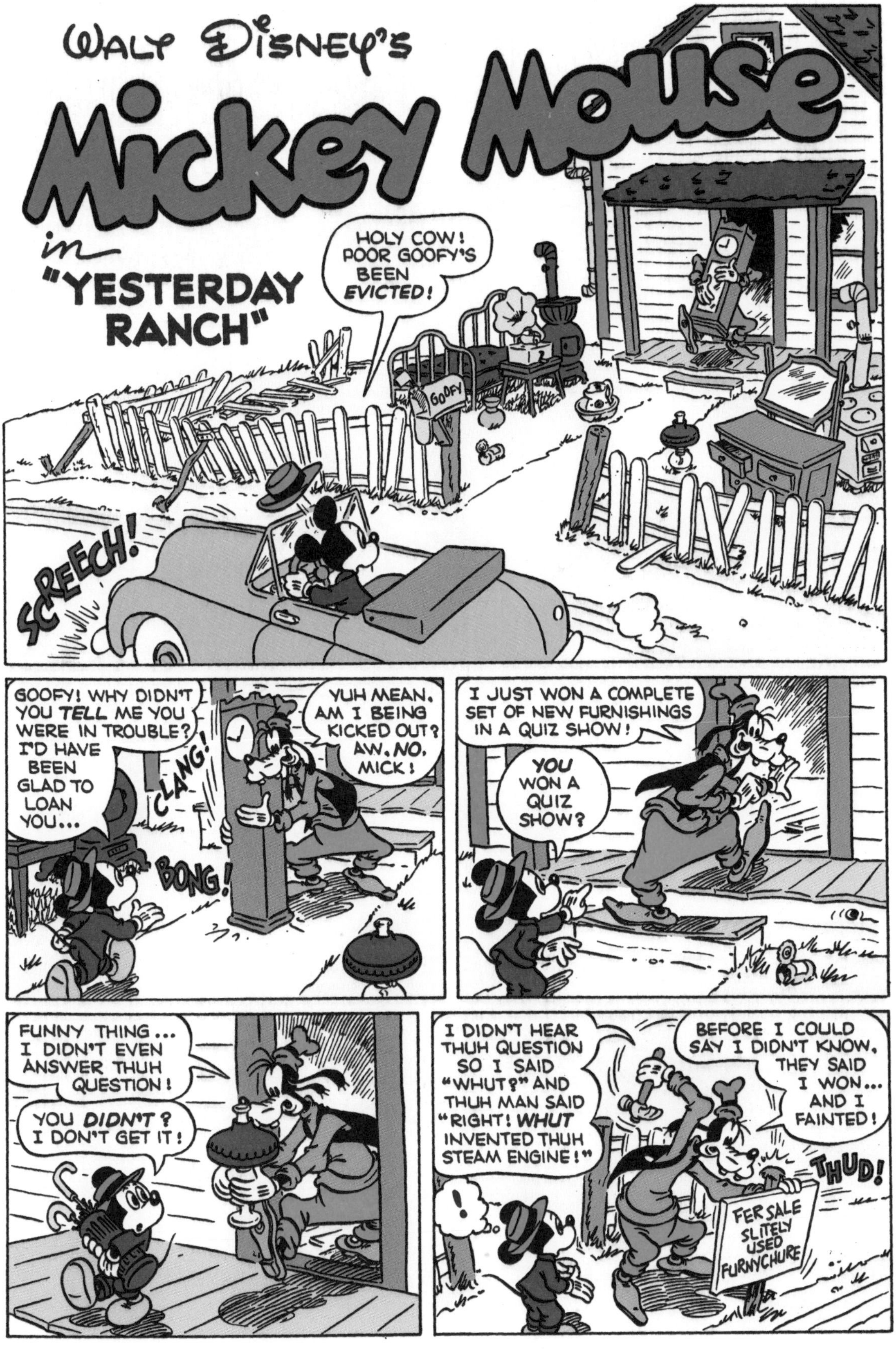
WALT DISNEY'S
Mickey Mouse
in "YESTERDAY RANCH"
HOLY COW! POOR GOOFY'S BEEN *EVICTED*!
GOOFY
SCREECH!
GOOFY! WHY DIDN'T YOU *TELL* ME YOU WERE IN TROUBLE? I'D HAVE BEEN GLAD TO LOAN YOU...
CLANG!
BONG!
YUH MEAN, AM I BEING KICKED OUT? AW, *NO*, MICK!
I JUST WON A COMPLETE SET OF NEW FURNISHINGS IN A QUIZ SHOW!
YOU WON A QUIZ SHOW?
FUNNY THING... I DIDN'T EVEN ANSWER THUH QUESTION!
YOU *DIDN'T*? I DON'T GET IT!
I DIDN'T HEAR THUH QUESTION SO I SAID "WHUT?" AND THUH MAN SAID "RIGHT! *WHUT* INVENTED THUH STEAM ENGINE!"
BEFORE I COULD SAY I DIDN'T KNOW, THEY SAID I WON... AND I FAINTED!
THUD!
!
FER SALE SLITELY USED FURNYCHURE

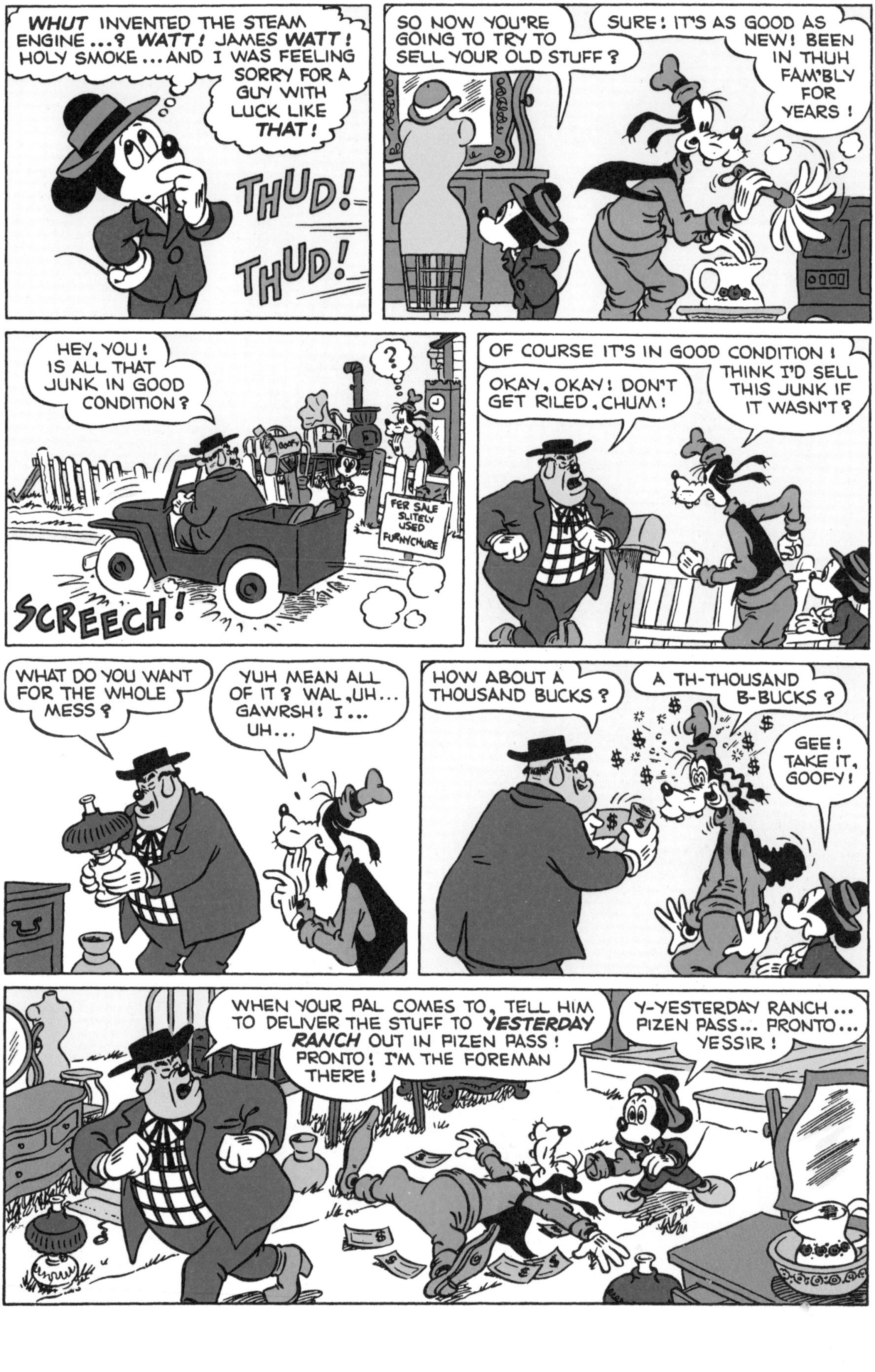
WHUT INVENTED THE STEAM ENGINE...? WATT! JAMES WATT! HOLY SMOKE... AND I WAS FEELING SORRY FOR A GUY WITH LUCK LIKE THAT!
THUD!
THUD!
SO NOW YOU'RE GOING TO TRY TO SELL YOUR OLD STUFF?
SURE! IT'S AS GOOD AS NEW! BEEN IN THUH FAM'BLY FOR YEARS!
HEY, YOU! IS ALL THAT JUNK IN GOOD CONDITION?
?
GOOFY
FER SALE SLITELY USED FURNYCHURE
SCREECH!
OF COURSE IT'S IN GOOD CONDITION! THINK I'D SELL THIS JUNK IF IT WASN'T?
OKAY, OKAY! DON'T GET RILED, CHUM!
WHAT DO YOU WANT FOR THE WHOLE MESS?
YUH MEAN ALL OF IT? WAL, UH... GAWRSH! I... UH...
HOW ABOUT A THOUSAND BUCKS?
A TH-THOUSAND B-BUCKS?
GEE! TAKE IT, GOOFY!
WHEN YOUR PAL COMES TO, TELL HIM TO DELIVER THE STUFF TO YESTERDAY RANCH OUT IN PIZEN PASS! PRONTO! I'M THE FOREMAN THERE!
Y-YESTERDAY RANCH... PIZEN PASS... PRONTO... YESSIR!

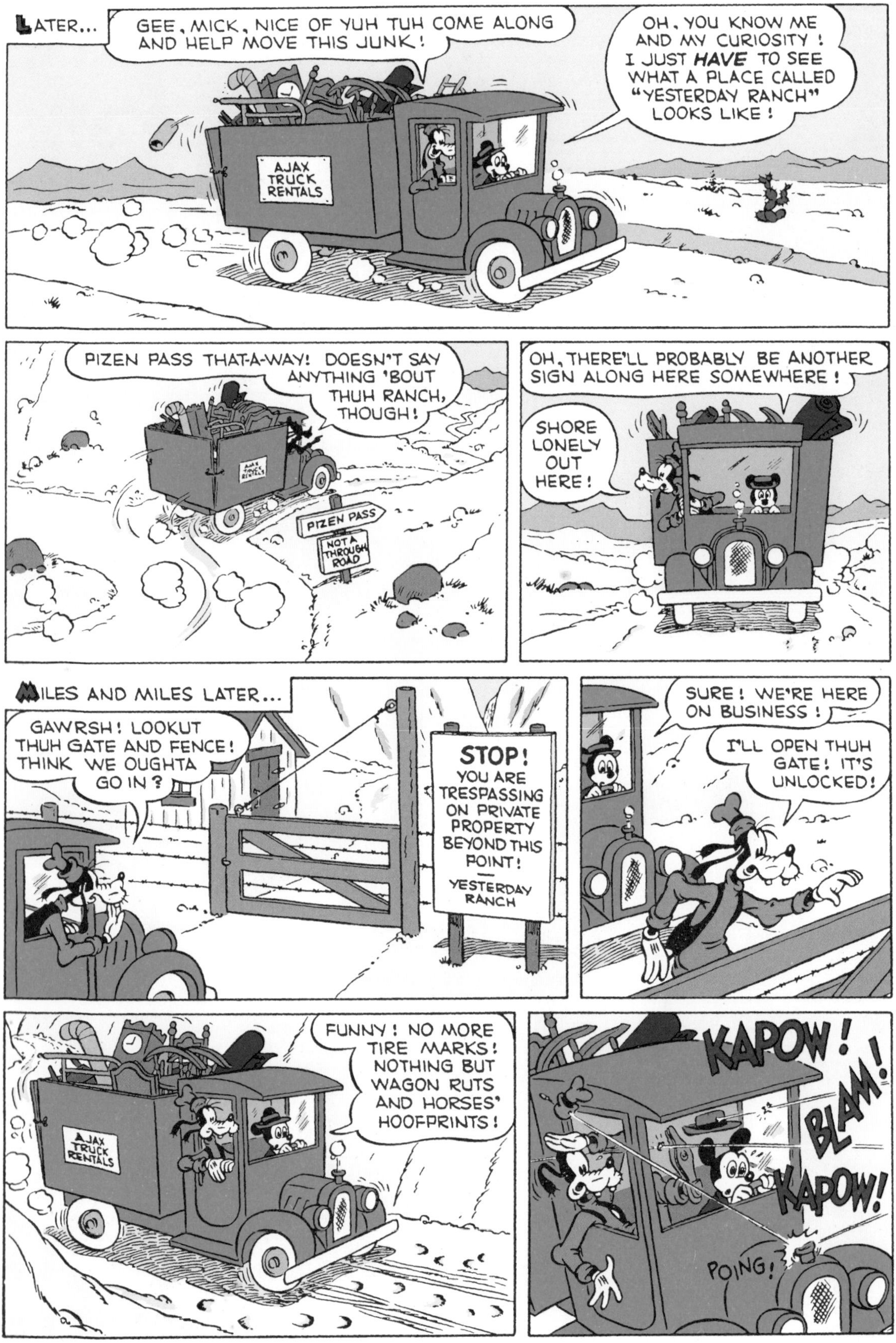
LATER...
GEE, MICK, NICE OF YUH TUH COME ALONG AND HELP MOVE THIS JUNK!
OH, YOU KNOW ME AND MY CURIOSITY! I JUST HAVE TO SEE WHAT A PLACE CALLED "YESTERDAY RANCH" LOOKS LIKE!
AJAX TRUCK RENTALS
PIZEN PASS THAT-A-WAY! DOESN'T SAY ANYTHING 'BOUT THUH RANCH, THOUGH!
PIZEN PASS
NOT A THROUGH ROAD
OH, THERE'LL PROBABLY BE ANOTHER SIGN ALONG HERE SOMEWHERE!
SHORE LONELY OUT HERE!
MILES AND MILES LATER...
GAWRSH! LOOKUT THUH GATE AND FENCE! THINK WE OUGHTA GO IN?
STOP! YOU ARE TRESPASSING ON PRIVATE PROPERTY BEYOND THIS POINT! — YESTERDAY RANCH
SURE! WE'RE HERE ON BUSINESS!
I'LL OPEN THUH GATE! IT'S UNLOCKED!
FUNNY! NO MORE TIRE MARKS! NOTHING BUT WAGON RUTS AND HORSES' HOOFPRINTS!
AJAX TRUCK RENTALS
KAPOW!
BLAM!
KAPOW!
POING!

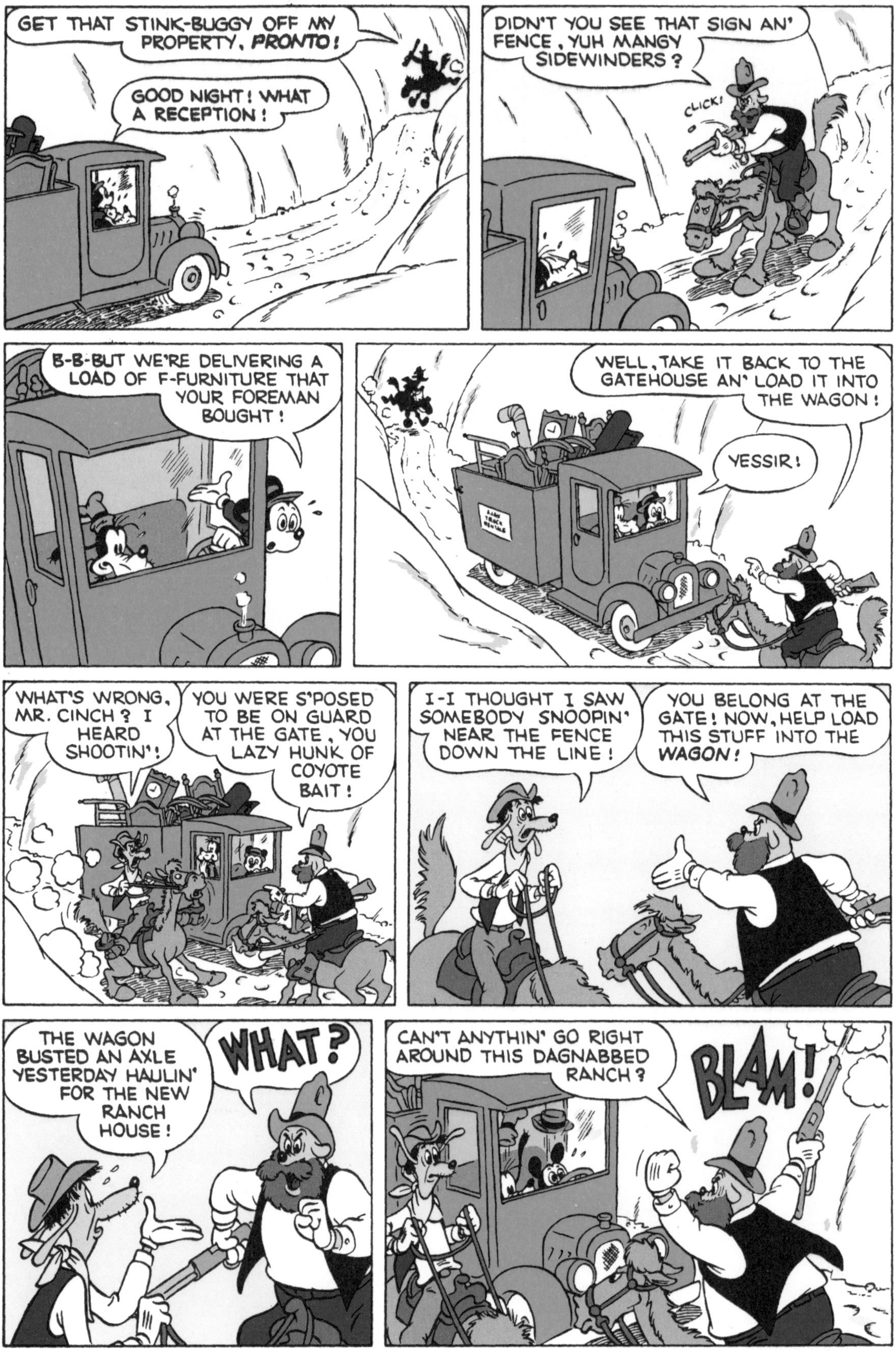
GET THAT STINK-BUGGY OFF MY PROPERTY, PRONTO!
GOOD NIGHT! WHAT A RECEPTION!
DIDN'T YOU SEE THAT SIGN AN' FENCE, YUH MANGY SIDEWINDERS?
CLICK!
B-B-BUT WE'RE DELIVERING A LOAD OF F-FURNITURE THAT YOUR FOREMAN BOUGHT!
WELL, TAKE IT BACK TO THE GATEHOUSE AN' LOAD IT INTO THE WAGON!
YESSIR!
WHAT'S WRONG, MR. CINCH? I HEARD SHOOTIN'!
YOU WERE S'POSED TO BE ON GUARD AT THE GATE, YOU LAZY HUNK OF COYOTE BAIT!
I-I THOUGHT I SAW SOMEBODY SNOOPIN' NEAR THE FENCE DOWN THE LINE!
YOU BELONG AT THE GATE! NOW, HELP LOAD THIS STUFF INTO THE WAGON!
THE WAGON BUSTED AN AXLE YESTERDAY HAULIN' FOR THE NEW RANCH HOUSE!
WHAT?
CAN'T ANYTHIN' GO RIGHT AROUND THIS DAGNABBED RANCH?
BLAM!

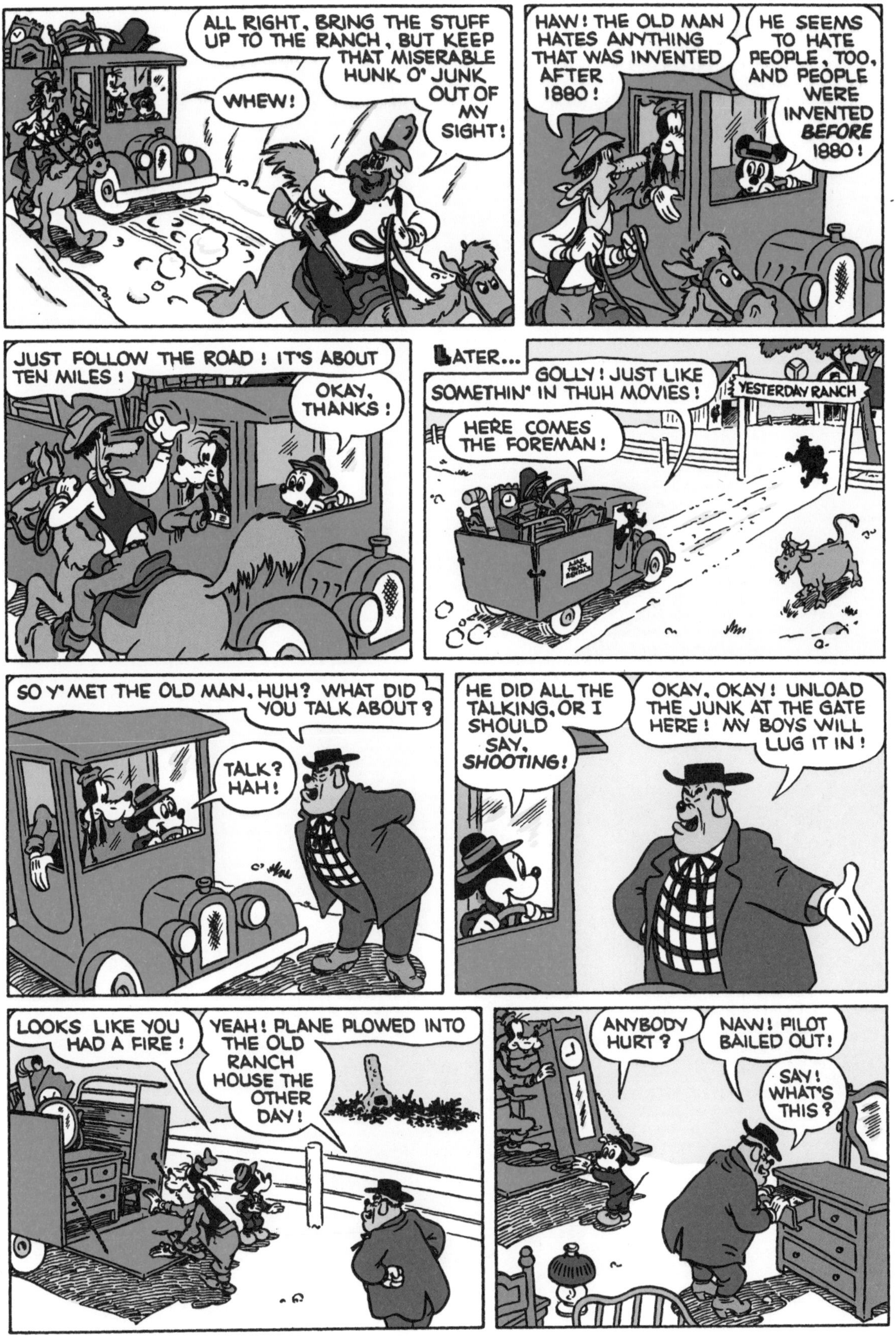

ALL RIGHT, BRING THE STUFF UP TO THE RANCH, BUT KEEP THAT MISERABLE HUNK O' JUNK OUT OF MY SIGHT!
WHEW!
HAW! THE OLD MAN HATES ANYTHING THAT WAS INVENTED AFTER 1880!
HE SEEMS TO HATE PEOPLE, TOO, AND PEOPLE WERE INVENTED *BEFORE* 1880!
JUST FOLLOW THE ROAD! IT'S ABOUT TEN MILES!
OKAY, THANKS!
LATER...
GOLLY! JUST LIKE SOMETHIN' IN THUH MOVIES!
HERE COMES THE FOREMAN!
YESTERDAY RANCH
SO Y' MET THE OLD MAN, HUH? WHAT DID YOU TALK ABOUT?
TALK? HAH!
HE DID ALL THE TALKING, OR I SHOULD SAY, *SHOOTING*!
OKAY, OKAY! UNLOAD THE JUNK AT THE GATE HERE! MY BOYS WILL LUG IT IN!
LOOKS LIKE YOU HAD A FIRE!
YEAH! PLANE PLOWED INTO THE OLD RANCH HOUSE THE OTHER DAY!
ANYBODY HURT?
NAW! PILOT BAILED OUT!
SAY! WHAT'S THIS?

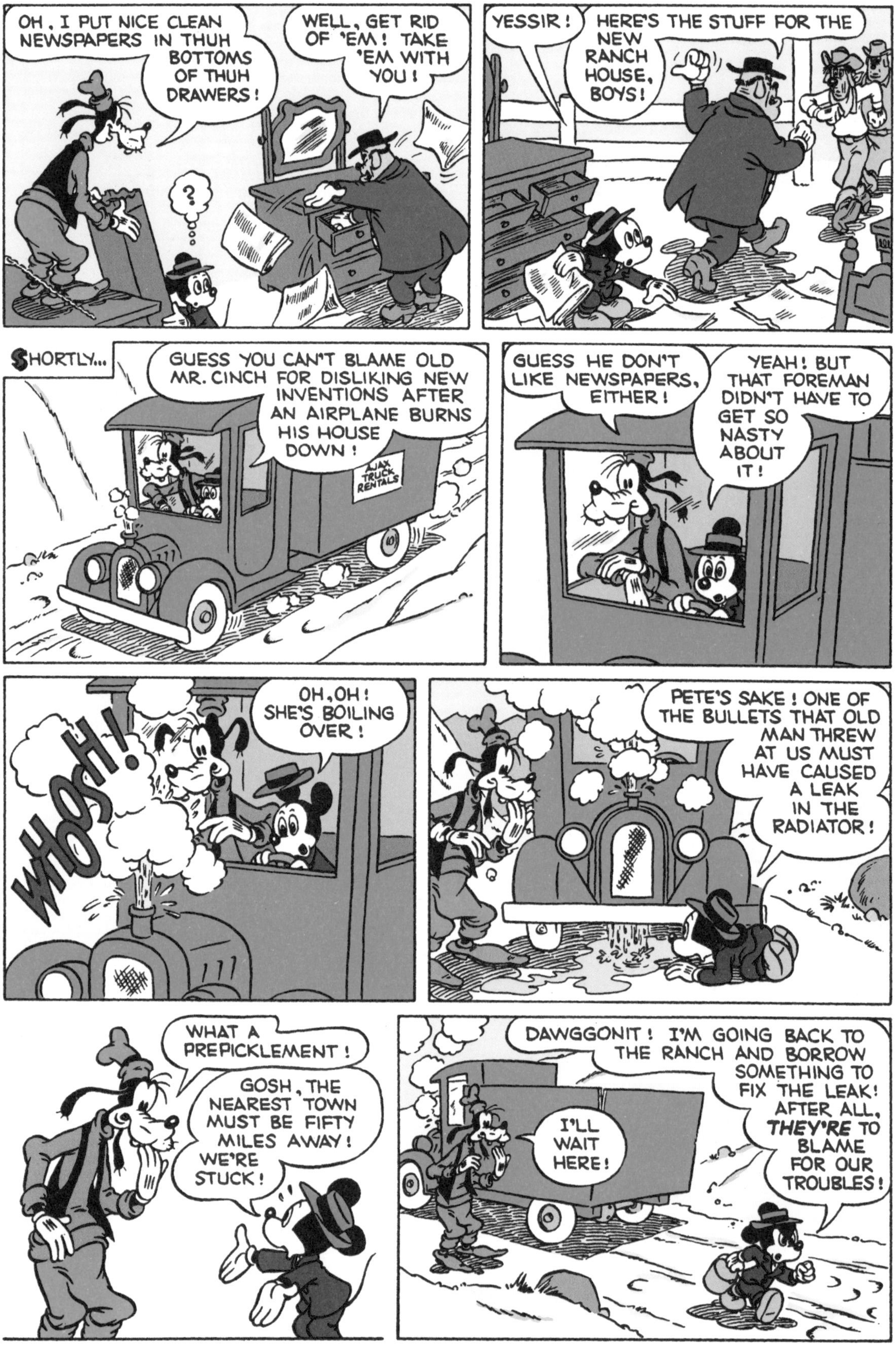
OH, I PUT NICE CLEAN NEWSPAPERS IN THUH BOTTOMS OF THUH DRAWERS!
?
WELL, GET RID OF 'EM! TAKE 'EM WITH YOU!
YESSIR!
HERE'S THE STUFF FOR THE NEW RANCH HOUSE, BOYS!
SHORTLY...
GUESS YOU CAN'T BLAME OLD MR. CINCH FOR DISLIKING NEW INVENTIONS AFTER AN AIRPLANE BURNS HIS HOUSE DOWN!
AJAX TRUCK RENTALS
GUESS HE DON'T LIKE NEWSPAPERS, EITHER!
YEAH! BUT THAT FOREMAN DIDN'T HAVE TO GET SO NASTY ABOUT IT!
WHOOSH!
OH, OH! SHE'S BOILING OVER!
PETE'S SAKE! ONE OF THE BULLETS THAT OLD MAN THREW AT US MUST HAVE CAUSED A LEAK IN THE RADIATOR!
WHAT A PREPICKLEMENT!
GOSH, THE NEAREST TOWN MUST BE FIFTY MILES AWAY! WE'RE STUCK!
DAWGGONIT! I'M GOING BACK TO THE RANCH AND BORROW SOMETHING TO FIX THE LEAK! AFTER ALL, THEY'RE TO BLAME FOR OUR TROUBLES!
I'LL WAIT HERE!

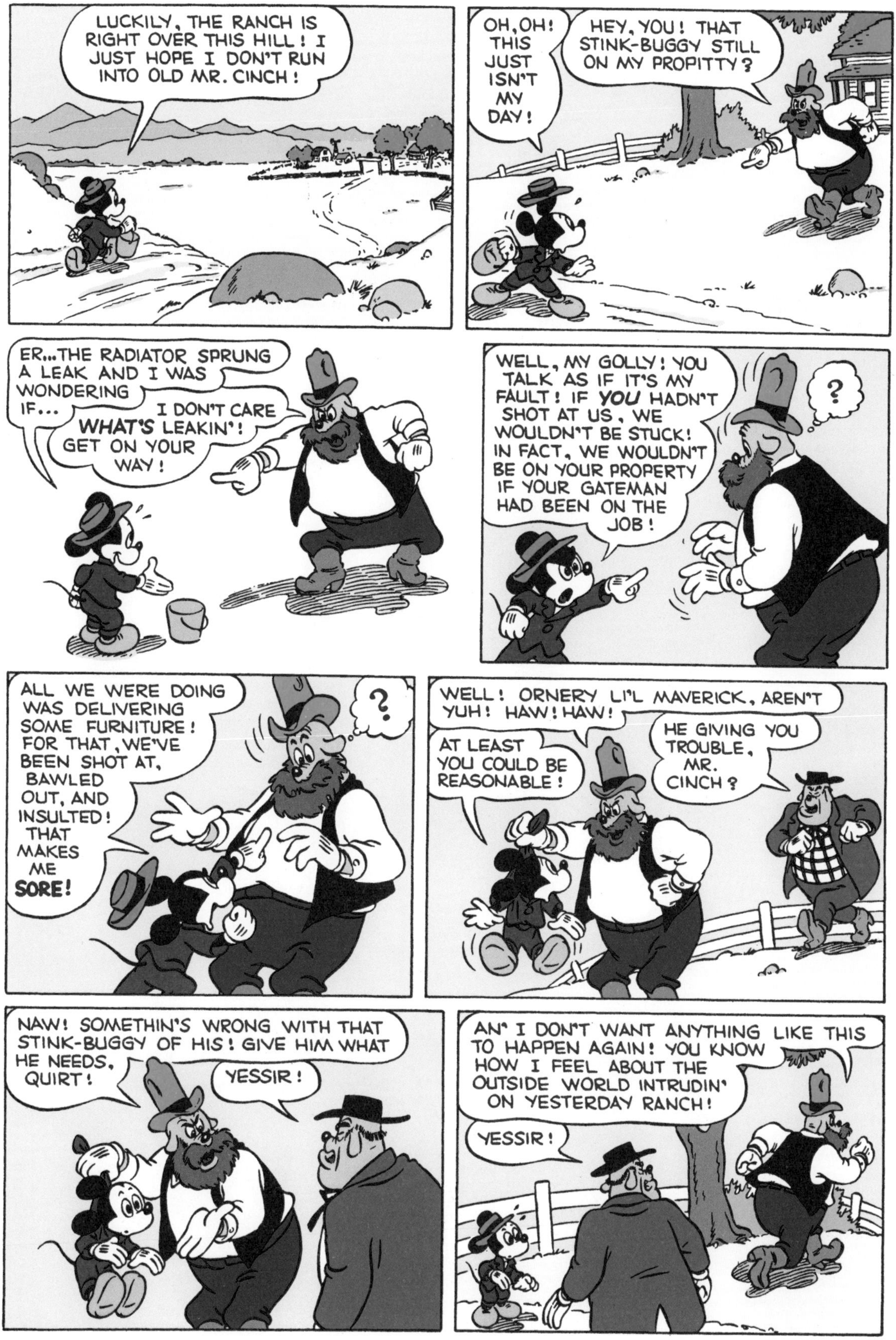

LUCKILY, THE RANCH IS RIGHT OVER THIS HILL! I JUST HOPE I DON'T RUN INTO OLD MR. CINCH!
HEY, YOU! THAT STINK-BUGGY STILL ON MY PROPITTY?
OH, OH! THIS JUST ISN'T MY DAY!
ER...THE RADIATOR SPRUNG A LEAK AND I WAS WONDERING IF...
I DON'T CARE WHAT'S LEAKIN'! GET ON YOUR WAY!
WELL, MY GOLLY! YOU TALK AS IF IT'S MY FAULT! IF YOU HADN'T SHOT AT US, WE WOULDN'T BE STUCK! IN FACT, WE WOULDN'T BE ON YOUR PROPERTY IF YOUR GATEMAN HAD BEEN ON THE JOB!
?
ALL WE WERE DOING WAS DELIVERING SOME FURNITURE! FOR THAT, WE'VE BEEN SHOT AT, BAWLED OUT, AND INSULTED! THAT MAKES ME SORE!
?
WELL! ORNERY LI'L MAVERICK, AREN'T YUH! HAW! HAW!
AT LEAST YOU COULD BE REASONABLE!
HE GIVING YOU TROUBLE, MR. CINCH?
NAW! SOMETHIN'S WRONG WITH THAT STINK-BUGGY OF HIS! GIVE HIM WHAT HE NEEDS, QUIRT!
YESSIR!
AN' I DON'T WANT ANYTHING LIKE THIS TO HAPPEN AGAIN! YOU KNOW HOW I FEEL ABOUT THE OUTSIDE WORLD INTRUDIN' ON YESTERDAY RANCH!
YESSIR!

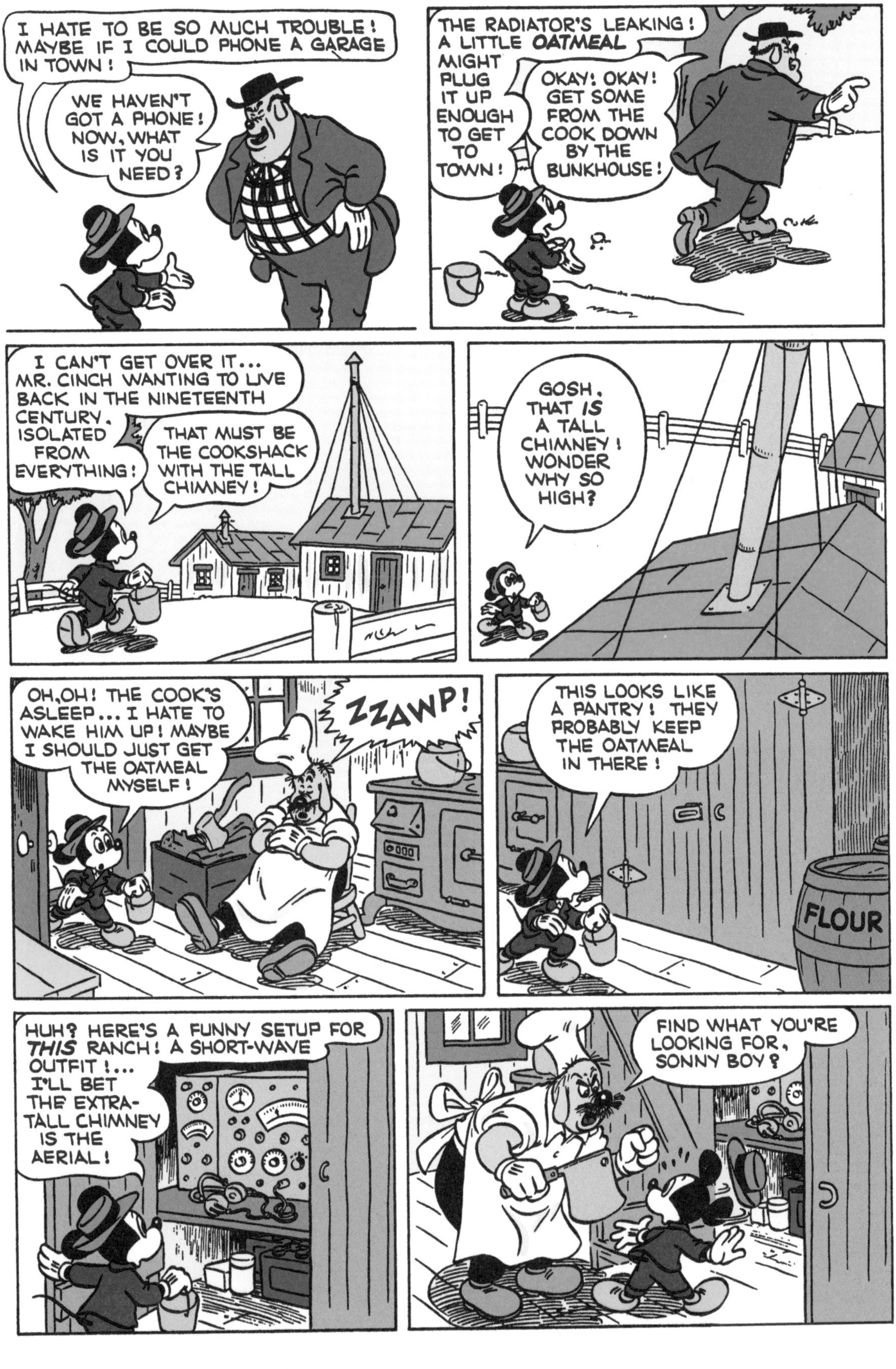
I HATE TO BE SO MUCH TROUBLE! MAYBE IF I COULD PHONE A GARAGE IN TOWN!
WE HAVEN'T GOT A PHONE! NOW, WHAT IS IT YOU NEED?
THE RADIATOR'S LEAKING! A LITTLE OATMEAL MIGHT PLUG IT UP ENOUGH TO GET TO TOWN!
OKAY! OKAY! GET SOME FROM THE COOK DOWN BY THE BUNKHOUSE!
I CAN'T GET OVER IT... MR. CINCH WANTING TO LIVE BACK IN THE NINETEENTH CENTURY, ISOLATED FROM EVERYTHING!
THAT MUST BE THE COOKSHACK WITH THE TALL CHIMNEY!
GOSH, THAT IS A TALL CHIMNEY! WONDER WHY SO HIGH?
OH,OH! THE COOK'S ASLEEP... I HATE TO WAKE HIM UP! MAYBE I SHOULD JUST GET THE OATMEAL MYSELF!
ZZAWP!
THIS LOOKS LIKE A PANTRY! THEY PROBABLY KEEP THE OATMEAL IN THERE!
FLOUR
HUH? HERE'S A FUNNY SETUP FOR THIS RANCH! A SHORT-WAVE OUTFIT!... I'LL BET THE EXTRA-TALL CHIMNEY IS THE AERIAL!
FIND WHAT YOU'RE LOOKING FOR, SONNY BOY?

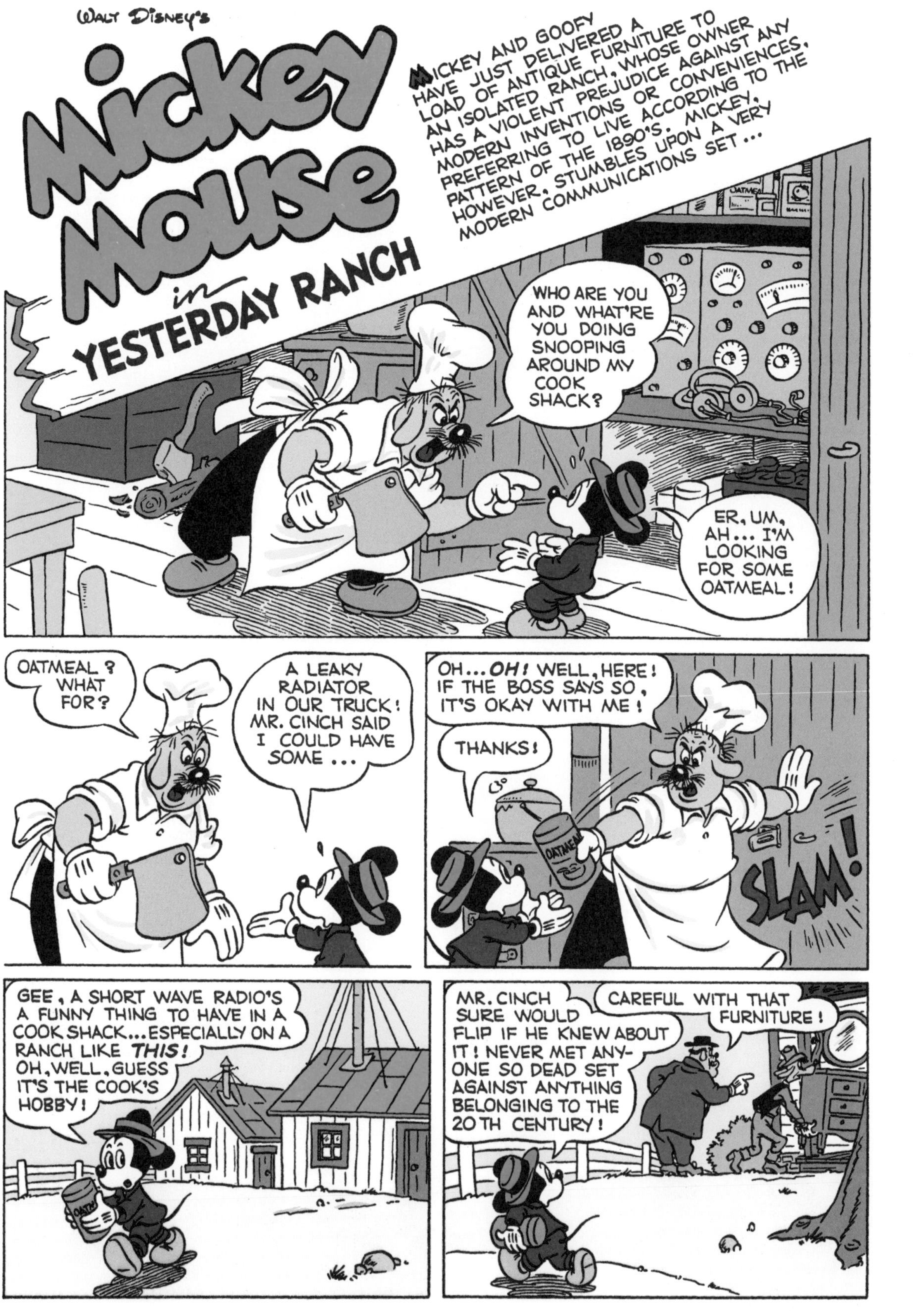
WALT DISNEY'S
MICKEY MOUSE
in
YESTERDAY RANCH
MICKEY AND GOOFY HAVE JUST DELIVERED A LOAD OF ANTIQUE FURNITURE TO AN ISOLATED RANCH, WHOSE OWNER HAS A VIOLENT PREJUDICE AGAINST ANY MODERN INVENTIONS OR CONVENIENCES, PREFERRING TO LIVE ACCORDING TO THE PATTERN OF THE 1890'S. MICKEY, HOWEVER, STUMBLES UPON A VERY MODERN COMMUNICATIONS SET...
WHO ARE YOU AND WHAT'RE YOU DOING SNOOPING AROUND MY COOK SHACK?
ER, UM, AH... I'M LOOKING FOR SOME OATMEAL!
OATMEAL? WHAT FOR?
A LEAKY RADIATOR IN OUR TRUCK! MR. CINCH SAID I COULD HAVE SOME...
OH... OH! WELL, HERE! IF THE BOSS SAYS SO, IT'S OKAY WITH ME!
THANKS!
OATMEAL
SLAM!
GEE, A SHORT WAVE RADIO'S A FUNNY THING TO HAVE IN A COOK SHACK... ESPECIALLY ON A RANCH LIKE THIS! OH, WELL, GUESS IT'S THE COOK'S HOBBY!
MR. CINCH SURE WOULD FLIP IF HE KNEW ABOUT IT! NEVER MET ANYONE SO DEAD SET AGAINST ANYTHING BELONGING TO THE 20TH CENTURY!
CAREFUL WITH THAT FURNITURE!

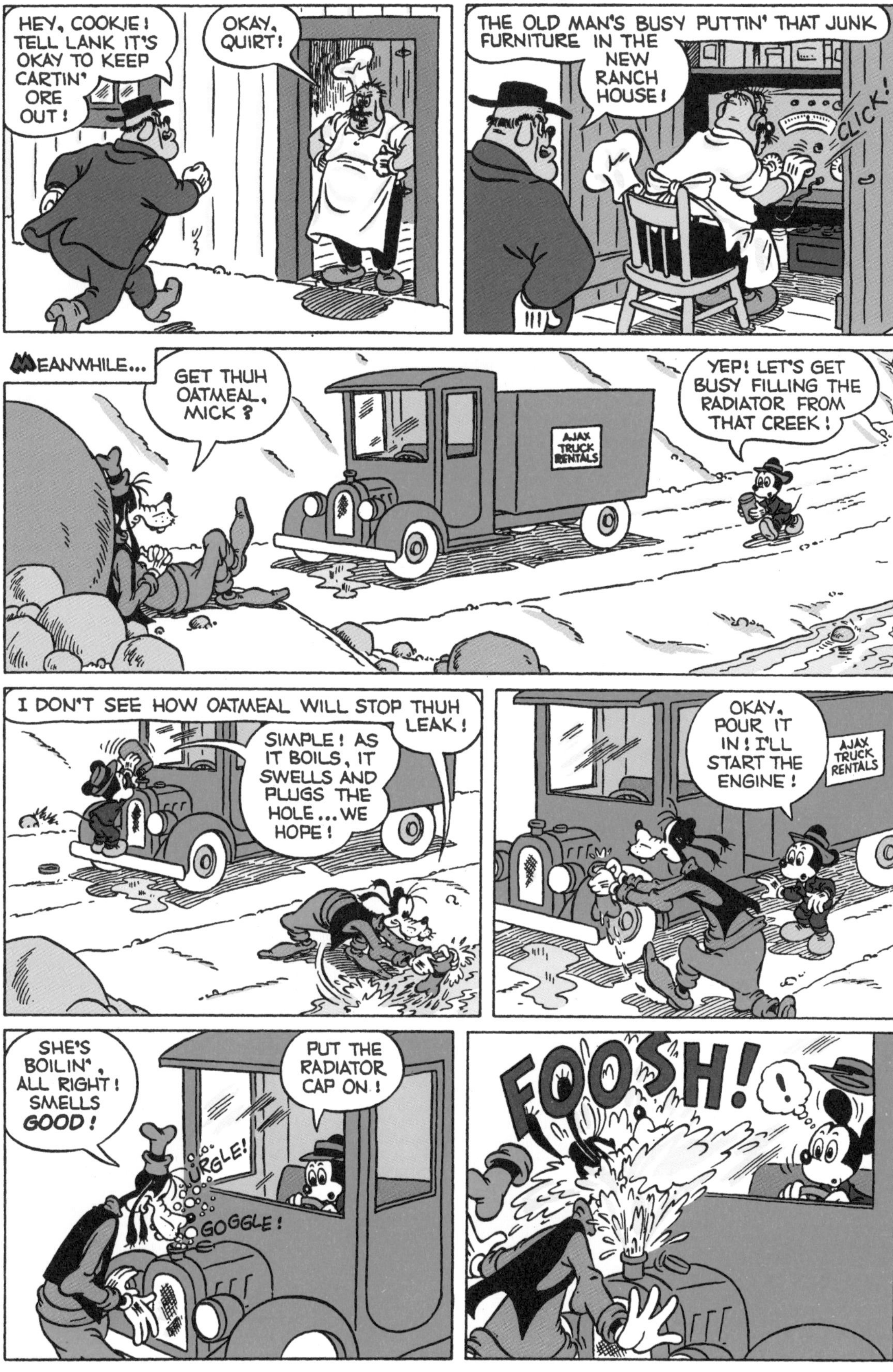
HEY, COOKIE! TELL LANK IT'S OKAY TO KEEP CARTIN' ORE OUT!
OKAY, QUIRT!
THE OLD MAN'S BUSY PUTTIN' THAT JUNK FURNITURE IN THE NEW RANCH HOUSE!
CLICK!
MEANWHILE...
GET THUH OATMEAL, MICK?
AJAX TRUCK RENTALS
YEP! LET'S GET BUSY FILLING THE RADIATOR FROM THAT CREEK!
I DON'T SEE HOW OATMEAL WILL STOP THUH LEAK!
SIMPLE! AS IT BOILS, IT SWELLS AND PLUGS THE HOLE... WE HOPE!
OKAY. POUR IT IN! I'LL START THE ENGINE!
AJAX TRUCK RENTALS
SHE'S BOILIN', ALL RIGHT! SMELLS GOOD!
PUT THE RADIATOR CAP ON!
URGLE!
GOGGLE!
FOOSH!
!

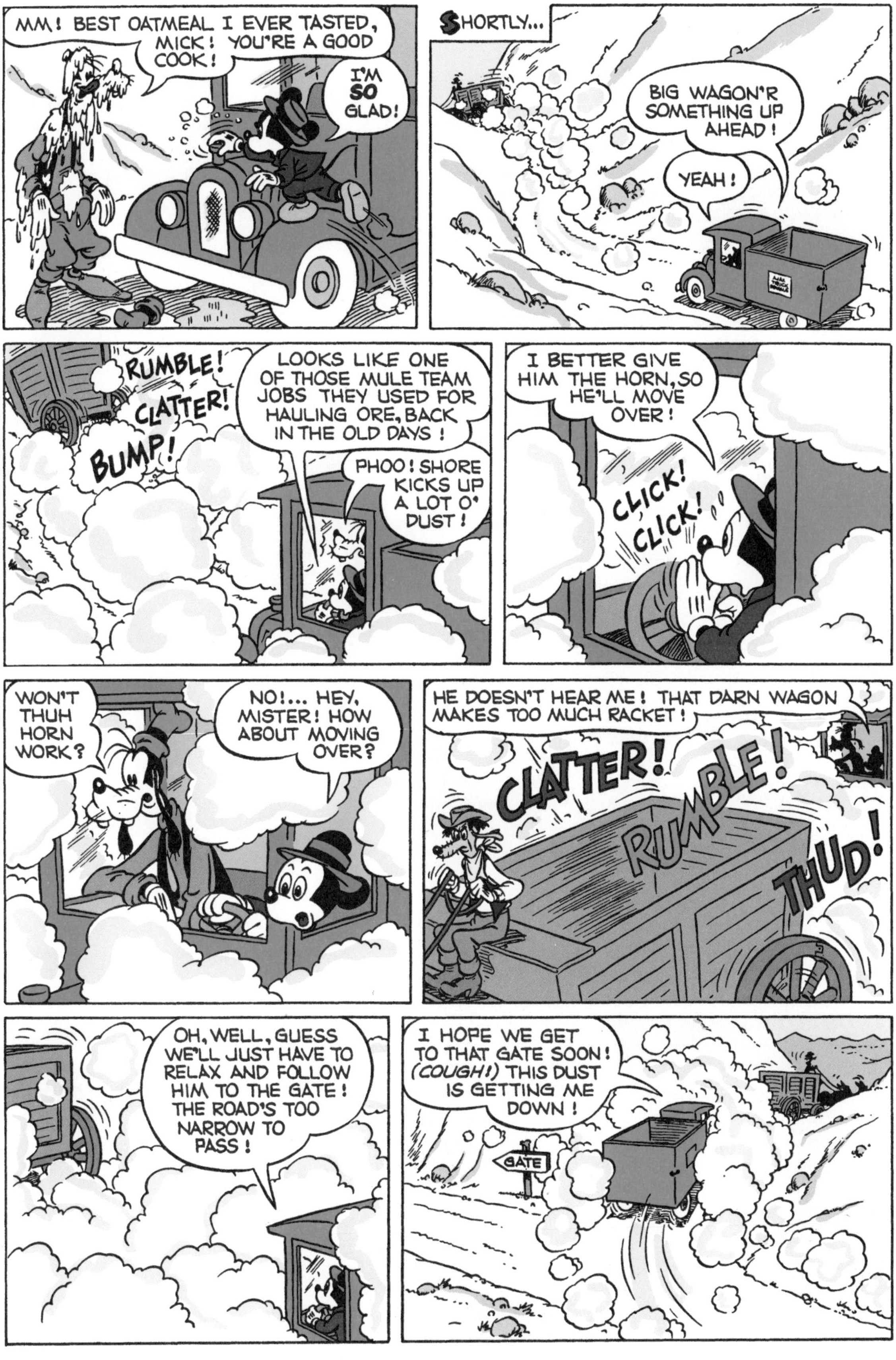
MM! BEST OATMEAL I EVER TASTED, MICK! YOU'RE A GOOD COOK!
I'M SO GLAD!
SHORTLY...
BIG WAGON'R SOMETHING UP AHEAD!
YEAH!
RUMBLE!
CLATTER!
BUMP!
LOOKS LIKE ONE OF THOSE MULE TEAM JOBS THEY USED FOR HAULING ORE, BACK IN THE OLD DAYS!
PHOO! SHORE KICKS UP A LOT O' DUST!
I BETTER GIVE HIM THE HORN, SO HE'LL MOVE OVER!
CLICK!
CLICK!
WON'T THUH HORN WORK?
NO!... HEY, MISTER! HOW ABOUT MOVING OVER?
HE DOESN'T HEAR ME! THAT DARN WAGON MAKES TOO MUCH RACKET!
CLATTER!
RUMBLE!
THUD!
OH, WELL, GUESS WE'LL JUST HAVE TO RELAX AND FOLLOW HIM TO THE GATE! THE ROAD'S TOO NARROW TO PASS!
I HOPE WE GET TO THAT GATE SOON! (COUGH!) THIS DUST IS GETTING ME DOWN!
GATE

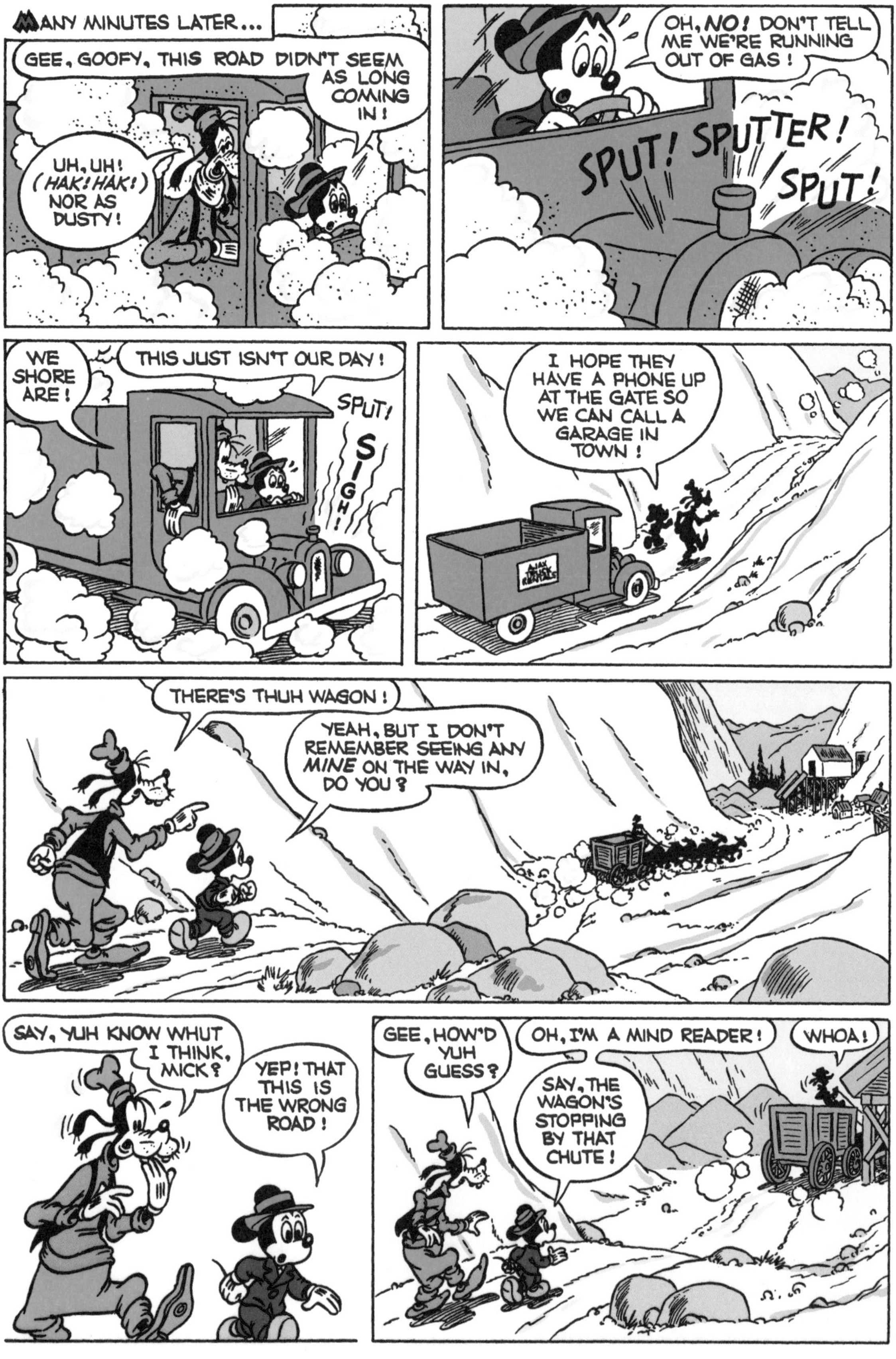
MANY MINUTES LATER...
GEE, GOOFY, THIS ROAD DIDN'T SEEM AS LONG COMING IN!
UH, UH! (HAK! HAK!) NOR AS DUSTY!
OH, NO! DON'T TELL ME WE'RE RUNNING OUT OF GAS!
SPUT! SPUTTER! SPUT!
WE SHORE ARE!
THIS JUST ISN'T OUR DAY!
SPUT!
SIGH!
I HOPE THEY HAVE A PHONE UP AT THE GATE SO WE CAN CALL A GARAGE IN TOWN!
THERE'S THUH WAGON!
YEAH, BUT I DON'T REMEMBER SEEING ANY MINE ON THE WAY IN, DO YOU?
SAY, YUH KNOW WHUT I THINK, MICK?
YEP! THAT THIS IS THE WRONG ROAD!
GEE, HOW'D YUH GUESS?
OH, I'M A MIND READER!
WHOA!
SAY, THE WAGON'S STOPPING BY THAT CHUTE!

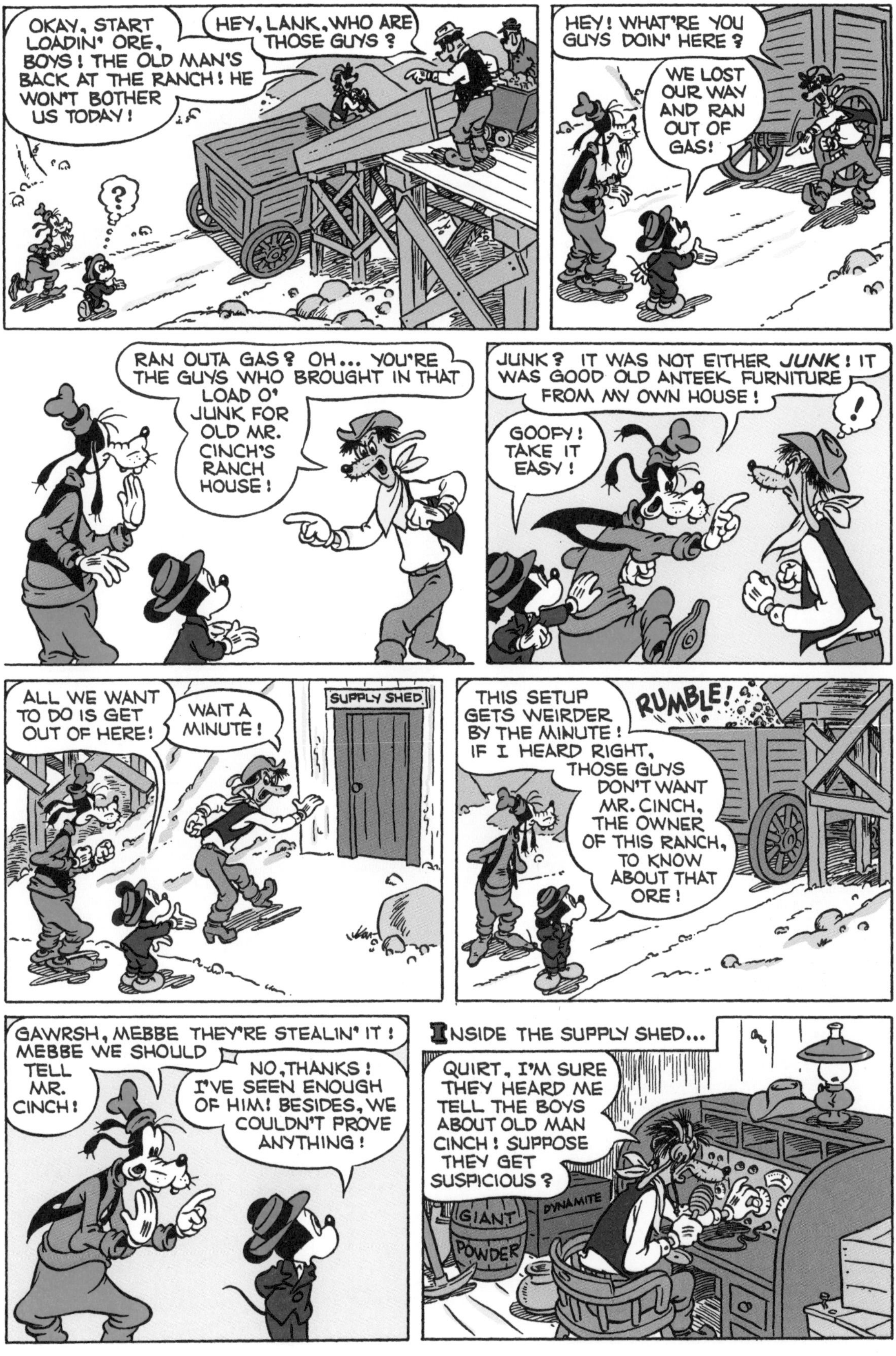

OKAY, START LOADIN' ORE, BOYS! THE OLD MAN'S BACK AT THE RANCH! HE WON'T BOTHER US TODAY!
HEY, LANK, WHO ARE THOSE GUYS?
?
HEY! WHAT'RE YOU GUYS DOIN' HERE?
WE LOST OUR WAY AND RAN OUT OF GAS!
RAN OUTA GAS? OH... YOU'RE THE GUYS WHO BROUGHT IN THAT LOAD O' JUNK FOR OLD MR. CINCH'S RANCH HOUSE!
JUNK? IT WAS NOT EITHER JUNK! IT WAS GOOD OLD ANTEEK FURNITURE FROM MY OWN HOUSE!
!
GOOFY! TAKE IT EASY!
ALL WE WANT TO DO IS GET OUT OF HERE!
WAIT A MINUTE!
SUPPLY SHED
THIS SETUP GETS WEIRDER BY THE MINUTE! IF I HEARD RIGHT, THOSE GUYS DON'T WANT MR. CINCH, THE OWNER OF THIS RANCH, TO KNOW ABOUT THAT ORE!
RUMBLE!
GAWRSH, MEBBE THEY'RE STEALIN' IT! MEBBE WE SHOULD TELL MR. CINCH!
NO, THANKS! I'VE SEEN ENOUGH OF HIM! BESIDES, WE COULDN'T PROVE ANYTHING!
INSIDE THE SUPPLY SHED...
QUIRT, I'M SURE THEY HEARD ME TELL THE BOYS ABOUT OLD MAN CINCH! SUPPOSE THEY GET SUSPICIOUS?
GIANT POWDER
DYNAMITE

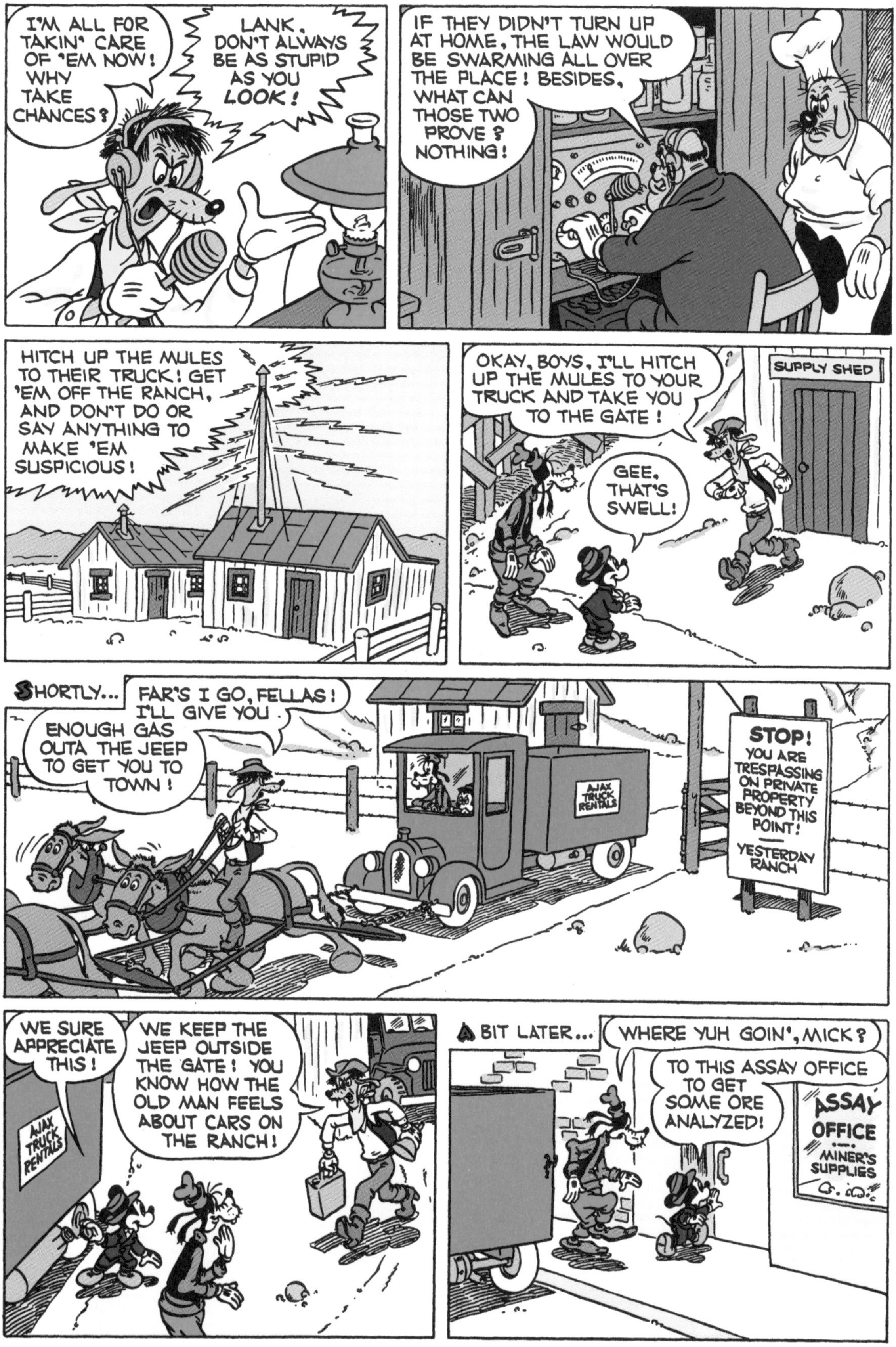
I'M ALL FOR TAKIN' CARE OF 'EM NOW! WHY TAKE CHANCES?
LANK. DON'T ALWAYS BE AS STUPID AS YOU LOOK!
IF THEY DIDN'T TURN UP AT HOME, THE LAW WOULD BE SWARMING ALL OVER THE PLACE! BESIDES, WHAT CAN THOSE TWO PROVE? NOTHING!
HITCH UP THE MULES TO THEIR TRUCK! GET 'EM OFF THE RANCH, AND DON'T DO OR SAY ANYTHING TO MAKE 'EM SUSPICIOUS!
OKAY, BOYS, I'LL HITCH UP THE MULES TO YOUR TRUCK AND TAKE YOU TO THE GATE!
SUPPLY SHED
GEE, THAT'S SWELL!
SHORTLY...
FAR'S I GO, FELLAS! I'LL GIVE YOU ENOUGH GAS OUTA THE JEEP TO GET YOU TO TOWN!
AJAX TRUCK RENTALS
STOP! YOU ARE TRESPASSING ON PRIVATE PROPERTY BEYOND THIS POINT! YESTERDAY RANCH
WE SURE APPRECIATE THIS!
WE KEEP THE JEEP OUTSIDE THE GATE! YOU KNOW HOW THE OLD MAN FEELS ABOUT CARS ON THE RANCH!
AJAX TRUCK RENTALS
A BIT LATER...
WHERE YUH GOIN', MICK?
TO THIS ASSAY OFFICE TO GET SOME ORE ANALYZED!
ASSAY OFFICE MINER'S SUPPLIES

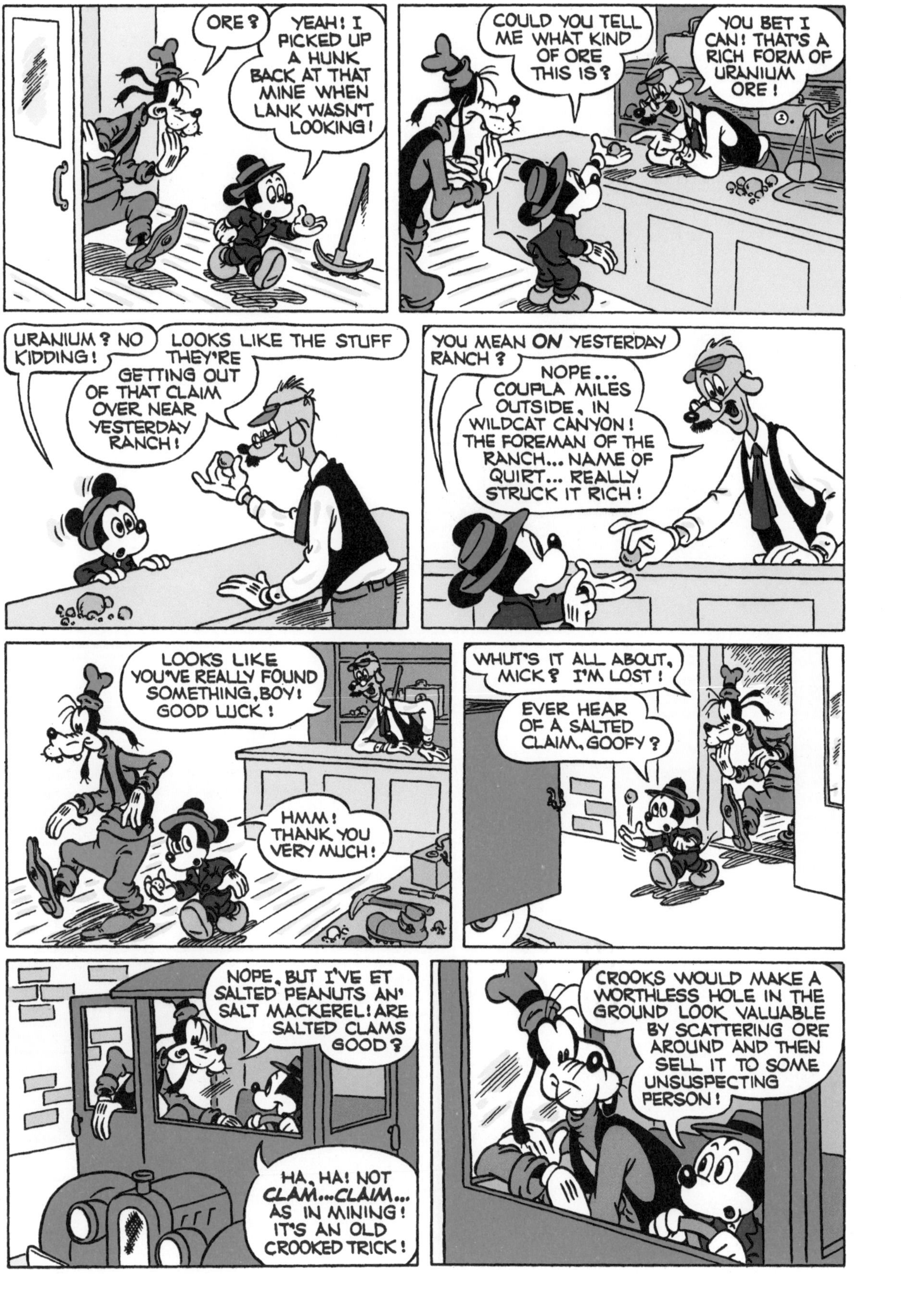
ORE?
YEAH! I PICKED UP A HUNK BACK AT THAT MINE WHEN LANK WASN'T LOOKING!
COULD YOU TELL ME WHAT KIND OF ORE THIS IS?
YOU BET I CAN! THAT'S A RICH FORM OF URANIUM ORE!
URANIUM? NO KIDDING!
LOOKS LIKE THE STUFF THEY'RE GETTING OUT OF THAT CLAIM OVER NEAR YESTERDAY RANCH!
YOU MEAN ON YESTERDAY RANCH?
NOPE... COUPLA MILES OUTSIDE, IN WILDCAT CANYON! THE FOREMAN OF THE RANCH... NAME OF QUIRT... REALLY STRUCK IT RICH!
LOOKS LIKE YOU'VE REALLY FOUND SOMETHING, BOY! GOOD LUCK!
HMM! THANK YOU VERY MUCH!
WHUT'S IT ALL ABOUT, MICK? I'M LOST!
EVER HEAR OF A SALTED CLAIM, GOOFY?
NOPE, BUT I'VE ET SALTED PEANUTS AN' SALT MACKEREL! ARE SALTED CLAMS GOOD?
HA, HA! NOT CLAM...CLAIM... AS IN MINING! IT'S AN OLD CROOKED TRICK!
CROOKS WOULD MAKE A WORTHLESS HOLE IN THE GROUND LOOK VALUABLE BY SCATTERING ORE AROUND AND THEN SELL IT TO SOME UNSUSPECTING PERSON!

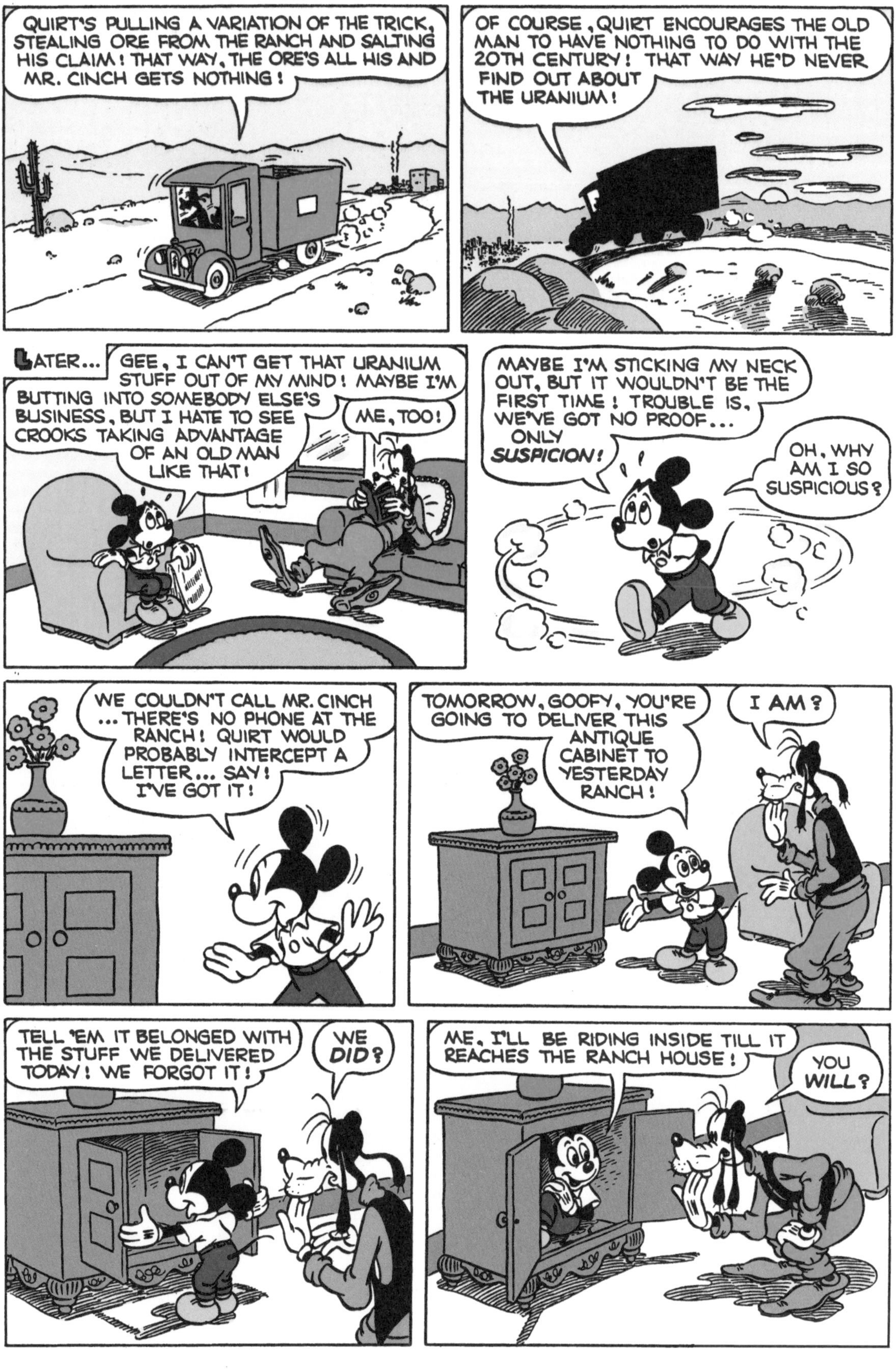

QUIRT'S PULLING A VARIATION OF THE TRICK, STEALING ORE FROM THE RANCH AND SALTING HIS CLAIM! THAT WAY, THE ORE'S ALL HIS AND MR. CINCH GETS NOTHING!
OF COURSE, QUIRT ENCOURAGES THE OLD MAN TO HAVE NOTHING TO DO WITH THE 20TH CENTURY! THAT WAY HE'D NEVER FIND OUT ABOUT THE URANIUM!
LATER...
GEE, I CAN'T GET THAT URANIUM STUFF OUT OF MY MIND! MAYBE I'M BUTTING INTO SOMEBODY ELSE'S BUSINESS, BUT I HATE TO SEE CROOKS TAKING ADVANTAGE OF AN OLD MAN LIKE THAT!
ME, TOO!
MAYBE I'M STICKING MY NECK OUT, BUT IT WOULDN'T BE THE FIRST TIME! TROUBLE IS, WE'VE GOT NO PROOF... ONLY *SUSPICION!*
OH, WHY AM I SO SUSPICIOUS?
WE COULDN'T CALL MR. CINCH ... THERE'S NO PHONE AT THE RANCH! QUIRT WOULD PROBABLY INTERCEPT A LETTER... SAY! I'VE GOT IT!
TOMORROW, GOOFY, YOU'RE GOING TO DELIVER THIS ANTIQUE CABINET TO YESTERDAY RANCH!
I AM?
TELL 'EM IT BELONGED WITH THE STUFF WE DELIVERED TODAY! WE FORGOT IT!
WE *DID*?
ME, I'LL BE RIDING INSIDE TILL IT REACHES THE RANCH HOUSE!
YOU *WILL*?

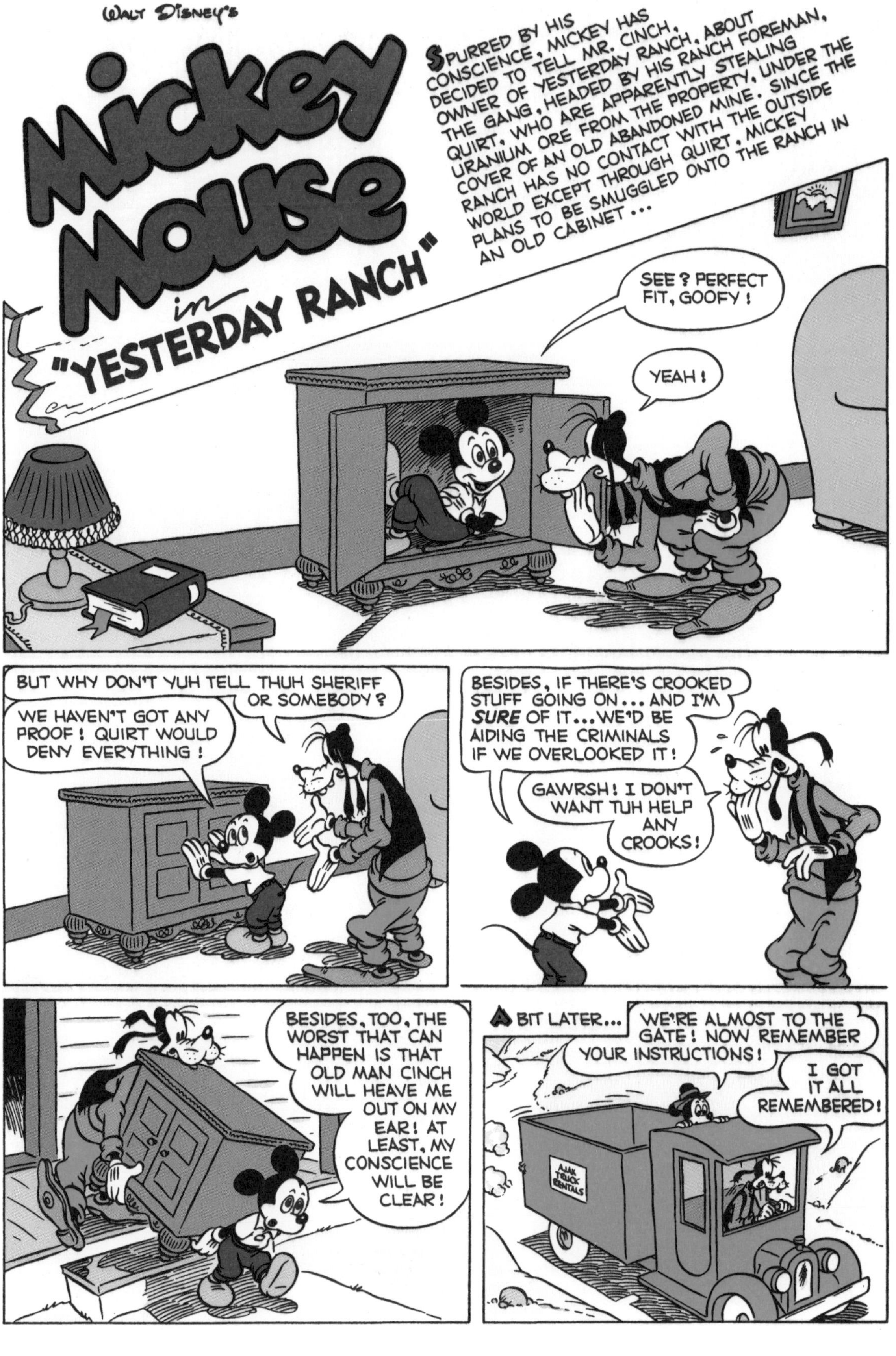
WALT DISNEY'S
Mickey Mouse
in
"YESTERDAY RANCH"
SPURRED BY HIS CONSCIENCE, MICKEY HAS DECIDED TO TELL MR. CINCH, OWNER OF YESTERDAY RANCH, ABOUT THE GANG, HEADED BY HIS RANCH FOREMAN, QUIRT, WHO ARE APPARENTLY STEALING URANIUM ORE FROM THE PROPERTY, UNDER THE COVER OF AN OLD ABANDONED MINE. SINCE THE RANCH HAS NO CONTACT WITH THE OUTSIDE WORLD EXCEPT THROUGH QUIRT, MICKEY PLANS TO BE SMUGGLED ONTO THE RANCH IN AN OLD CABINET ...
SEE? PERFECT FIT, GOOFY!
YEAH!
BUT WHY DON'T YUH TELL THUH SHERIFF OR SOMEBODY?
WE HAVEN'T GOT ANY PROOF! QUIRT WOULD DENY EVERYTHING!
BESIDES, IF THERE'S CROOKED STUFF GOING ON... AND I'M SURE OF IT... WE'D BE AIDING THE CRIMINALS IF WE OVERLOOKED IT!
GAWRSH! I DON'T WANT TUH HELP ANY CROOKS!
BESIDES, TOO, THE WORST THAT CAN HAPPEN IS THAT OLD MAN CINCH WILL HEAVE ME OUT ON MY EAR! AT LEAST, MY CONSCIENCE WILL BE CLEAR!
A BIT LATER...
WE'RE ALMOST TO THE GATE! NOW REMEMBER YOUR INSTRUCTIONS!
I GOT IT ALL REMEMBERED!
AJAX TRUCK RENTALS

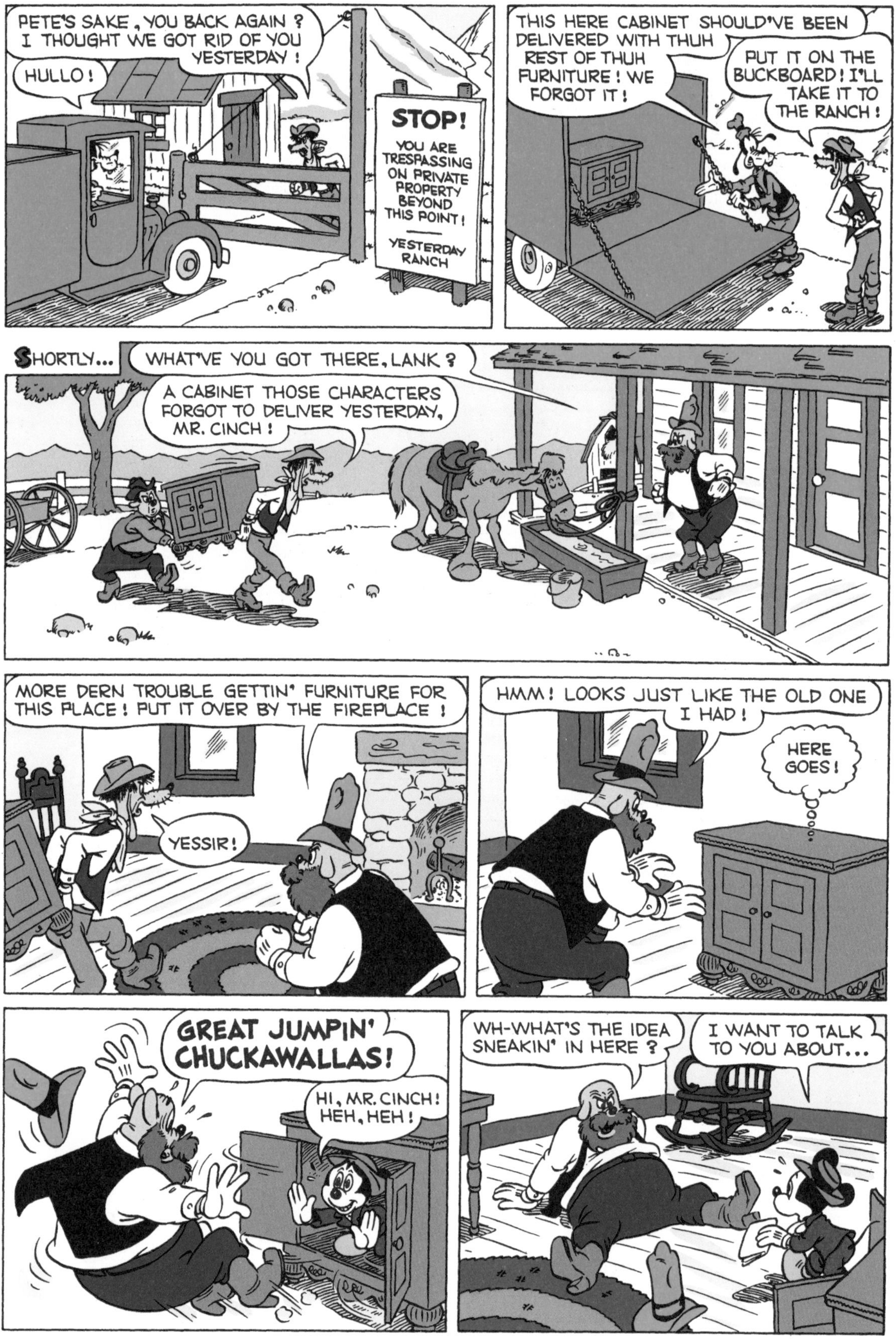
PETE'S SAKE, YOU BACK AGAIN? I THOUGHT WE GOT RID OF YOU YESTERDAY!
HULLO!
STOP! YOU ARE TRESPASSING ON PRIVATE PROPERTY BEYOND THIS POINT! YESTERDAY RANCH
THIS HERE CABINET SHOULD'VE BEEN DELIVERED WITH THUH REST OF THUH FURNITURE! WE FORGOT IT!
PUT IT ON THE BUCKBOARD! I'LL TAKE IT TO THE RANCH!
SHORTLY...
WHAT'VE YOU GOT THERE, LANK?
A CABINET THOSE CHARACTERS FORGOT TO DELIVER YESTERDAY, MR. CINCH!
MORE DERN TROUBLE GETTIN' FURNITURE FOR THIS PLACE! PUT IT OVER BY THE FIREPLACE!
YESSIR!
HMM! LOOKS JUST LIKE THE OLD ONE I HAD!
HERE GOES!
GREAT JUMPIN' CHUCKAWALLAS!
HI, MR. CINCH! HEH, HEH!
WH-WHAT'S THE IDEA SNEAKIN' IN HERE?
I WANT TO TALK TO YOU ABOUT...

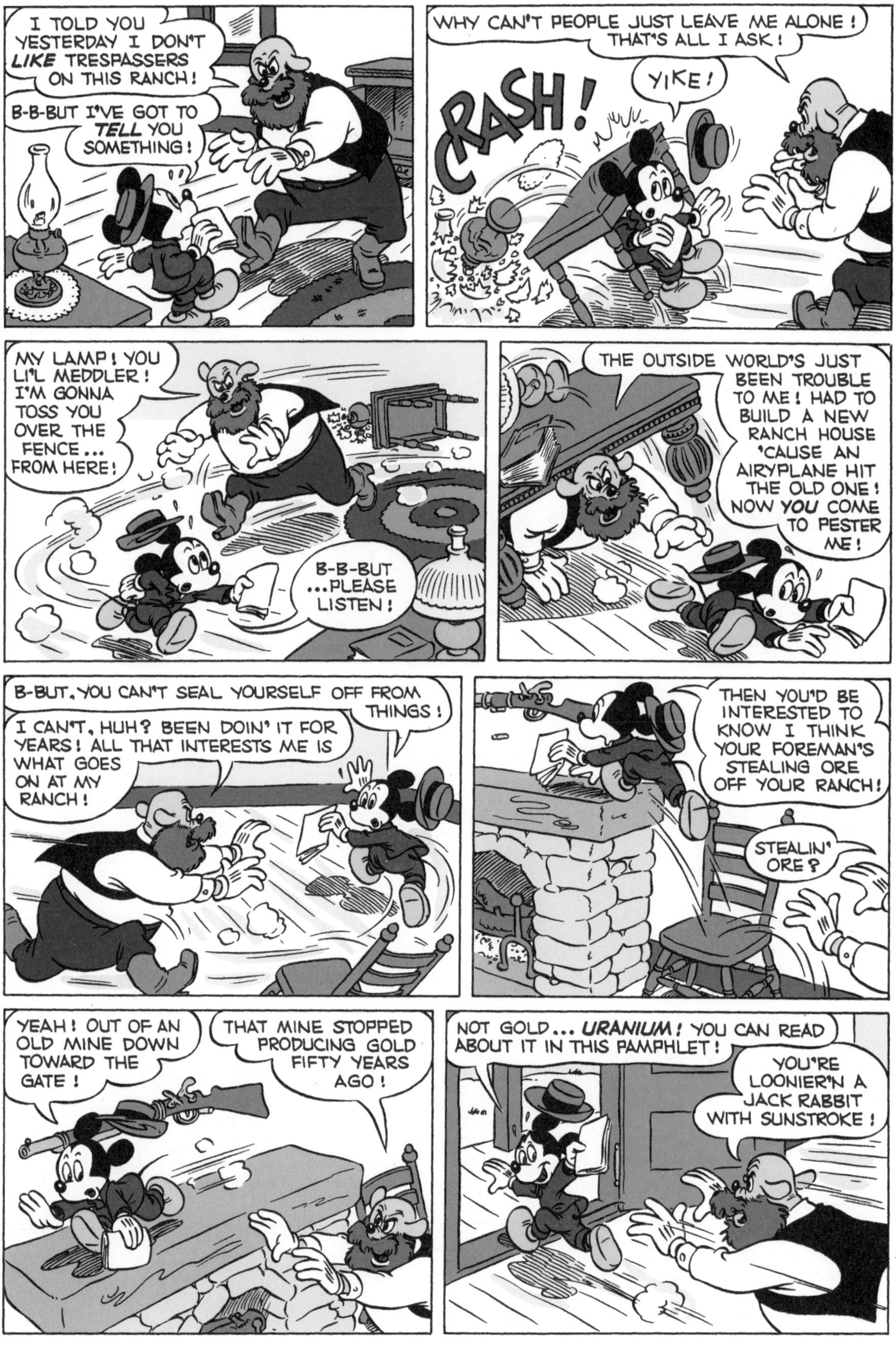

I TOLD YOU YESTERDAY I DON'T *LIKE* TRESPASSERS ON THIS RANCH!
B-B-BUT I'VE GOT TO *TELL* YOU SOMETHING!
WHY CAN'T PEOPLE JUST LEAVE ME ALONE! THAT'S ALL I ASK!
CRASH!
YIKE!
MY LAMP! YOU LI'L MEDDLER! I'M GONNA TOSS YOU OVER THE FENCE... FROM HERE!
B-B-BUT ...PLEASE LISTEN!
THE OUTSIDE WORLD'S JUST BEEN TROUBLE TO ME! HAD TO BUILD A NEW RANCH HOUSE 'CAUSE AN AIRYPLANE HIT THE OLD ONE! NOW *YOU* COME TO PESTER ME!
B-BUT, YOU CAN'T SEAL YOURSELF OFF FROM THINGS!
I CAN'T, HUH? BEEN DOIN' IT FOR YEARS! ALL THAT INTERESTS ME IS WHAT GOES ON AT MY RANCH!
THEN YOU'D BE INTERESTED TO KNOW I THINK YOUR FOREMAN'S STEALING ORE OFF YOUR RANCH!
STEALIN' ORE?
YEAH! OUT OF AN OLD MINE DOWN TOWARD THE GATE!
THAT MINE STOPPED PRODUCING GOLD FIFTY YEARS AGO!
NOT GOLD... *URANIUM!* YOU CAN READ ABOUT IT IN THIS PAMPHLET!
YOU'RE LOONIER'N A JACK RABBIT WITH SUNSTROKE!

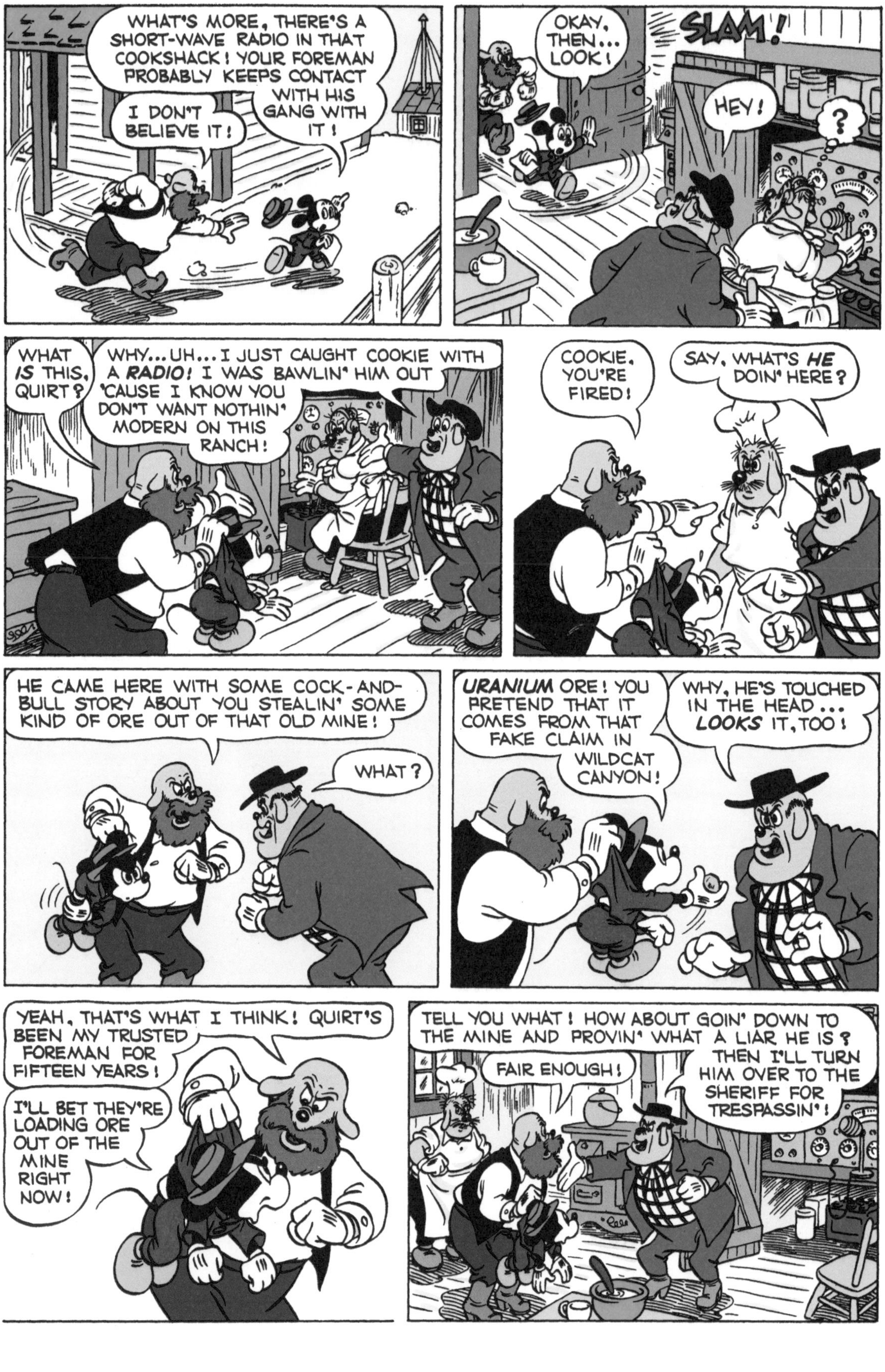
WHAT'S MORE, THERE'S A SHORT-WAVE RADIO IN THAT COOKSHACK! YOUR FOREMAN PROBABLY KEEPS CONTACT WITH HIS GANG WITH IT!
I DON'T BELIEVE IT!
OKAY, THEN... LOOK!
SLAM!
HEY!
?
WHAT IS THIS, QUIRT?
WHY... UH... I JUST CAUGHT COOKIE WITH A RADIO! I WAS BAWLIN' HIM OUT 'CAUSE I KNOW YOU DON'T WANT NOTHIN' MODERN ON THIS RANCH!
COOKIE, YOU'RE FIRED!
SAY, WHAT'S HE DOIN' HERE?
HE CAME HERE WITH SOME COCK-AND-BULL STORY ABOUT YOU STEALIN' SOME KIND OF ORE OUT OF THAT OLD MINE!
WHAT?
URANIUM ORE! YOU PRETEND THAT IT COMES FROM THAT FAKE CLAIM IN WILDCAT CANYON!
WHY, HE'S TOUCHED IN THE HEAD... LOOKS IT, TOO!
YEAH, THAT'S WHAT I THINK! QUIRT'S BEEN MY TRUSTED FOREMAN FOR FIFTEEN YEARS!
I'LL BET THEY'RE LOADING ORE OUT OF THE MINE RIGHT NOW!
TELL YOU WHAT! HOW ABOUT GOIN' DOWN TO THE MINE AND PROVIN' WHAT A LIAR HE IS?
FAIR ENOUGH!
THEN I'LL TURN HIM OVER TO THE SHERIFF FOR TRESPASSIN'!

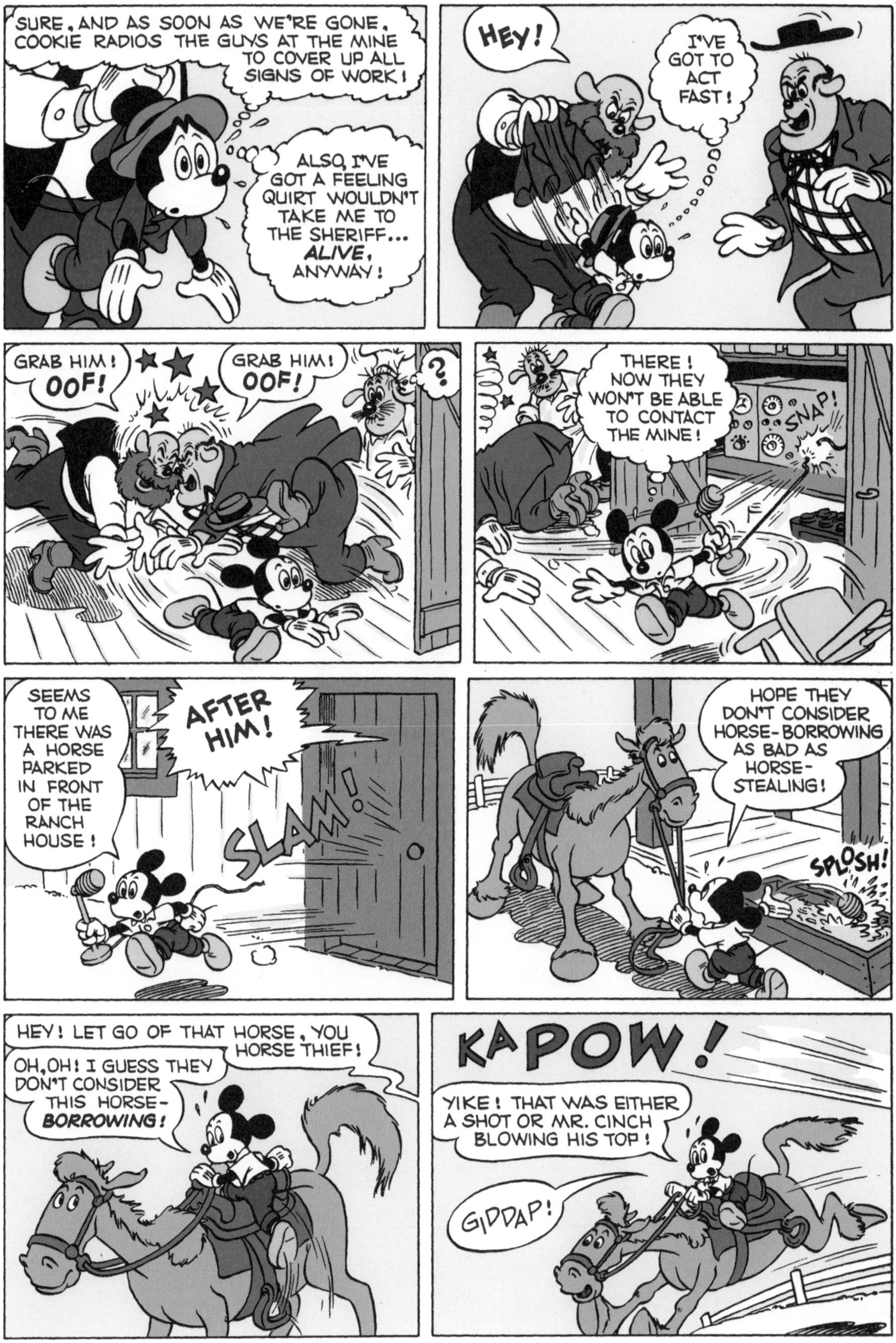
SURE, AND AS SOON AS WE'RE GONE, COOKIE RADIOS THE GUYS AT THE MINE TO COVER UP ALL SIGNS OF WORK!
ALSO, I'VE GOT A FEELING QUIRT WOULDN'T TAKE ME TO THE SHERIFF... ALIVE, ANYWAY!
HEY!
I'VE GOT TO ACT FAST!
GRAB HIM! OOF!
GRAB HIM! OOF!
?
THERE! NOW THEY WON'T BE ABLE TO CONTACT THE MINE!
SNAP!
SEEMS TO ME THERE WAS A HORSE PARKED IN FRONT OF THE RANCH HOUSE!
AFTER HIM!
SLAM!
HOPE THEY DON'T CONSIDER HORSE-BORROWING AS BAD AS HORSE-STEALING!
SPLOSH!
HEY! LET GO OF THAT HORSE, YOU HORSE THIEF!
OH, OH! I GUESS THEY DON'T CONSIDER THIS HORSE-BORROWING!
KAPOW!
YIKE! THAT WAS EITHER A SHOT OR MR. CINCH BLOWING HIS TOP!
GIDDAP!

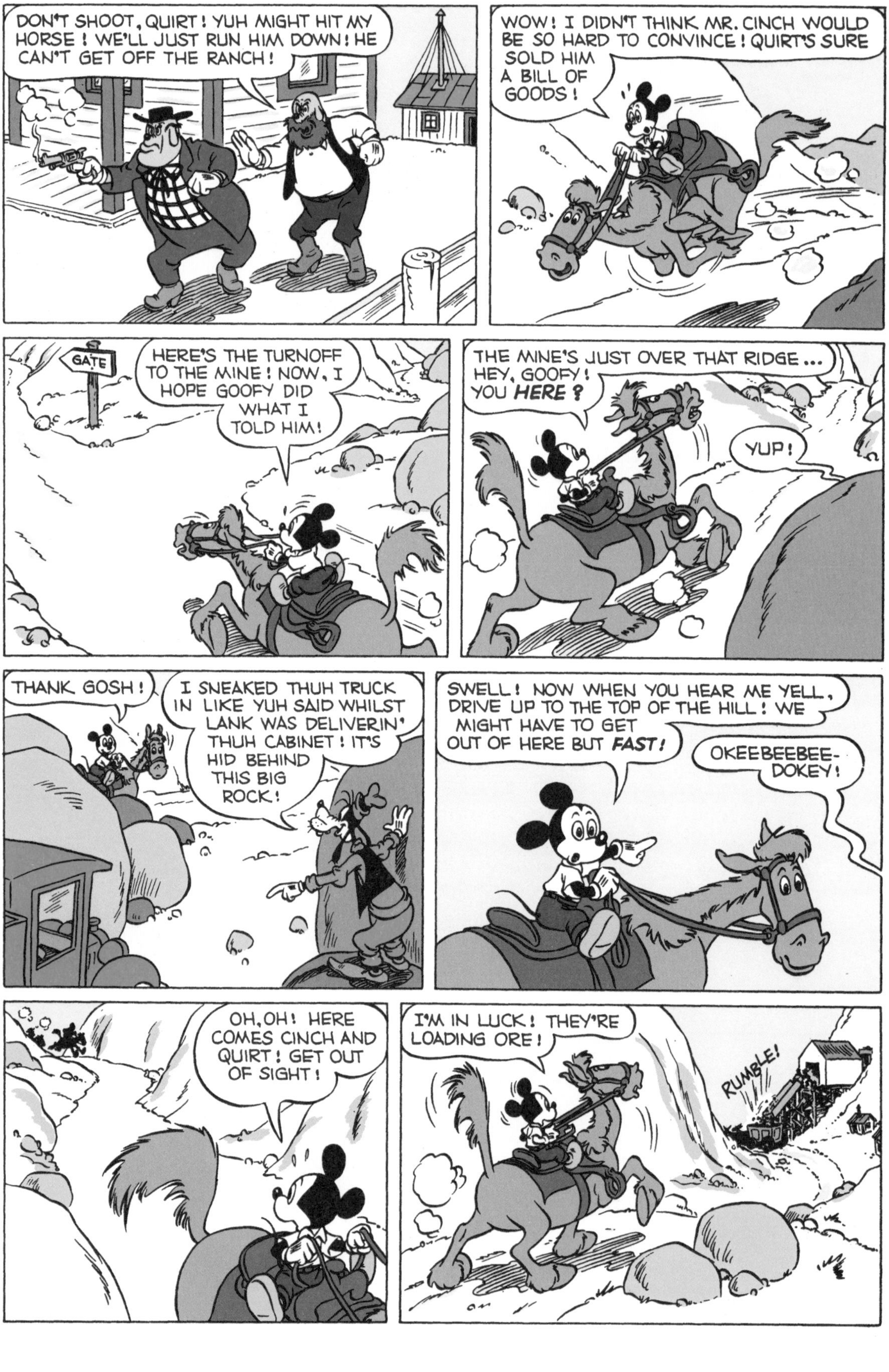
DON'T SHOOT, QUIRT! YUH MIGHT HIT MY HORSE! WE'LL JUST RUN HIM DOWN! HE CAN'T GET OFF THE RANCH!
WOW! I DIDN'T THINK MR. CINCH WOULD BE SO HARD TO CONVINCE! QUIRT'S SURE SOLD HIM A BILL OF GOODS!
GATE
HERE'S THE TURNOFF TO THE MINE! NOW, I HOPE GOOFY DID WHAT I TOLD HIM!
THE MINE'S JUST OVER THAT RIDGE... HEY, GOOFY! YOU HERE?
YUP!
THANK GOSH!
I SNEAKED THUH TRUCK IN LIKE YUH SAID WHILST LANK WAS DELIVERIN' THUH CABINET! IT'S HID BEHIND THIS BIG ROCK!
SWELL! NOW WHEN YOU HEAR ME YELL, DRIVE UP TO THE TOP OF THE HILL! WE MIGHT HAVE TO GET OUT OF HERE BUT FAST!
OKEEBEEBEE-DOKEY!
OH, OH! HERE COMES CINCH AND QUIRT! GET OUT OF SIGHT!
I'M IN LUCK! THEY'RE LOADING ORE!
RUMBLE!

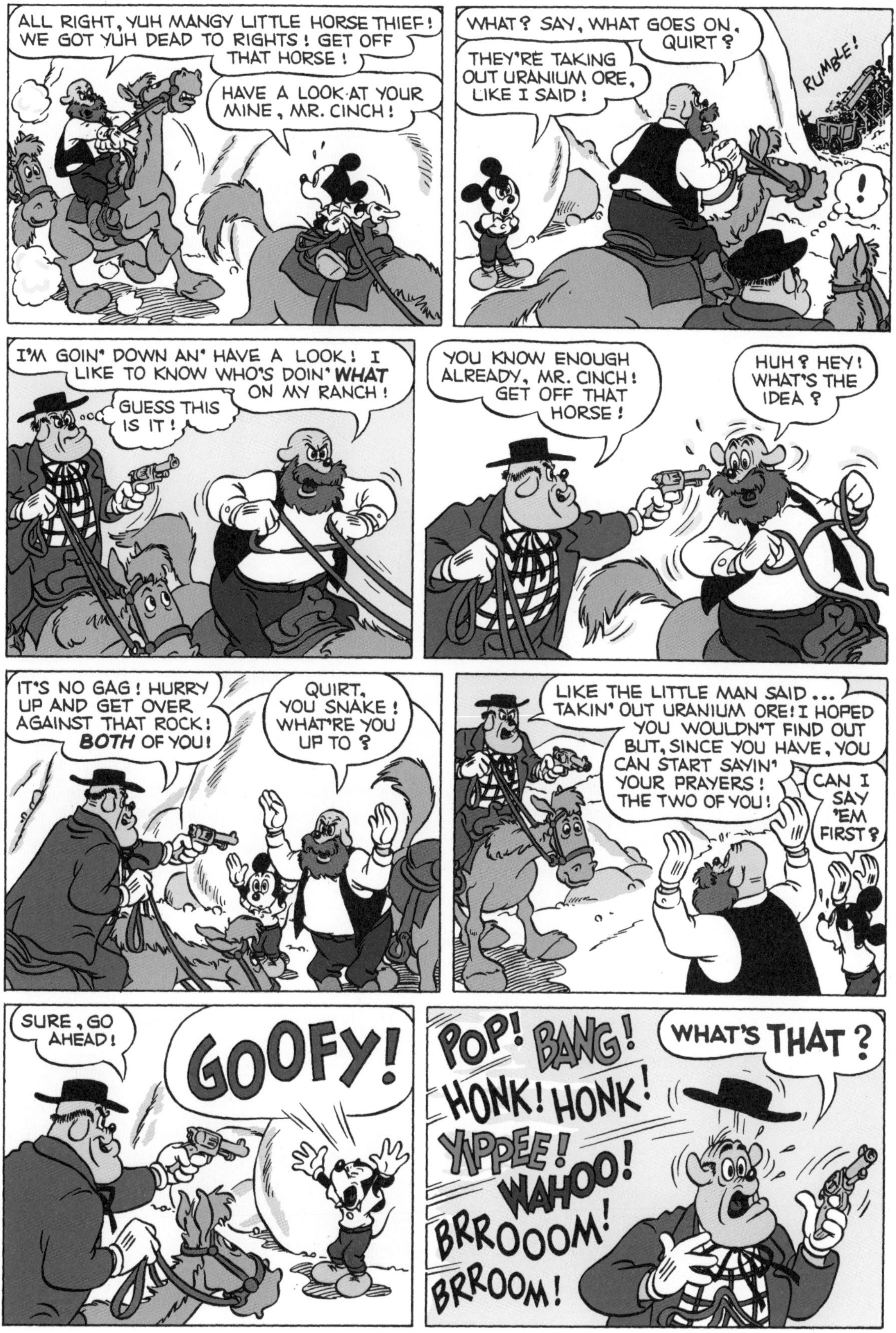

ALL RIGHT, YUH MANGY LITTLE HORSE THIEF! WE GOT YUH DEAD TO RIGHTS! GET OFF THAT HORSE!
HAVE A LOOK AT YOUR MINE, MR. CINCH!
WHAT? SAY, WHAT GOES ON, QUIRT?
THEY'RE TAKING OUT URANIUM ORE, LIKE I SAID!
RUMBLE!
!
I'M GOIN' DOWN AN' HAVE A LOOK! I LIKE TO KNOW WHO'S DOIN' **WHAT** ON MY RANCH!
GUESS THIS IS IT!
YOU KNOW ENOUGH ALREADY, MR. CINCH! GET OFF THAT HORSE!
HUH? HEY! WHAT'S THE IDEA?
IT'S NO GAG! HURRY UP AND GET OVER AGAINST THAT ROCK! ***BOTH*** OF YOU!
QUIRT, YOU SNAKE! WHAT'RE YOU UP TO?
LIKE THE LITTLE MAN SAID ... TAKIN' OUT URANIUM ORE! I HOPED YOU WOULDN'T FIND OUT BUT, SINCE YOU HAVE, YOU CAN START SAYIN' YOUR PRAYERS! THE TWO OF YOU!
CAN I SAY 'EM FIRST?
SURE, GO AHEAD!
GOOFY!
POP! BANG!
HONK! HONK!
YIPPEE!
WAHOO!
BRROOOM!
BRROOM!
WHAT'S THAT?

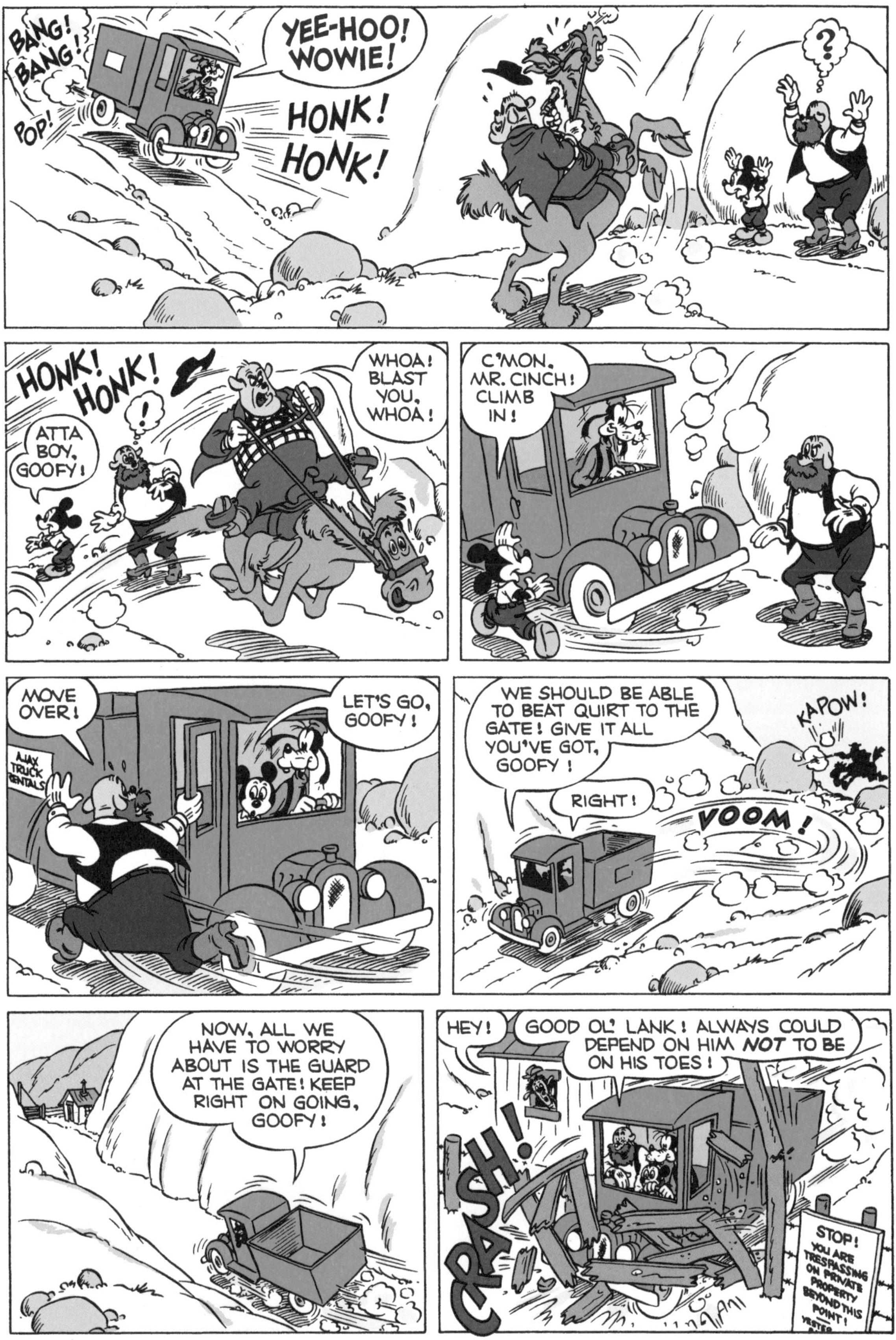
BANG! BANG!
POP!
YEE-HOO! WOWIE!
HONK! HONK!
?
HONK! HONK!
!
ATTA BOY, GOOFY!
WHOA! BLAST YOU, WHOA!
C'MON, MR. CINCH! CLIMB IN!
MOVE OVER!
AJAX TRUCK RENTALS
LET'S GO, GOOFY!
WE SHOULD BE ABLE TO BEAT QUIRT TO THE GATE! GIVE IT ALL YOU'VE GOT, GOOFY!
RIGHT!
VOOM!
KAPOW!
NOW, ALL WE HAVE TO WORRY ABOUT IS THE GUARD AT THE GATE! KEEP RIGHT ON GOING, GOOFY!
HEY!
GOOD OL' LANK! ALWAYS COULD DEPEND ON HIM ***NOT*** TO BE ON HIS TOES!
CRASH!
STOP! YOU ARE TRESPASSING ON PRIVATE PROPERTY BEYOND THIS POINT!

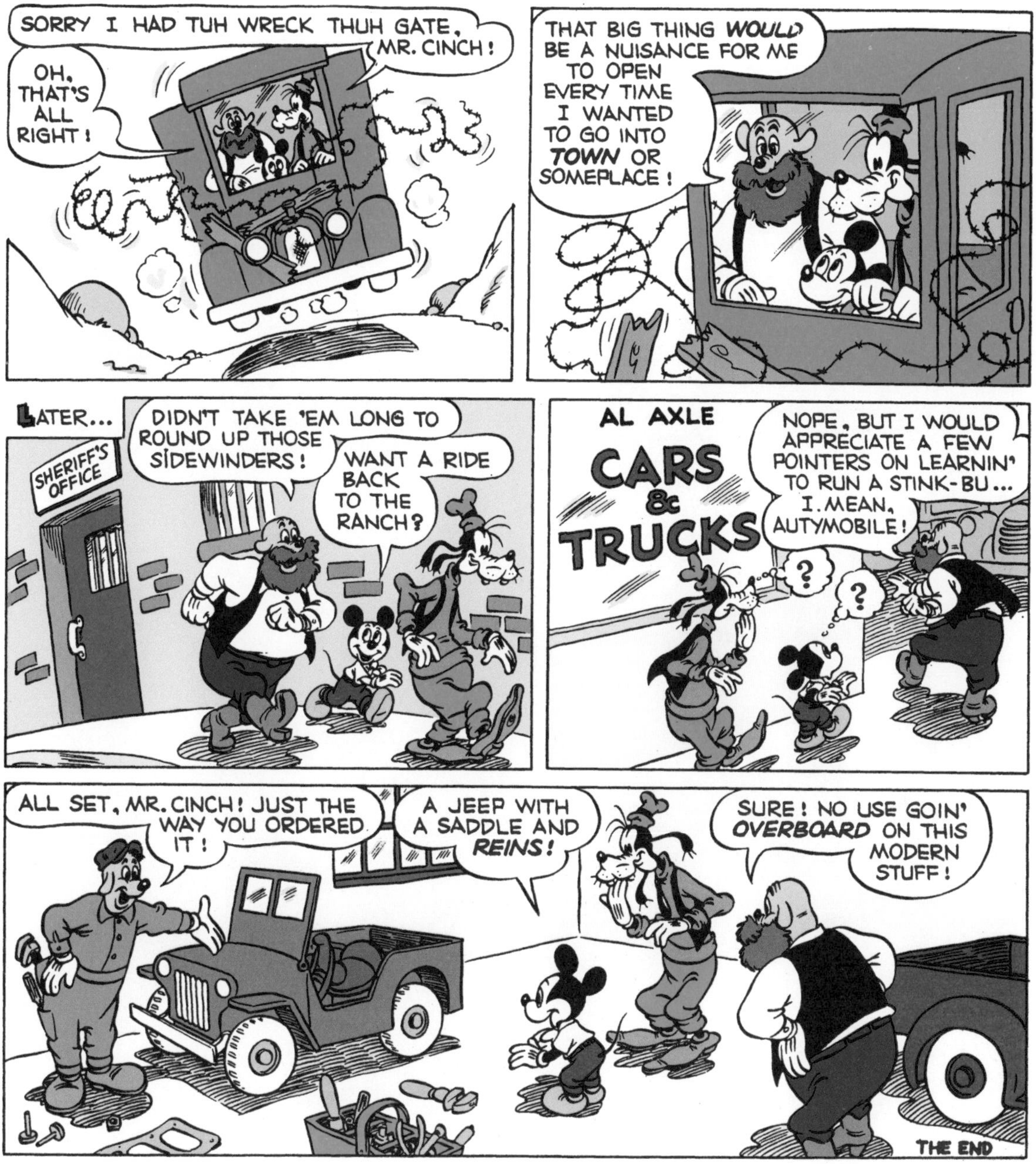
SORRY I HAD TUH WRECK THUH GATE, MR. CINCH!
OH, THAT'S ALL RIGHT!
THAT BIG THING **WOULD** BE A NUISANCE FOR ME TO OPEN EVERY TIME I WANTED TO GO INTO **TOWN** OR SOMEPLACE!
LATER...
SHERIFF'S OFFICE
DIDN'T TAKE 'EM LONG TO ROUND UP THOSE SIDEWINDERS!
WANT A RIDE BACK TO THE RANCH?
AL AXLE
CARS & TRUCKS
NOPE, BUT I WOULD APPRECIATE A FEW POINTERS ON LEARNIN' TO RUN A STINK-BU... I. MEAN, AUTYMOBILE!
ALL SET, MR. CINCH! JUST THE WAY YOU ORDERED IT!
A JEEP WITH A SADDLE AND **REINS!**
SURE! NO USE GOIN' **OVERBOARD** ON THIS MODERN STUFF!
THE END

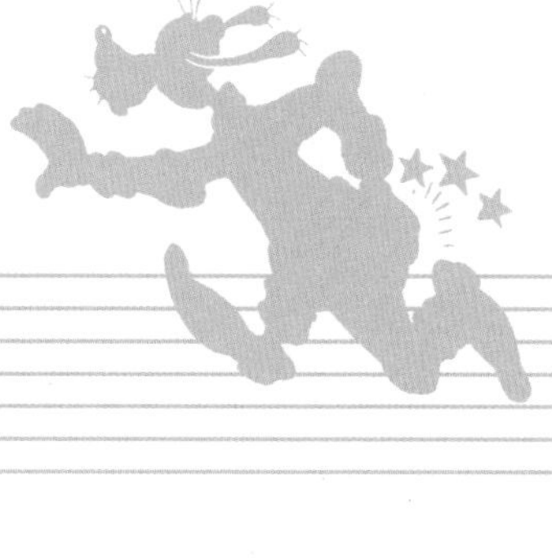

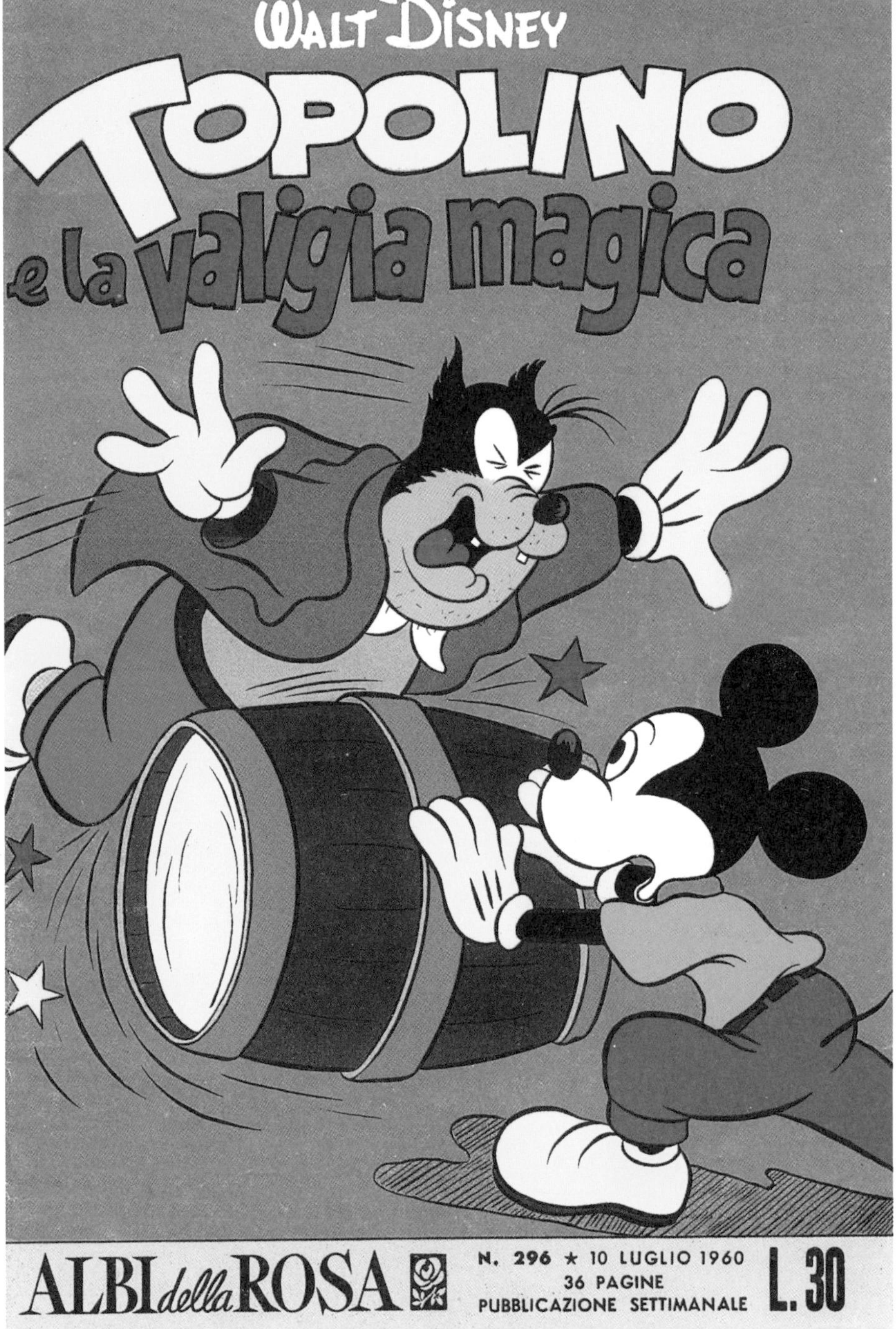
WALT DISNEY
TOPOLINO
e la valigia magica
ALBI della ROSA
N. 296 ★ 10 LUGLIO 1960
36 PAGINE
PUBBLICAZIONE SETTIMANALE
L. 30

Ouch! Paul Murry didn't draw his own cover for "The Marvelous Magnet," the story you're about to read—but Italian artists created this action-packed (if slightly crude) cover for their local edition (*Walt Disney Albi d'oro* 15, 1956).

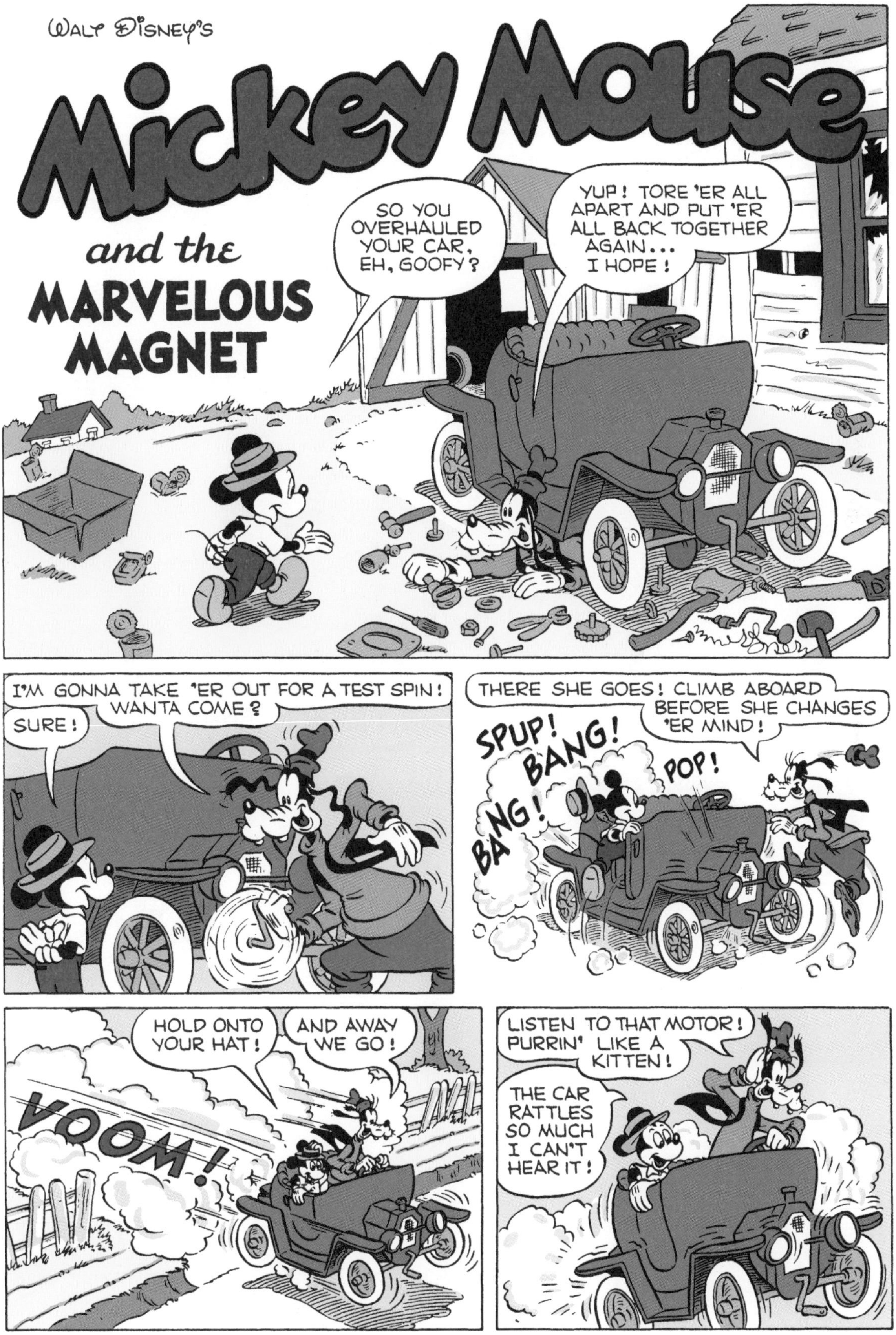

WALT DISNEY'S
Mickey Mouse
and the
MARVELOUS
MAGNET
SO YOU OVERHAULED YOUR CAR, EH, GOOFY?
YUP! TORE 'ER ALL APART AND PUT 'ER ALL BACK TOGETHER AGAIN... I HOPE!
I'M GONNA TAKE 'ER OUT FOR A TEST SPIN! WANTA COME?
SURE!
THERE SHE GOES! CLIMB ABOARD BEFORE SHE CHANGES 'ER MIND!
SPUP! BANG! BANG! POP! BANG!
HOLD ONTO YOUR HAT!
AND AWAY WE GO!
VOOM!
LISTEN TO THAT MOTOR! PURRIN' LIKE A KITTEN!
THE CAR RATTLES SO MUCH I CAN'T HEAR IT!

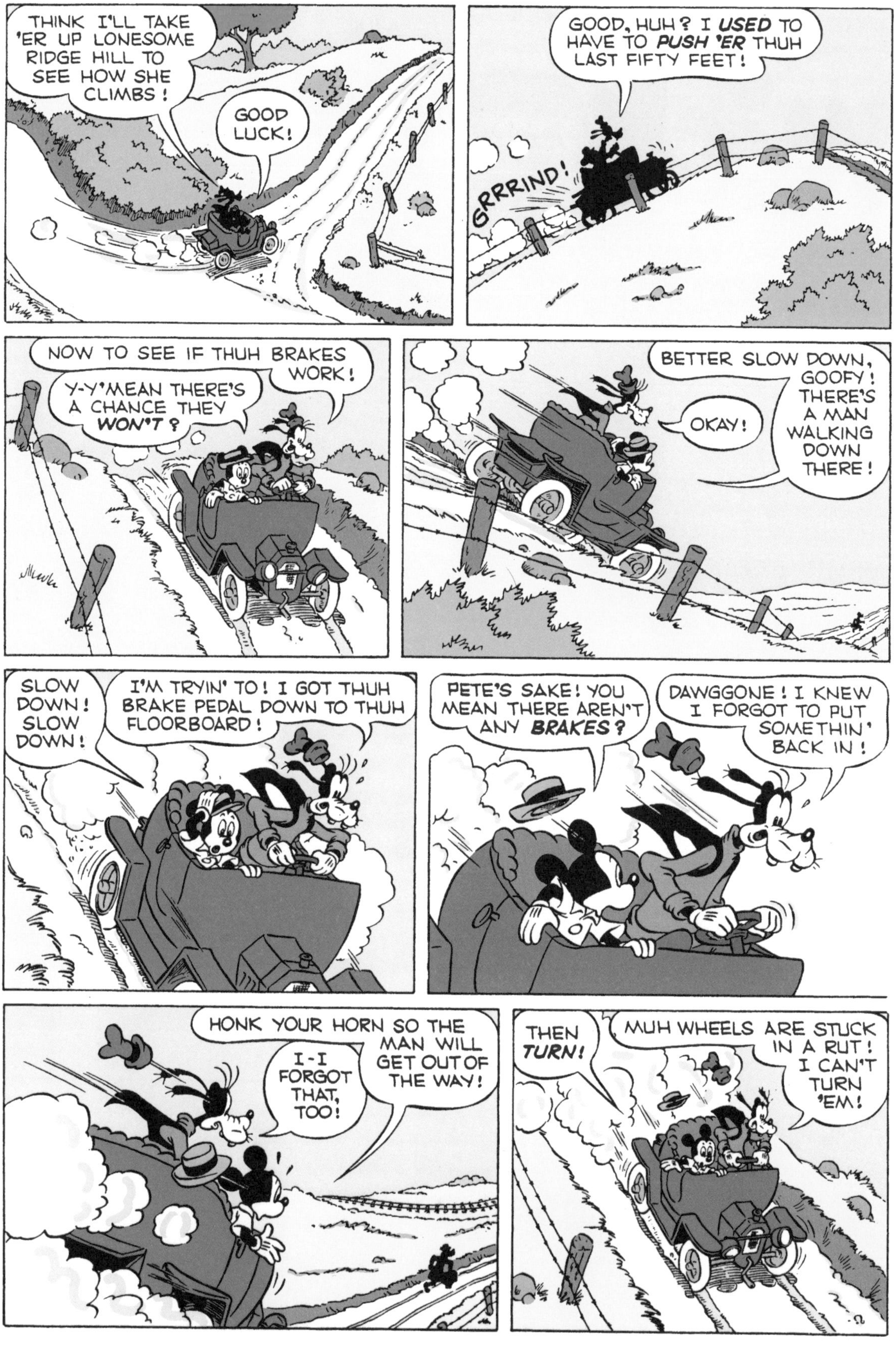
THINK I'LL TAKE 'ER UP LONESOME RIDGE HILL TO SEE HOW SHE CLIMBS!
GOOD LUCK!
GOOD, HUH? I USED TO HAVE TO PUSH 'ER THUH LAST FIFTY FEET!
GRRRIND!
NOW TO SEE IF THUH BRAKES WORK!
Y-Y'MEAN THERE'S A CHANCE THEY WON'T?
BETTER SLOW DOWN, GOOFY! THERE'S A MAN WALKING DOWN THERE!
OKAY!
SLOW DOWN! SLOW DOWN!
I'M TRYIN' TO! I GOT THUH BRAKE PEDAL DOWN TO THUH FLOORBOARD!
PETE'S SAKE! YOU MEAN THERE AREN'T ANY BRAKES?
DAWGGONE! I KNEW I FORGOT TO PUT SOMETHIN' BACK IN!
HONK YOUR HORN SO THE MAN WILL GET OUT OF THE WAY!
I-I FORGOT THAT, TOO!
THEN TURN!
MUH WHEELS ARE STUCK IN A RUT! I CAN'T TURN 'EM!

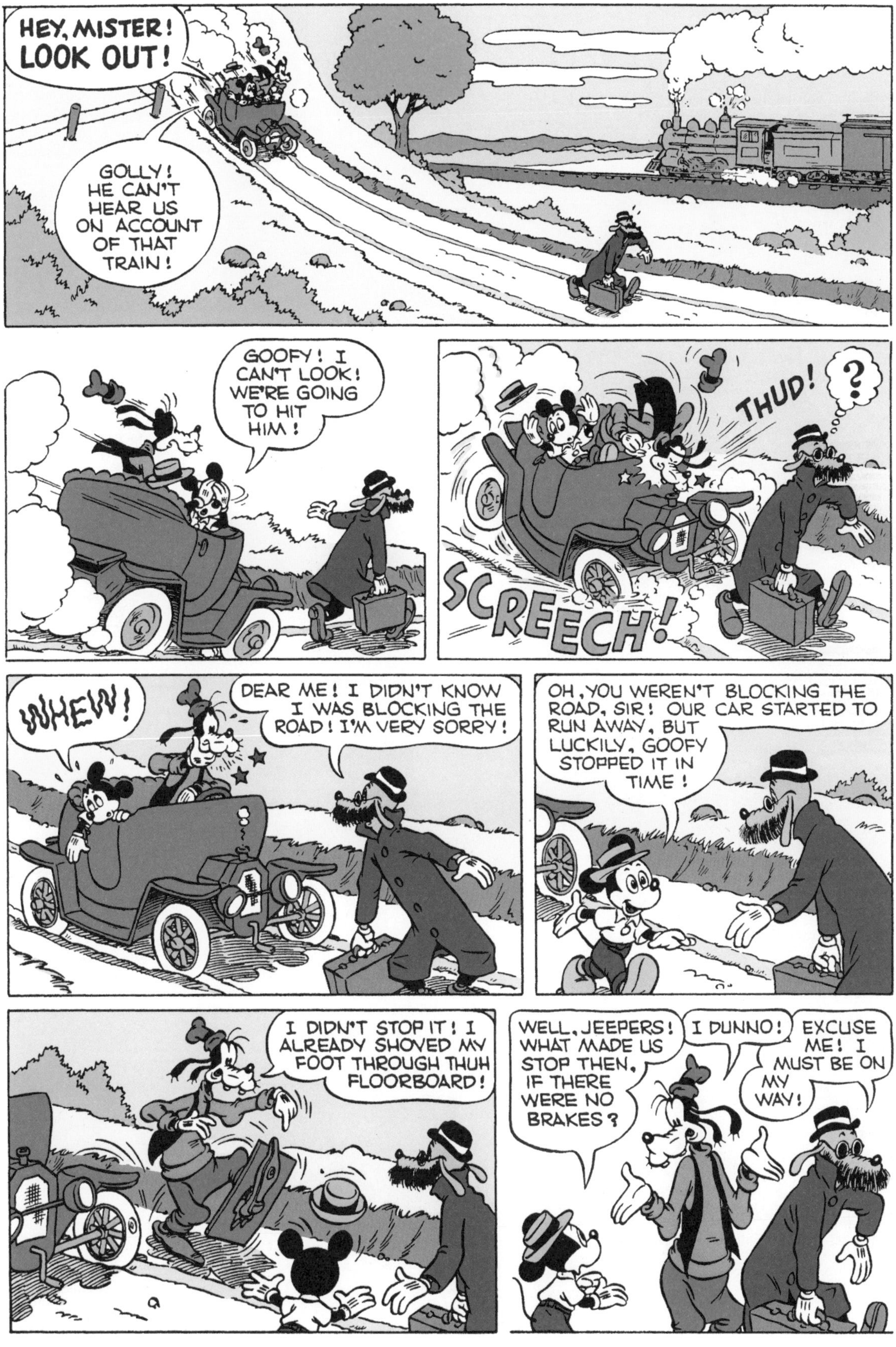
HEY, MISTER! LOOK OUT!
GOLLY! HE CAN'T HEAR US ON ACCOUNT OF THAT TRAIN!
GOOFY! I CAN'T LOOK! WE'RE GOING TO HIT HIM!
THUD!
?
SCREECH!
WHEW!
DEAR ME! I DIDN'T KNOW I WAS BLOCKING THE ROAD! I'M VERY SORRY!
OH, YOU WEREN'T BLOCKING THE ROAD, SIR! OUR CAR STARTED TO RUN AWAY, BUT LUCKILY, GOOFY STOPPED IT IN TIME!
I DIDN'T STOP IT! I ALREADY SHOVED MY FOOT THROUGH THUH FLOORBOARD!
WELL, JEEPERS! WHAT MADE US STOP THEN, IF THERE WERE NO BRAKES?
I DUNNO!
EXCUSE ME! I MUST BE ON MY WAY!

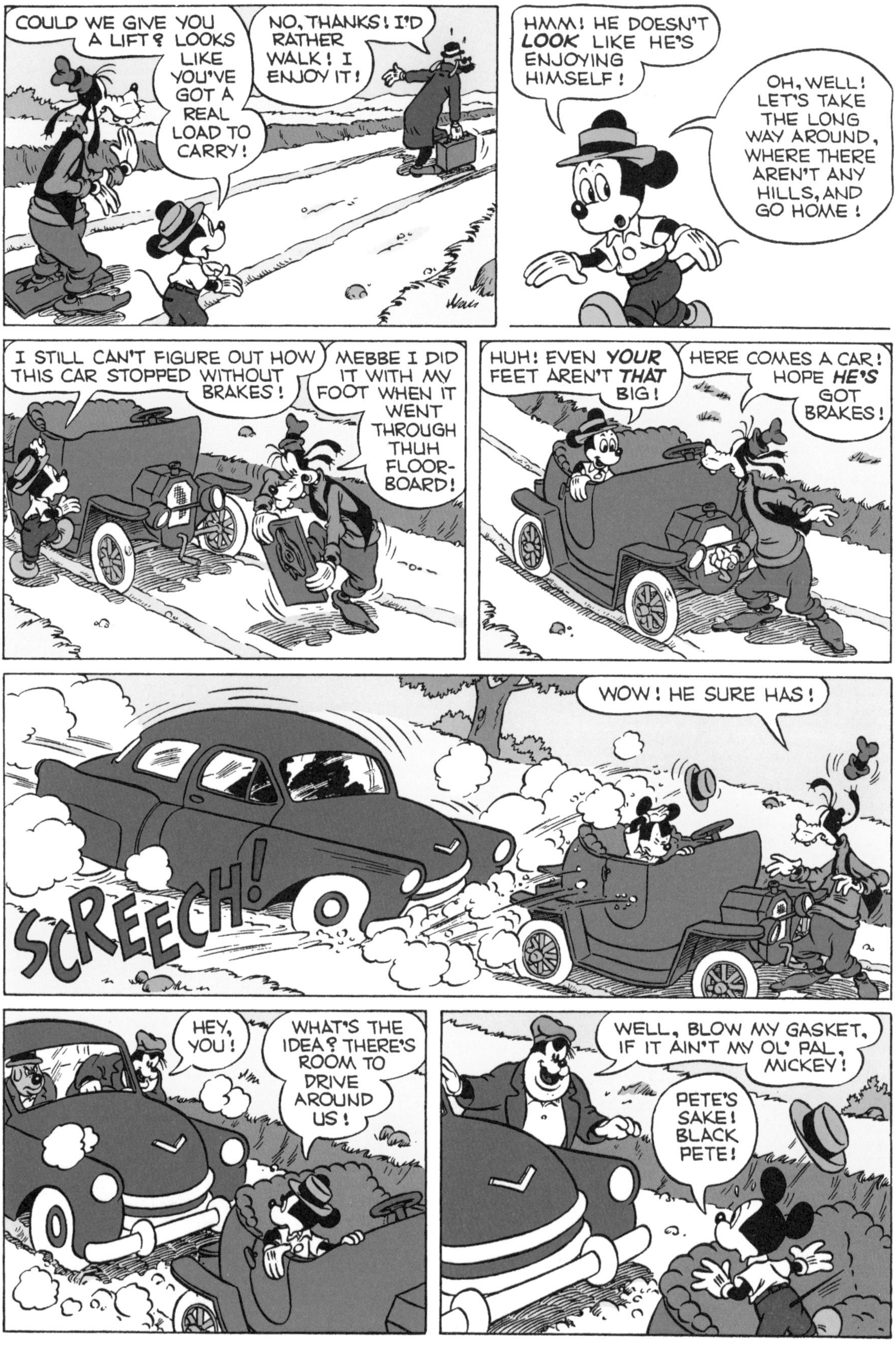

COULD WE GIVE YOU A LIFT? LOOKS LIKE YOU'VE GOT A REAL LOAD TO CARRY!
NO, THANKS! I'D RATHER WALK! I ENJOY IT!
HMM! HE DOESN'T LOOK LIKE HE'S ENJOYING HIMSELF!
OH, WELL! LET'S TAKE THE LONG WAY AROUND, WHERE THERE AREN'T ANY HILLS, AND GO HOME!
I STILL CAN'T FIGURE OUT HOW THIS CAR STOPPED WITHOUT BRAKES!
MEBBE I DID IT WITH MY FOOT WHEN IT WENT THROUGH THUH FLOOR-BOARD!
HUH! EVEN YOUR FEET AREN'T THAT BIG!
HERE COMES A CAR! HOPE HE'S GOT BRAKES!
WOW! HE SURE HAS!
SCREECH!
HEY, YOU!
WHAT'S THE IDEA? THERE'S ROOM TO DRIVE AROUND US!
WELL, BLOW MY GASKET, IF IT AIN'T MY OL' PAL, MICKEY!
PETE'S SAKE! BLACK PETE!

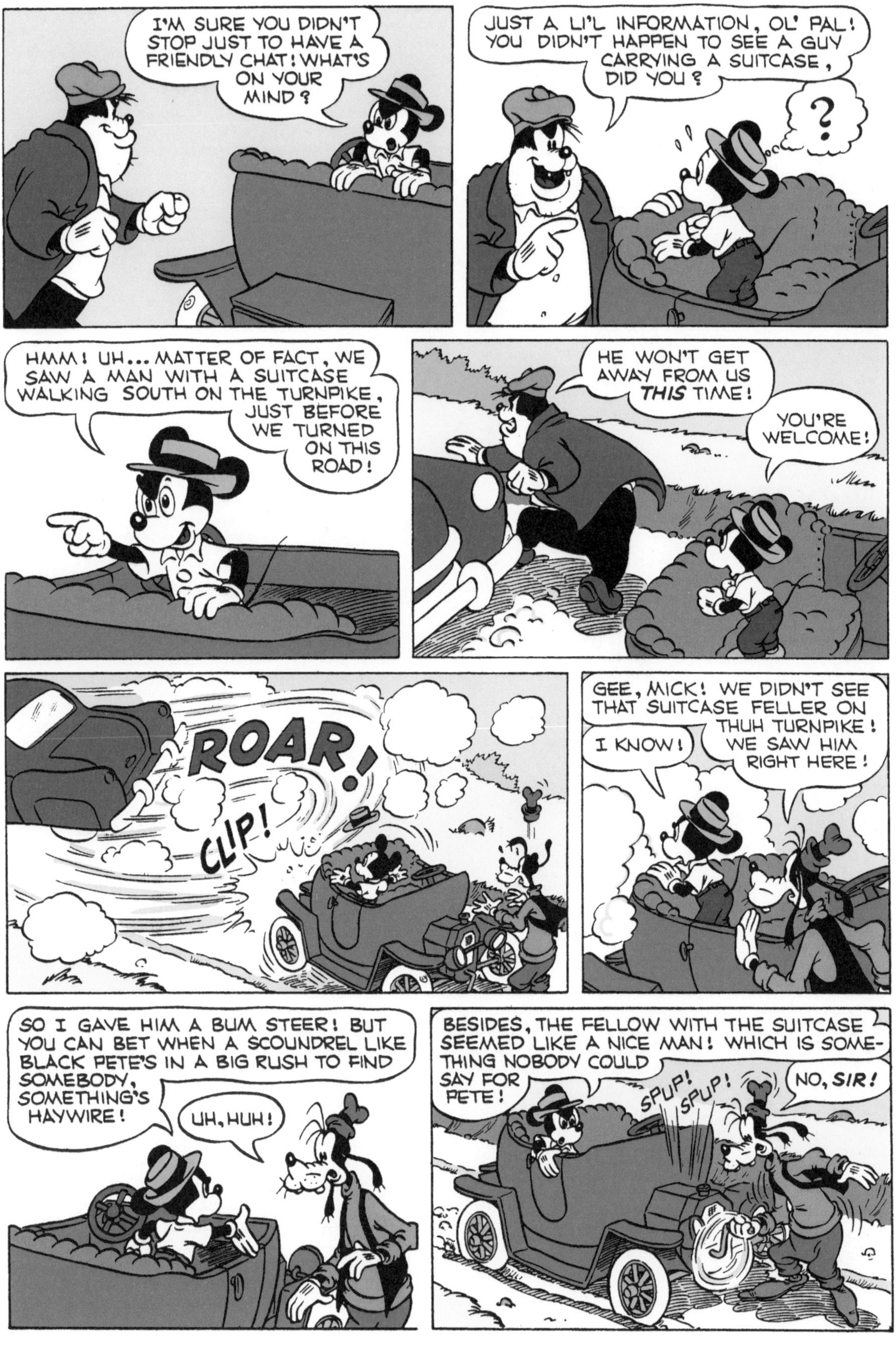

I'M SURE YOU DIDN'T STOP JUST TO HAVE A FRIENDLY CHAT! WHAT'S ON YOUR MIND?
JUST A LI'L INFORMATION, OL' PAL! YOU DIDN'T HAPPEN TO SEE A GUY CARRYING A SUITCASE, DID YOU?
?
HMM! UH... MATTER OF FACT, WE SAW A MAN WITH A SUITCASE WALKING SOUTH ON THE TURNPIKE, JUST BEFORE WE TURNED ON THIS ROAD!
HE WON'T GET AWAY FROM US ***THIS*** TIME!
YOU'RE WELCOME!
ROAR!
CLIP!
GEE, MICK! WE DIDN'T SEE THAT SUITCASE FELLER ON THUH TURNPIKE! WE SAW HIM RIGHT HERE!
I KNOW!
SO I GAVE HIM A BUM STEER! BUT YOU CAN BET WHEN A SCOUNDREL LIKE BLACK PETE'S IN A BIG RUSH TO FIND SOMEBODY, SOMETHING'S HAYWIRE!
UH, HUH!
BESIDES, THE FELLOW WITH THE SUITCASE SEEMED LIKE A NICE MAN! WHICH IS SOMETHING NOBODY COULD SAY FOR PETE!
SPUP! SPUP!
NO, ***SIR!***

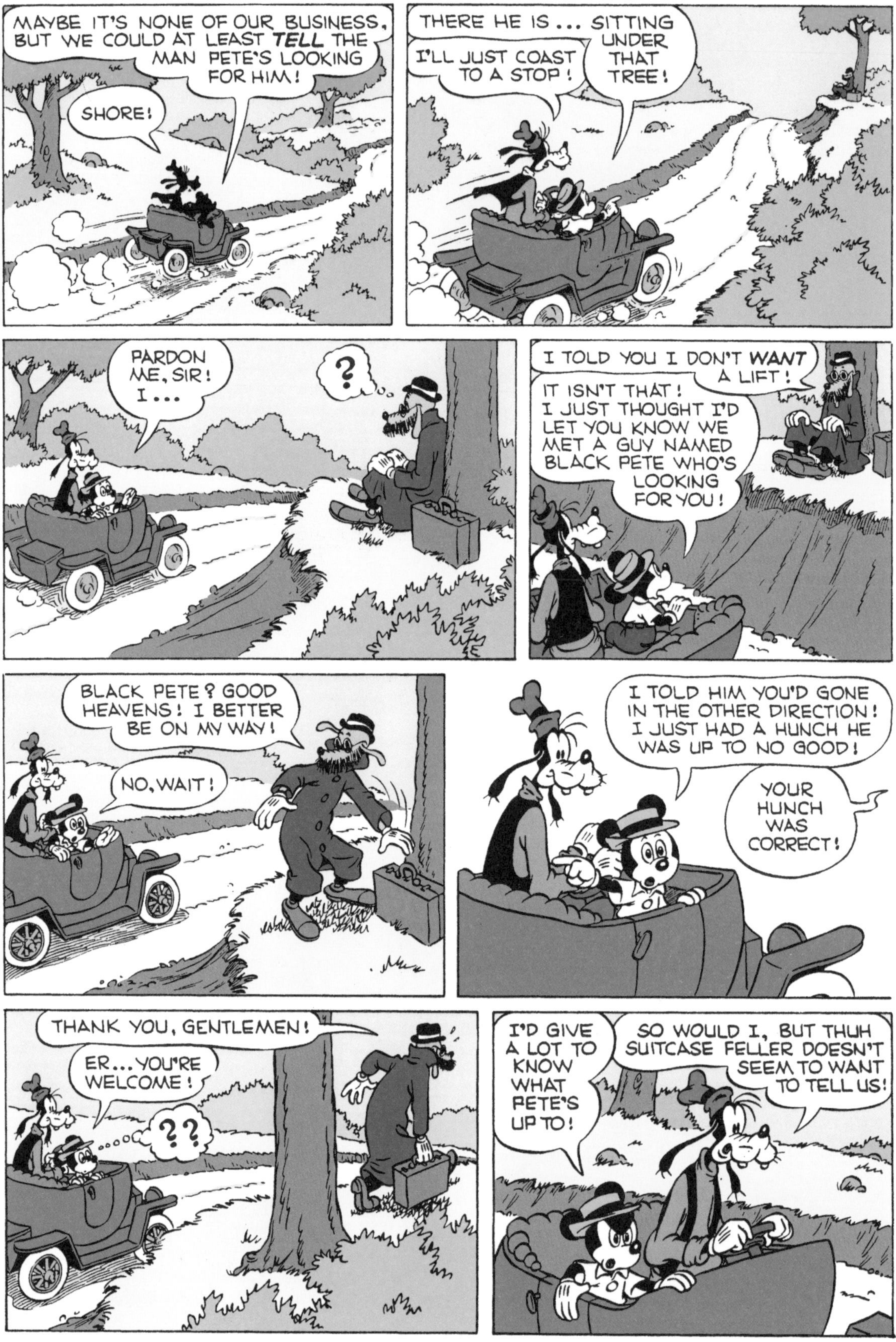
MAYBE IT'S NONE OF OUR BUSINESS, BUT WE COULD AT LEAST TELL THE MAN PETE'S LOOKING FOR HIM!
SHORE!
THERE HE IS ... SITTING UNDER THAT TREE!
I'LL JUST COAST TO A STOP!
PARDON ME, SIR! I ...
?
I TOLD YOU I DON'T WANT A LIFT!
IT ISN'T THAT! I JUST THOUGHT I'D LET YOU KNOW WE MET A GUY NAMED BLACK PETE WHO'S LOOKING FOR YOU!
BLACK PETE? GOOD HEAVENS! I BETTER BE ON MY WAY!
NO, WAIT!
I TOLD HIM YOU'D GONE IN THE OTHER DIRECTION! I JUST HAD A HUNCH HE WAS UP TO NO GOOD!
YOUR HUNCH WAS CORRECT!
THANK YOU, GENTLEMEN!
ER... YOU'RE WELCOME!
??
I'D GIVE A LOT TO KNOW WHAT PETE'S UP TO!
SO WOULD I, BUT THUH SUITCASE FELLER DOESN'T SEEM TO WANT TO TELL US!

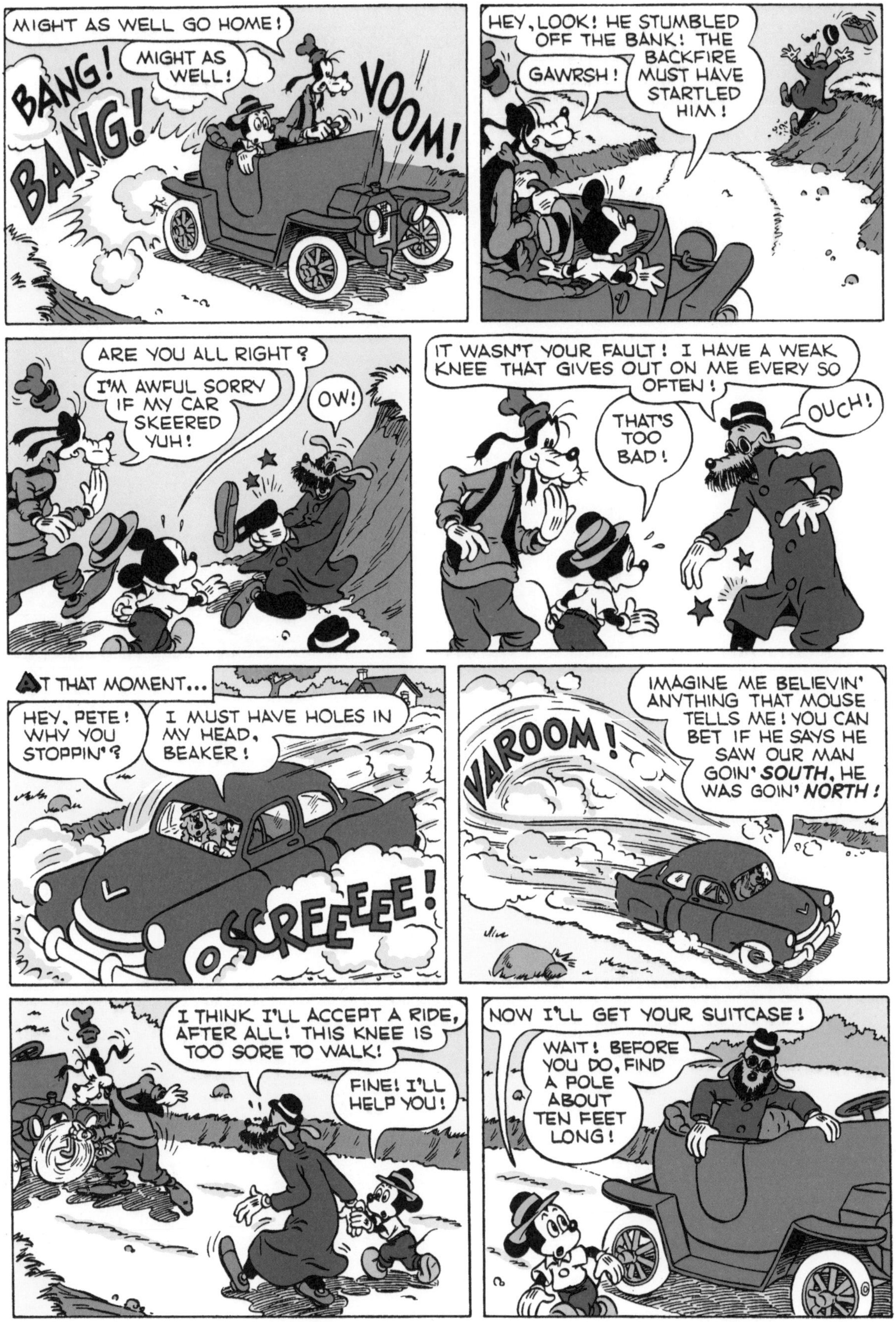
MIGHT AS WELL GO HOME!
MIGHT AS WELL!
BANG! BANG!
VOOM!
HEY, LOOK! HE STUMBLED OFF THE BANK! THE BACKFIRE MUST HAVE STARTLED HIM!
GAWRSH!
ARE YOU ALL RIGHT?
I'M AWFUL SORRY IF MY CAR SKEERED YUH!
OW!
IT WASN'T YOUR FAULT! I HAVE A WEAK KNEE THAT GIVES OUT ON ME EVERY SO OFTEN!
THAT'S TOO BAD!
OUCH!
AT THAT MOMENT...
HEY, PETE! WHY YOU STOPPIN'?
I MUST HAVE HOLES IN MY HEAD, BEAKER!
SCREEEEE!
VAROOM!
IMAGINE ME BELIEVIN' ANYTHING THAT MOUSE TELLS ME! YOU CAN BET IF HE SAYS HE SAW OUR MAN GOIN' **SOUTH**, HE WAS GOIN' **NORTH**!
I THINK I'LL ACCEPT A RIDE, AFTER ALL! THIS KNEE IS TOO SORE TO WALK!
FINE! I'LL HELP YOU!
NOW I'LL GET YOUR SUITCASE!
WAIT! BEFORE YOU DO, FIND A POLE ABOUT TEN FEET LONG!

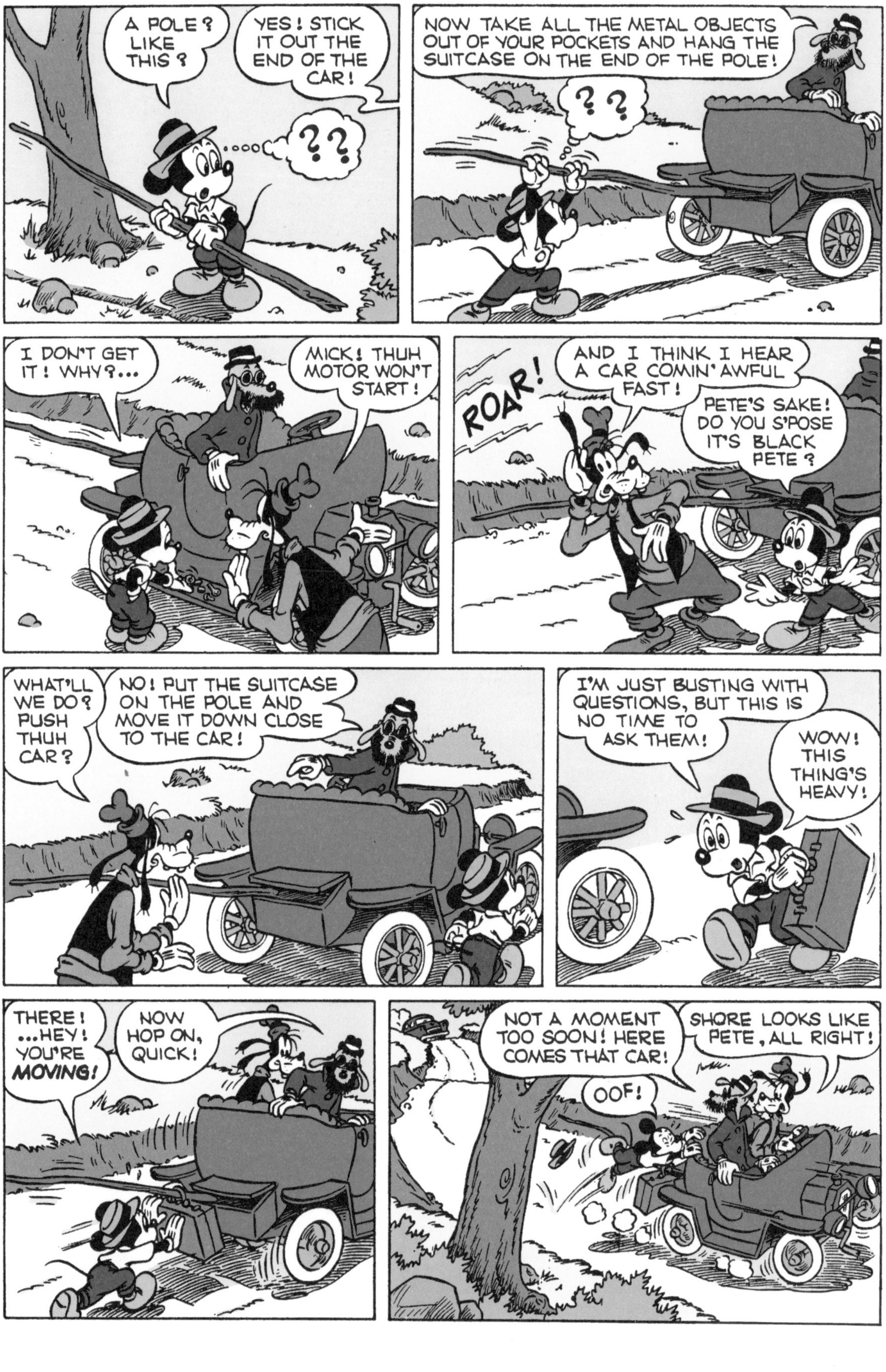
A POLE? LIKE THIS?
YES! STICK IT OUT THE END OF THE CAR!
??
NOW TAKE ALL THE METAL OBJECTS OUT OF YOUR POCKETS AND HANG THE SUITCASE ON THE END OF THE POLE!
??
I DON'T GET IT! WHY?...
MICK! THUH MOTOR WON'T START!
ROAR!
AND I THINK I HEAR A CAR COMIN' AWFUL FAST!
PETE'S SAKE! DO YOU S'POSE IT'S BLACK PETE?
WHAT'LL WE DO? PUSH THUH CAR?
NO! PUT THE SUITCASE ON THE POLE AND MOVE IT DOWN CLOSE TO THE CAR!
I'M JUST BUSTING WITH QUESTIONS, BUT THIS IS NO TIME TO ASK THEM!
WOW! THIS THING'S HEAVY!
THERE! ...HEY! YOU'RE *MOVING*!
NOW HOP ON, QUICK!
NOT A MOMENT TOO SOON! HERE COMES THAT CAR!
SHORE LOOKS LIKE PETE, ALL RIGHT!
OOF!

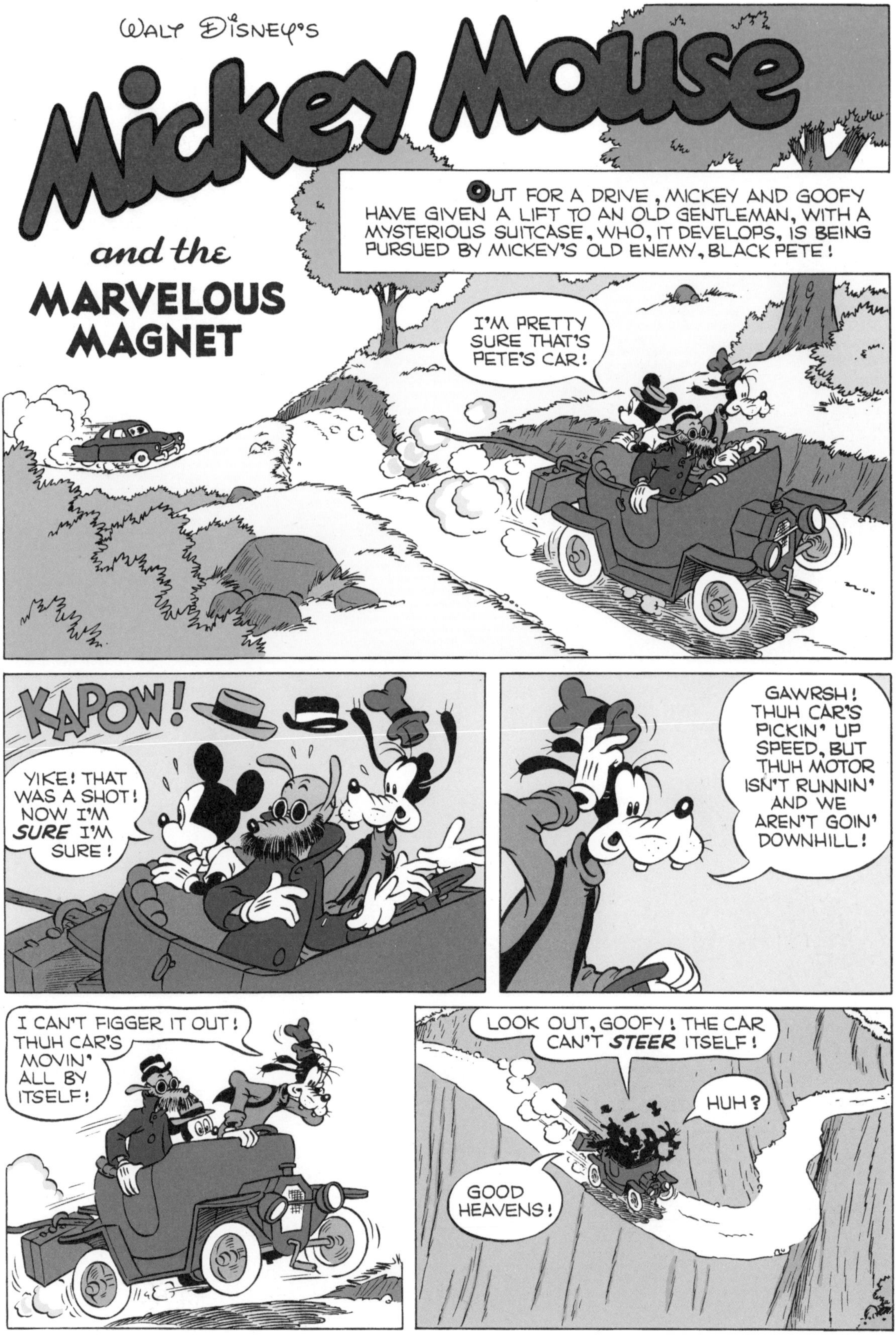
WALT DISNEY'S
Mickey Mouse
and the
MARVELOUS MAGNET
OUT FOR A DRIVE, MICKEY AND GOOFY HAVE GIVEN A LIFT TO AN OLD GENTLEMAN, WITH A MYSTERIOUS SUITCASE, WHO, IT DEVELOPS, IS BEING PURSUED BY MICKEY'S OLD ENEMY, BLACK PETE!
I'M PRETTY SURE THAT'S PETE'S CAR!
KAPOW!
YIKE! THAT WAS A SHOT! NOW I'M SURE I'M SURE!
GAWRSH! THUH CAR'S PICKIN' UP SPEED, BUT THUH MOTOR ISN'T RUNNIN' AND WE AREN'T GOIN' DOWNHILL!
I CAN'T FIGGER IT OUT! THUH CAR'S MOVIN' ALL BY ITSELF!
LOOK OUT, GOOFY! THE CAR CAN'T STEER ITSELF!
HUH?
GOOD HEAVENS!

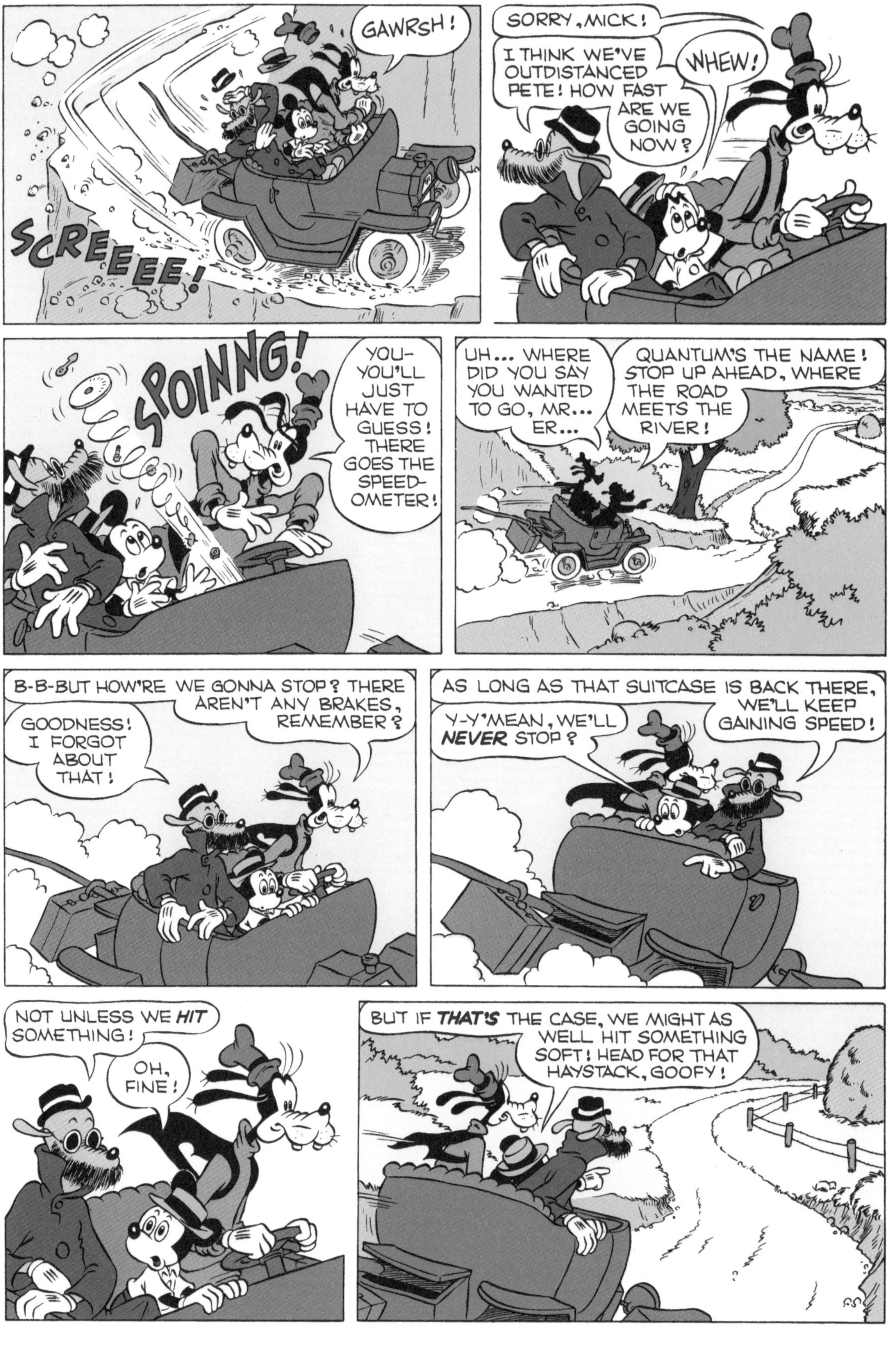
GAWRSH!
SCREEEEE!
SORRY, MICK!
I THINK WE'VE OUTDISTANCED PETE! HOW FAST ARE WE GOING NOW?
WHEW!
SPOINNG!
YOU—YOU'LL JUST HAVE TO GUESS! THERE GOES THE SPEEDOMETER!
UH... WHERE DID YOU SAY YOU WANTED TO GO, MR... ER...
QUANTUM'S THE NAME! STOP UP AHEAD, WHERE THE ROAD MEETS THE RIVER!
B-B-BUT HOW'RE WE GONNA STOP? THERE AREN'T ANY BRAKES, REMEMBER?
GOODNESS! I FORGOT ABOUT THAT!
AS LONG AS THAT SUITCASE IS BACK THERE, WE'LL KEEP GAINING SPEED!
Y-Y'MEAN, WE'LL NEVER STOP?
NOT UNLESS WE HIT SOMETHING!
OH, FINE!
BUT IF THAT'S THE CASE, WE MIGHT AS WELL HIT SOMETHING SOFT! HEAD FOR THAT HAYSTACK, GOOFY!

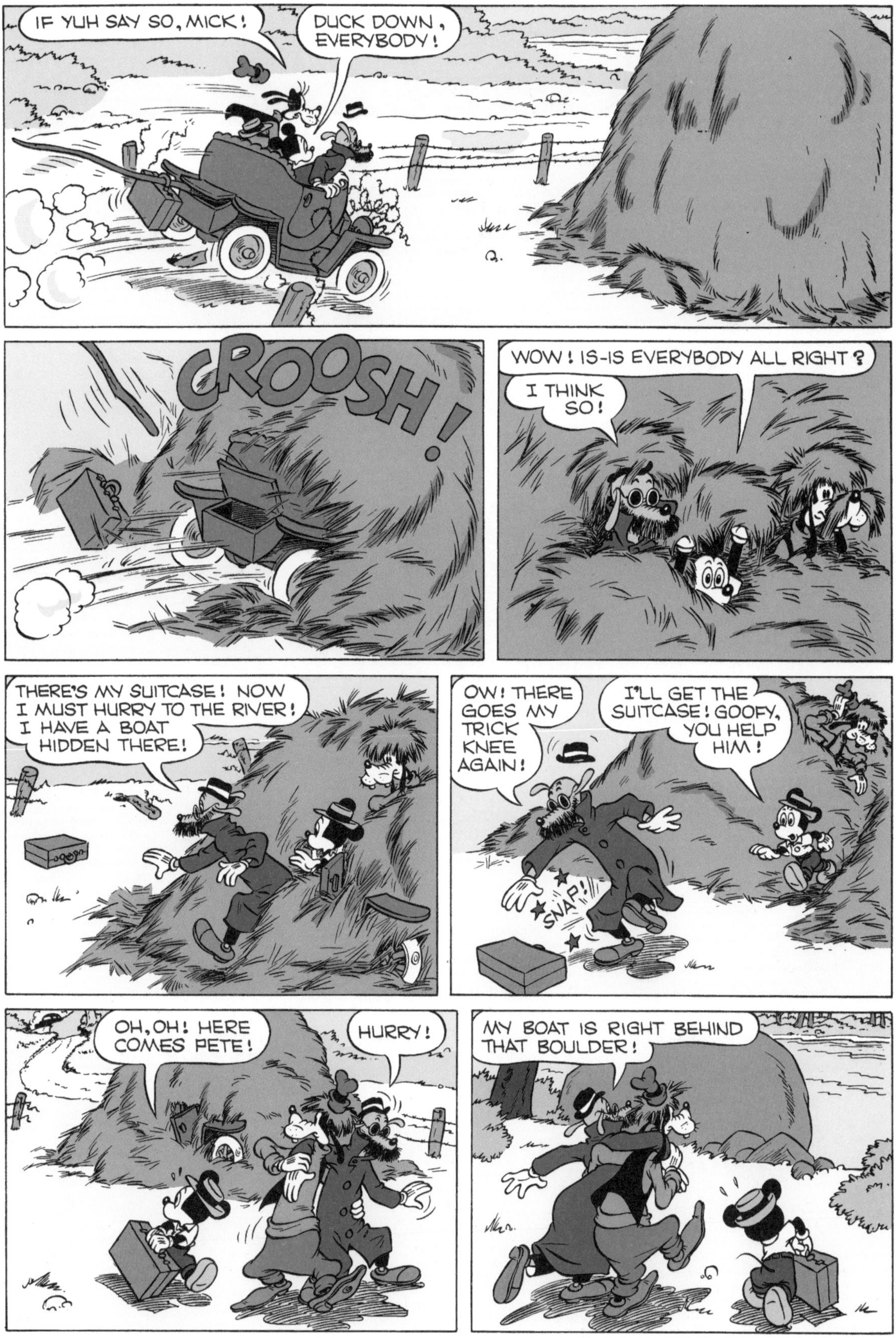
IF YUH SAY SO, MICK!
DUCK DOWN, EVERYBODY!
CROOSH!
WOW! IS-IS EVERYBODY ALL RIGHT?
I THINK SO!
THERE'S MY SUITCASE! NOW I MUST HURRY TO THE RIVER! I HAVE A BOAT HIDDEN THERE!
OW! THERE GOES MY TRICK KNEE AGAIN!
I'LL GET THE SUITCASE! GOOFY, YOU HELP HIM!
SNAP!
OH, OH! HERE COMES PETE!
HURRY!
MY BOAT IS RIGHT BEHIND THAT BOULDER!

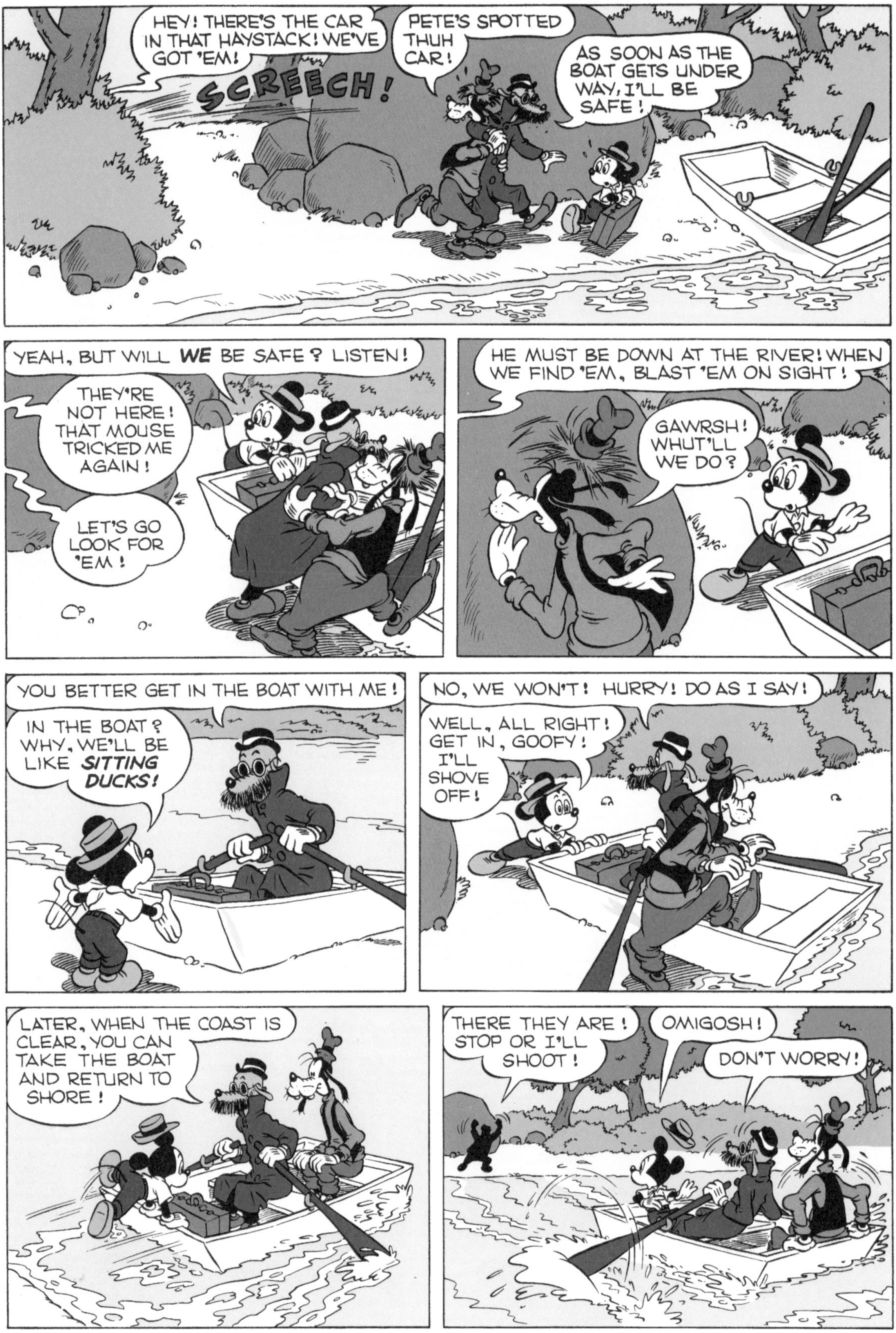
HEY! THERE'S THE CAR IN THAT HAYSTACK! WE'VE GOT 'EM!
SCREECH!
PETE'S SPOTTED THUH CAR!
AS SOON AS THE BOAT GETS UNDER WAY, I'LL BE SAFE!
YEAH, BUT WILL WE BE SAFE? LISTEN!
THEY'RE NOT HERE! THAT MOUSE TRICKED ME AGAIN!
LET'S GO LOOK FOR 'EM!
HE MUST BE DOWN AT THE RIVER! WHEN WE FIND 'EM, BLAST 'EM ON SIGHT!
GAWRSH! WHUT'LL WE DO?
YOU BETTER GET IN THE BOAT WITH ME!
IN THE BOAT? WHY, WE'LL BE LIKE SITTING DUCKS!
NO, WE WON'T! HURRY! DO AS I SAY!
WELL, ALL RIGHT! GET IN, GOOFY! I'LL SHOVE OFF!
LATER, WHEN THE COAST IS CLEAR, YOU CAN TAKE THE BOAT AND RETURN TO SHORE!
THERE THEY ARE! STOP OR I'LL SHOOT!
OMIGOSH!
DON'T WORRY!

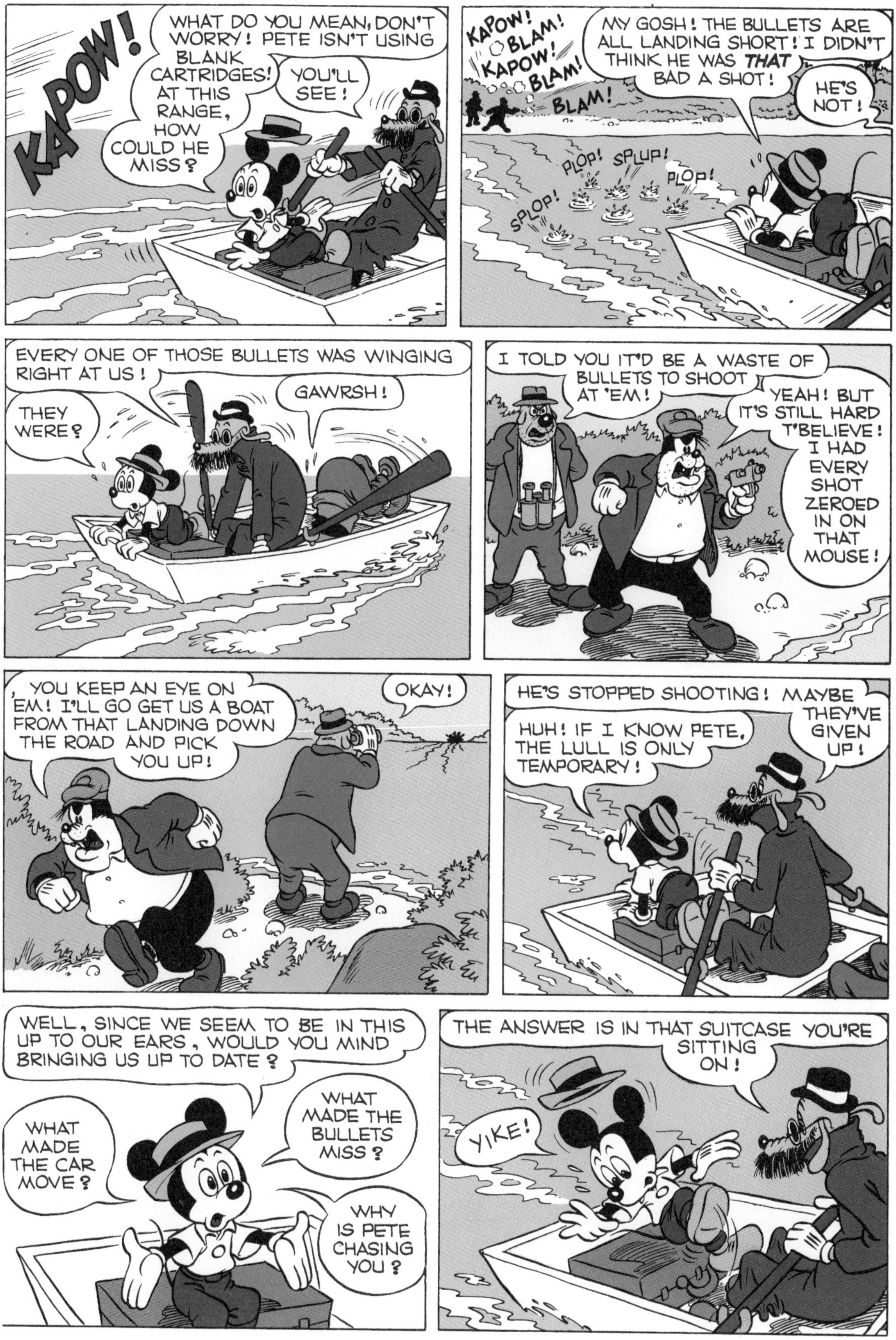
KAPOW!
WHAT DO YOU MEAN, DON'T WORRY! PETE ISN'T USING BLANK CARTRIDGES! AT THIS RANGE, HOW COULD HE MISS?
YOU'LL SEE!
KAPOW! BLAM! KAPOW! BLAM! BLAM!
MY GOSH! THE BULLETS ARE ALL LANDING SHORT! I DIDN'T THINK HE WAS THAT BAD A SHOT!
HE'S NOT!
PLOP! SPLUP! PLOP! SPLOP!
EVERY ONE OF THOSE BULLETS WAS WINGING RIGHT AT US!
THEY WERE?
GAWRSH!
I TOLD YOU IT'D BE A WASTE OF BULLETS TO SHOOT AT 'EM!
YEAH! BUT IT'S STILL HARD T'BELIEVE! I HAD EVERY SHOT ZEROED IN ON THAT MOUSE!
YOU KEEP AN EYE ON 'EM! I'LL GO GET US A BOAT FROM THAT LANDING DOWN THE ROAD AND PICK YOU UP!
OKAY!
HE'S STOPPED SHOOTING! MAYBE THEY'VE GIVEN UP!
HUH! IF I KNOW PETE, THE LULL IS ONLY TEMPORARY!
WELL, SINCE WE SEEM TO BE IN THIS UP TO OUR EARS, WOULD YOU MIND BRINGING US UP TO DATE?
WHAT MADE THE CAR MOVE?
WHAT MADE THE BULLETS MISS?
WHY IS PETE CHASING YOU?
THE ANSWER IS IN THAT SUITCASE YOU'RE SITTING ON!
YIKE!

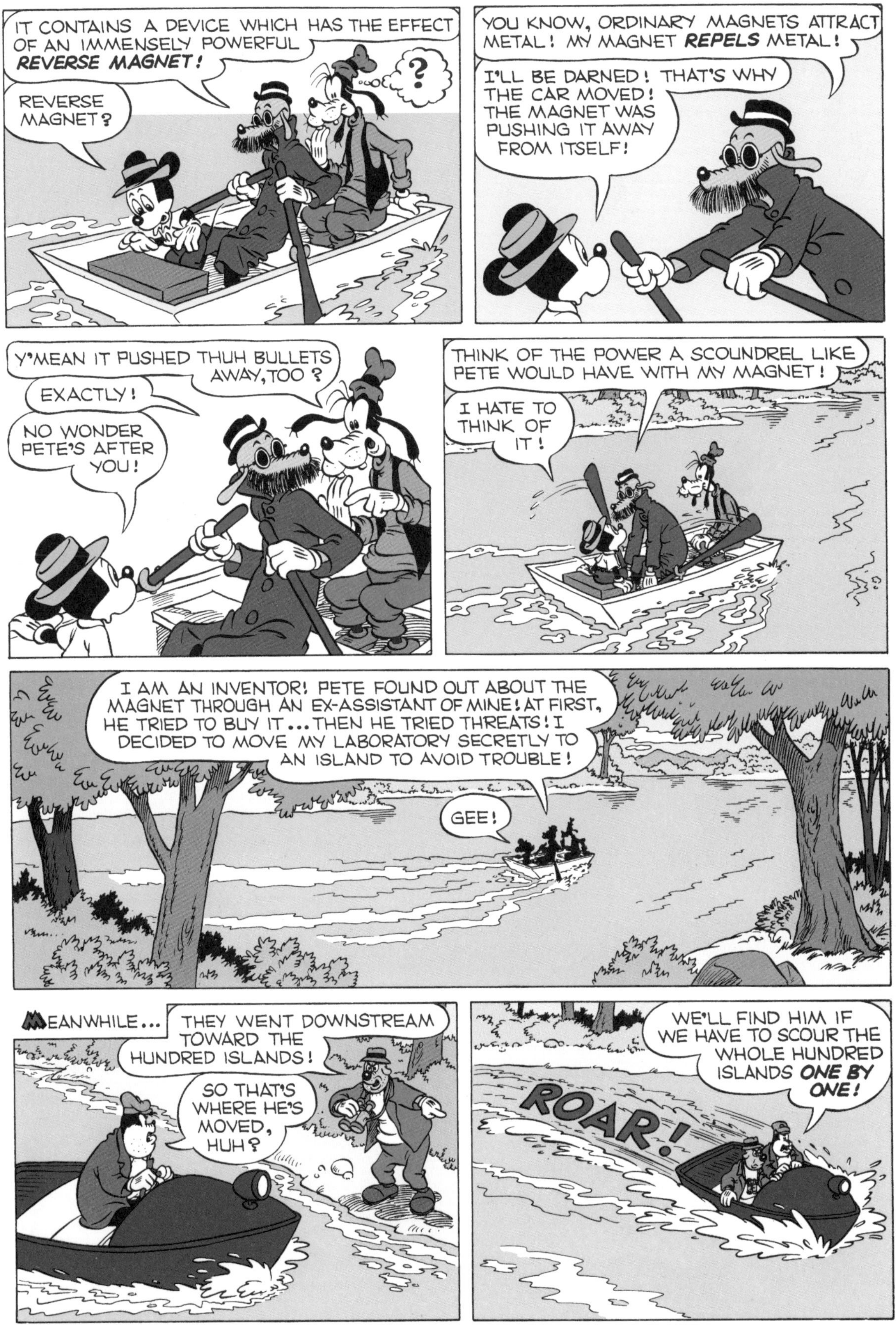
IT CONTAINS A DEVICE WHICH HAS THE EFFECT OF AN IMMENSELY POWERFUL REVERSE MAGNET!
REVERSE MAGNET?
?
YOU KNOW, ORDINARY MAGNETS ATTRACT METAL! MY MAGNET REPELS METAL!
I'LL BE DARNED! THAT'S WHY THE CAR MOVED! THE MAGNET WAS PUSHING IT AWAY FROM ITSELF!
Y'MEAN IT PUSHED THUH BULLETS AWAY, TOO?
EXACTLY!
NO WONDER PETE'S AFTER YOU!
THINK OF THE POWER A SCOUNDREL LIKE PETE WOULD HAVE WITH MY MAGNET!
I HATE TO THINK OF IT!
I AM AN INVENTOR! PETE FOUND OUT ABOUT THE MAGNET THROUGH AN EX-ASSISTANT OF MINE! AT FIRST, HE TRIED TO BUY IT... THEN HE TRIED THREATS! I DECIDED TO MOVE MY LABORATORY SECRETLY TO AN ISLAND TO AVOID TROUBLE!
GEE!
MEANWHILE...
THEY WENT DOWNSTREAM TOWARD THE HUNDRED ISLANDS!
SO THAT'S WHERE HE'S MOVED, HUH?
ROAR!
WE'LL FIND HIM IF WE HAVE TO SCOUR THE WHOLE HUNDRED ISLANDS ONE BY ONE!

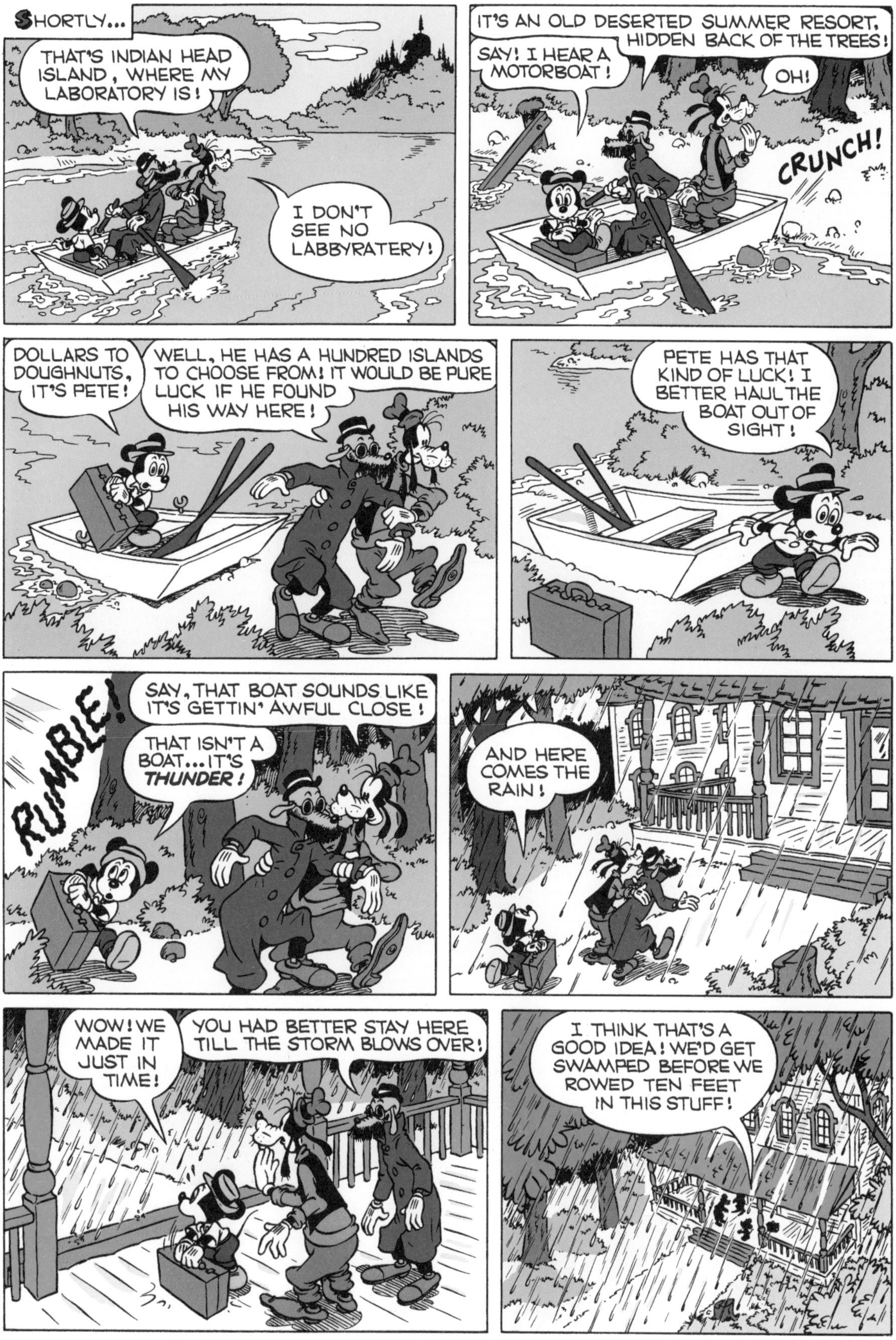
SHORTLY...
THAT'S INDIAN HEAD ISLAND, WHERE MY LABORATORY IS!
I DON'T SEE NO LABBYRATERY!
IT'S AN OLD DESERTED SUMMER RESORT, HIDDEN BACK OF THE TREES!
SAY! I HEAR A MOTORBOAT!
OH!
CRUNCH!
DOLLARS TO DOUGHNUTS, IT'S PETE!
WELL, HE HAS A HUNDRED ISLANDS TO CHOOSE FROM! IT WOULD BE PURE LUCK IF HE FOUND HIS WAY HERE!
PETE HAS THAT KIND OF LUCK! I BETTER HAUL THE BOAT OUT OF SIGHT!
RUMBLE!
SAY, THAT BOAT SOUNDS LIKE IT'S GETTIN' AWFUL CLOSE!
THAT ISN'T A BOAT...IT'S *THUNDER*!
AND HERE COMES THE RAIN!
WOW! WE MADE IT JUST IN TIME!
YOU HAD BETTER STAY HERE TILL THE STORM BLOWS OVER!
I THINK THAT'S A GOOD IDEA! WE'D GET SWAMPED BEFORE WE ROWED TEN FEET IN THIS STUFF!

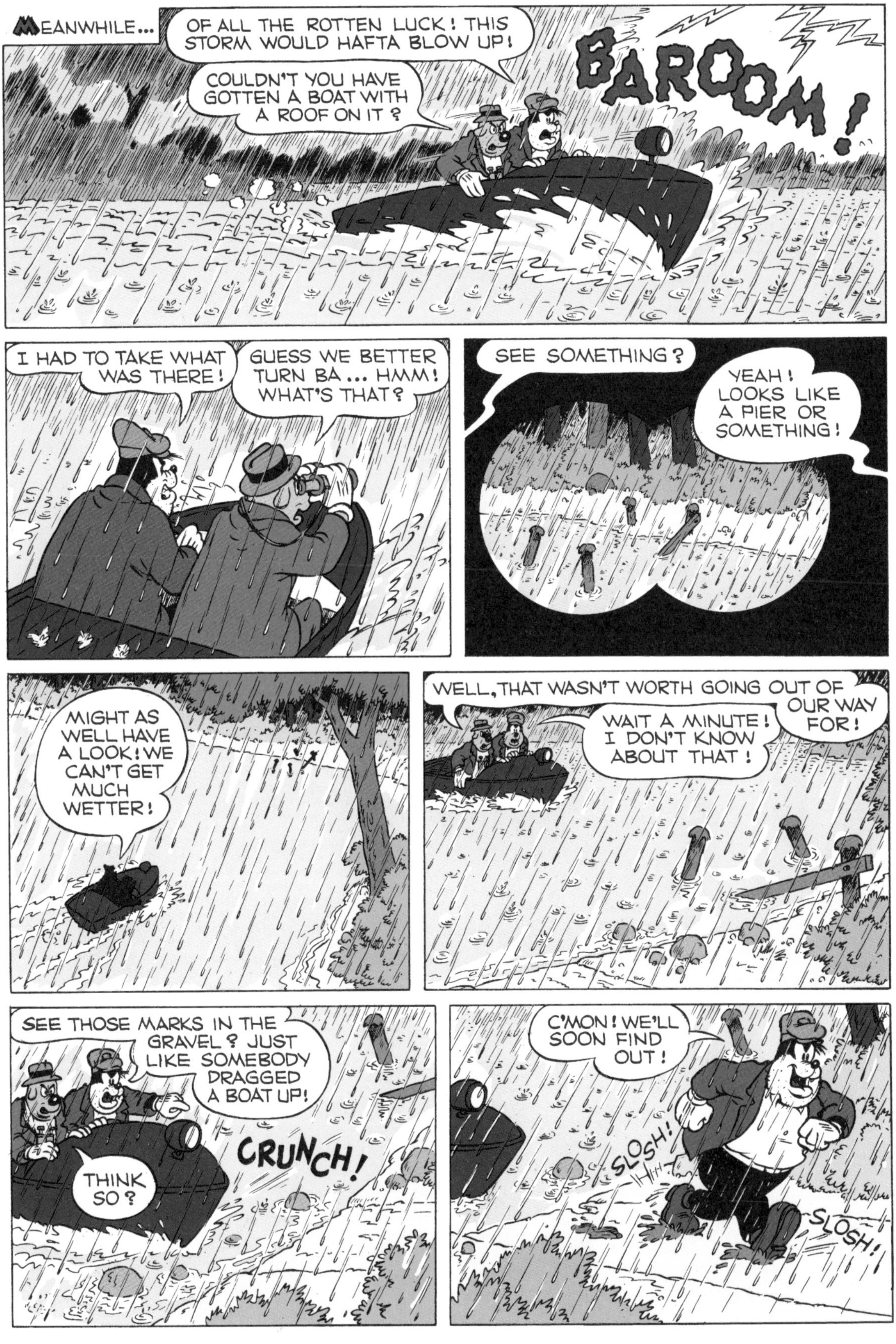
MEANWHILE...
OF ALL THE ROTTEN LUCK! THIS STORM WOULD HAFTA BLOW UP!
COULDN'T YOU HAVE GOTTEN A BOAT WITH A ROOF ON IT?
BAROOM!
I HAD TO TAKE WHAT WAS THERE!
GUESS WE BETTER TURN BA... HMM! WHAT'S THAT?
SEE SOMETHING?
YEAH! LOOKS LIKE A PIER OR SOMETHING!
MIGHT AS WELL HAVE A LOOK! WE CAN'T GET MUCH WETTER!
WELL, THAT WASN'T WORTH GOING OUT OF OUR WAY FOR!
WAIT A MINUTE! I DON'T KNOW ABOUT THAT!
SEE THOSE MARKS IN THE GRAVEL? JUST LIKE SOMEBODY DRAGGED A BOAT UP!
THINK SO?
CRUNCH!
C'MON! WE'LL SOON FIND OUT!
SLOSH!
SLOSH!

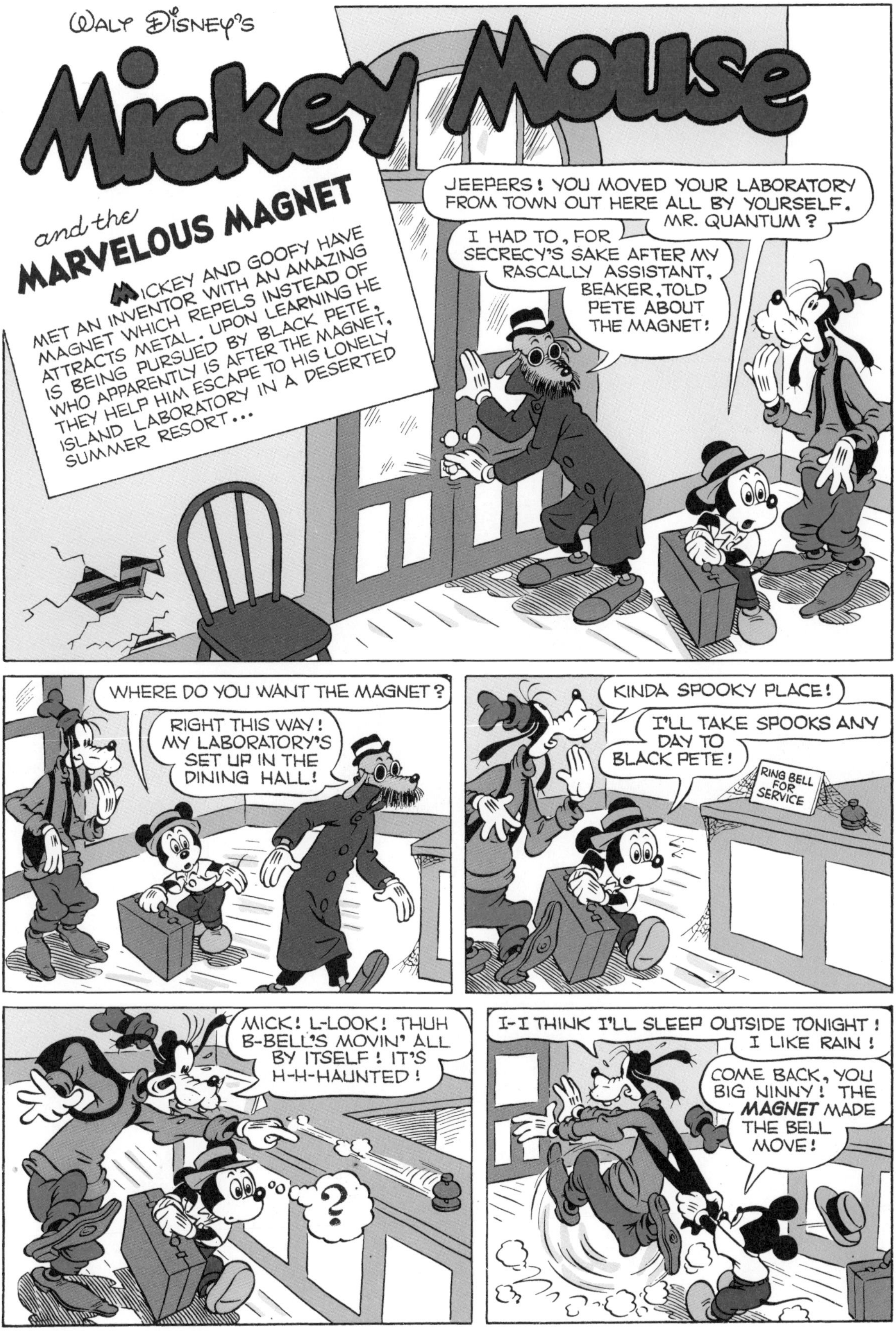

WALT DISNEY'S
Mickey Mouse
and the MARVELOUS MAGNET
MICKEY AND GOOFY HAVE MET AN INVENTOR WITH AN AMAZING MAGNET WHICH REPELS INSTEAD OF ATTRACTS METAL. UPON LEARNING HE IS BEING PURSUED BY BLACK PETE, WHO APPARENTLY IS AFTER THE MAGNET, THEY HELP HIM ESCAPE TO HIS LONELY ISLAND LABORATORY IN A DESERTED SUMMER RESORT...
JEEPERS! YOU MOVED YOUR LABORATORY FROM TOWN OUT HERE ALL BY YOURSELF, MR. QUANTUM?
I HAD TO, FOR SECRECY'S SAKE AFTER MY RASCALLY ASSISTANT, BEAKER, TOLD PETE ABOUT THE MAGNET!
WHERE DO YOU WANT THE MAGNET?
RIGHT THIS WAY! MY LABORATORY'S SET UP IN THE DINING HALL!
KINDA SPOOKY PLACE!
I'LL TAKE SPOOKS ANY DAY TO BLACK PETE!
RING BELL FOR SERVICE
MICK! L-LOOK! THUH B-BELL'S MOVIN' ALL BY ITSELF! IT'S H-H-HAUNTED!
?
I-I THINK I'LL SLEEP OUTSIDE TONIGHT! I LIKE RAIN!
COME BACK, YOU BIG NINNY! THE MAGNET MADE THE BELL MOVE!

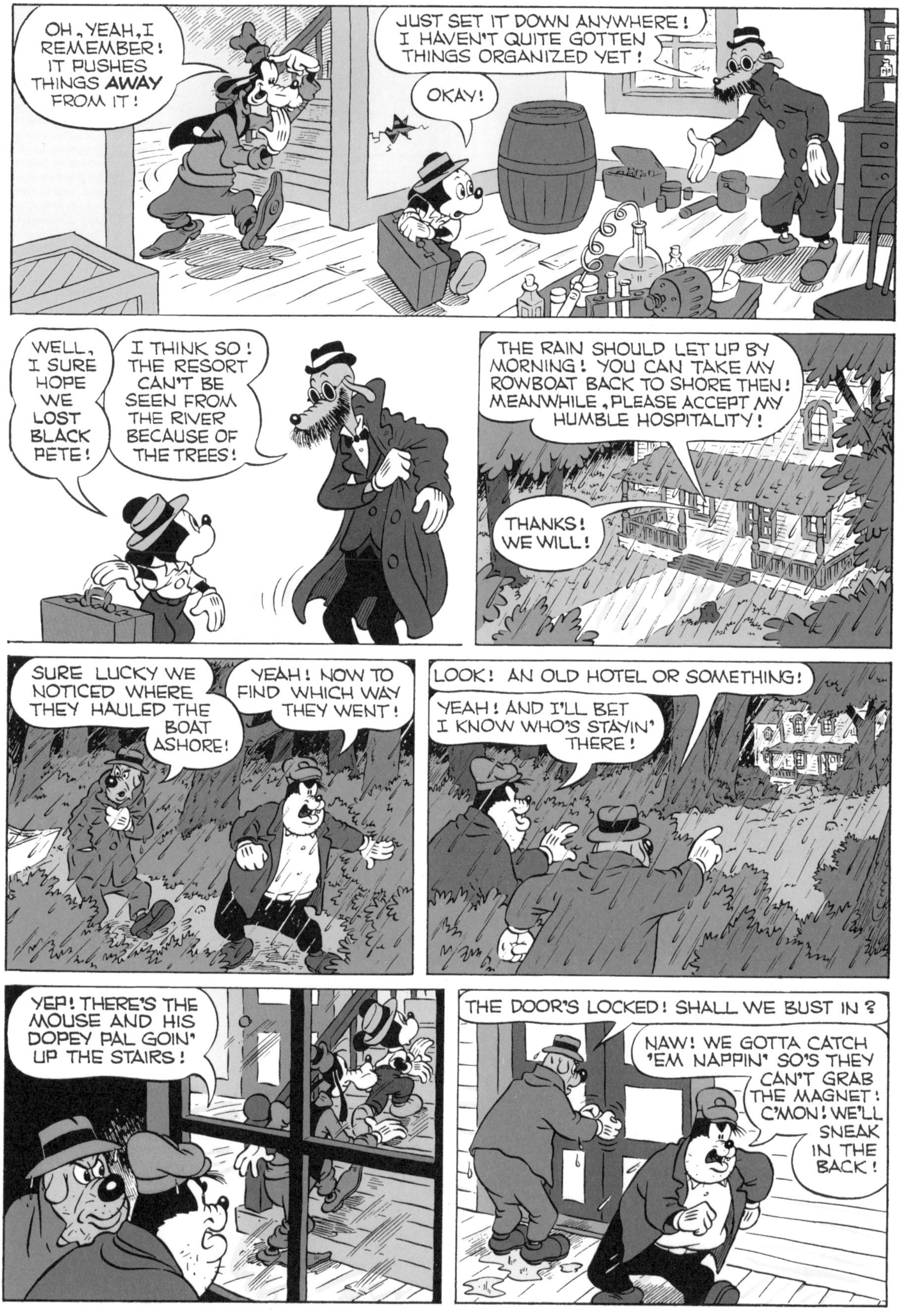

OH, YEAH, I REMEMBER! IT PUSHES THINGS **AWAY** FROM IT!
JUST SET IT DOWN ANYWHERE! I HAVEN'T QUITE GOTTEN THINGS ORGANIZED YET!
OKAY!
WELL, I SURE HOPE WE LOST BLACK PETE!
I THINK SO! THE RESORT CAN'T BE SEEN FROM THE RIVER BECAUSE OF THE TREES!
THE RAIN SHOULD LET UP BY MORNING! YOU CAN TAKE MY ROWBOAT BACK TO SHORE THEN! MEANWHILE, PLEASE ACCEPT MY HUMBLE HOSPITALITY!
THANKS! WE WILL!
SURE LUCKY WE NOTICED WHERE THEY HAULED THE BOAT ASHORE!
YEAH! NOW TO FIND WHICH WAY THEY WENT!
LOOK! AN OLD HOTEL OR SOMETHING!
YEAH! AND I'LL BET I KNOW WHO'S STAYIN' THERE!
YEP! THERE'S THE MOUSE AND HIS DOPEY PAL GOIN' UP THE STAIRS!
THE DOOR'S LOCKED! SHALL WE BUST IN?
NAW! WE GOTTA CATCH 'EM NAPPIN' SO'S THEY CAN'T GRAB THE MAGNET! C'MON! WE'LL SNEAK IN THE BACK!

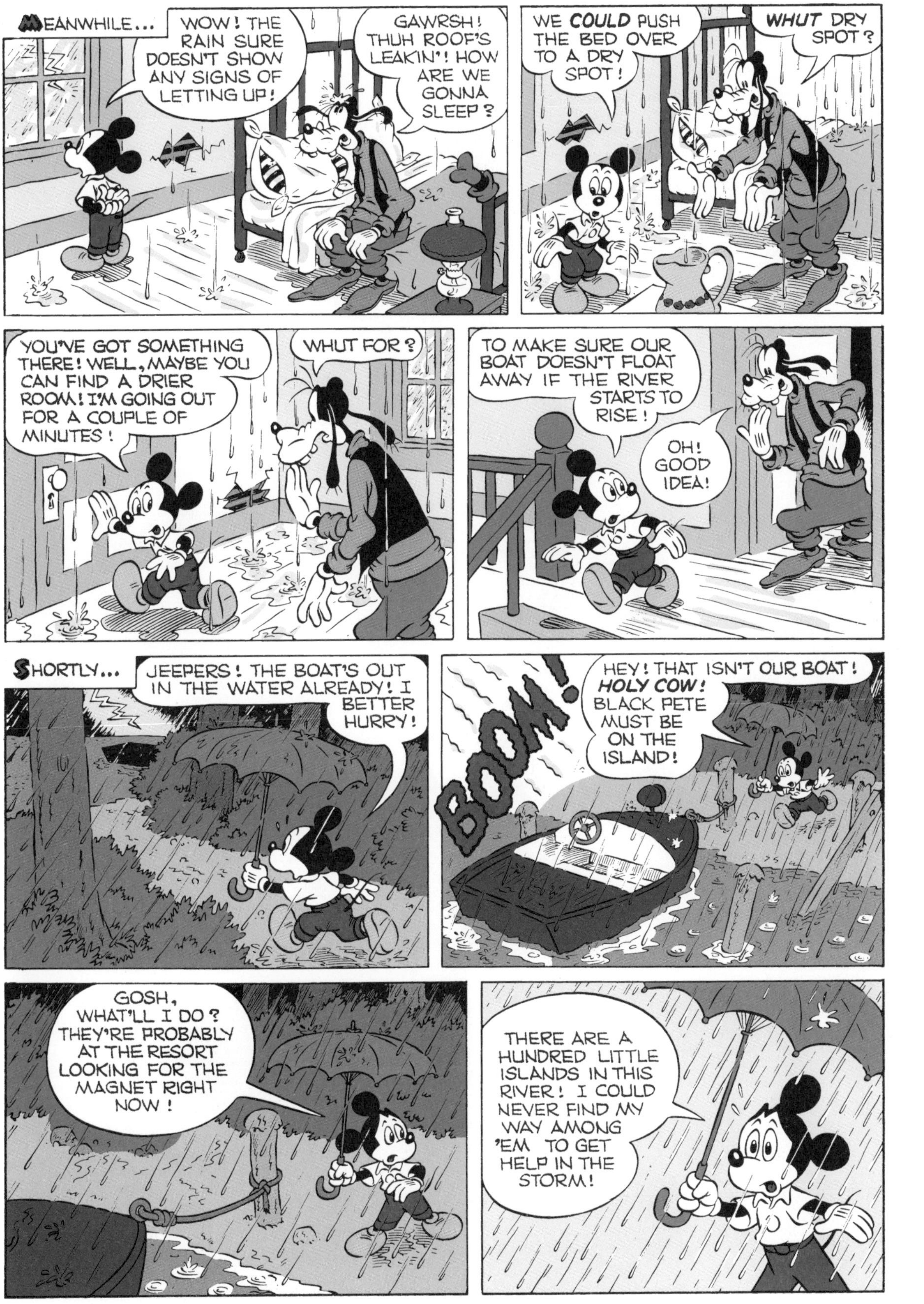
MEANWHILE...
WOW! THE RAIN SURE DOESN'T SHOW ANY SIGNS OF LETTING UP!
GAWRSH! THUH ROOF'S LEAKIN'! HOW ARE WE GONNA SLEEP?
WE COULD PUSH THE BED OVER TO A DRY SPOT!
WHUT DRY SPOT?
YOU'VE GOT SOMETHING THERE! WELL, MAYBE YOU CAN FIND A DRIER ROOM! I'M GOING OUT FOR A COUPLE OF MINUTES!
WHUT FOR?
TO MAKE SURE OUR BOAT DOESN'T FLOAT AWAY IF THE RIVER STARTS TO RISE!
OH! GOOD IDEA!
SHORTLY...
JEEPERS! THE BOAT'S OUT IN THE WATER ALREADY! I BETTER HURRY!
BOOM!
HEY! THAT ISN'T OUR BOAT! HOLY COW! BLACK PETE MUST BE ON THE ISLAND!
GOSH, WHAT'LL I DO? THEY'RE PROBABLY AT THE RESORT LOOKING FOR THE MAGNET RIGHT NOW!
THERE ARE A HUNDRED LITTLE ISLANDS IN THIS RIVER! I COULD NEVER FIND MY WAY AMONG 'EM TO GET HELP IN THE STORM!

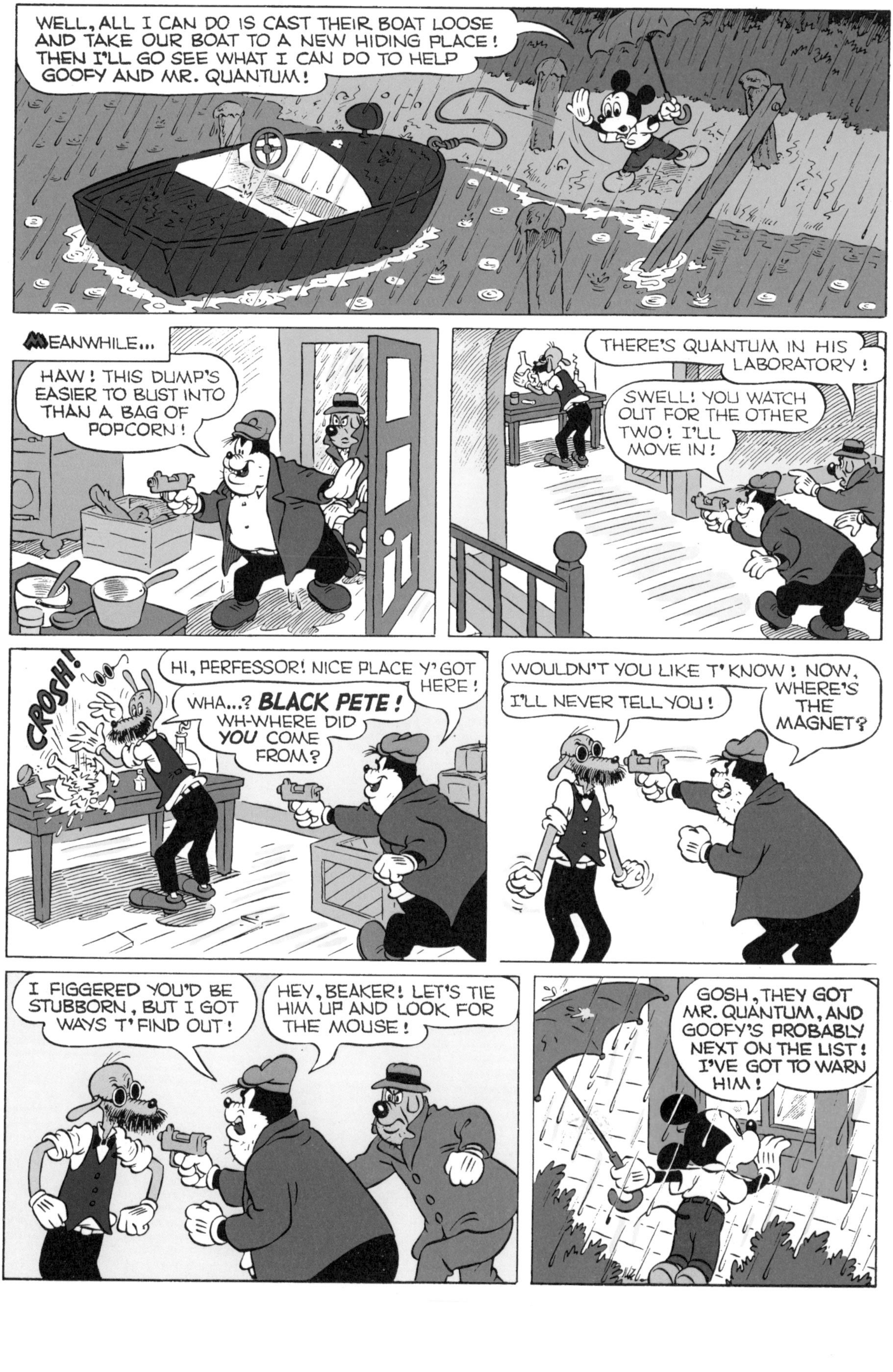
WELL, ALL I CAN DO IS CAST THEIR BOAT LOOSE AND TAKE OUR BOAT TO A NEW HIDING PLACE! THEN I'LL GO SEE WHAT I CAN DO TO HELP GOOFY AND MR. QUANTUM!
MEANWHILE...
HAW! THIS DUMP'S EASIER TO BUST INTO THAN A BAG OF POPCORN!
THERE'S QUANTUM IN HIS LABORATORY!
SWELL! YOU WATCH OUT FOR THE OTHER TWO! I'LL MOVE IN!
CROSH!
HI, PERFESSOR! NICE PLACE Y' GOT HERE!
WHA...? BLACK PETE! WH-WHERE DID YOU COME FROM?
WOULDN'T YOU LIKE T' KNOW! NOW, WHERE'S THE MAGNET?
I'LL NEVER TELL YOU!
I FIGGERED YOU'D BE STUBBORN, BUT I GOT WAYS T' FIND OUT!
HEY, BEAKER! LET'S TIE HIM UP AND LOOK FOR THE MOUSE!
GOSH, THEY GOT MR. QUANTUM, AND GOOFY'S PROBABLY NEXT ON THE LIST! I'VE GOT TO WARN HIM!

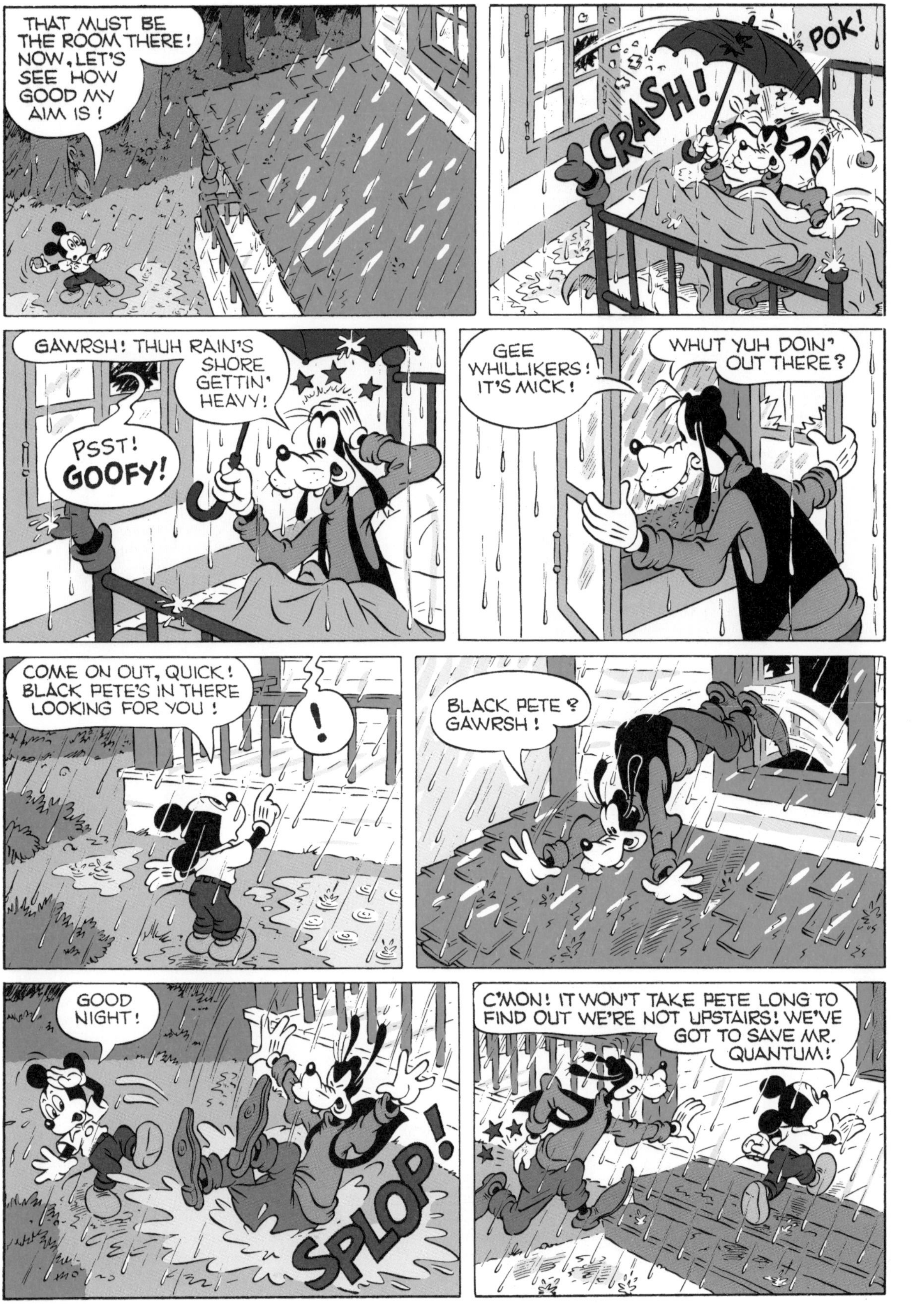
THAT MUST BE THE ROOM THERE! NOW, LET'S SEE HOW GOOD MY AIM IS!
CRASH!
POK!
GAWRSH! THUH RAIN'S SHORE GETTIN' HEAVY!
PSST! GOOFY!
GEE WHILLIKERS! IT'S MICK!
WHUT YUH DOIN' OUT THERE?
COME ON OUT, QUICK! BLACK PETE'S IN THERE LOOKING FOR YOU!
!
BLACK PETE? GAWRSH!
GOOD NIGHT!
SPLOP!
C'MON! IT WON'T TAKE PETE LONG TO FIND OUT WE'RE NOT UPSTAIRS! WE'VE GOT TO SAVE MR. QUANTUM!

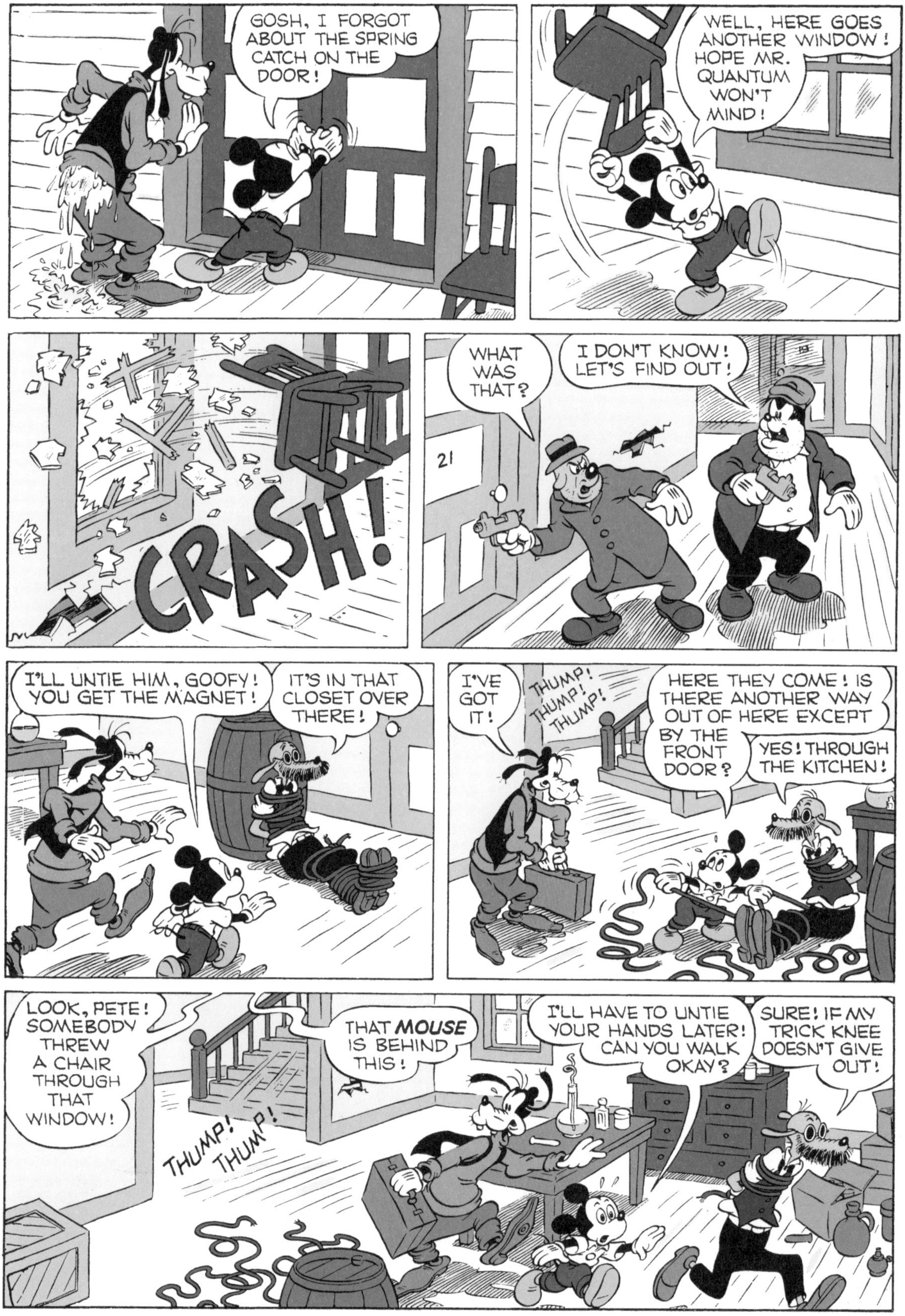
GOSH, I FORGOT ABOUT THE SPRING CATCH ON THE DOOR!
WELL, HERE GOES ANOTHER WINDOW! HOPE MR. QUANTUM WON'T MIND!
CRASH!
WHAT WAS THAT?
I DON'T KNOW! LET'S FIND OUT!
21
I'LL UNTIE HIM, GOOFY! YOU GET THE MAGNET!
IT'S IN THAT CLOSET OVER THERE!
I'VE GOT IT!
THUMP! THUMP! THUMP!
HERE THEY COME! IS THERE ANOTHER WAY OUT OF HERE EXCEPT BY THE FRONT DOOR?
YES! THROUGH THE KITCHEN!
LOOK, PETE! SOMEBODY THREW A CHAIR THROUGH THAT WINDOW!
THAT MOUSE IS BEHIND THIS!
THUMP! THUMP!
I'LL HAVE TO UNTIE YOUR HANDS LATER! CAN YOU WALK OKAY?
SURE! IF MY TRICK KNEE DOESN'T GIVE OUT!

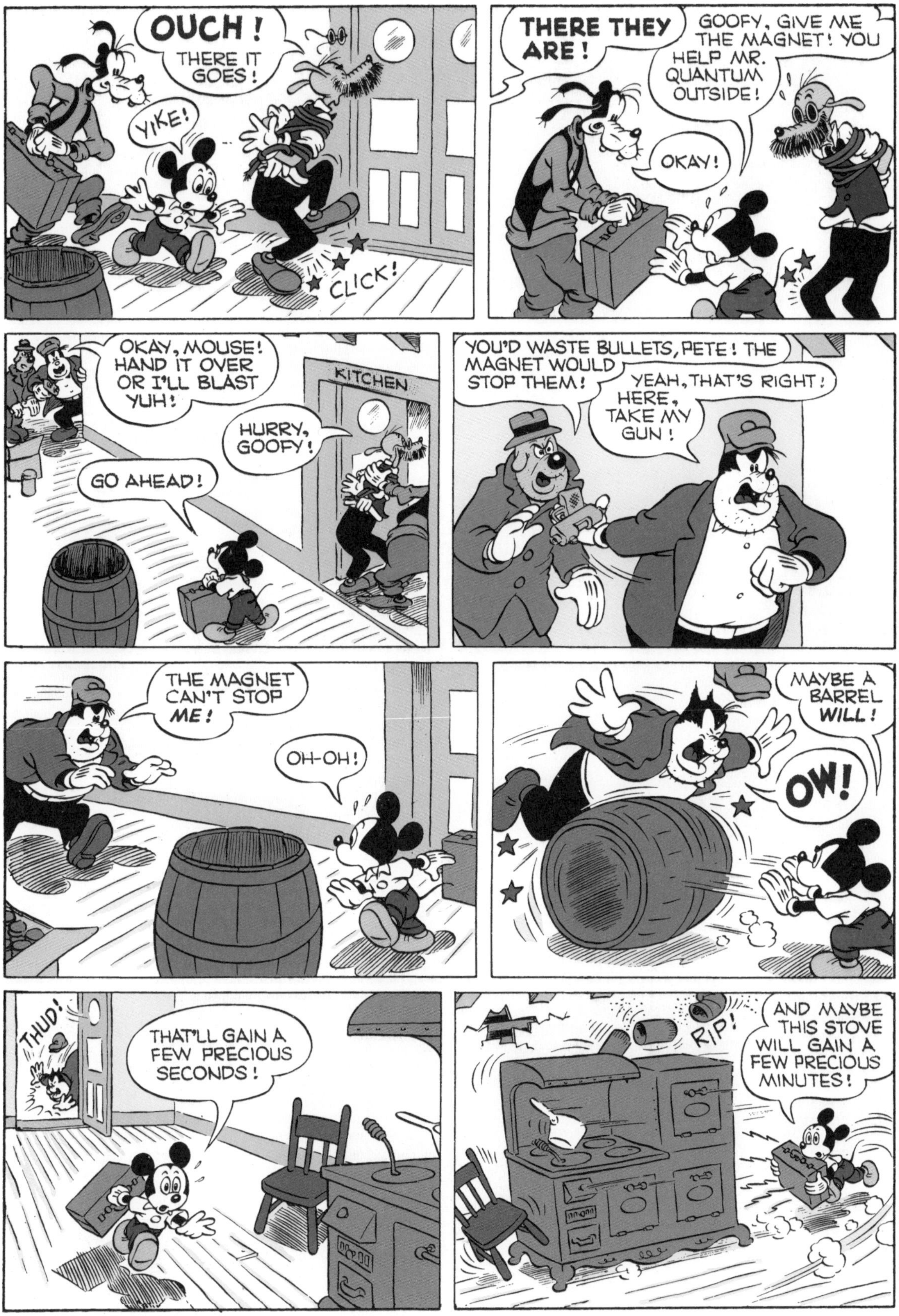
OUCH!
THERE IT GOES!
YIKE!
CLICK!
THERE THEY ARE!
GOOFY, GIVE ME THE MAGNET! YOU HELP MR. QUANTUM OUTSIDE!
OKAY!
OKAY, MOUSE! HAND IT OVER OR I'LL BLAST YUH!
KITCHEN
HURRY, GOOFY!
GO AHEAD!
YOU'D WASTE BULLETS, PETE! THE MAGNET WOULD STOP THEM!
YEAH, THAT'S RIGHT! HERE, TAKE MY GUN!
THE MAGNET CAN'T STOP ME!
OH-OH!
MAYBE A BARREL WILL!
OW!
THUD!
THAT'LL GAIN A FEW PRECIOUS SECONDS!
RIP!
AND MAYBE THIS STOVE WILL GAIN A FEW PRECIOUS MINUTES!

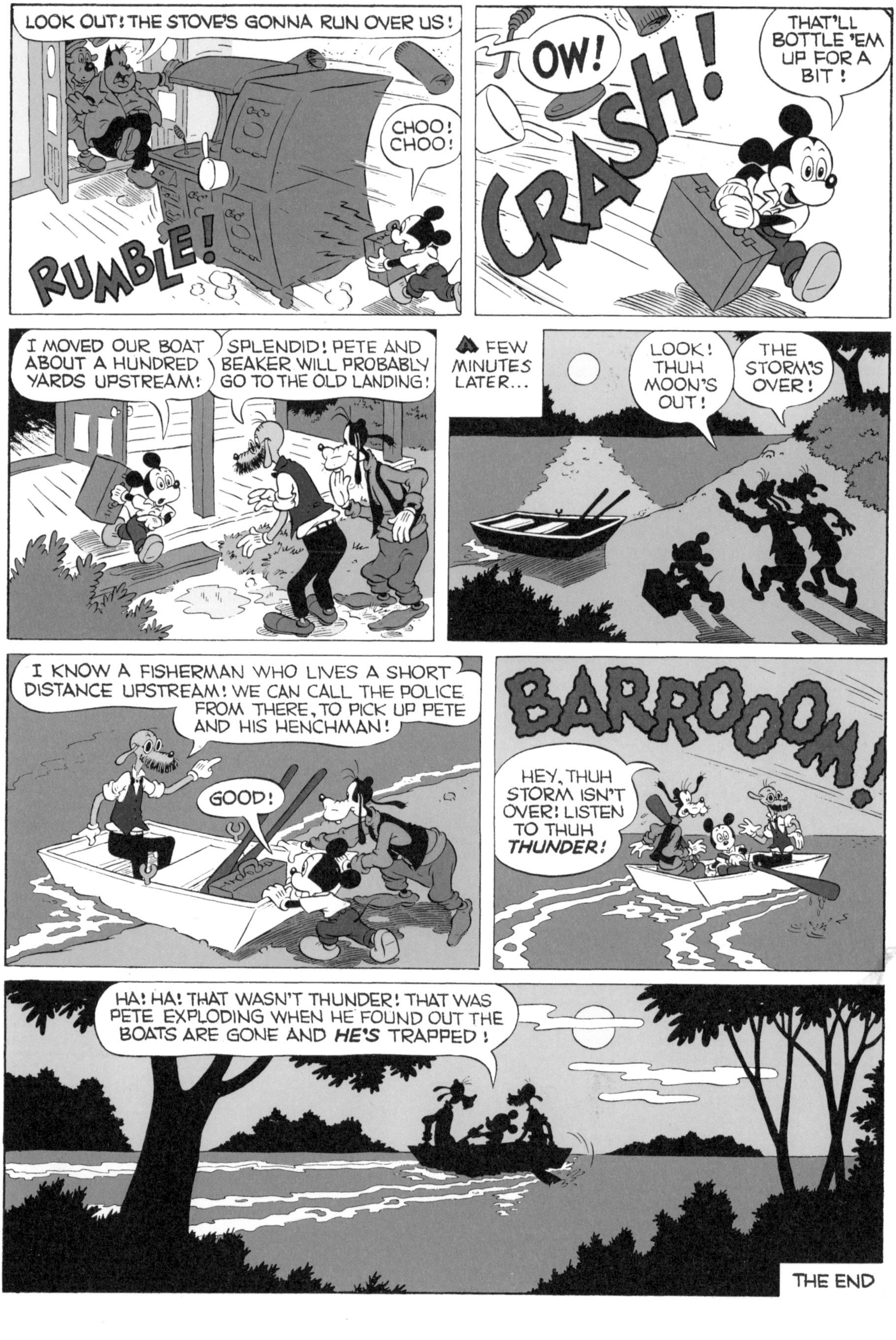
LOOK OUT! THE STOVE'S GONNA RUN OVER US!
CHOO! CHOO!
RUMBLE!
OW!
CRASH!
THAT'LL BOTTLE 'EM UP FOR A BIT!
I MOVED OUR BOAT ABOUT A HUNDRED YARDS UPSTREAM!
SPLENDID! PETE AND BEAKER WILL PROBABLY GO TO THE OLD LANDING!
A FEW MINUTES LATER...
LOOK! THUH MOON'S OUT!
THE STORM'S OVER!
I KNOW A FISHERMAN WHO LIVES A SHORT DISTANCE UPSTREAM! WE CAN CALL THE POLICE FROM THERE, TO PICK UP PETE AND HIS HENCHMAN!
GOOD!
BARROOOM!
HEY, THUH STORM ISN'T OVER! LISTEN TO THUH THUNDER!
HA! HA! THAT WASN'T THUNDER! THAT WAS PETE EXPLODING WHEN HE FOUND OUT THE BOATS ARE GONE AND HE'S TRAPPED!
THE END

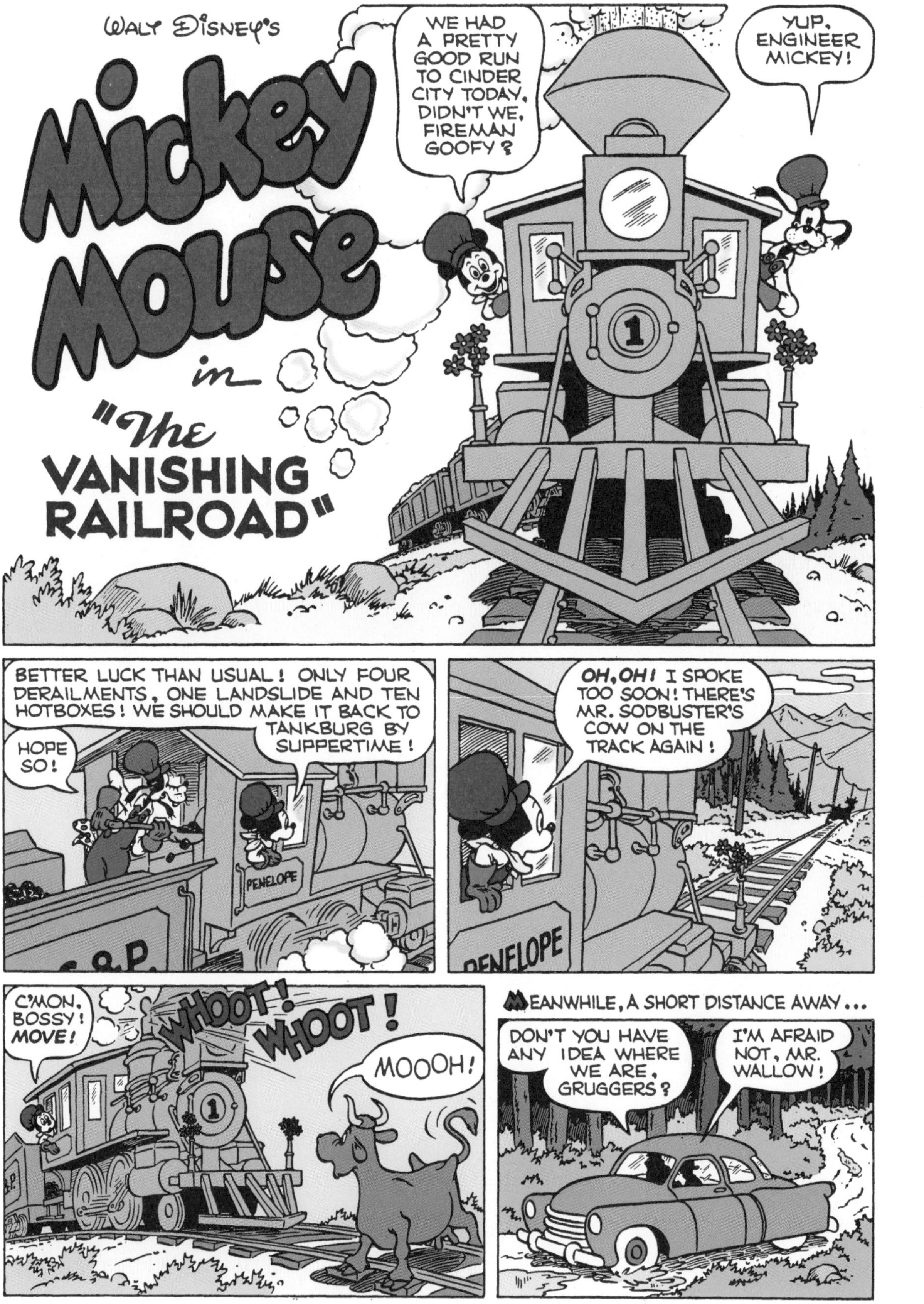
WALT DISNEY'S
Mickey Mouse
in
"The VANISHING RAILROAD"
WE HAD A PRETTY GOOD RUN TO CINDER CITY TODAY, DIDN'T WE, FIREMAN GOOFY?
YUP, ENGINEER MICKEY!
BETTER LUCK THAN USUAL! ONLY FOUR DERAILMENTS, ONE LANDSLIDE AND TEN HOTBOXES! WE SHOULD MAKE IT BACK TO TANKBURG BY SUPPERTIME!
HOPE SO!
PENELOPE
OH, OH! I SPOKE TOO SOON! THERE'S MR. SODBUSTER'S COW ON THE TRACK AGAIN!
PENELOPE
C'MON, BOSSY! MOVE!
WHOOT! WHOOT!
MOOOH!
MEANWHILE, A SHORT DISTANCE AWAY...
DON'T YOU HAVE ANY IDEA WHERE WE ARE, GRUGGERS?
I'M AFRAID NOT, MR. WALLOW!

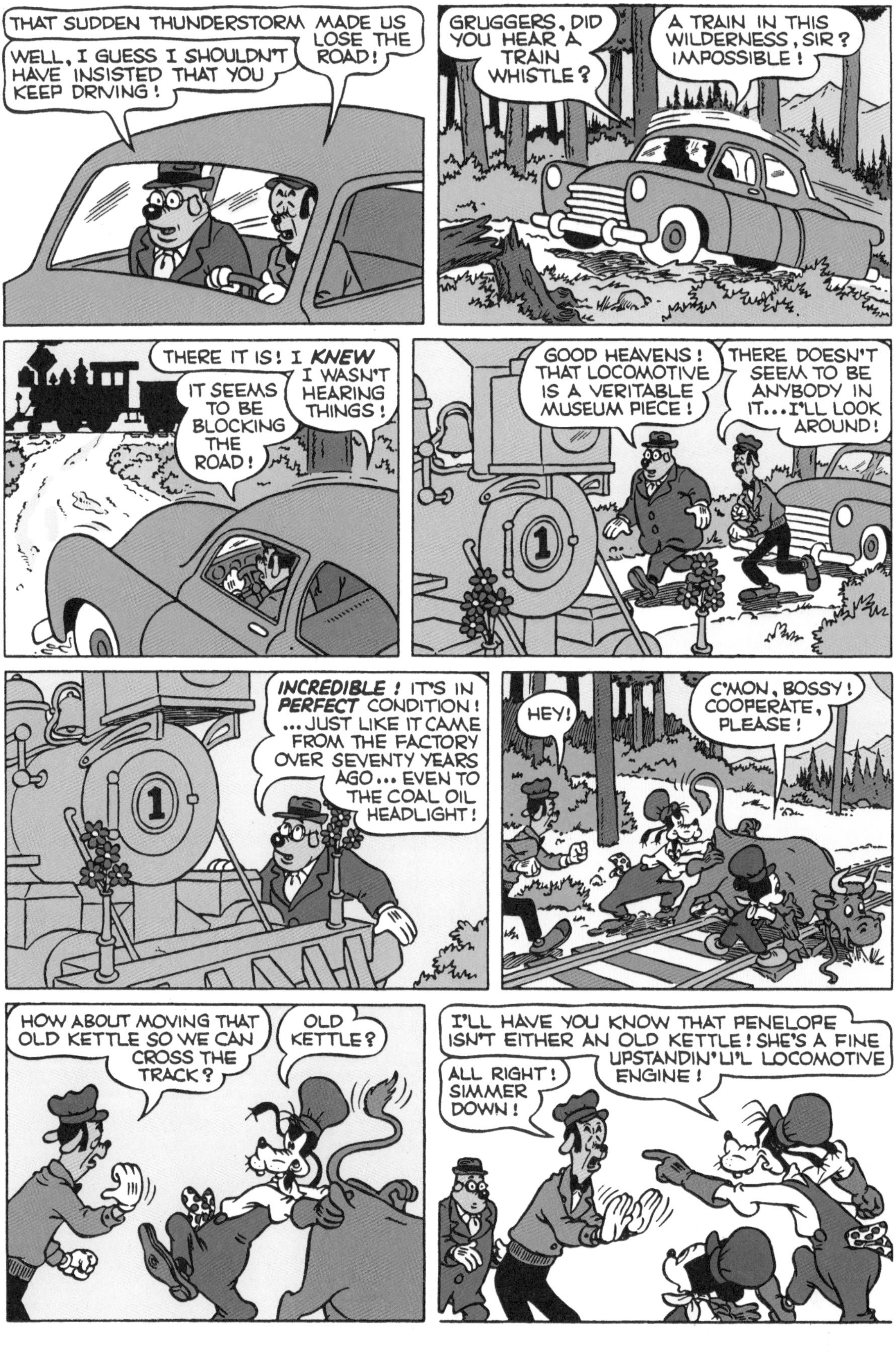

THAT SUDDEN THUNDERSTORM MADE US LOSE THE ROAD!
WELL, I GUESS I SHOULDN'T HAVE INSISTED THAT YOU KEEP DRIVING!
GRUGGERS, DID YOU HEAR A TRAIN WHISTLE?
A TRAIN IN THIS WILDERNESS, SIR? IMPOSSIBLE!
THERE IT IS! I *KNEW* I WASN'T HEARING THINGS!
IT SEEMS TO BE BLOCKING THE ROAD!
GOOD HEAVENS! THAT LOCOMOTIVE IS A VERITABLE MUSEUM PIECE!
THERE DOESN'T SEEM TO BE ANYBODY IN IT... I'LL LOOK AROUND!
1
INCREDIBLE! IT'S IN ***PERFECT*** CONDITION! ...JUST LIKE IT CAME FROM THE FACTORY OVER SEVENTY YEARS AGO... EVEN TO THE COAL OIL HEADLIGHT!
1
HEY!
C'MON, BOSSY! COOPERATE, PLEASE!
HOW ABOUT MOVING THAT OLD KETTLE SO WE CAN CROSS THE TRACK?
OLD KETTLE?
I'LL HAVE YOU KNOW THAT PENELOPE ISN'T EITHER AN OLD KETTLE! SHE'S A FINE UPSTANDIN' LI'L LOCOMOTIVE ENGINE!
ALL RIGHT! SIMMER DOWN!

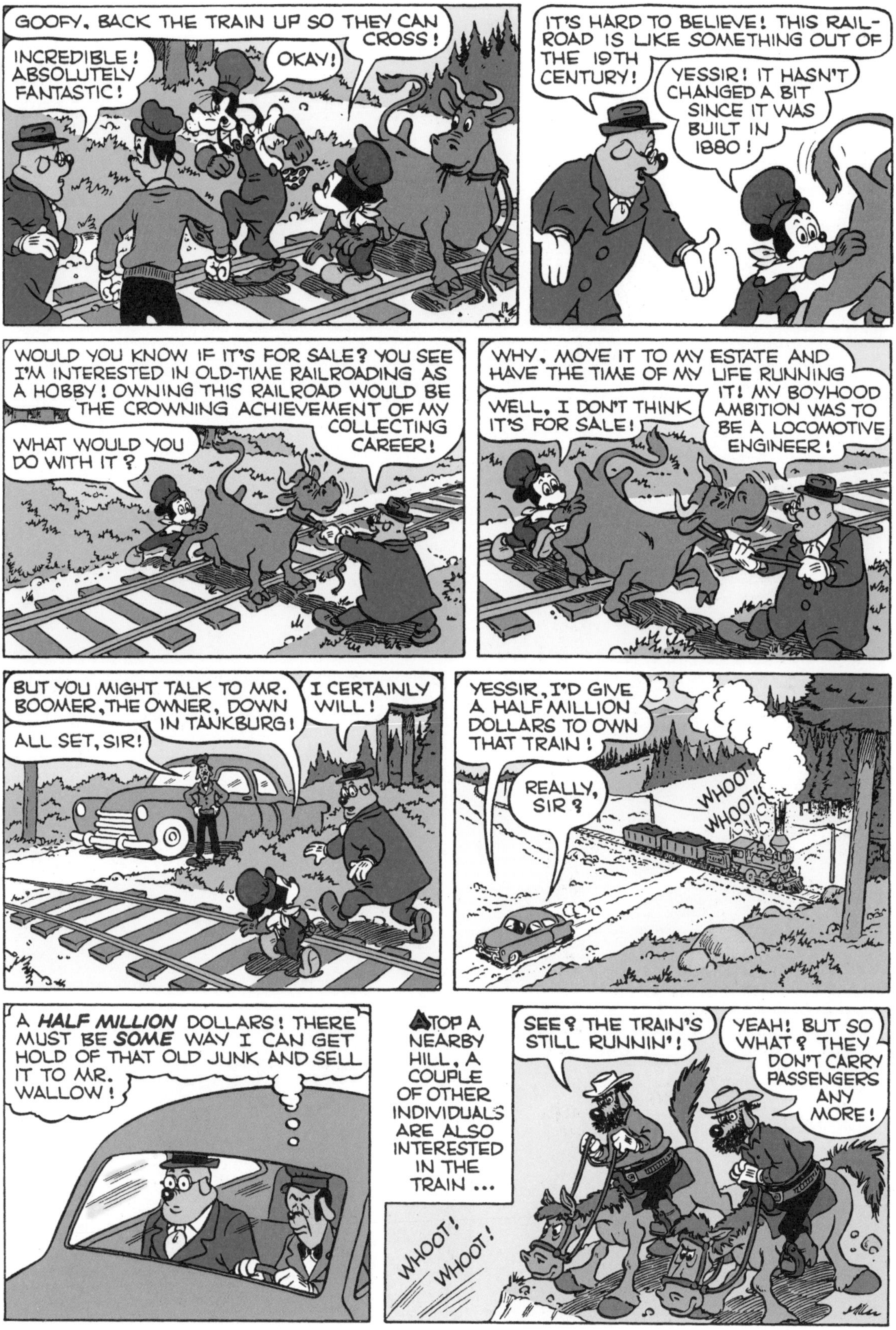
GOOFY, BACK THE TRAIN UP SO THEY CAN CROSS!
INCREDIBLE! ABSOLUTELY FANTASTIC!
OKAY!
IT'S HARD TO BELIEVE! THIS RAILROAD IS LIKE SOMETHING OUT OF THE 19TH CENTURY!
YESSIR! IT HASN'T CHANGED A BIT SINCE IT WAS BUILT IN 1880!
WOULD YOU KNOW IF IT'S FOR SALE? YOU SEE I'M INTERESTED IN OLD-TIME RAILROADING AS A HOBBY! OWNING THIS RAILROAD WOULD BE THE CROWNING ACHIEVEMENT OF MY COLLECTING CAREER!
WHAT WOULD YOU DO WITH IT?
WHY, MOVE IT TO MY ESTATE AND HAVE THE TIME OF MY LIFE RUNNING IT! MY BOYHOOD AMBITION WAS TO BE A LOCOMOTIVE ENGINEER!
WELL, I DON'T THINK IT'S FOR SALE!
BUT YOU MIGHT TALK TO MR. BOOMER, THE OWNER, DOWN IN TANKBURG!
I CERTAINLY WILL!
ALL SET, SIR!
YESSIR, I'D GIVE A HALF MILLION DOLLARS TO OWN THAT TRAIN!
REALLY, SIR?
WHOOT! WHOOT!
A HALF MILLION DOLLARS! THERE MUST BE SOME WAY I CAN GET HOLD OF THAT OLD JUNK AND SELL IT TO MR. WALLOW!
ATOP A NEARBY HILL, A COUPLE OF OTHER INDIVIDUALS ARE ALSO INTERESTED IN THE TRAIN ...
SEE? THE TRAIN'S STILL RUNNIN'!
YEAH! BUT SO WHAT? THEY DON'T CARRY PASSENGERS ANY MORE!
WHOOT! WHOOT!

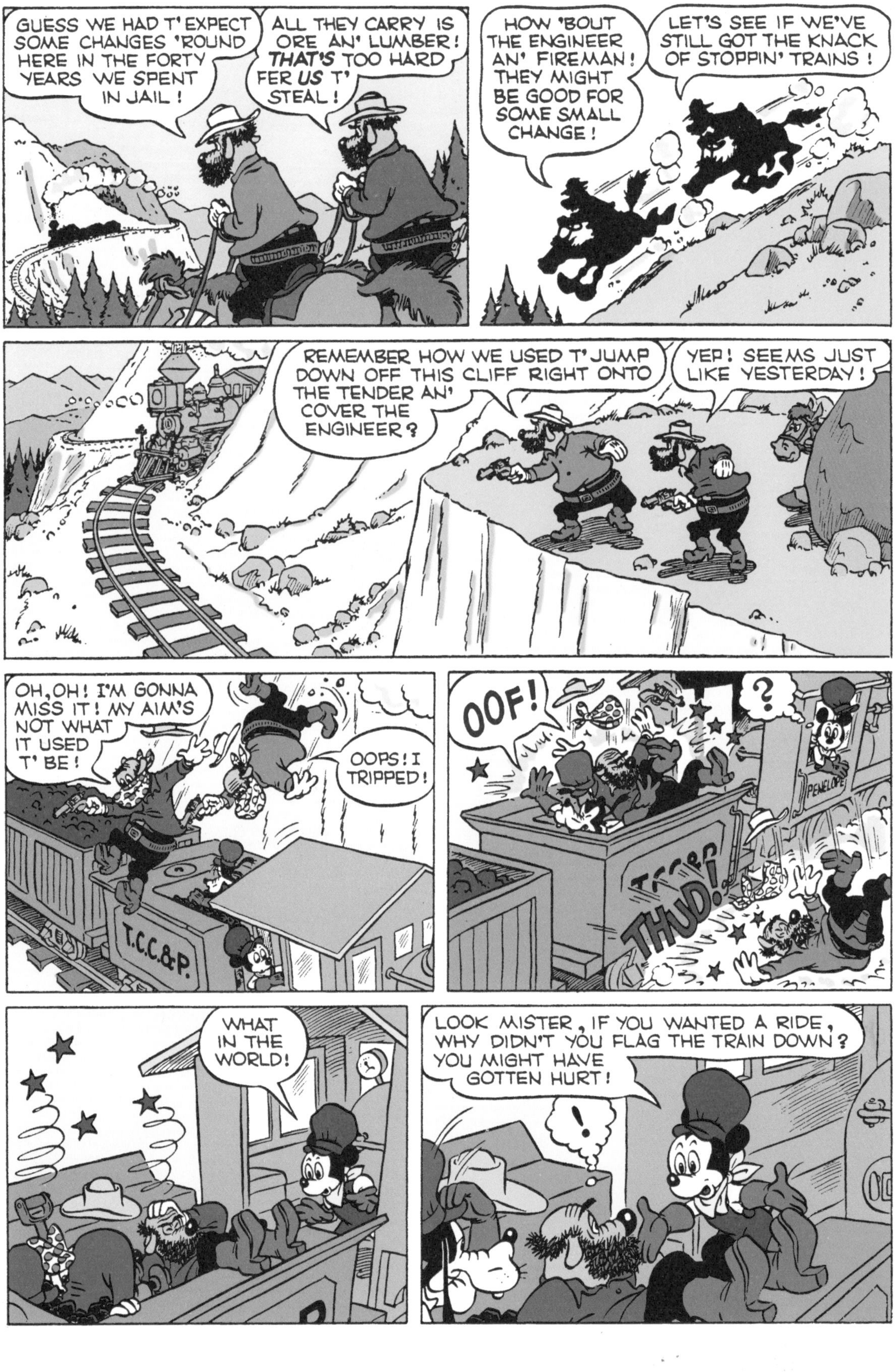
GUESS WE HAD T' EXPECT SOME CHANGES 'ROUND HERE IN THE FORTY YEARS WE SPENT IN JAIL!
ALL THEY CARRY IS ORE AN' LUMBER! THAT'S TOO HARD FER US T' STEAL!
HOW 'BOUT THE ENGINEER AN' FIREMAN! THEY MIGHT BE GOOD FOR SOME SMALL CHANGE!
LET'S SEE IF WE'VE STILL GOT THE KNACK OF STOPPIN' TRAINS!
REMEMBER HOW WE USED T' JUMP DOWN OFF THIS CLIFF RIGHT ONTO THE TENDER AN' COVER THE ENGINEER?
YEP! SEEMS JUST LIKE YESTERDAY!
OH, OH! I'M GONNA MISS IT! MY AIM'S NOT WHAT IT USED T' BE!
OOPS! I TRIPPED!
T.C.C.&P.
OOF!
?
PENELOPE
THUD!
WHAT IN THE WORLD!
LOOK MISTER, IF YOU WANTED A RIDE, WHY DIDN'T YOU FLAG THE TRAIN DOWN? YOU MIGHT HAVE GOTTEN HURT!
!

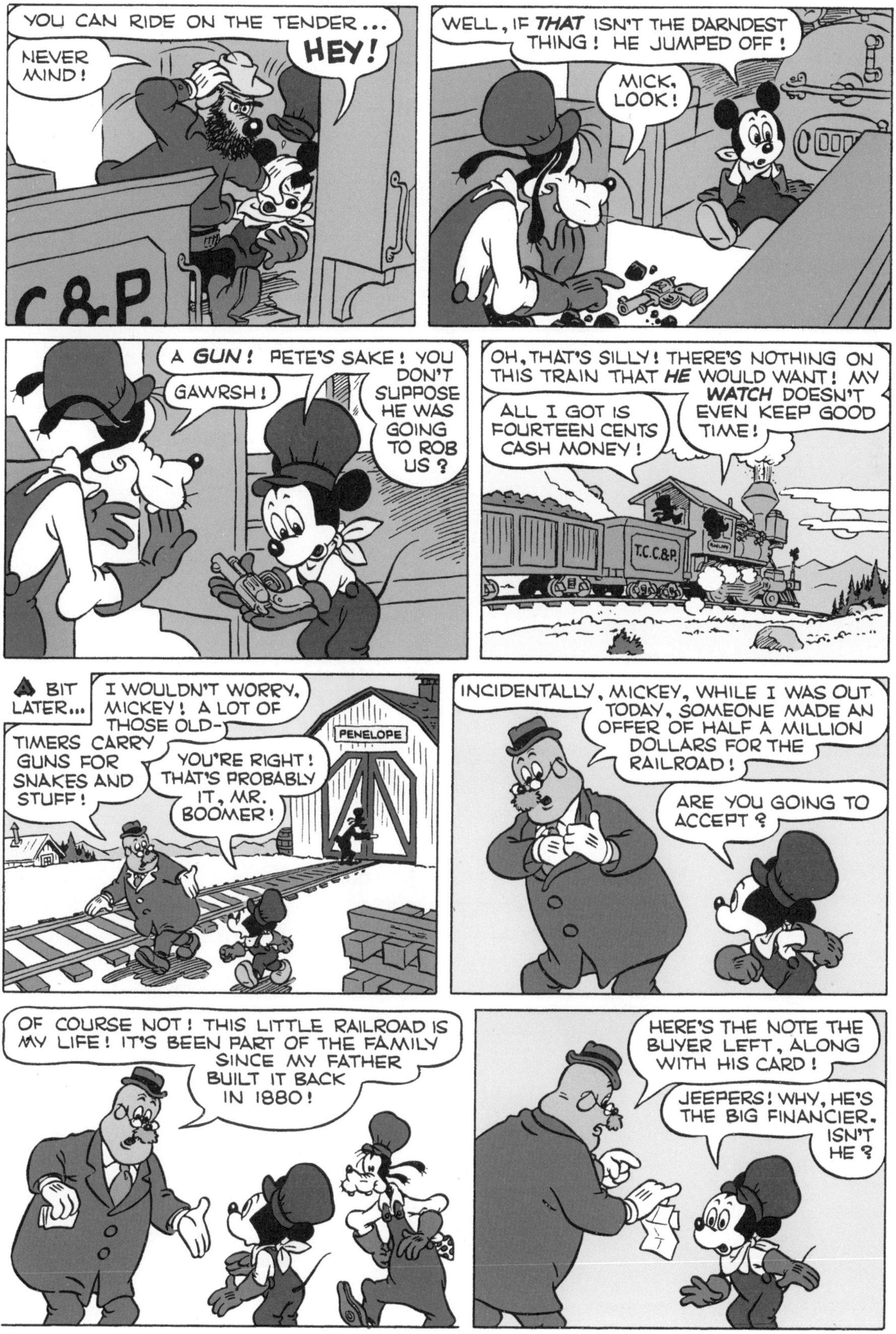
YOU CAN RIDE ON THE TENDER...
NEVER MIND!
HEY!
WELL, IF THAT ISN'T THE DARNDEST THING! HE JUMPED OFF!
MICK, LOOK!
A GUN! PETE'S SAKE! YOU DON'T SUPPOSE HE WAS GOING TO ROB US?
GAWRSH!
OH, THAT'S SILLY! THERE'S NOTHING ON THIS TRAIN THAT HE WOULD WANT! MY WATCH DOESN'T EVEN KEEP GOOD TIME!
ALL I GOT IS FOURTEEN CENTS CASH MONEY!
T.C.C.&P.
A BIT LATER...
I WOULDN'T WORRY, MICKEY! A LOT OF THOSE OLD-TIMERS CARRY GUNS FOR SNAKES AND STUFF!
YOU'RE RIGHT! THAT'S PROBABLY IT, MR. BOOMER!
PENELOPE
INCIDENTALLY, MICKEY, WHILE I WAS OUT TODAY, SOMEONE MADE AN OFFER OF HALF A MILLION DOLLARS FOR THE RAILROAD!
ARE YOU GOING TO ACCEPT?
OF COURSE NOT! THIS LITTLE RAILROAD IS MY LIFE! IT'S BEEN PART OF THE FAMILY SINCE MY FATHER BUILT IT BACK IN 1880!
HERE'S THE NOTE THE BUYER LEFT, ALONG WITH HIS CARD!
JEEPERS! WHY, HE'S THE BIG FINANCIER. ISN'T HE?

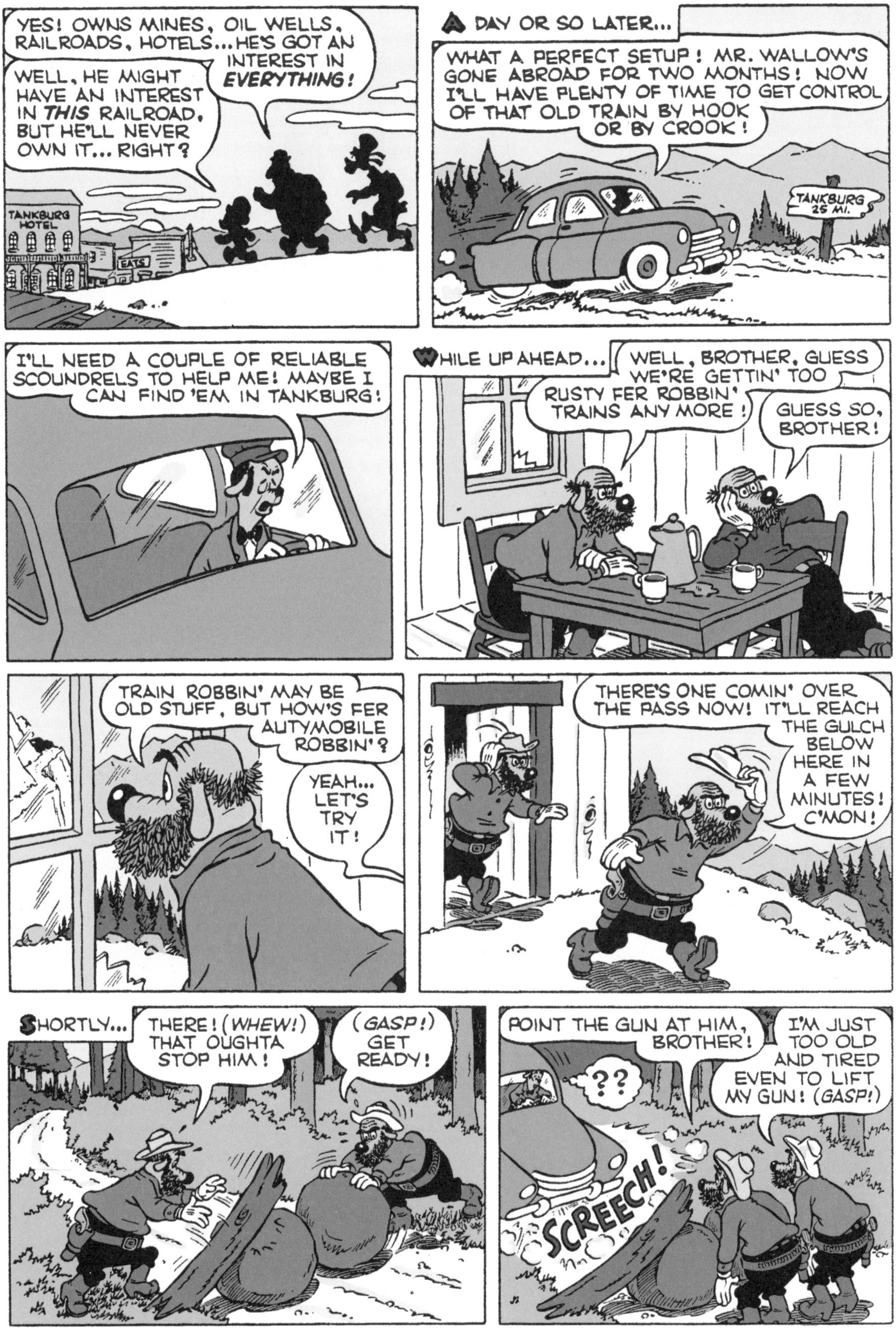

YES! OWNS MINES, OIL WELLS, RAILROADS, HOTELS...HE'S GOT AN INTEREST IN EVERYTHING!
WELL, HE MIGHT HAVE AN INTEREST IN THIS RAILROAD, BUT HE'LL NEVER OWN IT... RIGHT?
TANKBURG HOTEL
EATS
A DAY OR SO LATER...
WHAT A PERFECT SETUP! MR. WALLOW'S GONE ABROAD FOR TWO MONTHS! NOW I'LL HAVE PLENTY OF TIME TO GET CONTROL OF THAT OLD TRAIN BY HOOK OR BY CROOK!
TANKBURG 25 MI.
I'LL NEED A COUPLE OF RELIABLE SCOUNDRELS TO HELP ME! MAYBE I CAN FIND 'EM IN TANKBURG!
WHILE UP AHEAD...
WELL, BROTHER, GUESS WE'RE GETTIN' TOO RUSTY FER ROBBIN' TRAINS ANY MORE!
GUESS SO, BROTHER!
TRAIN ROBBIN' MAY BE OLD STUFF, BUT HOW'S FER AUTYMOBILE ROBBIN'?
YEAH... LET'S TRY IT!
THERE'S ONE COMIN' OVER THE PASS NOW! IT'LL REACH THE GULCH BELOW HERE IN A FEW MINUTES! C'MON!
SHORTLY...
THERE! (WHEW!) THAT OUGHTA STOP HIM!
(GASP!) GET READY!
POINT THE GUN AT HIM, BROTHER!
I'M JUST TOO OLD AND TIRED EVEN TO LIFT MY GUN! (GASP!)
??
SCREECH!

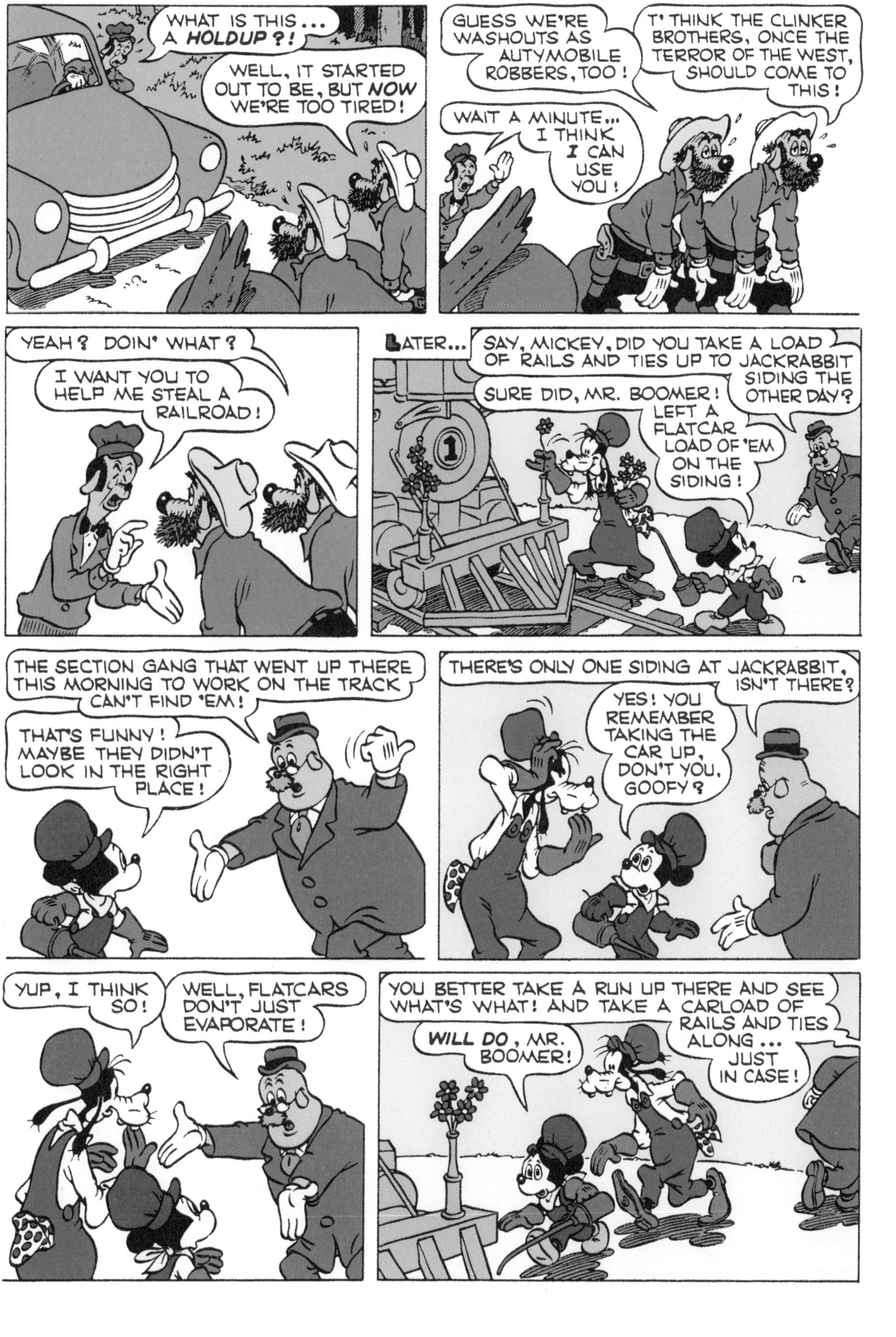
WHAT IS THIS ... A **HOLDUP** ?!
WELL, IT STARTED OUT TO BE, BUT **NOW** WE'RE TOO TIRED!
GUESS WE'RE WASHOUTS AS AUTYMOBILE ROBBERS, TOO!
T' THINK THE CLINKER BROTHERS, ONCE THE TERROR OF THE WEST, SHOULD COME TO THIS!
WAIT A MINUTE... I THINK **I** CAN USE YOU!
YEAH? DOIN' WHAT?
I WANT YOU TO HELP ME STEAL A RAILROAD!
LATER...
SAY, MICKEY, DID YOU TAKE A LOAD OF RAILS AND TIES UP TO JACKRABBIT SIDING THE OTHER DAY?
SURE DID, MR. BOOMER! LEFT A FLATCAR LOAD OF 'EM ON THE SIDING!
THE SECTION GANG THAT WENT UP THERE THIS MORNING TO WORK ON THE TRACK CAN'T FIND 'EM!
THAT'S FUNNY! MAYBE THEY DIDN'T LOOK IN THE RIGHT PLACE!
THERE'S ONLY ONE SIDING AT JACKRABBIT, ISN'T THERE?
YES! YOU REMEMBER TAKING THE CAR UP, DON'T YOU, GOOFY?
YUP, I THINK SO!
WELL, FLATCARS DON'T JUST EVAPORATE!
YOU BETTER TAKE A RUN UP THERE AND SEE WHAT'S WHAT! AND TAKE A CARLOAD OF RAILS AND TIES ALONG ... JUST IN CASE!
WILL DO, MR. BOOMER!

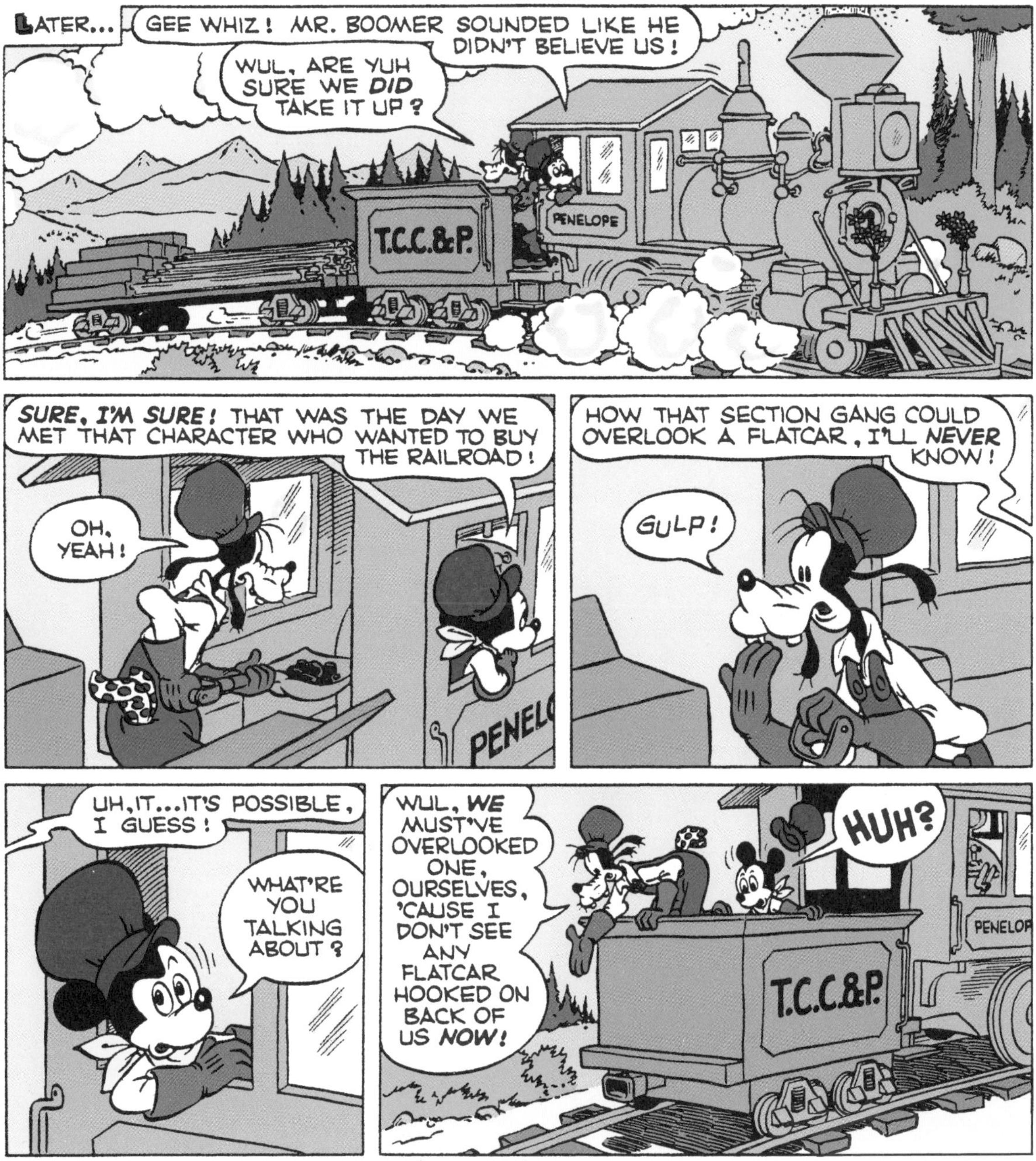

LATER...
GEE WHIZ! MR. BOOMER SOUNDED LIKE HE DIDN'T BELIEVE US!
WUL, ARE YUH SURE WE DID TAKE IT UP?
T.C.C.&P.
PENELOPE
SURE, I'M SURE! THAT WAS THE DAY WE MET THAT CHARACTER WHO WANTED TO BUY THE RAILROAD!
OH, YEAH!
PENELO
HOW THAT SECTION GANG COULD OVERLOOK A FLATCAR, I'LL NEVER KNOW!
GULP!
UH, IT...IT'S POSSIBLE, I GUESS!
WHAT'RE YOU TALKING ABOUT?
WUL, WE MUST'VE OVERLOOKED ONE, OURSELVES, 'CAUSE I DON'T SEE ANY FLATCAR HOOKED ON BACK OF US NOW!
HUH?
T.C.C.&P.
PENELOP

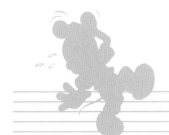

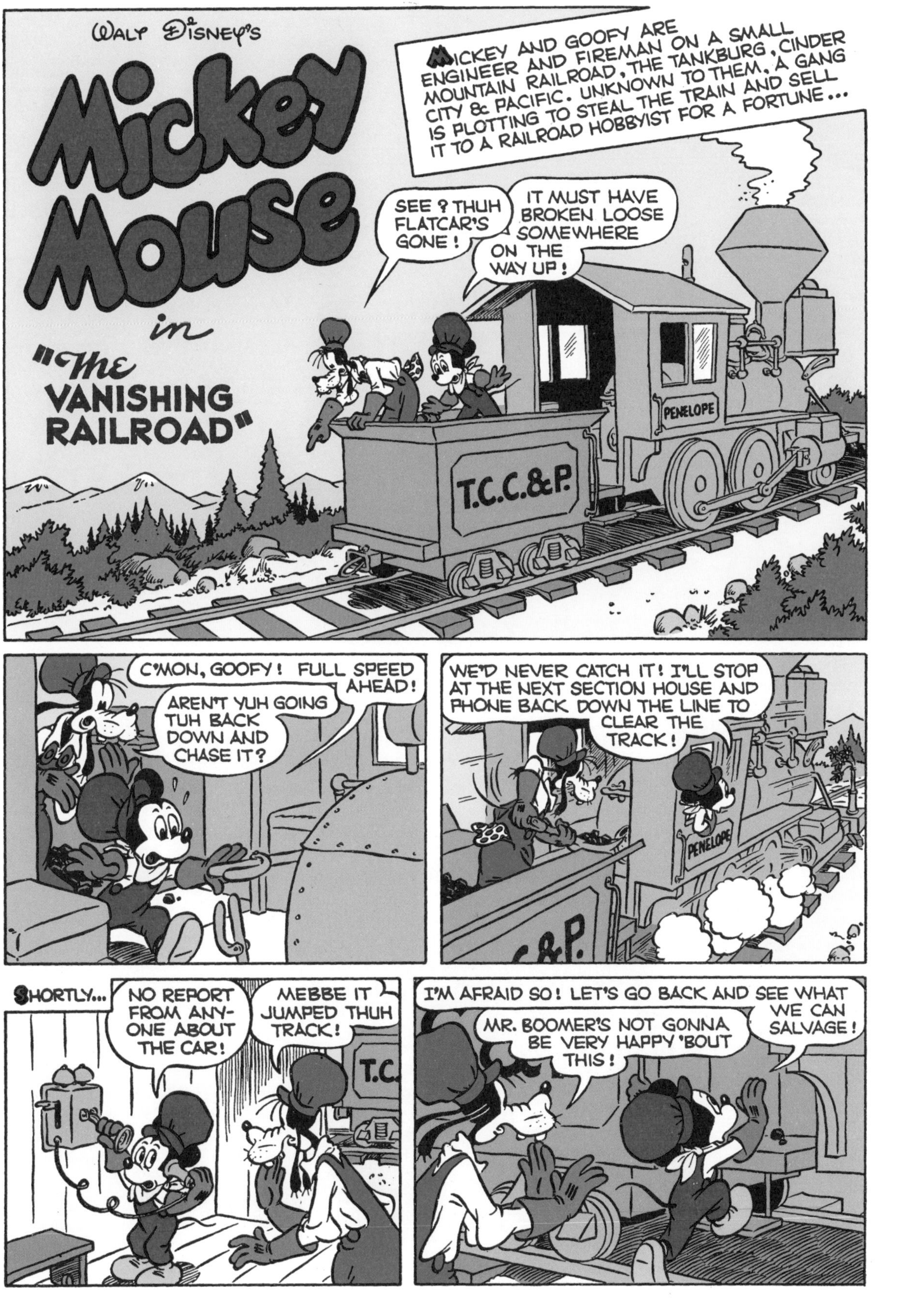

WALT DISNEY'S
Mickey Mouse
in
"The VANISHING RAILROAD"
MICKEY AND GOOFY ARE ENGINEER AND FIREMAN ON A SMALL MOUNTAIN RAILROAD, THE TANKBURG, CINDER CITY & PACIFIC. UNKNOWN TO THEM, A GANG IS PLOTTING TO STEAL THE TRAIN AND SELL IT TO A RAILROAD HOBBYIST FOR A FORTUNE...
SEE ? THUH FLATCAR'S GONE !
IT MUST HAVE BROKEN LOOSE SOMEWHERE ON THE WAY UP !
PENELOPE
T.C.C.&P.
C'MON, GOOFY ! FULL SPEED AHEAD !
AREN'T YUH GOING TUH BACK DOWN AND CHASE IT ?
WE'D NEVER CATCH IT ! I'LL STOP AT THE NEXT SECTION HOUSE AND PHONE BACK DOWN THE LINE TO CLEAR THE TRACK !
PENELOPE
C&P.
SHORTLY...
NO REPORT FROM ANY-ONE ABOUT THE CAR !
MEBBE IT JUMPED THUH TRACK !
T.C.
I'M AFRAID SO ! LET'S GO BACK AND SEE WHAT WE CAN SALVAGE !
MR. BOOMER'S NOT GONNA BE VERY HAPPY 'BOUT THIS !

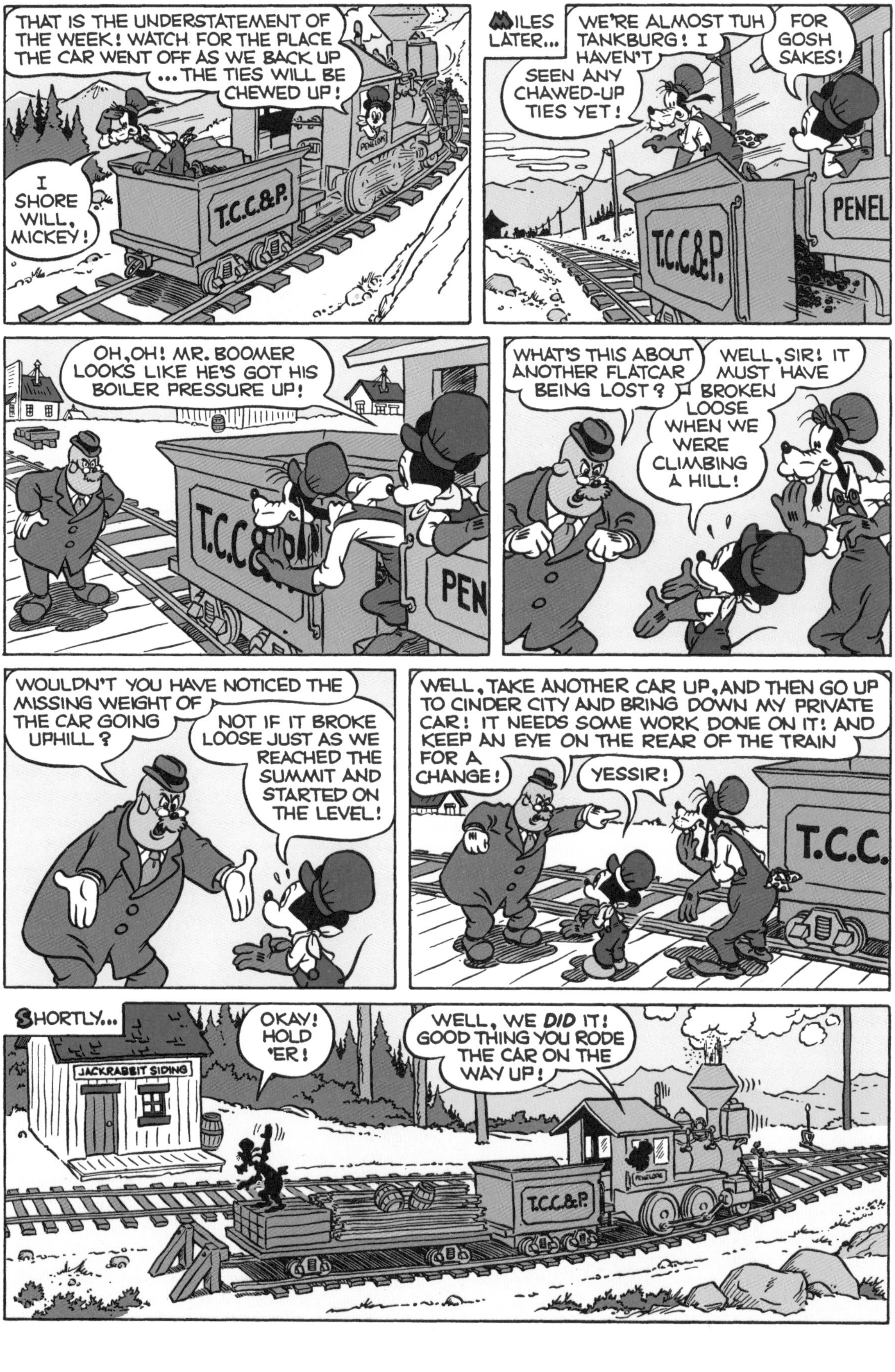
THAT IS THE UNDERSTATEMENT OF THE WEEK! WATCH FOR THE PLACE THE CAR WENT OFF AS WE BACK UP ...THE TIES WILL BE CHEWED UP!
I SHORE WILL, MICKEY!
T.C.C.&P.
MILES LATER...
WE'RE ALMOST TUH TANKBURG! I HAVEN'T SEEN ANY CHAWED-UP TIES YET!
FOR GOSH SAKES!
T.C.C.&P.
PENEL
OH, OH! MR. BOOMER LOOKS LIKE HE'S GOT HIS BOILER PRESSURE UP!
PEN
WHAT'S THIS ABOUT ANOTHER FLATCAR BEING LOST?
WELL, SIR! IT MUST HAVE BROKEN LOOSE WHEN WE WERE CLIMBING A HILL!
WOULDN'T YOU HAVE NOTICED THE MISSING WEIGHT OF THE CAR GOING UPHILL?
NOT IF IT BROKE LOOSE JUST AS WE REACHED THE SUMMIT AND STARTED ON THE LEVEL!
WELL, TAKE ANOTHER CAR UP, AND THEN GO UP TO CINDER CITY AND BRING DOWN MY PRIVATE CAR! IT NEEDS SOME WORK DONE ON IT! AND KEEP AN EYE ON THE REAR OF THE TRAIN FOR A CHANGE!
YESSIR!
T.C.C.
SHORTLY...
OKAY! HOLD 'ER!
WELL, WE DID IT! GOOD THING YOU RODE THE CAR ON THE WAY UP!
JACKRABBIT SIDING
T.C.C.&P.

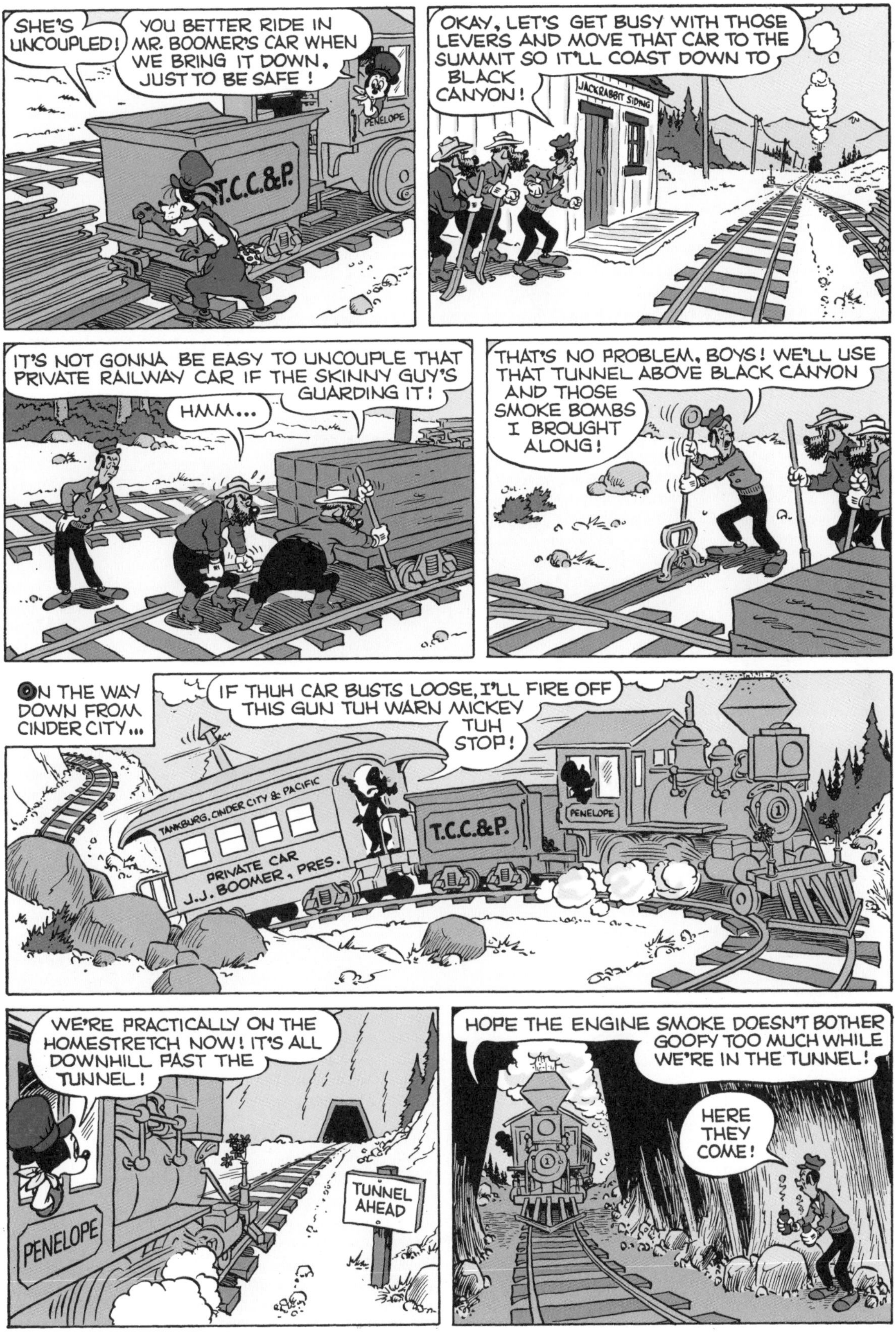
SHE'S UNCOUPLED!
YOU BETTER RIDE IN MR. BOOMER'S CAR WHEN WE BRING IT DOWN, JUST TO BE SAFE!
PENELOPE
T.C.C.&P.
OKAY, LET'S GET BUSY WITH THOSE LEVERS AND MOVE THAT CAR TO THE SUMMIT SO IT'LL COAST DOWN TO BLACK CANYON!
JACKRABBIT SIDING
IT'S NOT GONNA BE EASY TO UNCOUPLE THAT PRIVATE RAILWAY CAR IF THE SKINNY GUY'S GUARDING IT!
HMM...
THAT'S NO PROBLEM, BOYS! WE'LL USE THAT TUNNEL ABOVE BLACK CANYON AND THOSE SMOKE BOMBS I BROUGHT ALONG!
ON THE WAY DOWN FROM CINDER CITY...
IF THUH CAR BUSTS LOOSE, I'LL FIRE OFF THIS GUN TUH WARN MICKEY TUH STOP!
TANKBURG, CINDER CITY & PACIFIC
PRIVATE CAR
J.J. BOOMER, PRES.
T.C.C.&P.
PENELOPE
WE'RE PRACTICALLY ON THE HOMESTRETCH NOW! IT'S ALL DOWNHILL PAST THE TUNNEL!
TUNNEL AHEAD
PENELOPE
HOPE THE ENGINE SMOKE DOESN'T BOTHER GOOFY TOO MUCH WHILE WE'RE IN THE TUNNEL!
HERE THEY COME!

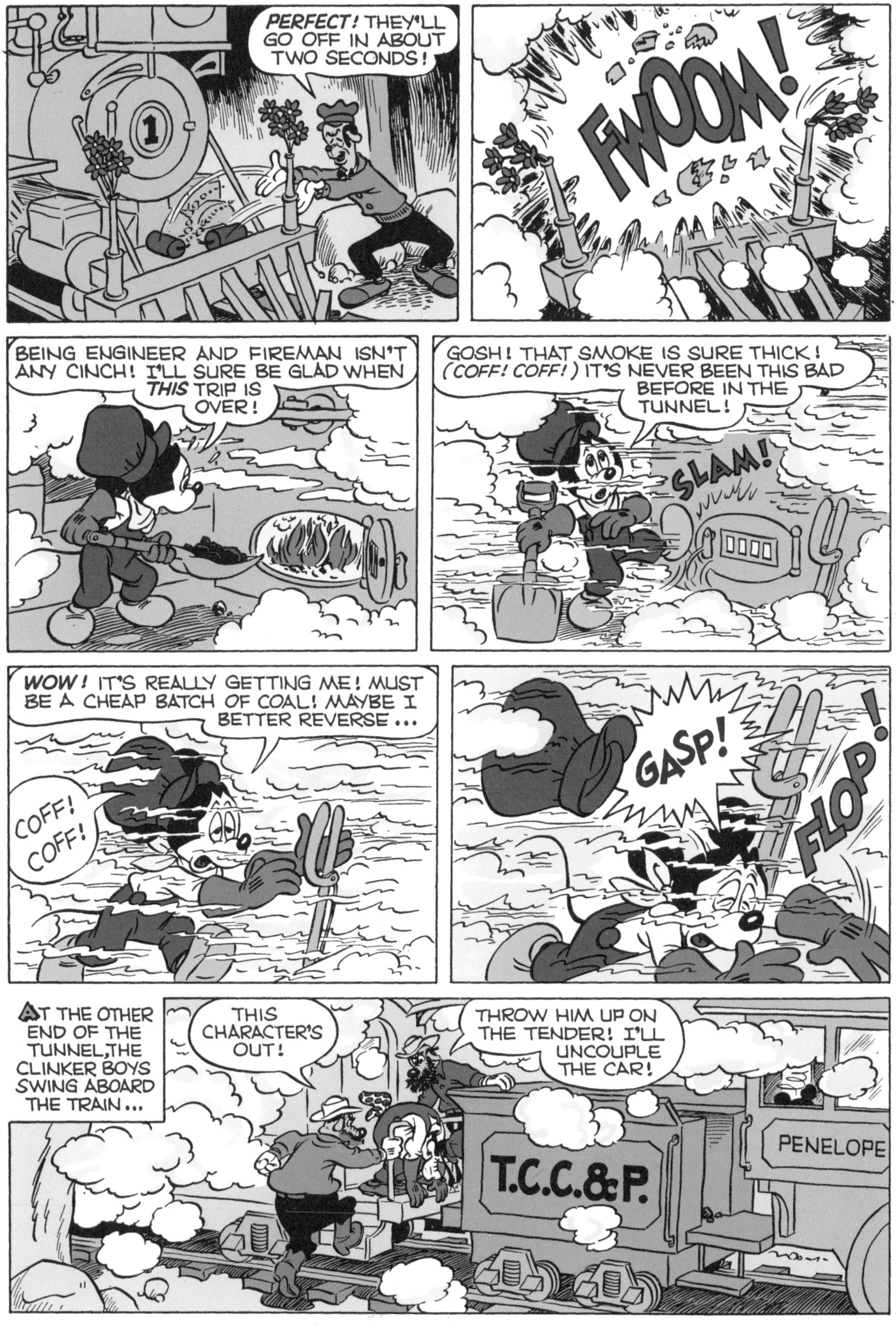
PERFECT! THEY'LL GO OFF IN ABOUT TWO SECONDS!
FWOOM!
BEING ENGINEER AND FIREMAN ISN'T ANY CINCH! I'LL SURE BE GLAD WHEN THIS TRIP IS OVER!
GOSH! THAT SMOKE IS SURE THICK! (COFF! COFF!) IT'S NEVER BEEN THIS BAD BEFORE IN THE TUNNEL!
SLAM!
WOW! IT'S REALLY GETTING ME! MUST BE A CHEAP BATCH OF COAL! MAYBE I BETTER REVERSE...
COFF! COFF!
GASP!
FLOP!
AT THE OTHER END OF THE TUNNEL, THE CLINKER BOYS SWING ABOARD THE TRAIN...
THIS CHARACTER'S OUT!
THROW HIM UP ON THE TENDER! I'LL UNCOUPLE THE CAR!
T.C.C.&P.
PENELOPE

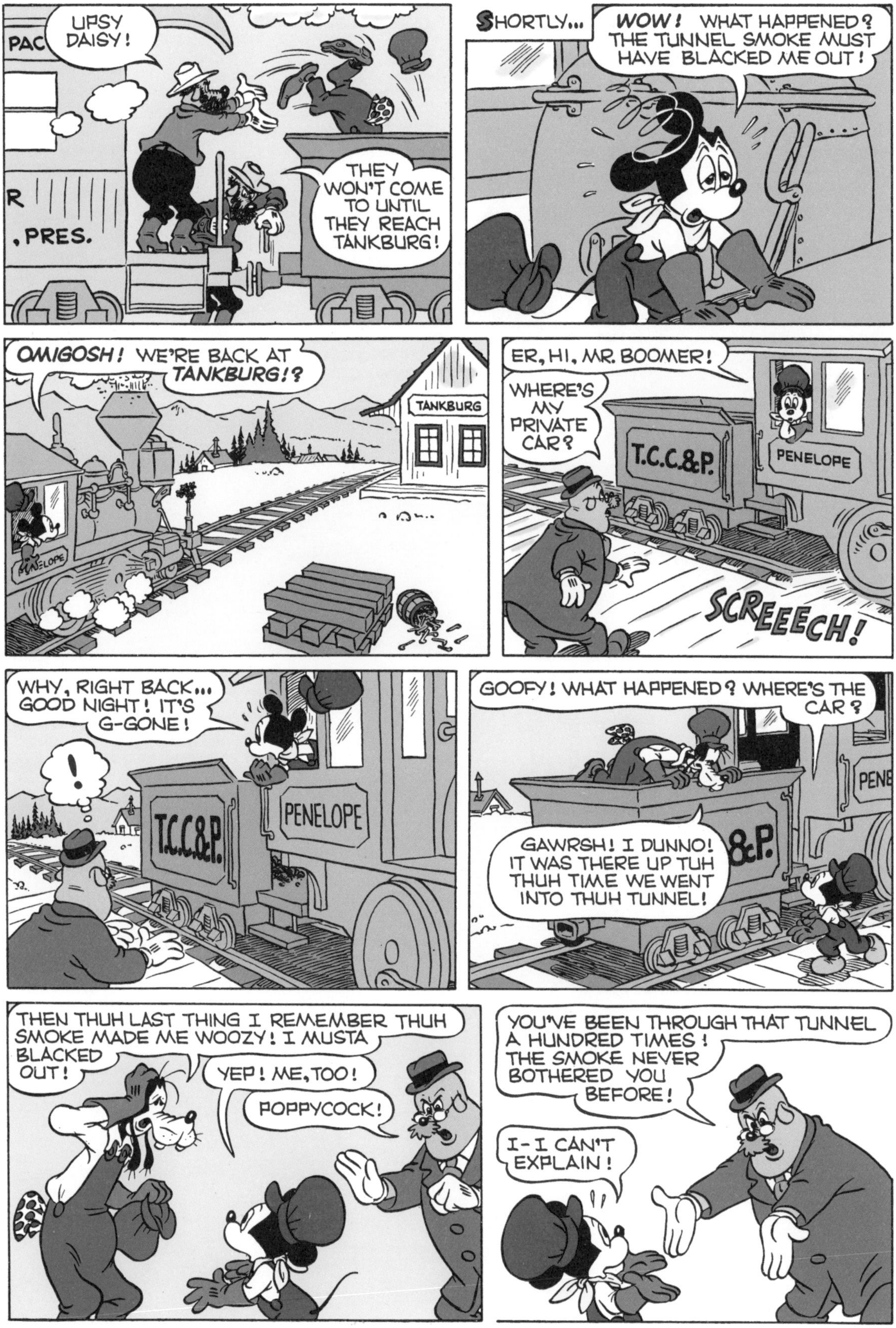
PAC
UPSY DAISY!
R
, PRES.
THEY WON'T COME TO UNTIL THEY REACH TANKBURG!
SHORTLY...
WOW! WHAT HAPPENED? THE TUNNEL SMOKE MUST HAVE BLACKED ME OUT!
OMIGOSH! WE'RE BACK AT TANKBURG!?
TANKBURG
ER, HI, MR. BOOMER!
WHERE'S MY PRIVATE CAR?
T.C.C.&P.
PENELOPE
SCREEECH!
WHY, RIGHT BACK... GOOD NIGHT! IT'S G-GONE!
!
T.C.C.&P.
PENELOPE
GOOFY! WHAT HAPPENED? WHERE'S THE CAR?
GAWRSH! I DUNNO! IT WAS THERE UP TUH THUH TIME WE WENT INTO THUH TUNNEL!
THEN THUH LAST THING I REMEMBER THUH SMOKE MADE ME WOOZY! I MUSTA BLACKED OUT!
YEP! ME, TOO!
POPPYCOCK!
YOU'VE BEEN THROUGH THAT TUNNEL A HUNDRED TIMES! THE SMOKE NEVER BOTHERED YOU BEFORE!
I- I CAN'T EXPLAIN!

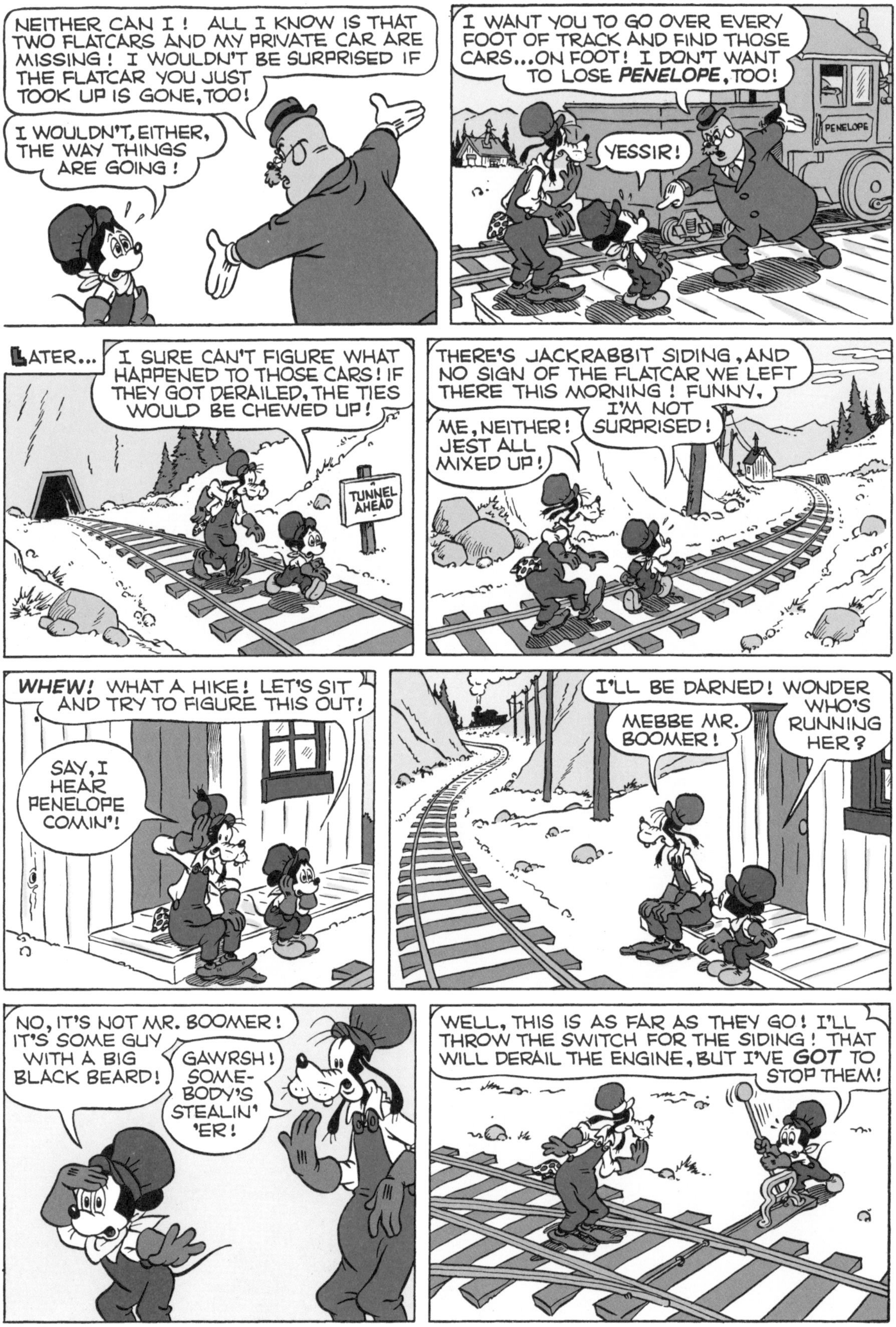
NEITHER CAN I! ALL I KNOW IS THAT TWO FLATCARS AND MY PRIVATE CAR ARE MISSING! I WOULDN'T BE SURPRISED IF THE FLATCAR YOU JUST TOOK UP IS GONE, TOO!
I WOULDN'T, EITHER, THE WAY THINGS ARE GOING!
I WANT YOU TO GO OVER EVERY FOOT OF TRACK AND FIND THOSE CARS...ON FOOT! I DON'T WANT TO LOSE *PENELOPE*, TOO!
YESSIR!
PENELOPE
LATER...
I SURE CAN'T FIGURE WHAT HAPPENED TO THOSE CARS! IF THEY GOT DERAILED, THE TIES WOULD BE CHEWED UP!
TUNNEL AHEAD
THERE'S JACKRABBIT SIDING, AND NO SIGN OF THE FLATCAR WE LEFT THERE THIS MORNING! FUNNY,
I'M NOT SURPRISED!
ME, NEITHER! JEST ALL MIXED UP!
WHEW! WHAT A HIKE! LET'S SIT AND TRY TO FIGURE THIS OUT!
SAY, I HEAR PENELOPE COMIN'!
I'LL BE DARNED! WONDER WHO'S RUNNING HER?
MEBBE MR. BOOMER!
NO, IT'S NOT MR. BOOMER! IT'S SOME GUY WITH A BIG BLACK BEARD!
GAWRSH! SOME-BODY'S STEALIN' 'ER!
WELL, THIS IS AS FAR AS THEY GO! I'LL THROW THE SWITCH FOR THE SIDING! THAT WILL DERAIL THE ENGINE, BUT I'VE *GOT* TO STOP THEM!

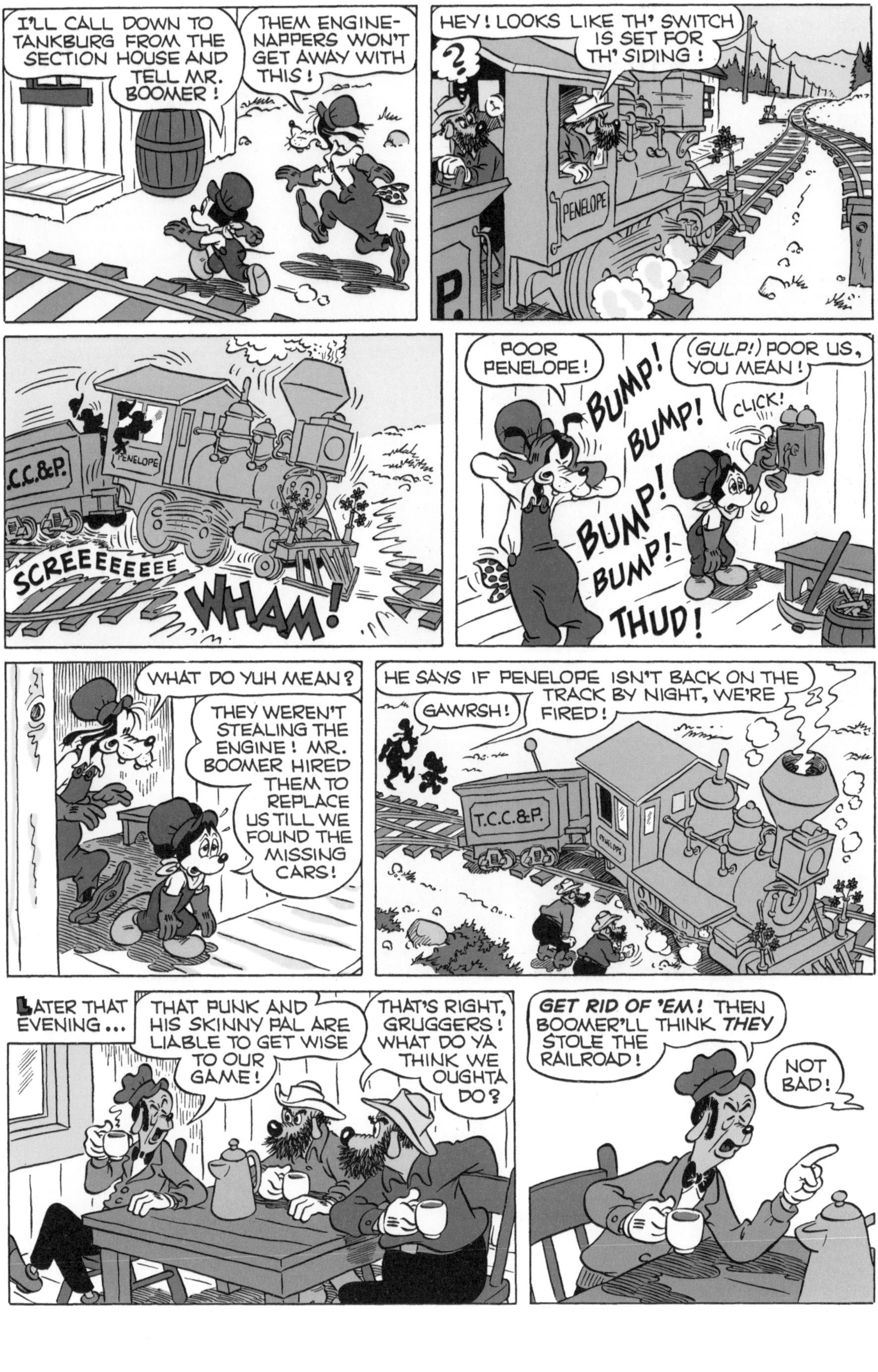
I'LL CALL DOWN TO TANKBURG FROM THE SECTION HOUSE AND TELL MR. BOOMER!
THEM ENGINE-NAPPERS WON'T GET AWAY WITH THIS!
HEY! LOOKS LIKE TH' SWITCH IS SET FOR TH' SIDING!
?
PENELOPE
P.
PENELOPE
T.C.C.&P.
SCREEEEEEEE
WHAM!
POOR PENELOPE!
(GULP!) POOR US, YOU MEAN!
BUMP!
BUMP!
CLICK!
BUMP!
BUMP!
THUD!
WHAT DO YUH MEAN?
THEY WEREN'T STEALING THE ENGINE! MR. BOOMER HIRED THEM TO REPLACE US TILL WE FOUND THE MISSING CARS!
HE SAYS IF PENELOPE ISN'T BACK ON THE TRACK BY NIGHT, WE'RE FIRED!
GAWRSH!
T.C.C.&P.
LATER THAT EVENING...
THAT PUNK AND HIS SKINNY PAL ARE LIABLE TO GET WISE TO OUR GAME!
THAT'S RIGHT, GRUGGERS! WHAT DO YA THINK WE OUGHTA DO?
GET RID OF 'EM! THEN BOOMER'LL THINK THEY STOLE THE RAILROAD!
NOT BAD!

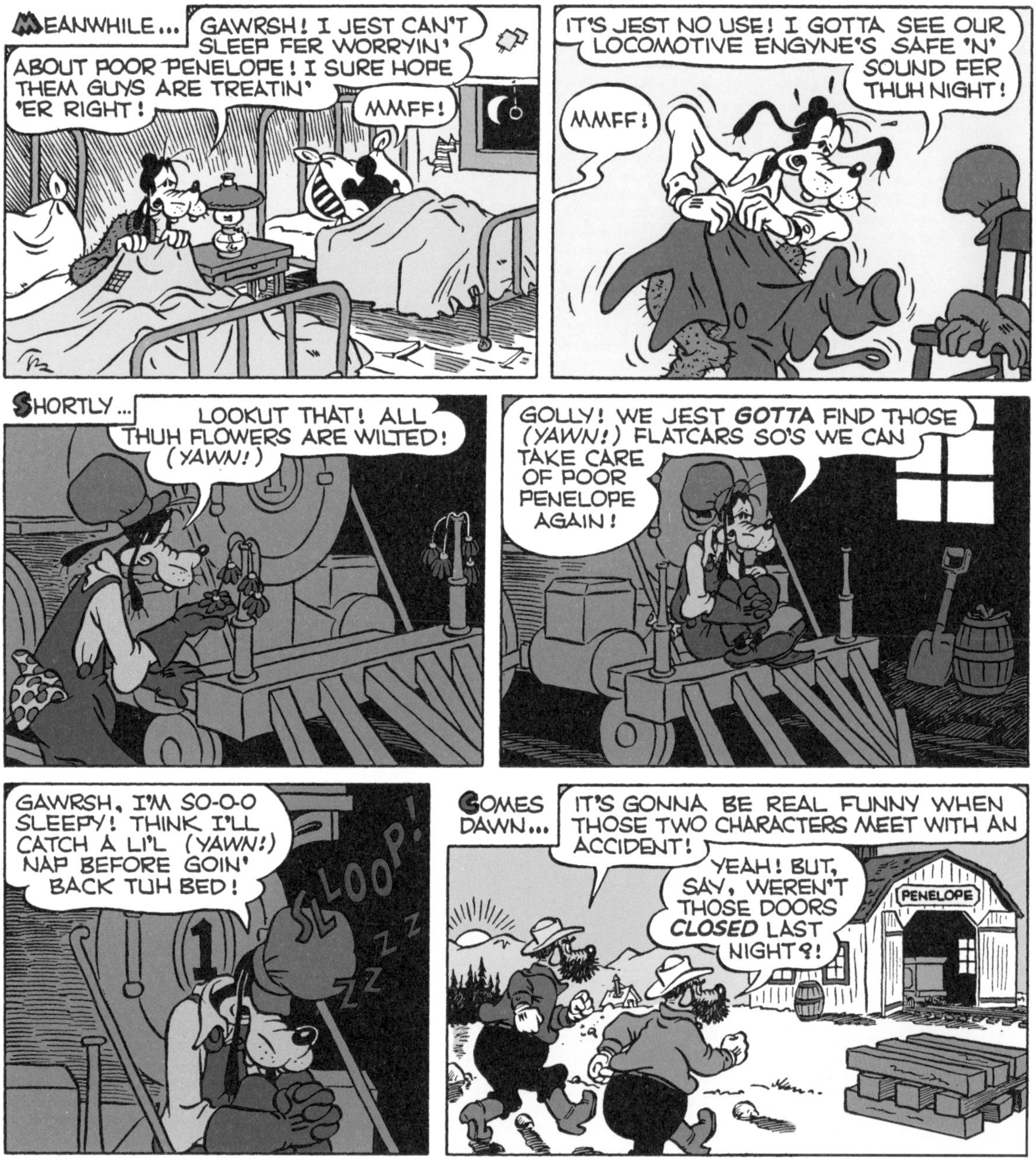
MEANWHILE...
GAWRSH! I JEST CAN'T SLEEP FER WORRYIN' ABOUT POOR PENELOPE! I SURE HOPE THEM GUYS ARE TREATIN' 'ER RIGHT!
MMFF!
IT'S JEST NO USE! I GOTTA SEE OUR LOCOMOTIVE ENGYNE'S SAFE 'N' SOUND FER THUH NIGHT!
MMFF!
SHORTLY...
LOOKUT THAT! ALL THUH FLOWERS ARE WILTED! (YAWN!)
GOLLY! WE JEST GOTTA FIND THOSE (YAWN!) FLATCARS SO'S WE CAN TAKE CARE OF POOR PENELOPE AGAIN!
GAWRSH, I'M SO-O-O SLEEPY! THINK I'LL CATCH A LI'L (YAWN!) NAP BEFORE GOIN' BACK TUH BED!
SLOOP!
Z Z Z
COMES DAWN...
IT'S GONNA BE REAL FUNNY WHEN THOSE TWO CHARACTERS MEET WITH AN ACCIDENT!
YEAH! BUT, SAY, WEREN'T THOSE DOORS CLOSED LAST NIGHT?!
PENELOPE

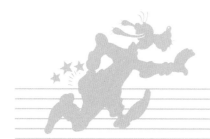

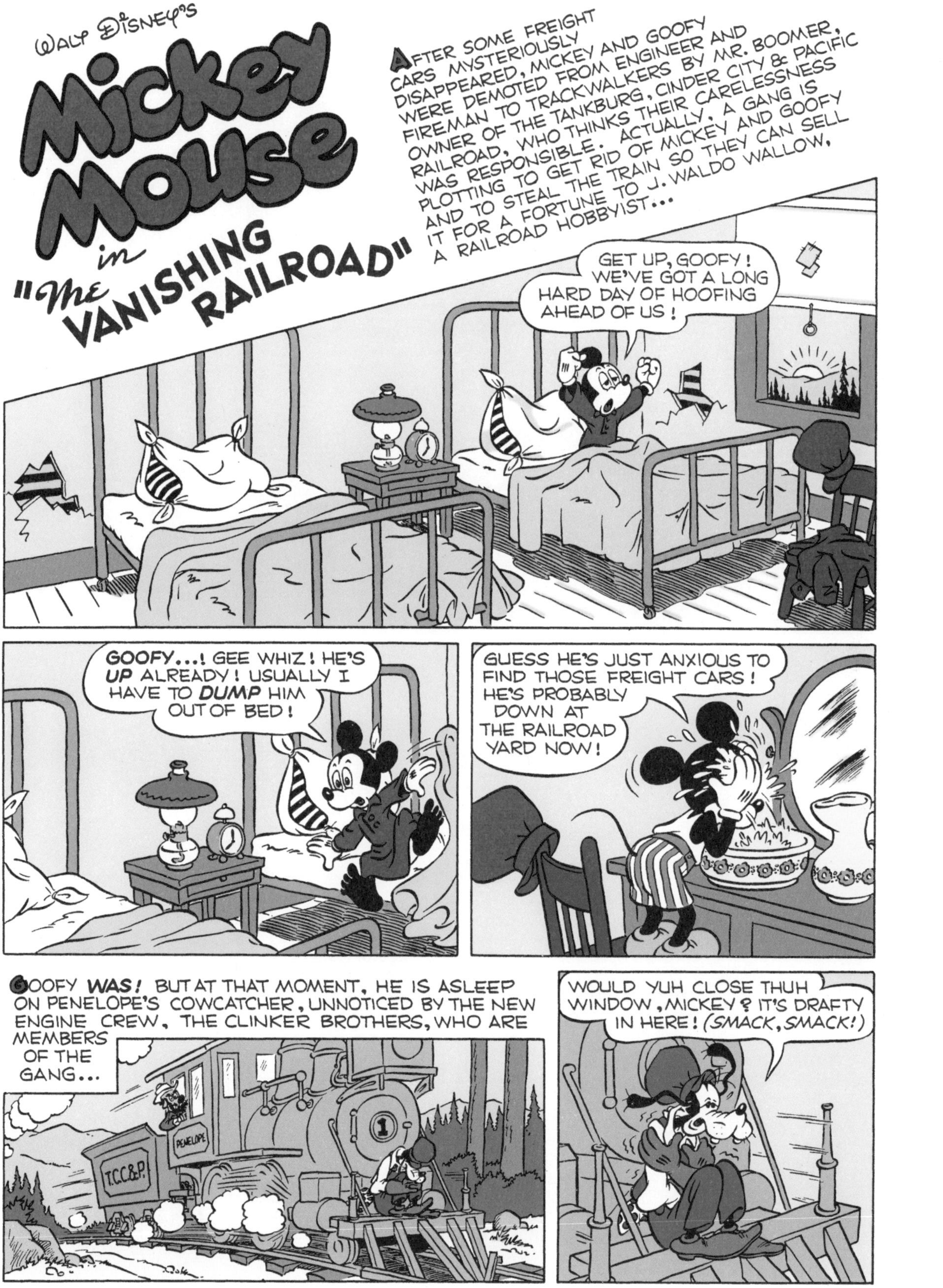
WALT DISNEY'S
Mickey Mouse
in
"The VANISHING RAILROAD"
AFTER SOME FREIGHT CARS MYSTERIOUSLY DISAPPEARED, MICKEY AND GOOFY WERE DEMOTED FROM ENGINEER AND FIREMAN TO TRACKWALKERS BY MR. BOOMER, OWNER OF THE TANKBURG, CINDER CITY & PACIFIC RAILROAD, WHO THINKS THEIR CARELESSNESS WAS RESPONSIBLE. ACTUALLY, A GANG IS PLOTTING TO GET RID OF MICKEY AND GOOFY AND TO STEAL THE TRAIN SO THEY CAN SELL IT FOR A FORTUNE TO J. WALDO WALLOW, A RAILROAD HOBBYIST...
GET UP, GOOFY! WE'VE GOT A LONG HARD DAY OF HOOFING AHEAD OF US!
GOOFY...! GEE WHIZ! HE'S UP ALREADY! USUALLY I HAVE TO DUMP HIM OUT OF BED!
GUESS HE'S JUST ANXIOUS TO FIND THOSE FREIGHT CARS! HE'S PROBABLY DOWN AT THE RAILROAD YARD NOW!
GOOFY WAS! BUT AT THAT MOMENT, HE IS ASLEEP ON PENELOPE'S COWCATCHER, UNNOTICED BY THE NEW ENGINE CREW, THE CLINKER BROTHERS, WHO ARE MEMBERS OF THE GANG...
PENELOPE
T.C.C.&P.
1
WOULD YUH CLOSE THUH WINDOW, MICKEY? IT'S DRAFTY IN HERE! (SMACK, SMACK!)

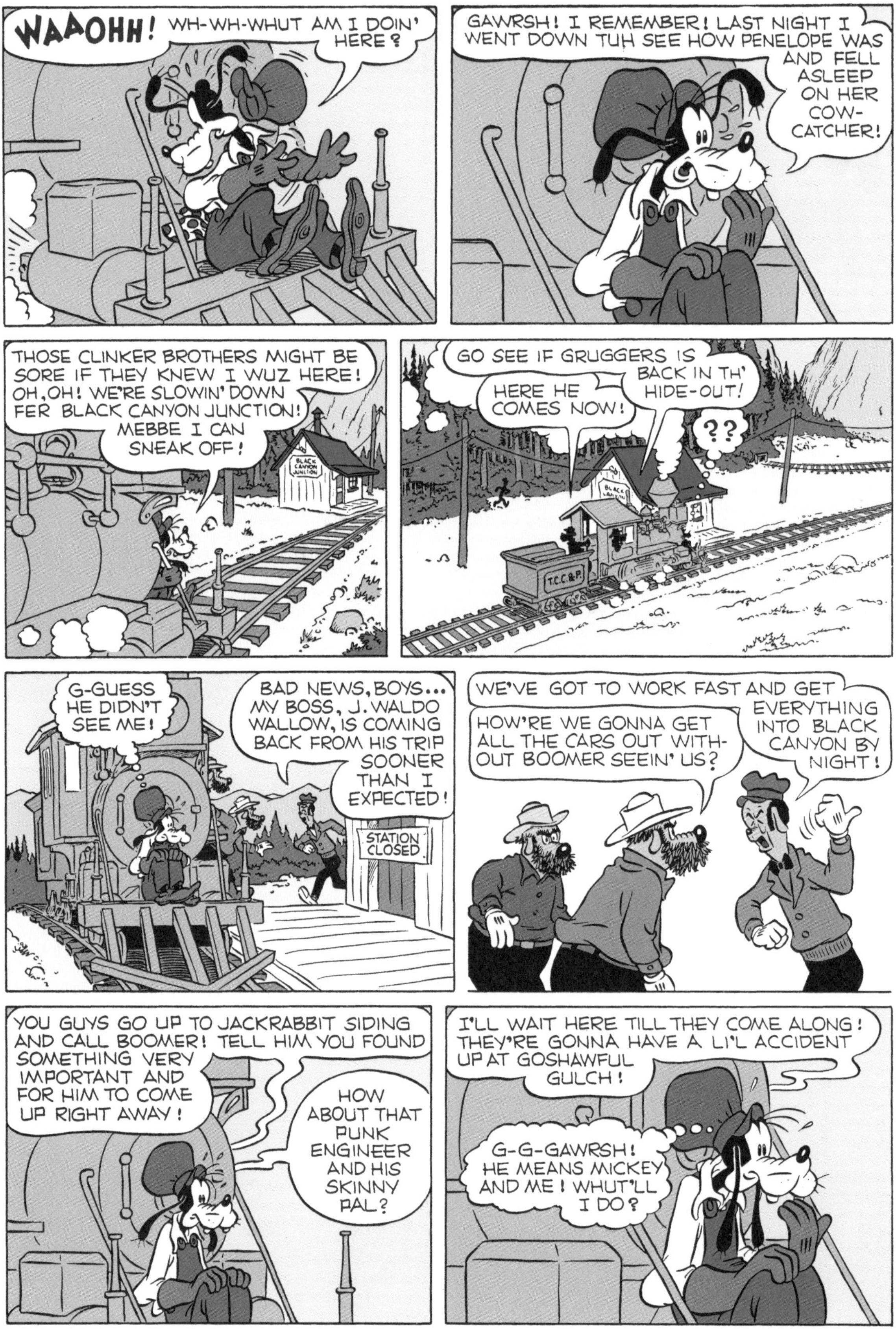
WAAOHH!
WH-WH-WHUT AM I DOIN' HERE?
GAWRSH! I REMEMBER! LAST NIGHT I WENT DOWN TUH SEE HOW PENELOPE WAS AND FELL ASLEEP ON HER COW-CATCHER!
THOSE CLINKER BROTHERS MIGHT BE SORE IF THEY KNEW I WUZ HERE! OH, OH! WE'RE SLOWIN' DOWN FER BLACK CANYON JUNCTION!
MEBBE I CAN SNEAK OFF!
BLACK CANYON JUNCTION
GO SEE IF GRUGGERS IS BACK IN TH' HIDE-OUT!
HERE HE COMES NOW!
??
T.C.C.&P.
G-GUESS HE DIDN'T SEE ME!
BAD NEWS, BOYS... MY BOSS, J. WALDO WALLOW, IS COMING BACK FROM HIS TRIP SOONER THAN I EXPECTED!
STATION CLOSED
WE'VE GOT TO WORK FAST AND GET EVERYTHING INTO BLACK CANYON BY NIGHT!
HOW'RE WE GONNA GET ALL THE CARS OUT WITH-OUT BOOMER SEEIN' US?
YOU GUYS GO UP TO JACKRABBIT SIDING AND CALL BOOMER! TELL HIM YOU FOUND SOMETHING VERY IMPORTANT AND FOR HIM TO COME UP RIGHT AWAY!
HOW ABOUT THAT PUNK ENGINEER AND HIS SKINNY PAL?
I'LL WAIT HERE TILL THEY COME ALONG! THEY'RE GONNA HAVE A LI'L ACCIDENT UP AT GOSHAWFUL GULCH!
G-G-GAWRSH! HE MEANS MICKEY AND ME! WHUT'LL I DO?

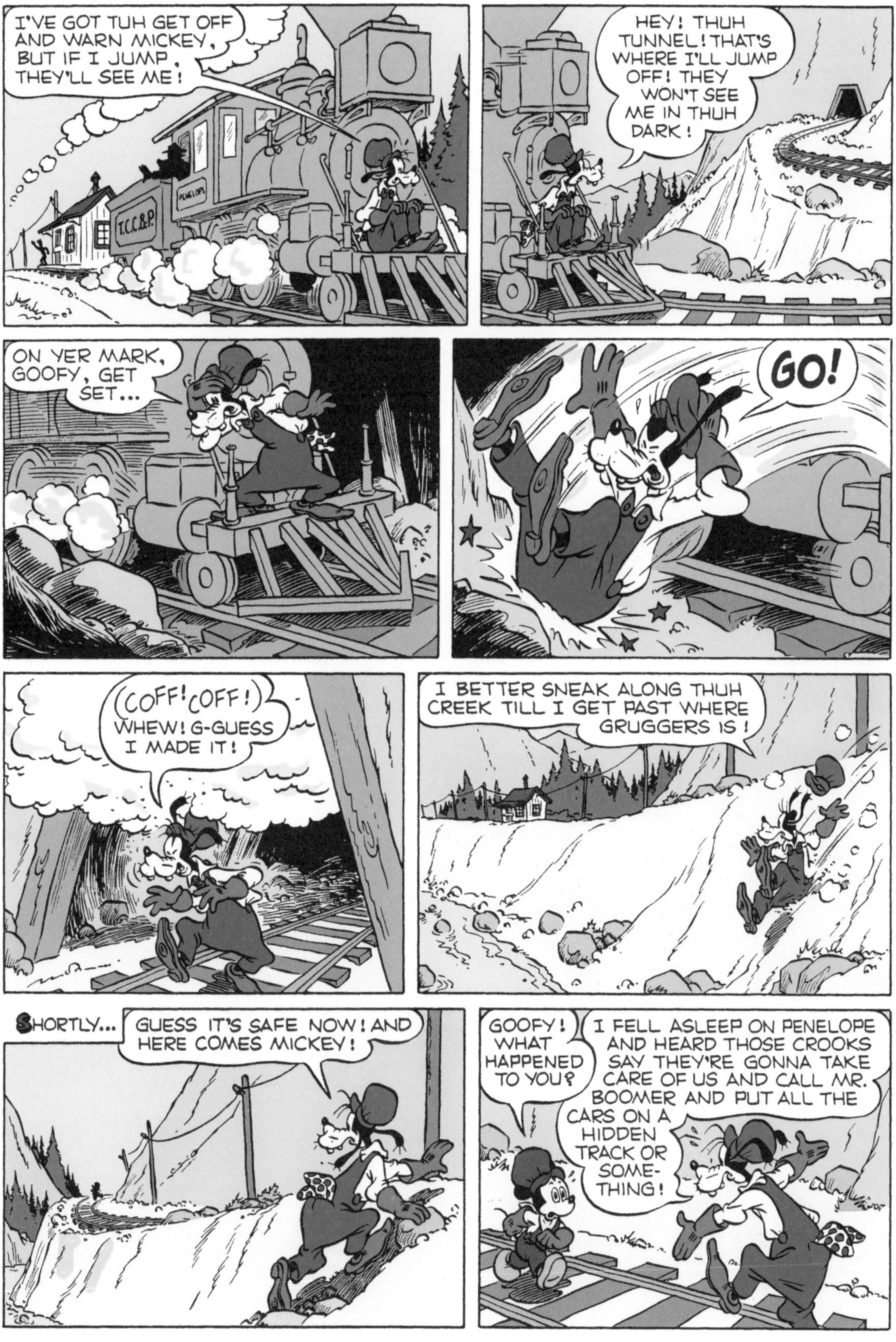
I'VE GOT TUH GET OFF AND WARN MICKEY, BUT IF I JUMP, THEY'LL SEE ME!
T.C.C.&P.
PENELOPE
HEY! THUH TUNNEL! THAT'S WHERE I'LL JUMP OFF! THEY WON'T SEE ME IN THUH DARK!
ON YER MARK, GOOFY, GET SET...
GO!
(COFF! COFF!) WHEW! G-GUESS I MADE IT!
I BETTER SNEAK ALONG THUH CREEK TILL I GET PAST WHERE GRUGGERS IS!
SHORTLY...
GUESS IT'S SAFE NOW! AND HERE COMES MICKEY!
GOOFY! WHAT HAPPENED TO YOU?
I FELL ASLEEP ON PENELOPE AND HEARD THOSE CROOKS SAY THEY'RE GONNA TAKE CARE OF US AND CALL MR. BOOMER AND PUT ALL THE CARS ON A HIDDEN TRACK OR SOME-THING!

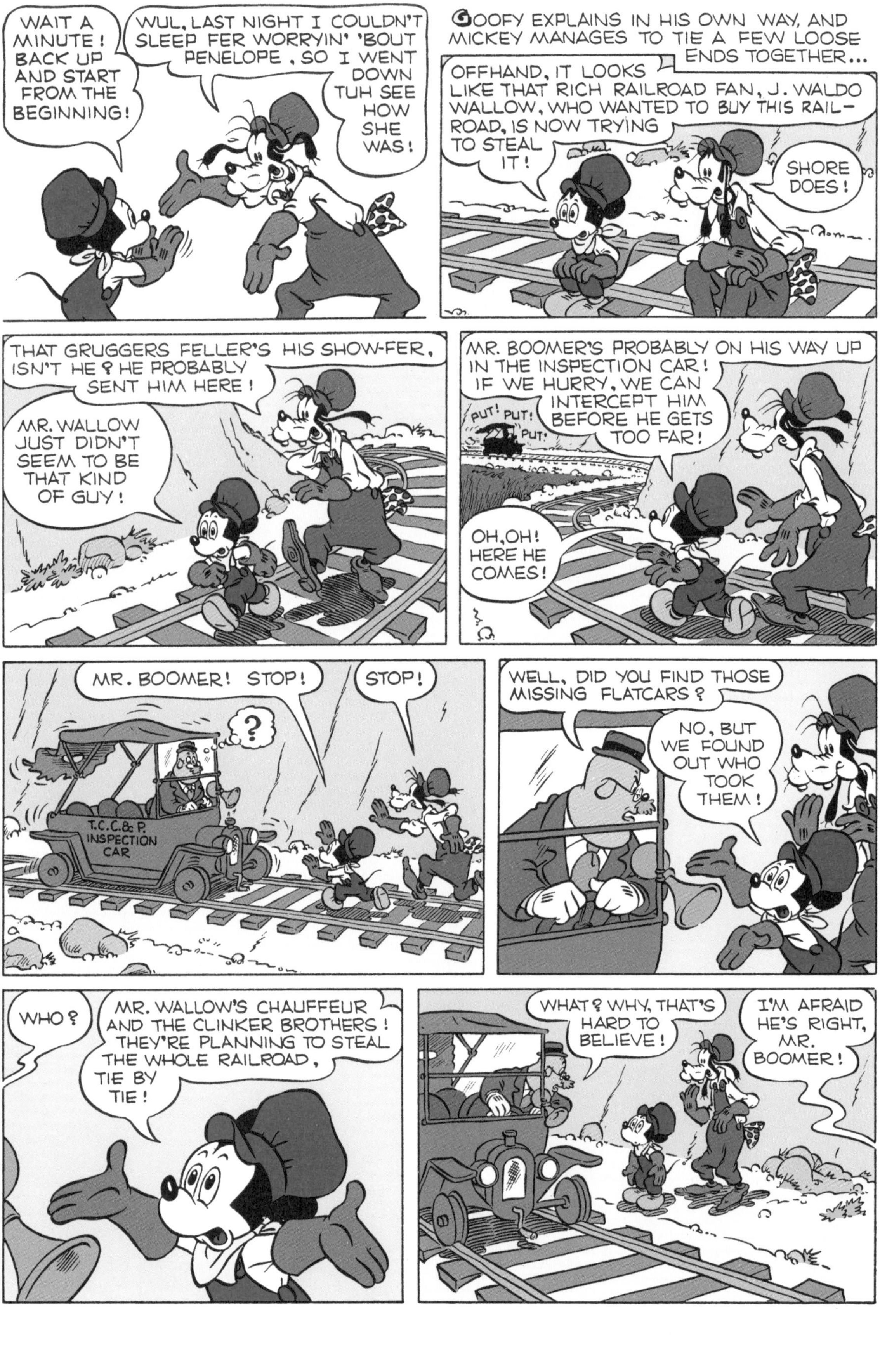
WAIT A MINUTE! BACK UP AND START FROM THE BEGINNING!
WUL, LAST NIGHT I COULDN'T SLEEP FER WORRYIN' 'BOUT PENELOPE, SO I WENT DOWN TUH SEE HOW SHE WAS!
GOOFY EXPLAINS IN HIS OWN WAY, AND MICKEY MANAGES TO TIE A FEW LOOSE ENDS TOGETHER...
OFFHAND, IT LOOKS LIKE THAT RICH RAILROAD FAN, J. WALDO WALLOW, WHO WANTED TO BUY THIS RAILROAD, IS NOW TRYING TO STEAL IT!
SHORE DOES!
THAT GRUGGERS FELLER'S HIS SHOW-FER, ISN'T HE? HE PROBABLY SENT HIM HERE!
MR. WALLOW JUST DIDN'T SEEM TO BE THAT KIND OF GUY!
MR. BOOMER'S PROBABLY ON HIS WAY UP IN THE INSPECTION CAR! IF WE HURRY, WE CAN INTERCEPT HIM BEFORE HE GETS TOO FAR!
PUT! PUT! PUT!
OH, OH! HERE HE COMES!
MR. BOOMER! STOP!
STOP!
?
T.C.C.& P. INSPECTION CAR
WELL, DID YOU FIND THOSE MISSING FLATCARS?
NO, BUT WE FOUND OUT WHO TOOK THEM!
WHO?
MR. WALLOW'S CHAUFFEUR AND THE CLINKER BROTHERS! THEY'RE PLANNING TO STEAL THE WHOLE RAILROAD, TIE BY TIE!
WHAT? WHY, THAT'S HARD TO BELIEVE!
I'M AFRAID HE'S RIGHT, MR. BOOMER!

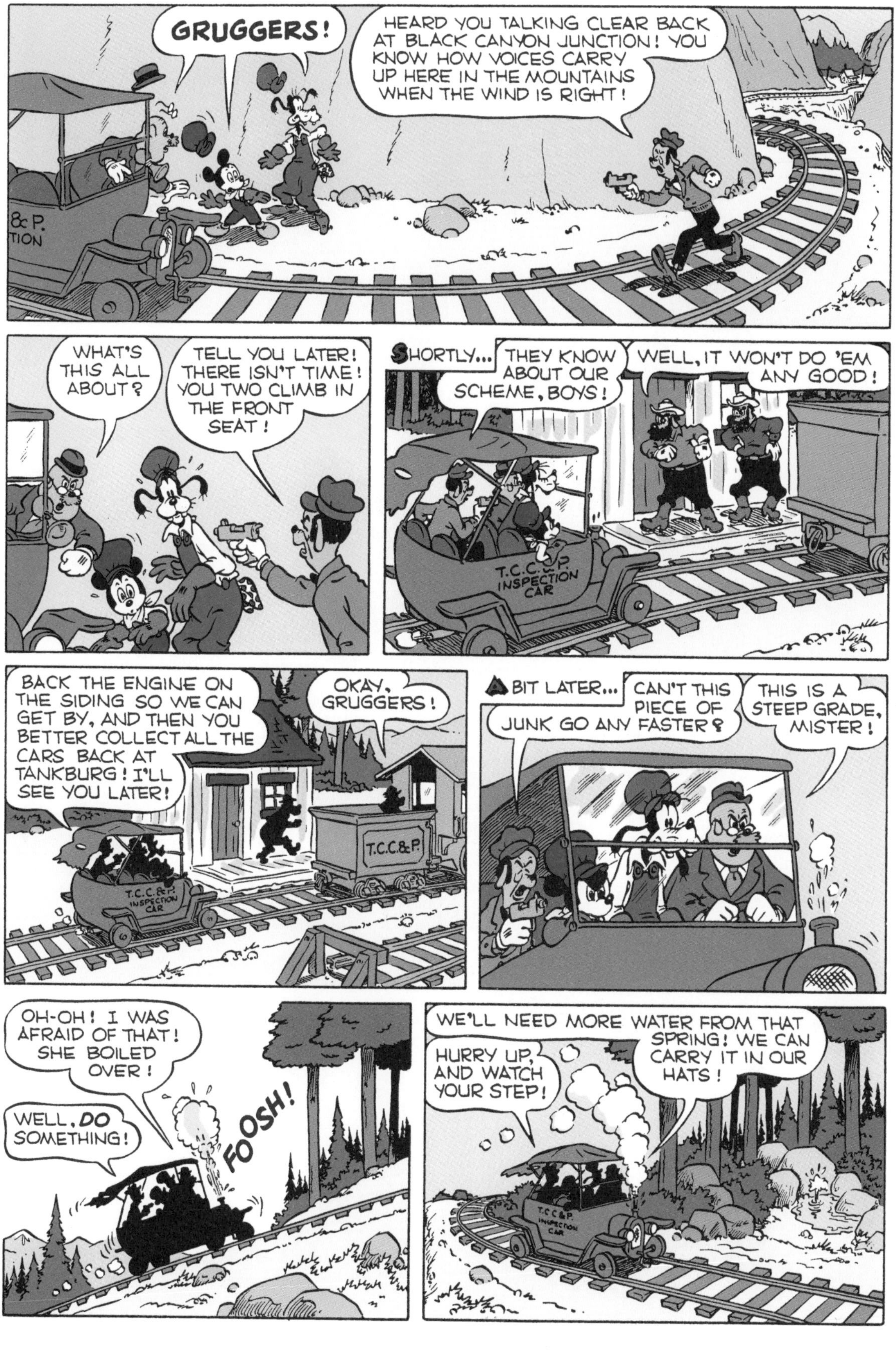
GRUGGERS!
HEARD YOU TALKING CLEAR BACK AT BLACK CANYON JUNCTION! YOU KNOW HOW VOICES CARRY UP HERE IN THE MOUNTAINS WHEN THE WIND IS RIGHT!
WHAT'S THIS ALL ABOUT?
TELL YOU LATER! THERE ISN'T TIME! YOU TWO CLIMB IN THE FRONT SEAT!
SHORTLY...
THEY KNOW ABOUT OUR SCHEME, BOYS!
WELL, IT WON'T DO 'EM ANY GOOD!
T.C.C.&P. INSPECTION CAR
BACK THE ENGINE ON THE SIDING SO WE CAN GET BY, AND THEN YOU BETTER COLLECT ALL THE CARS BACK AT TANKBURG! I'LL SEE YOU LATER!
OKAY, GRUGGERS!
T.C.C.&P.
A BIT LATER...
CAN'T THIS PIECE OF JUNK GO ANY FASTER?
THIS IS A STEEP GRADE, MISTER!
OH-OH! I WAS AFRAID OF THAT! SHE BOILED OVER!
WELL, DO SOMETHING!
FOOSH!
WE'LL NEED MORE WATER FROM THAT SPRING! WE CAN CARRY IT IN OUR HATS!
HURRY UP, AND WATCH YOUR STEP!
T.C.C.&P. INSPECTION CAR

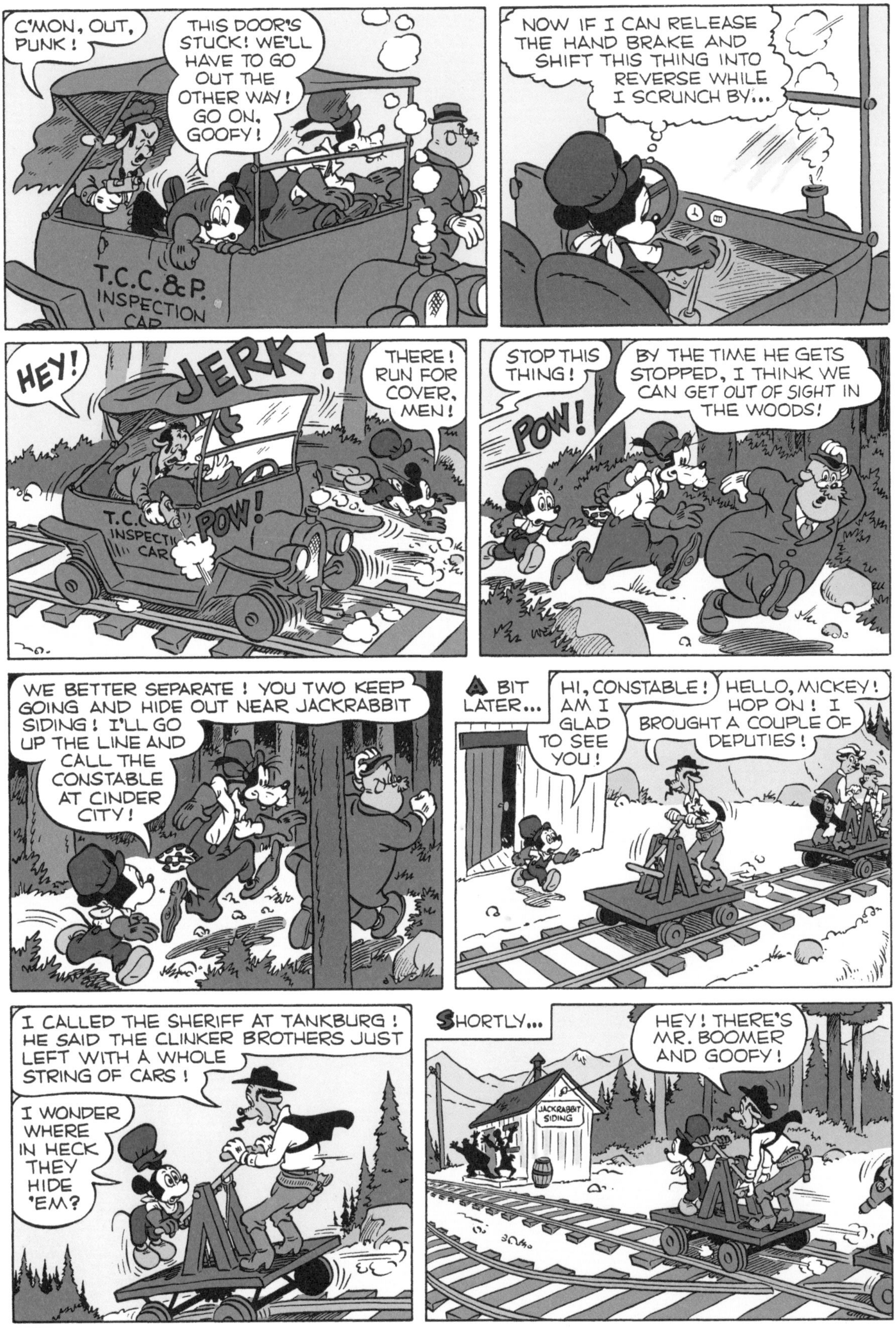
C'MON, OUT, PUNK!
THIS DOOR'S STUCK! WE'LL HAVE TO GO OUT THE OTHER WAY! GO ON, GOOFY!
T.C.C.&P. INSPECTION CAR
NOW IF I CAN RELEASE THE HAND BRAKE AND SHIFT THIS THING INTO REVERSE WHILE I SCRUNCH BY...
HEY!
JERK!
THERE! RUN FOR COVER, MEN!
POW!
STOP THIS THING!
BY THE TIME HE GETS STOPPED, I THINK WE CAN GET OUT OF SIGHT IN THE WOODS!
POW!
WE BETTER SEPARATE! YOU TWO KEEP GOING AND HIDE OUT NEAR JACKRABBIT SIDING! I'LL GO UP THE LINE AND CALL THE CONSTABLE AT CINDER CITY!
A BIT LATER...
HI, CONSTABLE! AM I GLAD TO SEE YOU!
HELLO, MICKEY! HOP ON! I BROUGHT A COUPLE OF DEPUTIES!
I CALLED THE SHERIFF AT TANKBURG! HE SAID THE CLINKER BROTHERS JUST LEFT WITH A WHOLE STRING OF CARS!
I WONDER WHERE IN HECK THEY HIDE 'EM?
SHORTLY...
HEY! THERE'S MR. BOOMER AND GOOFY!
JACKRABBIT SIDING

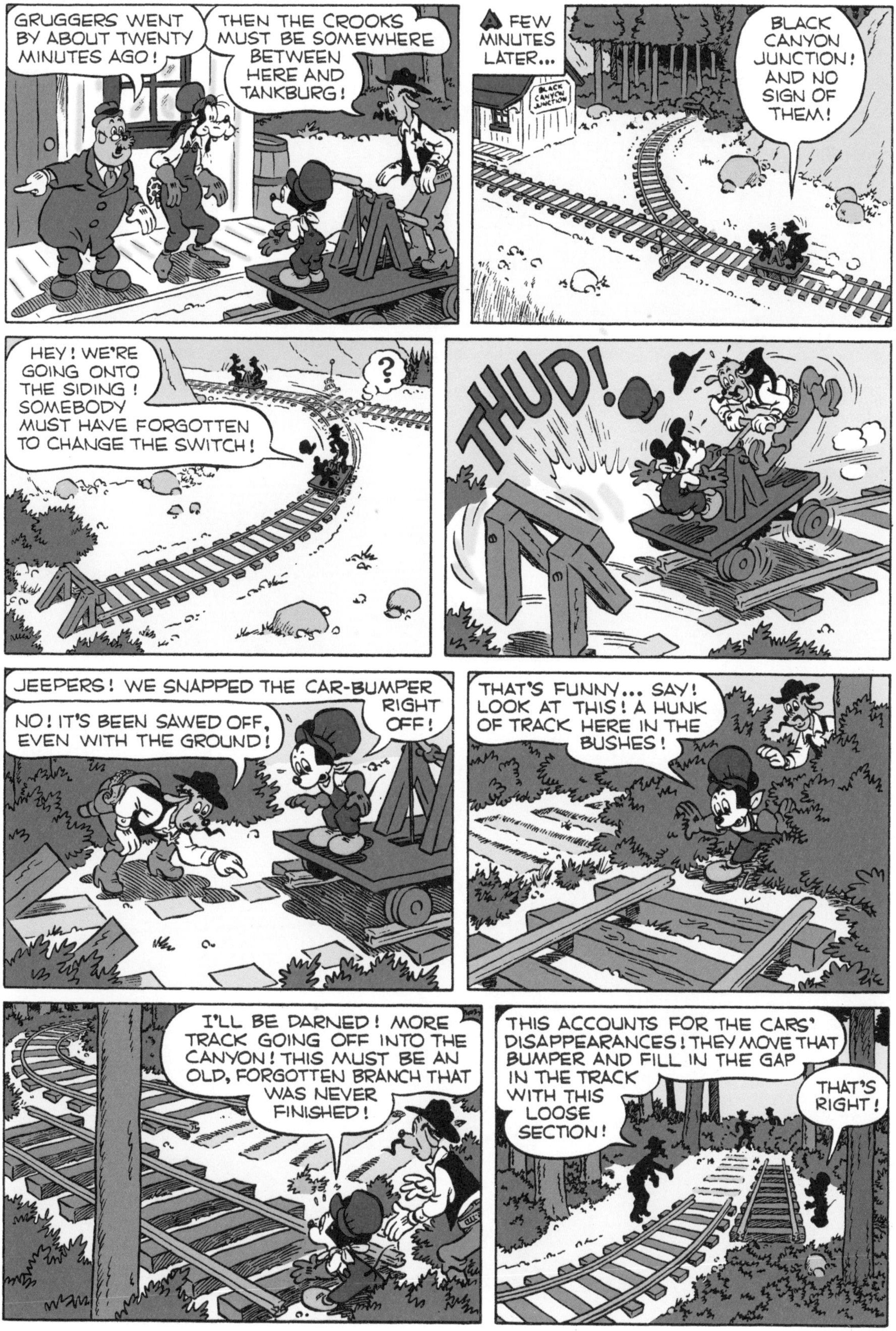
GRUGGERS WENT BY ABOUT TWENTY MINUTES AGO!
THEN THE CROOKS MUST BE SOMEWHERE BETWEEN HERE AND TANKBURG!
A FEW MINUTES LATER...
BLACK CANYON JUNCTION
BLACK CANYON JUNCTION! AND NO SIGN OF THEM!
HEY! WE'RE GOING ONTO THE SIDING! SOMEBODY MUST HAVE FORGOTTEN TO CHANGE THE SWITCH!
?
THUD!
JEEPERS! WE SNAPPED THE CAR-BUMPER RIGHT OFF!
NO! IT'S BEEN SAWED OFF, EVEN WITH THE GROUND!
THAT'S FUNNY... SAY! LOOK AT THIS! A HUNK OF TRACK HERE IN THE BUSHES!
I'LL BE DARNED! MORE TRACK GOING OFF INTO THE CANYON! THIS MUST BE AN OLD, FORGOTTEN BRANCH THAT WAS NEVER FINISHED!
THIS ACCOUNTS FOR THE CARS' DISAPPEARANCES! THEY MOVE THAT BUMPER AND FILL IN THE GAP IN THE TRACK WITH THIS LOOSE SECTION!
THAT'S RIGHT!

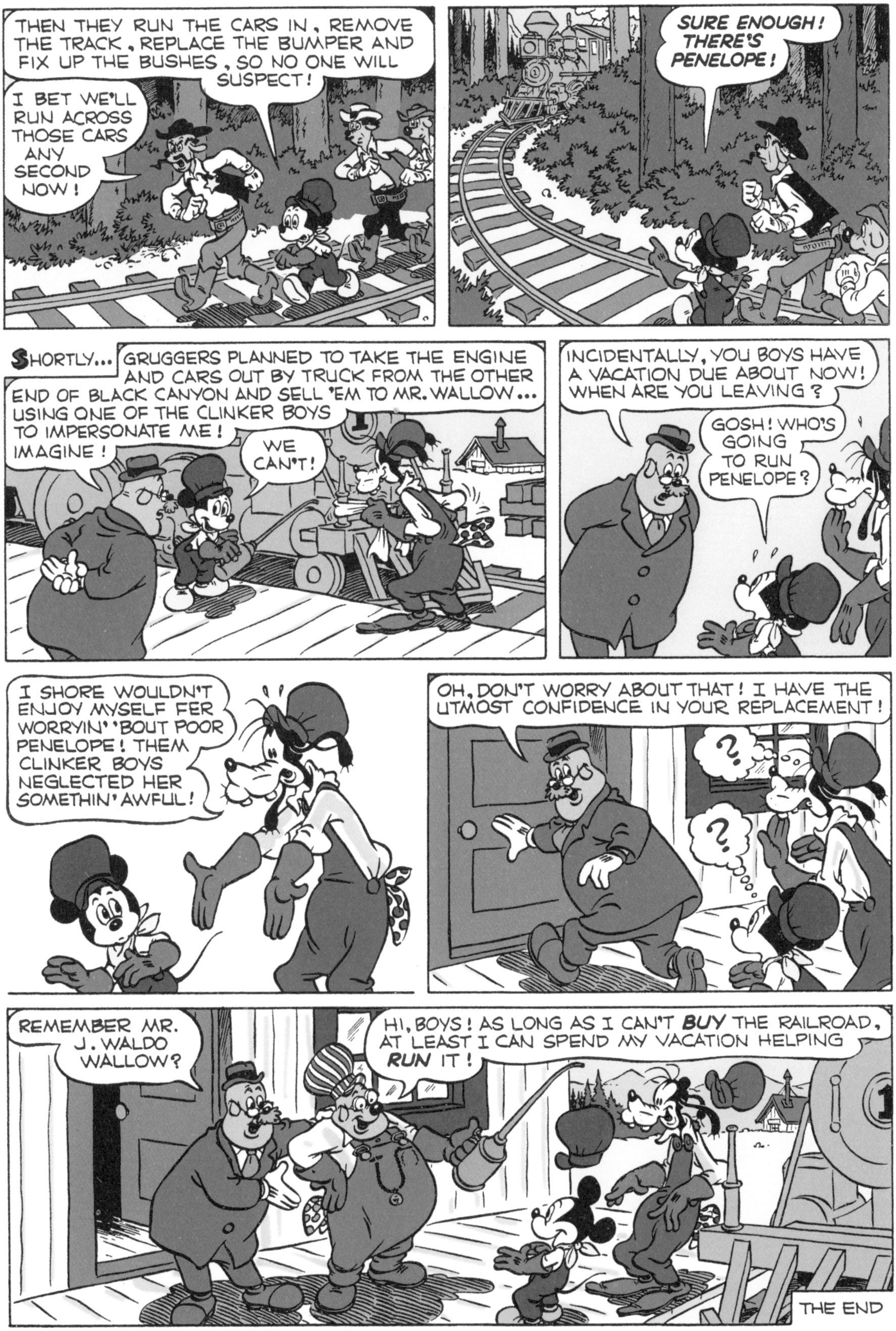
THEN THEY RUN THE CARS IN, REMOVE THE TRACK, REPLACE THE BUMPER AND FIX UP THE BUSHES, SO NO ONE WILL SUSPECT!
I BET WE'LL RUN ACROSS THOSE CARS ANY SECOND NOW!
SURE ENOUGH! THERE'S PENELOPE!
SHORTLY...
GRUGGERS PLANNED TO TAKE THE ENGINE AND CARS OUT BY TRUCK FROM THE OTHER END OF BLACK CANYON AND SELL 'EM TO MR. WALLOW... USING ONE OF THE CLINKER BOYS TO IMPERSONATE ME! IMAGINE!
WE CAN'T!
INCIDENTALLY, YOU BOYS HAVE A VACATION DUE ABOUT NOW! WHEN ARE YOU LEAVING?
GOSH! WHO'S GOING TO RUN PENELOPE?
I SHORE WOULDN'T ENJOY MYSELF FER WORRYIN' 'BOUT POOR PENELOPE! THEM CLINKER BOYS NEGLECTED HER SOMETHIN' AWFUL!
OH, DON'T WORRY ABOUT THAT! I HAVE THE UTMOST CONFIDENCE IN YOUR REPLACEMENT!
?
?
REMEMBER MR. J. WALDO WALLOW?
HI, BOYS! AS LONG AS I CAN'T BUY THE RAILROAD, AT LEAST I CAN SPEND MY VACATION HELPING RUN IT!
THE END

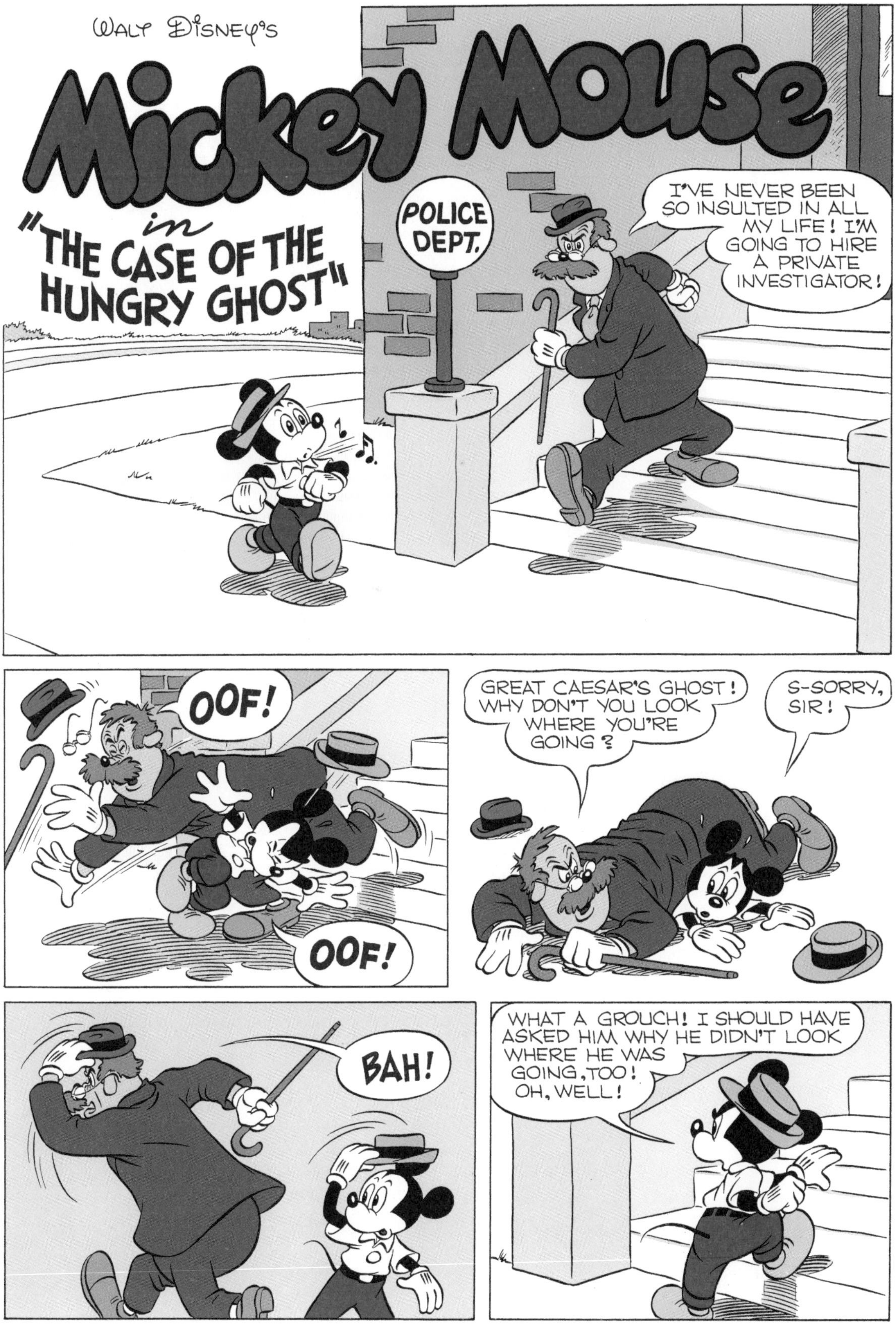
WALT DISNEY'S
Mickey Mouse
in
"THE CASE OF THE HUNGRY GHOST"
POLICE DEPT.
I'VE NEVER BEEN SO INSULTED IN ALL MY LIFE! I'M GOING TO HIRE A PRIVATE INVESTIGATOR!
OOF!
OOF!
GREAT CAESAR'S GHOST! WHY DON'T YOU LOOK WHERE YOU'RE GOING?
S-SORRY, SIR!
BAH!
WHAT A GROUCH! I SHOULD HAVE ASKED HIM WHY HE DIDN'T LOOK WHERE HE WAS GOING, TOO! OH, WELL!

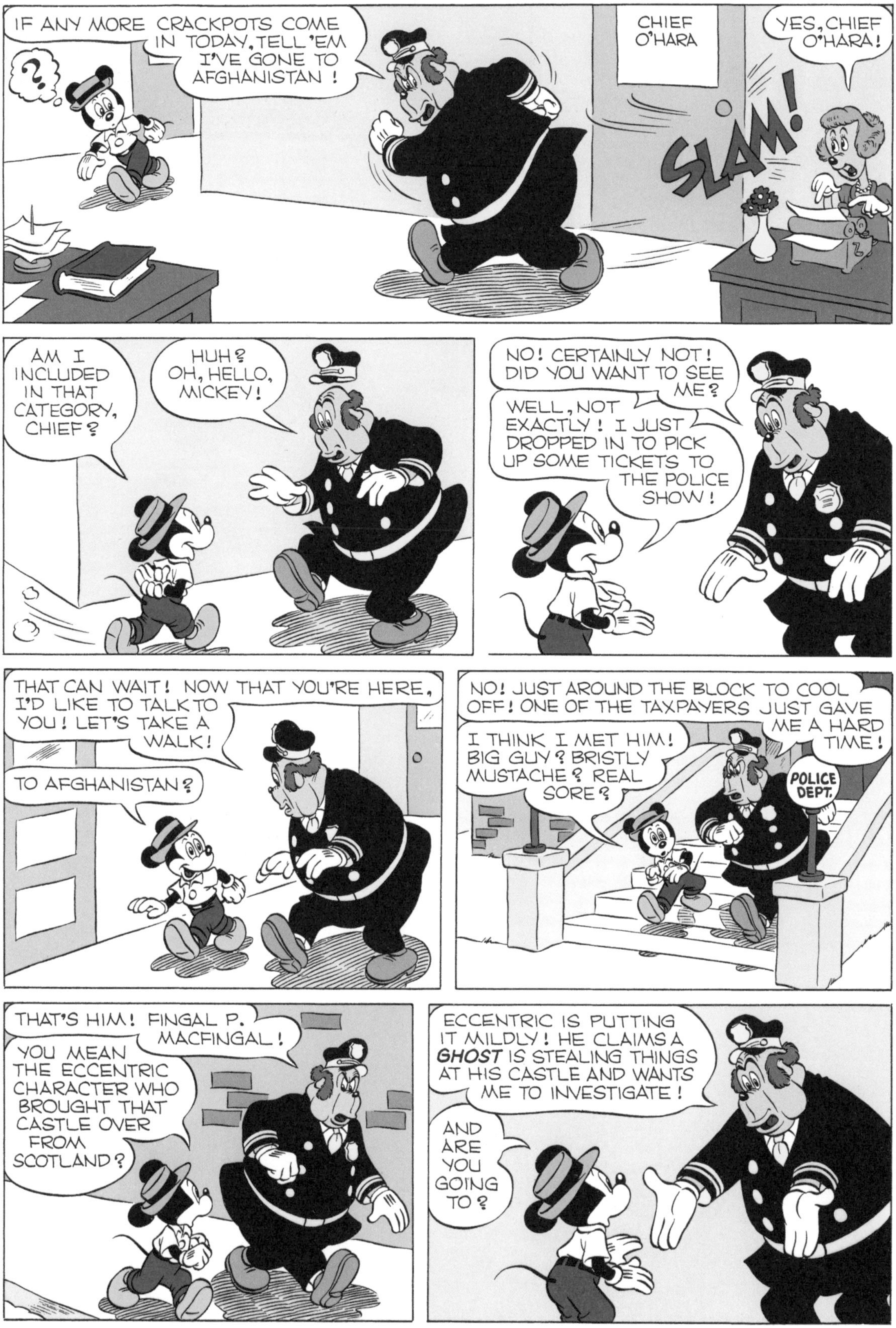
IF ANY MORE CRACKPOTS COME IN TODAY, TELL 'EM I'VE GONE TO AFGHANISTAN !
?
CHIEF O'HARA
YES, CHIEF O'HARA!
SLAM!
AM I INCLUDED IN THAT CATEGORY, CHIEF?
HUH? OH, HELLO, MICKEY!
NO! CERTAINLY NOT! DID YOU WANT TO SEE ME?
WELL, NOT EXACTLY! I JUST DROPPED IN TO PICK UP SOME TICKETS TO THE POLICE SHOW!
THAT CAN WAIT! NOW THAT YOU'RE HERE, I'D LIKE TO TALK TO YOU! LET'S TAKE A WALK!
TO AFGHANISTAN?
NO! JUST AROUND THE BLOCK TO COOL OFF! ONE OF THE TAXPAYERS JUST GAVE ME A HARD TIME!
I THINK I MET HIM! BIG GUY? BRISTLY MUSTACHE? REAL SORE?
POLICE DEPT.
THAT'S HIM! FINGAL P. MACFINGAL!
YOU MEAN THE ECCENTRIC CHARACTER WHO BROUGHT THAT CASTLE OVER FROM SCOTLAND?
ECCENTRIC IS PUTTING IT MILDLY! HE CLAIMS A **GHOST** IS STEALING THINGS AT HIS CASTLE AND WANTS ME TO INVESTIGATE!
AND ARE YOU GOING TO?

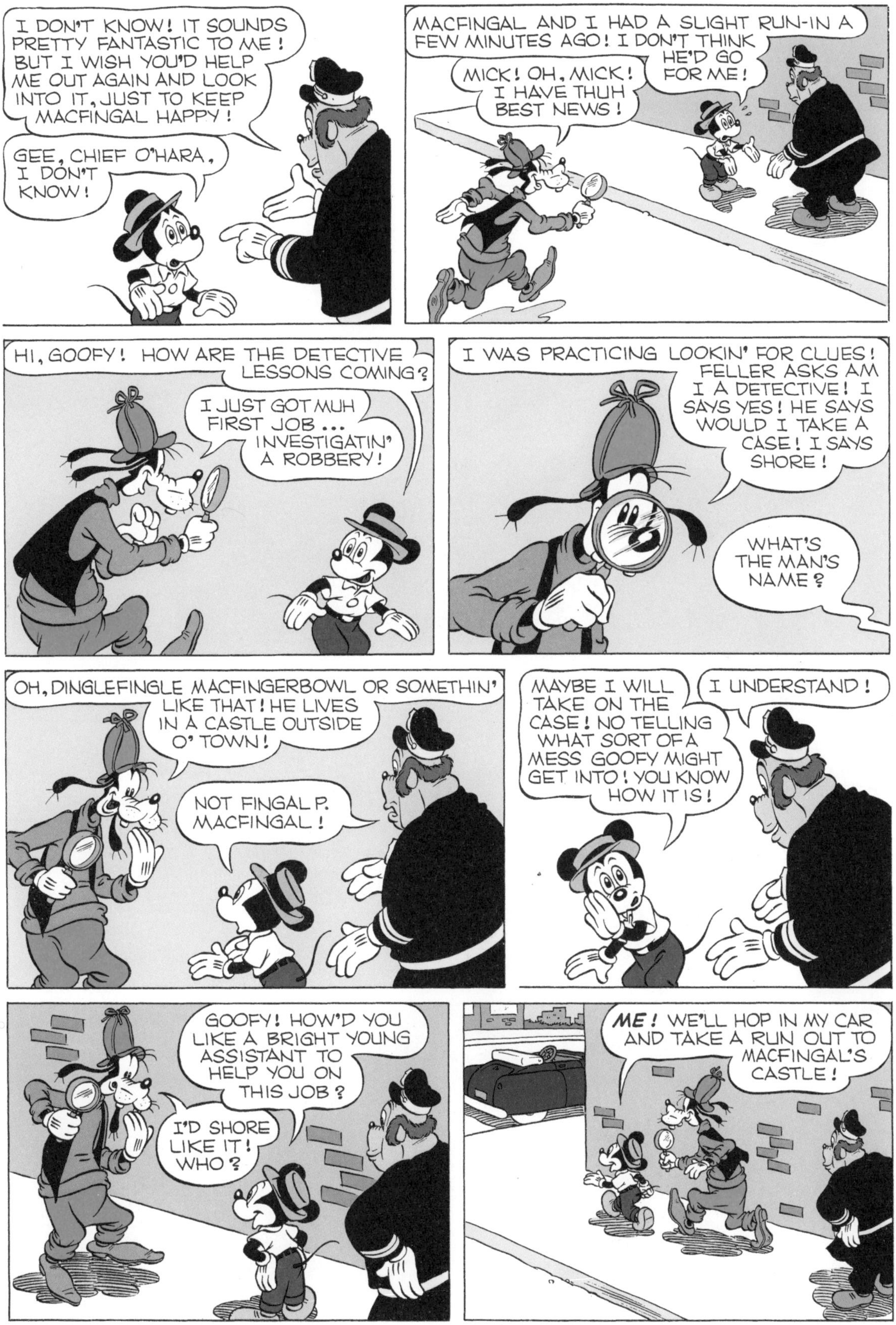
I DON'T KNOW! IT SOUNDS PRETTY FANTASTIC TO ME! BUT I WISH YOU'D HELP ME OUT AGAIN AND LOOK INTO IT, JUST TO KEEP MACFINGAL HAPPY!
GEE, CHIEF O'HARA, I DON'T KNOW!
MACFINGAL AND I HAD A SLIGHT RUN-IN A FEW MINUTES AGO! I DON'T THINK HE'D GO FOR ME!
MICK! OH, MICK! I HAVE THUH BEST NEWS!
HI, GOOFY! HOW ARE THE DETECTIVE LESSONS COMING?
I JUST GOT MUH FIRST JOB ... INVESTIGATIN' A ROBBERY!
I WAS PRACTICING LOOKIN' FOR CLUES! FELLER ASKS AM I A DETECTIVE! I SAYS YES! HE SAYS WOULD I TAKE A CASE! I SAYS SHORE!
WHAT'S THE MAN'S NAME?
OH, DINGLEFINGLE MACFINGERBOWL OR SOMETHIN' LIKE THAT! HE LIVES IN A CASTLE OUTSIDE O' TOWN!
NOT FINGAL P. MACFINGAL!
MAYBE I WILL TAKE ON THE CASE! NO TELLING WHAT SORT OF A MESS GOOFY MIGHT GET INTO! YOU KNOW HOW IT IS!
I UNDERSTAND!
GOOFY! HOW'D YOU LIKE A BRIGHT YOUNG ASSISTANT TO HELP YOU ON THIS JOB?
I'D SHORE LIKE IT! WHO?
ME! WE'LL HOP IN MY CAR AND TAKE A RUN OUT TO MACFINGAL'S CASTLE!

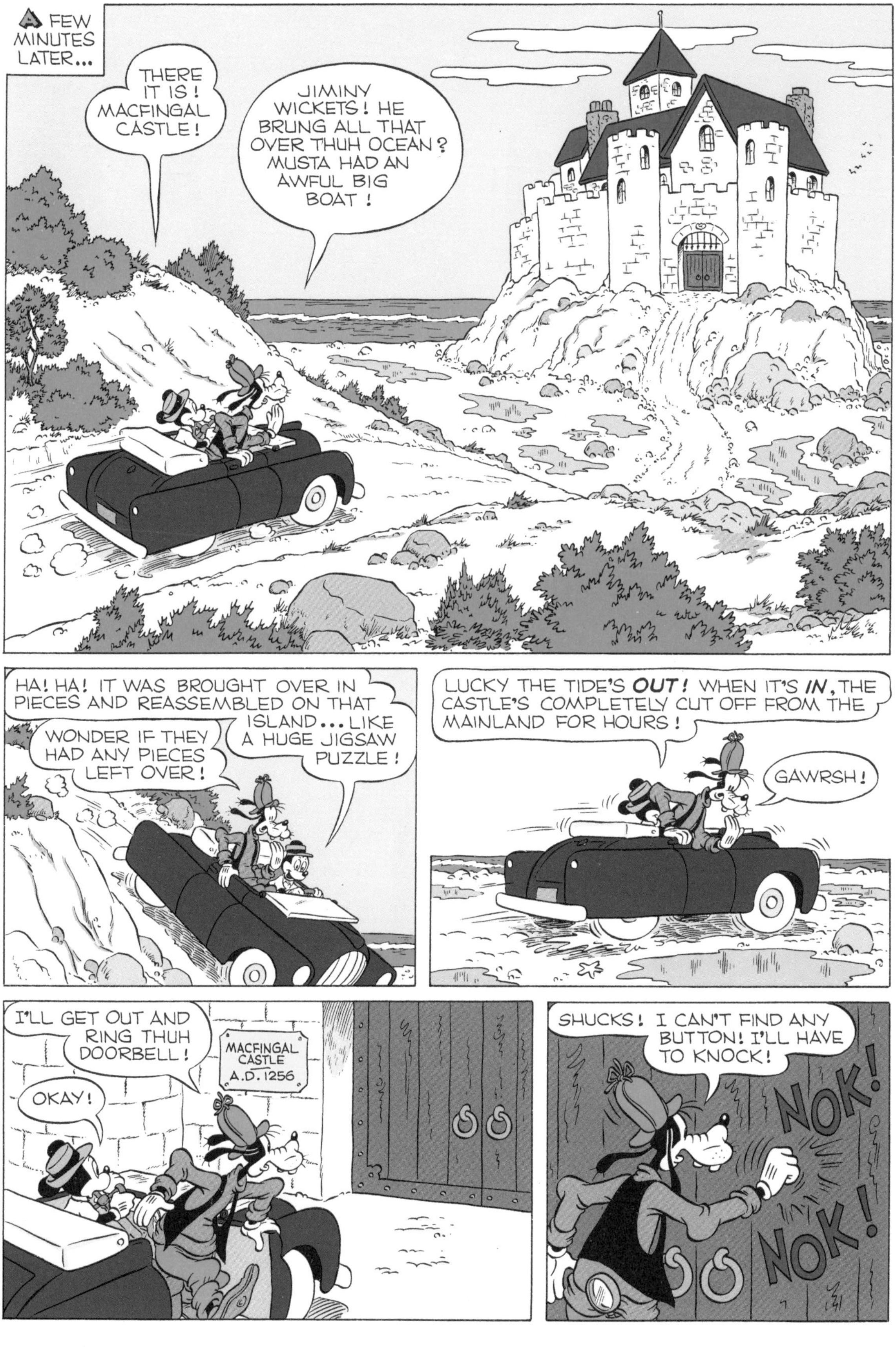

A FEW MINUTES LATER...
THERE IT IS! MACFINGAL CASTLE!
JIMINY WICKETS! HE BRUNG ALL THAT OVER THUH OCEAN? MUSTA HAD AN AWFUL BIG BOAT!
HA! HA! IT WAS BROUGHT OVER IN PIECES AND REASSEMBLED ON THAT ISLAND... LIKE A HUGE JIGSAW PUZZLE!
WONDER IF THEY HAD ANY PIECES LEFT OVER!
LUCKY THE TIDE'S **OUT!** WHEN IT'S **IN**, THE CASTLE'S COMPLETELY CUT OFF FROM THE MAINLAND FOR HOURS!
GAWRSH!
I'LL GET OUT AND RING THUH DOORBELL!
MACFINGAL CASTLE A.D. 1256
OKAY!
SHUCKS! I CAN'T FIND ANY BUTTON! I'LL HAVE TO KNOCK!
NOK!
NOK!

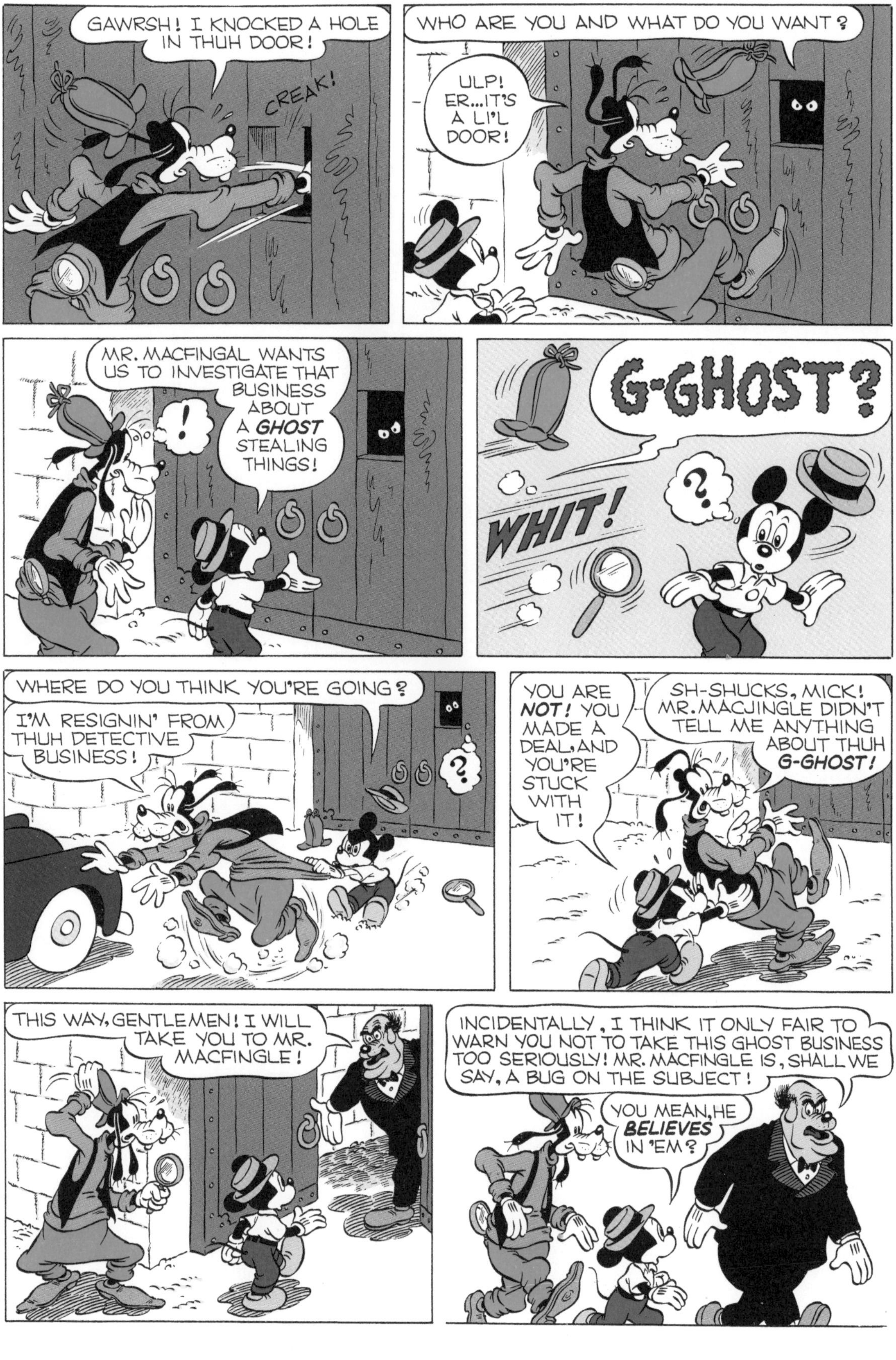
GAWRSH! I KNOCKED A HOLE IN THUH DOOR!
CREAK!
WHO ARE YOU AND WHAT DO YOU WANT?
ULP! ER...IT'S A LI'L DOOR!
MR. MACFINGAL WANTS US TO INVESTIGATE THAT BUSINESS ABOUT A GHOST STEALING THINGS!
!
G-GHOST?
WHIT!
?
WHERE DO YOU THINK YOU'RE GOING?
I'M RESIGNIN' FROM THUH DETECTIVE BUSINESS!
?
SH-SHUCKS, MICK! MR. MACJINGLE DIDN'T TELL ME ANYTHING ABOUT THUH G-GHOST!
YOU ARE NOT! YOU MADE A DEAL, AND YOU'RE STUCK WITH IT!
THIS WAY, GENTLEMEN! I WILL TAKE YOU TO MR. MACFINGLE!
INCIDENTALLY, I THINK IT ONLY FAIR TO WARN YOU NOT TO TAKE THIS GHOST BUSINESS TOO SERIOUSLY! MR. MACFINGLE IS, SHALL WE SAY, A BUG ON THE SUBJECT!
YOU MEAN, HE BELIEVES IN 'EM?

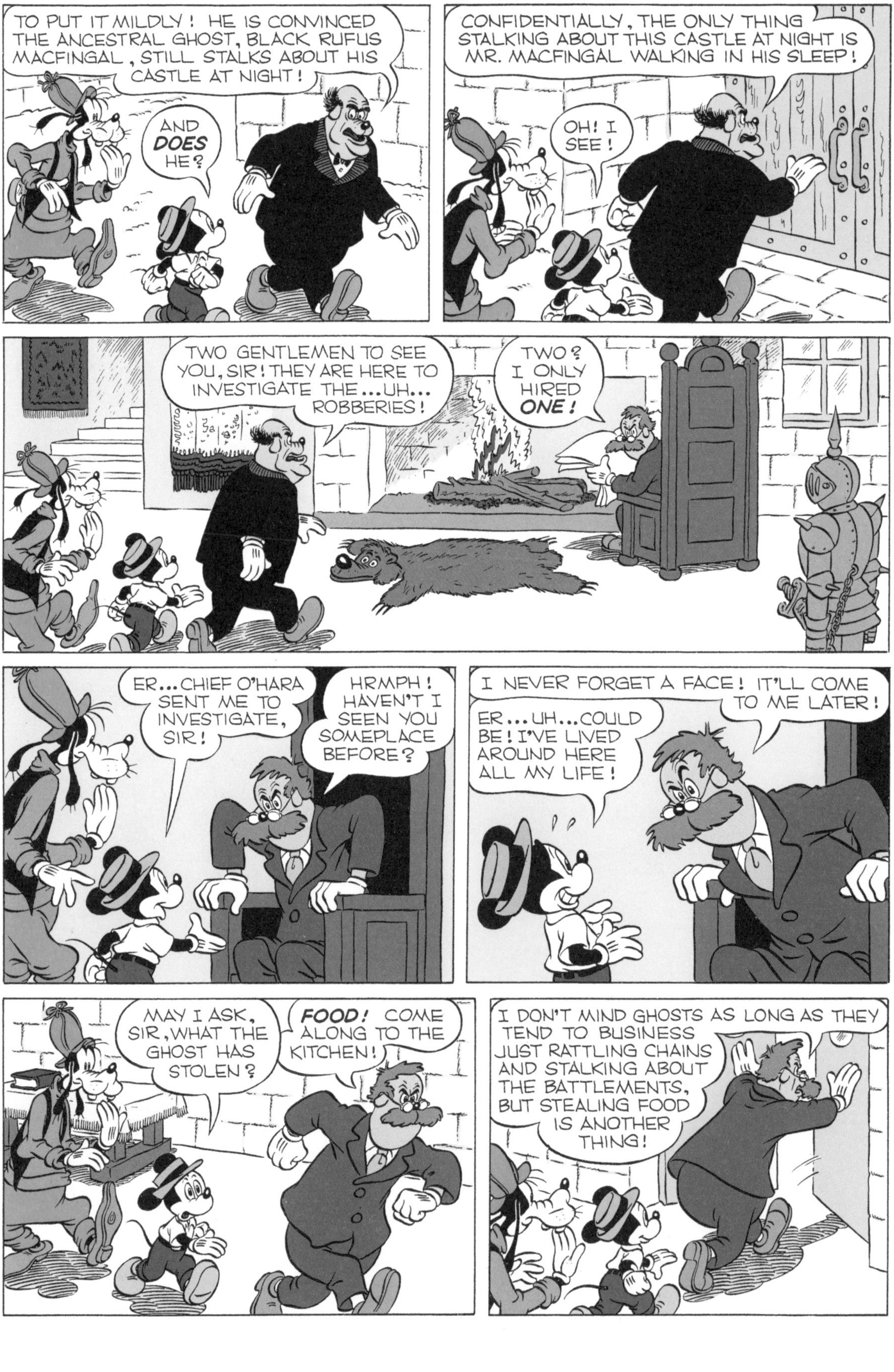
TO PUT IT MILDLY! HE IS CONVINCED THE ANCESTRAL GHOST, BLACK RUFUS MACFINGAL, STILL STALKS ABOUT HIS CASTLE AT NIGHT!
AND DOES HE?
CONFIDENTIALLY, THE ONLY THING STALKING ABOUT THIS CASTLE AT NIGHT IS MR. MACFINGAL WALKING IN HIS SLEEP!
OH! I SEE!
TWO GENTLEMEN TO SEE YOU, SIR! THEY ARE HERE TO INVESTIGATE THE...UH... ROBBERIES!
TWO? I ONLY HIRED ONE!
ER...CHIEF O'HARA SENT ME TO INVESTIGATE, SIR!
HRMPH! HAVEN'T I SEEN YOU SOMEPLACE BEFORE?
ER...UH...COULD BE! I'VE LIVED AROUND HERE ALL MY LIFE!
I NEVER FORGET A FACE! IT'LL COME TO ME LATER!
MAY I ASK, SIR, WHAT THE GHOST HAS STOLEN?
FOOD! COME ALONG TO THE KITCHEN!
I DON'T MIND GHOSTS AS LONG AS THEY TEND TO BUSINESS JUST RATTLING CHAINS AND STALKING ABOUT THE BATTLEMENTS, BUT STEALING FOOD IS ANOTHER THING!

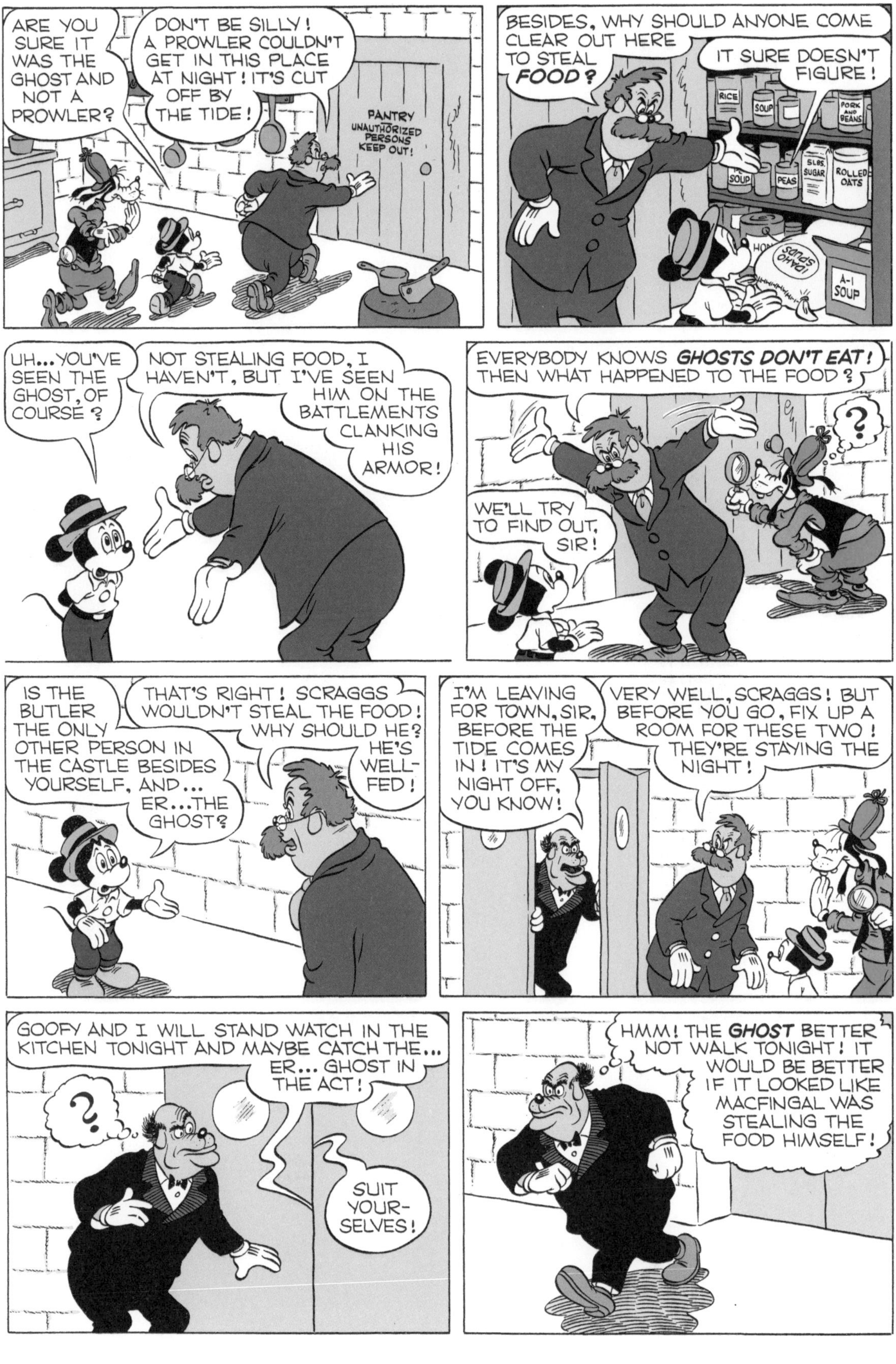

ARE YOU SURE IT WAS THE GHOST AND NOT A PROWLER?
DON'T BE SILLY! A PROWLER COULDN'T GET IN THIS PLACE AT NIGHT! IT'S CUT OFF BY THE TIDE!
PANTRY UNAUTHORIZED PERSONS KEEP OUT!
BESIDES, WHY SHOULD ANYONE COME CLEAR OUT HERE TO STEAL FOOD?
IT SURE DOESN'T FIGURE!
RICE
SOUP
PORK AND BEANS
SOUP
PEAS
5LBS. SUGAR
ROLLED OATS
IDAHO SPUDS
A-1 SOUP
UH... YOU'VE SEEN THE GHOST, OF COURSE?
NOT STEALING FOOD, I HAVEN'T, BUT I'VE SEEN HIM ON THE BATTLEMENTS CLANKING HIS ARMOR!
EVERYBODY KNOWS GHOSTS DON'T EAT! THEN WHAT HAPPENED TO THE FOOD?
?
WE'LL TRY TO FIND OUT, SIR!
IS THE BUTLER THE ONLY OTHER PERSON IN THE CASTLE BESIDES YOURSELF, AND... ER...THE GHOST?
THAT'S RIGHT! SCRAGGS WOULDN'T STEAL THE FOOD! WHY SHOULD HE? HE'S WELL-FED!
I'M LEAVING FOR TOWN, SIR, BEFORE THE TIDE COMES IN! IT'S MY NIGHT OFF, YOU KNOW!
VERY WELL, SCRAGGS! BUT BEFORE YOU GO, FIX UP A ROOM FOR THESE TWO! THEY'RE STAYING THE NIGHT!
GOOFY AND I WILL STAND WATCH IN THE KITCHEN TONIGHT AND MAYBE CATCH THE... ER... GHOST IN THE ACT!
?
SUIT YOURSELVES!
HMM! THE GHOST BETTER NOT WALK TONIGHT! IT WOULD BE BETTER IF IT LOOKED LIKE MACFINGAL WAS STEALING THE FOOD HIMSELF!

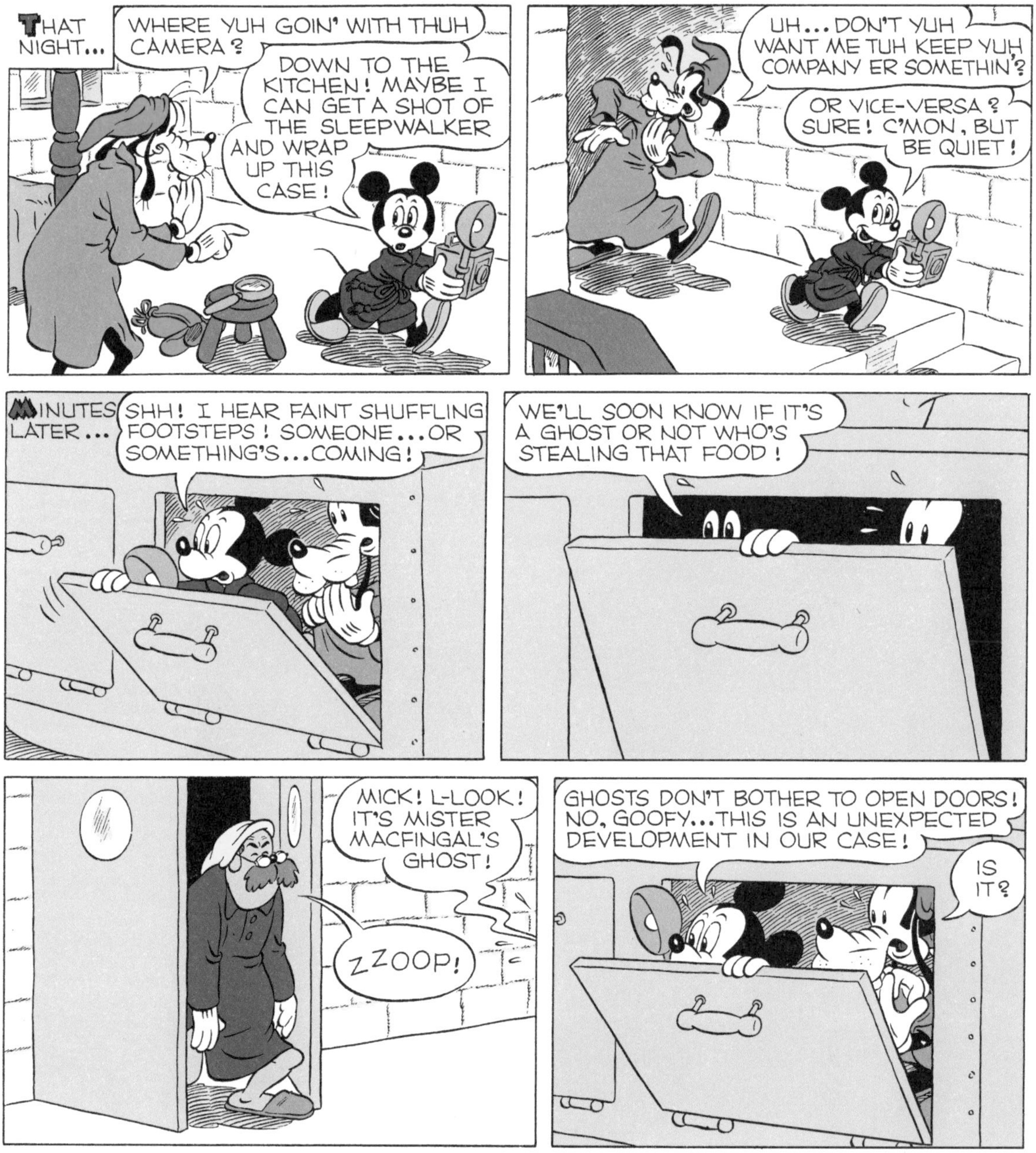
THAT NIGHT...
WHERE YUH GOIN' WITH THUH CAMERA?
DOWN TO THE KITCHEN! MAYBE I CAN GET A SHOT OF THE SLEEPWALKER AND WRAP UP THIS CASE!
UH... DON'T YUH WANT ME TUH KEEP YUH COMPANY ER SOMETHIN'?
OR VICE-VERSA? SURE! C'MON, BUT BE QUIET!
MINUTES LATER...
SHH! I HEAR FAINT SHUFFLING FOOTSTEPS! SOMEONE...OR SOMETHING'S...COMING!
WE'LL SOON KNOW IF IT'S A GHOST OR NOT WHO'S STEALING THAT FOOD!
MICK! L-LOOK! IT'S MISTER MACFINGAL'S GHOST!
ZZOOP!
GHOSTS DON'T BOTHER TO OPEN DOORS! NO, GOOFY...THIS IS AN UNEXPECTED DEVELOPMENT IN OUR CASE!
IS IT?

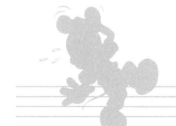

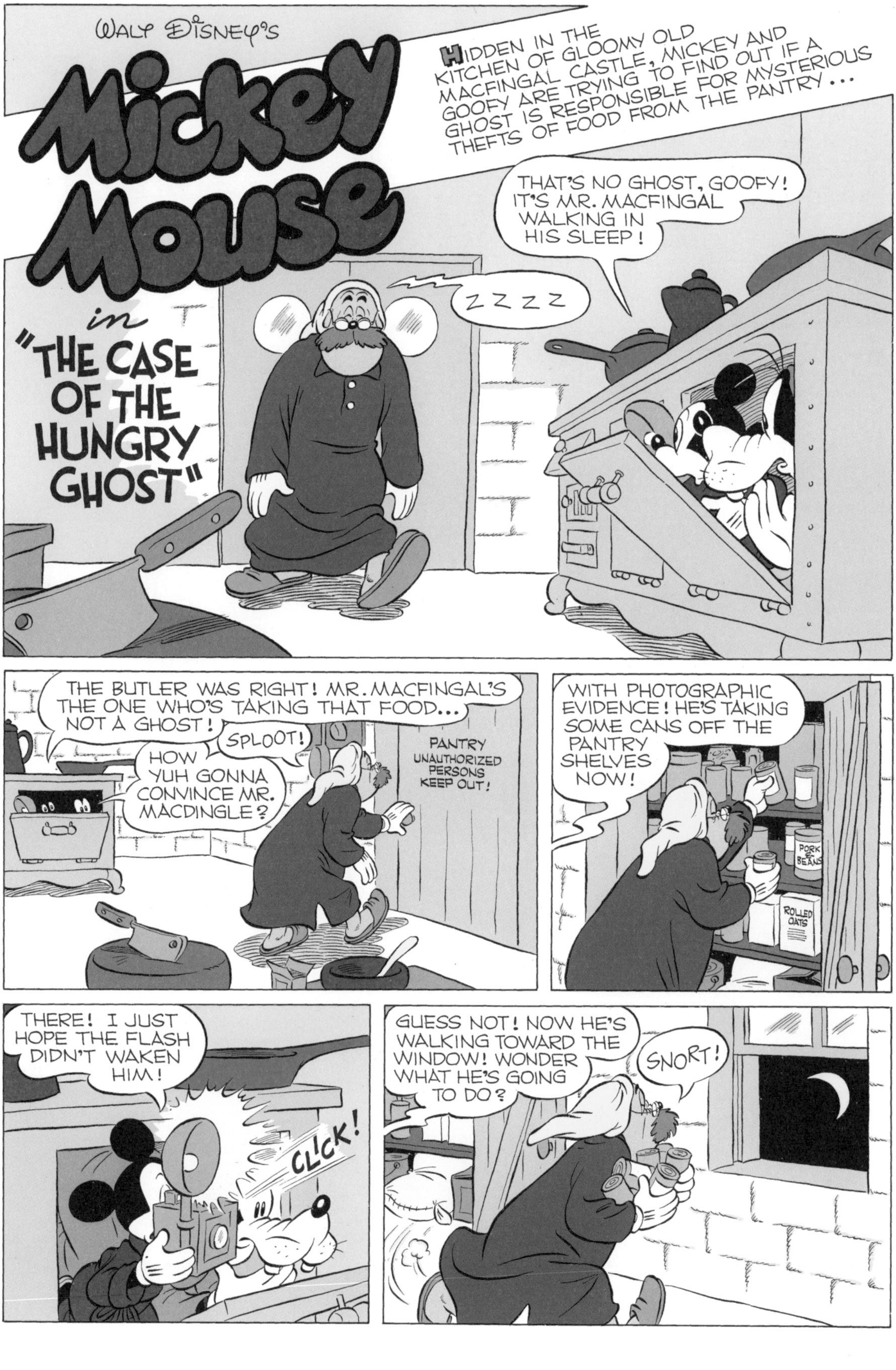
WALT DISNEY'S
Mickey Mouse
in
"THE CASE OF THE HUNGRY GHOST"
HIDDEN IN THE KITCHEN OF GLOOMY OLD MACFINGAL CASTLE, MICKEY AND GOOFY ARE TRYING TO FIND OUT IF A GHOST IS RESPONSIBLE FOR MYSTERIOUS THEFTS OF FOOD FROM THE PANTRY...
Z Z Z Z
THAT'S NO GHOST, GOOFY! IT'S MR. MACFINGAL WALKING IN HIS SLEEP!
THE BUTLER WAS RIGHT! MR. MACFINGAL'S THE ONE WHO'S TAKING THAT FOOD... NOT A GHOST!
HOW YUH GONNA CONVINCE MR. MACDINGLE?
SPLOOT!
PANTRY UNAUTHORIZED PERSONS KEEP OUT!
WITH PHOTOGRAPHIC EVIDENCE! HE'S TAKING SOME CANS OFF THE PANTRY SHELVES NOW!
PORK & BEANS
ROLLED OATS
THERE! I JUST HOPE THE FLASH DIDN'T WAKEN HIM!
CLICK!
GUESS NOT! NOW HE'S WALKING TOWARD THE WINDOW! WONDER WHAT HE'S GOING TO DO?
SNORT!

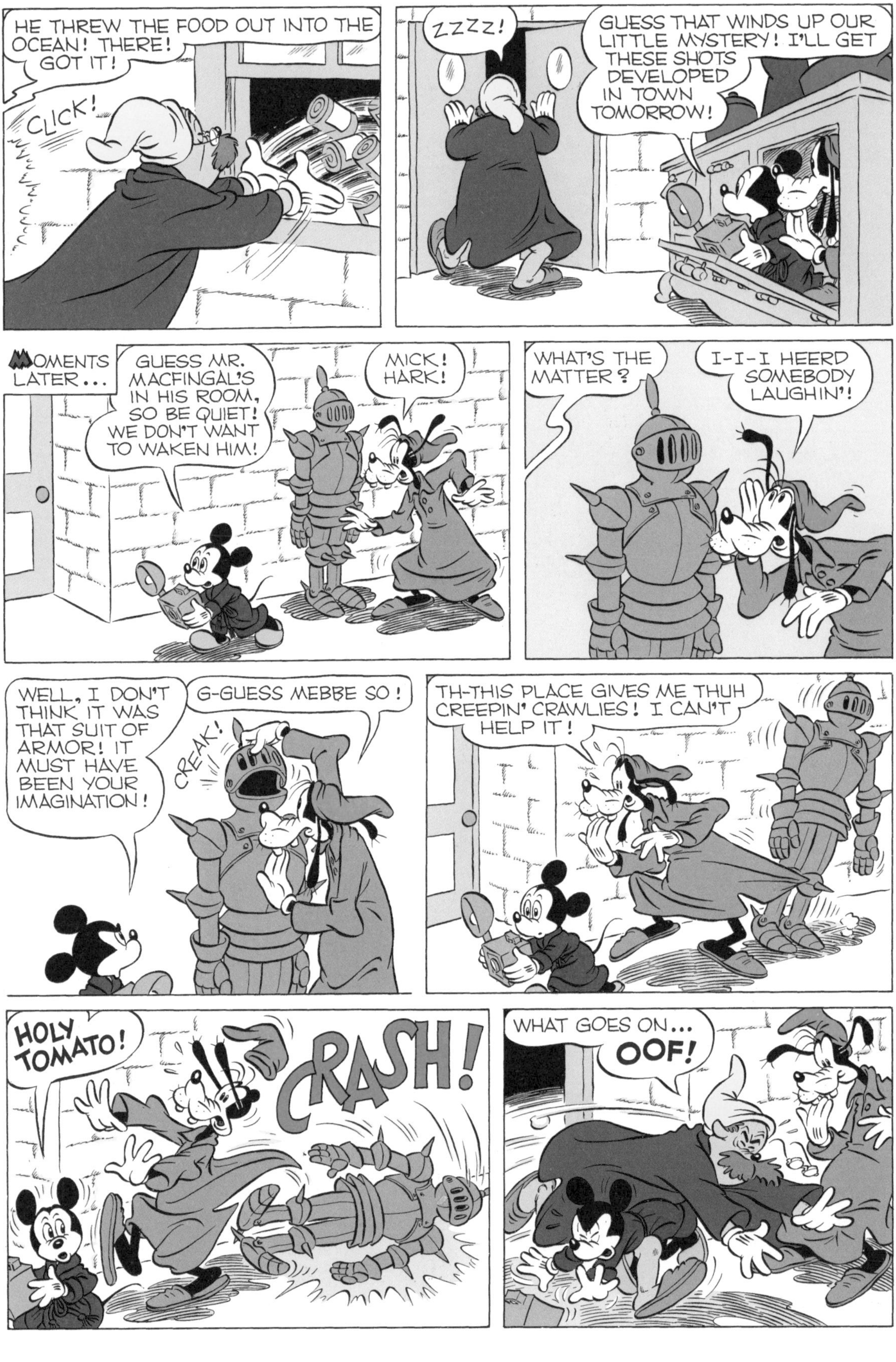
HE THREW THE FOOD OUT INTO THE OCEAN! THERE! GOT IT!
CLICK!
ZZZZ!
GUESS THAT WINDS UP OUR LITTLE MYSTERY! I'LL GET THESE SHOTS DEVELOPED IN TOWN TOMORROW!
MOMENTS LATER...
GUESS MR. MACFINGAL'S IN HIS ROOM, SO BE QUIET! WE DON'T WANT TO WAKEN HIM!
MICK! HARK!
WHAT'S THE MATTER?
I-I-I HEERD SOMEBODY LAUGHIN'!
WELL, I DON'T THINK IT WAS THAT SUIT OF ARMOR! IT MUST HAVE BEEN YOUR IMAGINATION!
G-GUESS MEBBE SO!
CREAK!
TH-THIS PLACE GIVES ME THUH CREEPIN' CRAWLIES! I CAN'T HELP IT!
HOLY TOMATO!
CRASH!
WHAT GOES ON... OOF!

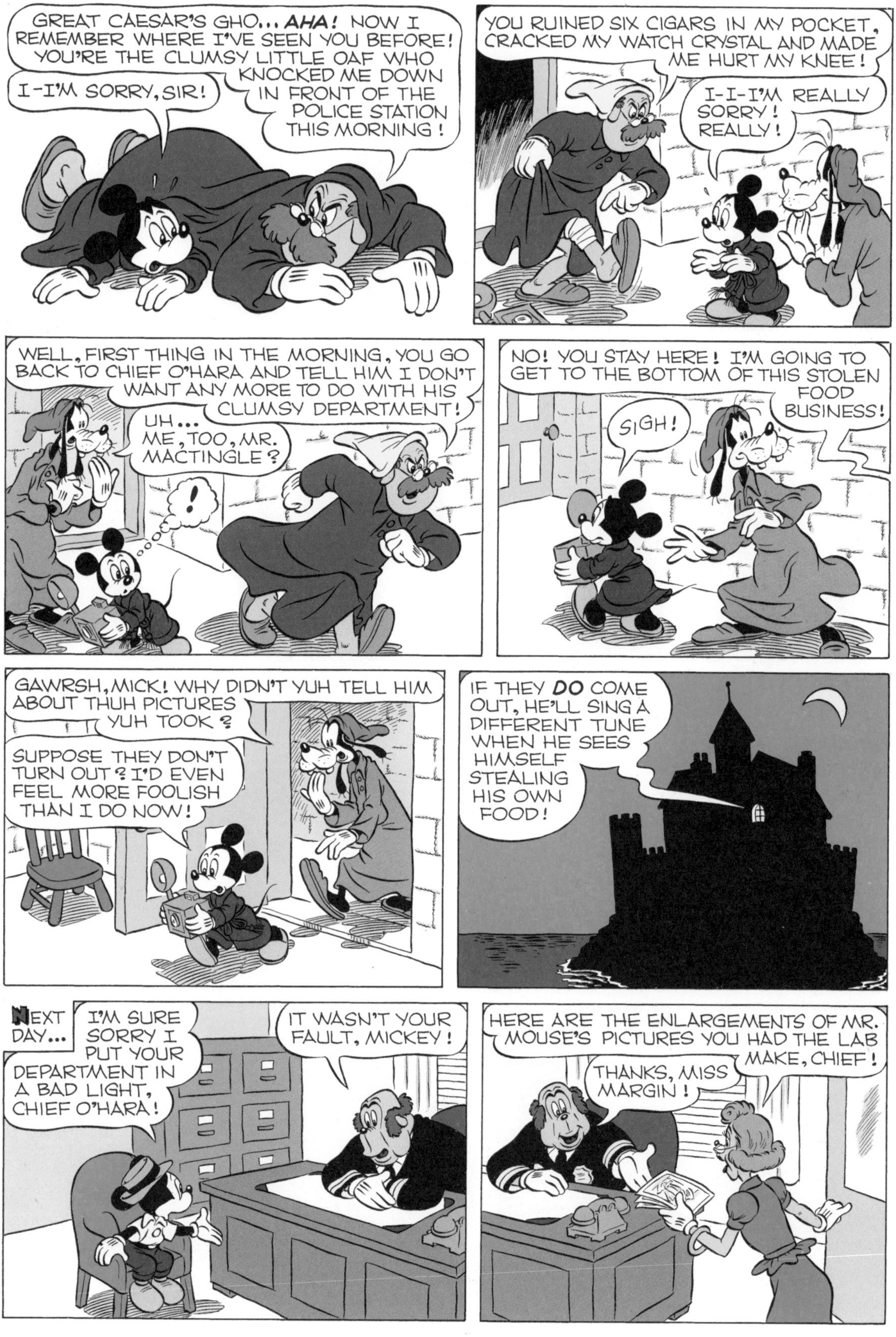
GREAT CAESAR'S GHO... AHA! NOW I REMEMBER WHERE I'VE SEEN YOU BEFORE! YOU'RE THE CLUMSY LITTLE OAF WHO KNOCKED ME DOWN IN FRONT OF THE POLICE STATION THIS MORNING!
I-I'M SORRY, SIR!
YOU RUINED SIX CIGARS IN MY POCKET, CRACKED MY WATCH CRYSTAL AND MADE ME HURT MY KNEE!
I-I-I'M REALLY SORRY! REALLY!
WELL, FIRST THING IN THE MORNING, YOU GO BACK TO CHIEF O'HARA AND TELL HIM I DON'T WANT ANY MORE TO DO WITH HIS CLUMSY DEPARTMENT!
UH... ME, TOO, MR. MACTINGLE?
!
NO! YOU STAY HERE! I'M GOING TO GET TO THE BOTTOM OF THIS STOLEN FOOD BUSINESS!
SIGH!
GAWRSH, MICK! WHY DIDN'T YUH TELL HIM ABOUT THUH PICTURES YUH TOOK?
SUPPOSE THEY DON'T TURN OUT? I'D EVEN FEEL MORE FOOLISH THAN I DO NOW!
IF THEY DO COME OUT, HE'LL SING A DIFFERENT TUNE WHEN HE SEES HIMSELF STEALING HIS OWN FOOD!
NEXT DAY...
I'M SURE SORRY I PUT YOUR DEPARTMENT IN A BAD LIGHT, CHIEF O'HARA!
IT WASN'T YOUR FAULT, MICKEY!
HERE ARE THE ENLARGEMENTS OF MR. MOUSE'S PICTURES YOU HAD THE LAB MAKE, CHIEF!
THANKS, MISS MARGIN!

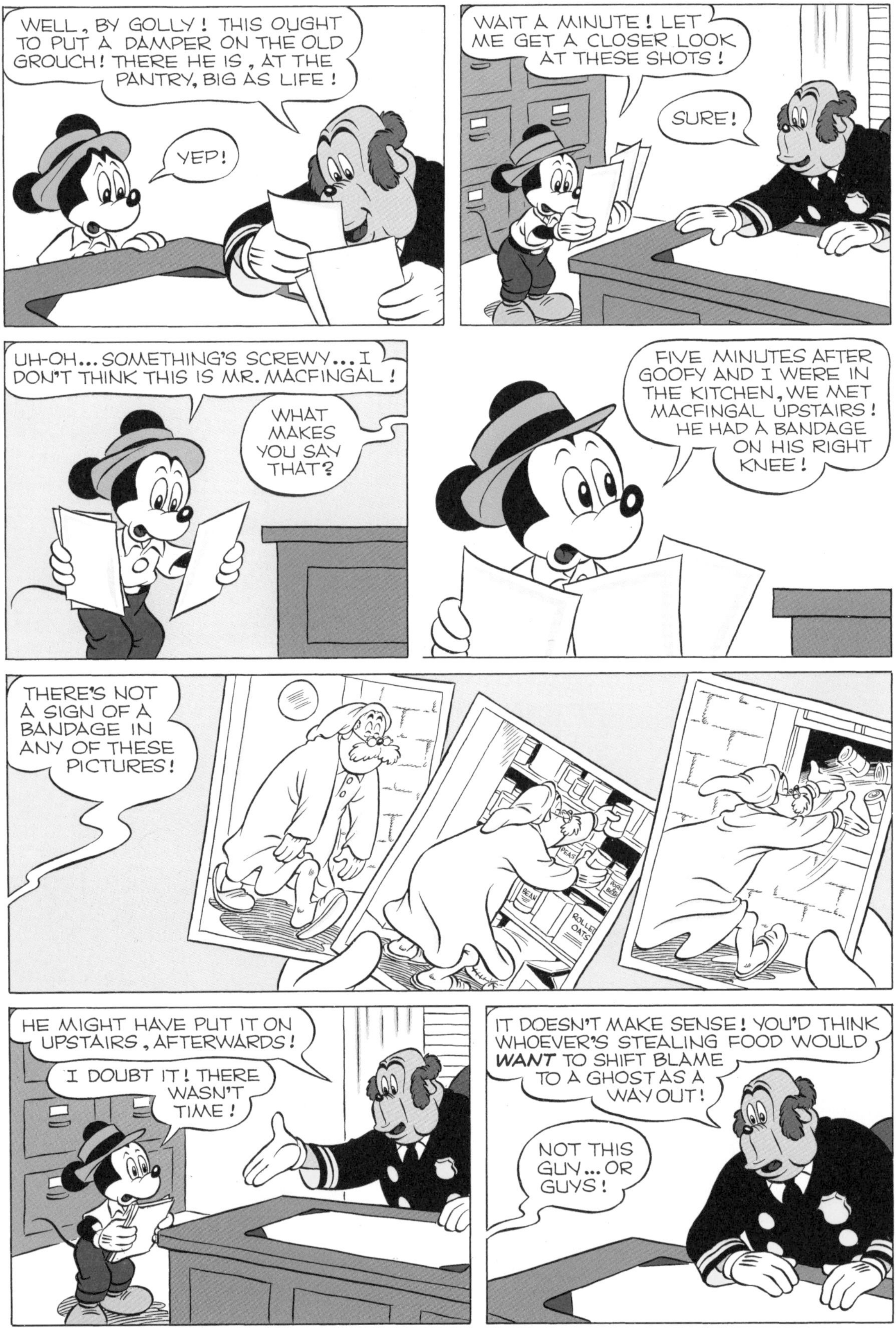
WELL, BY GOLLY! THIS OUGHT TO PUT A DAMPER ON THE OLD GROUCH! THERE HE IS, AT THE PANTRY, BIG AS LIFE!
YEP!
WAIT A MINUTE! LET ME GET A CLOSER LOOK AT THESE SHOTS!
SURE!
UH-OH... SOMETHING'S SCREWY... I DON'T THINK THIS IS MR. MACFINGAL!
WHAT MAKES YOU SAY THAT?
FIVE MINUTES AFTER GOOFY AND I WERE IN THE KITCHEN, WE MET MACFINGAL UPSTAIRS! HE HAD A BANDAGE ON HIS RIGHT KNEE!
THERE'S NOT A SIGN OF A BANDAGE IN ANY OF THESE PICTURES!
PEAS
BEAN
ROLLED OATS
HE MIGHT HAVE PUT IT ON UPSTAIRS, AFTERWARDS!
I DOUBT IT! THERE WASN'T TIME!
IT DOESN'T MAKE SENSE! YOU'D THINK WHOEVER'S STEALING FOOD WOULD WANT TO SHIFT BLAME TO A GHOST AS A WAY OUT!
NOT THIS GUY... OR GUYS!

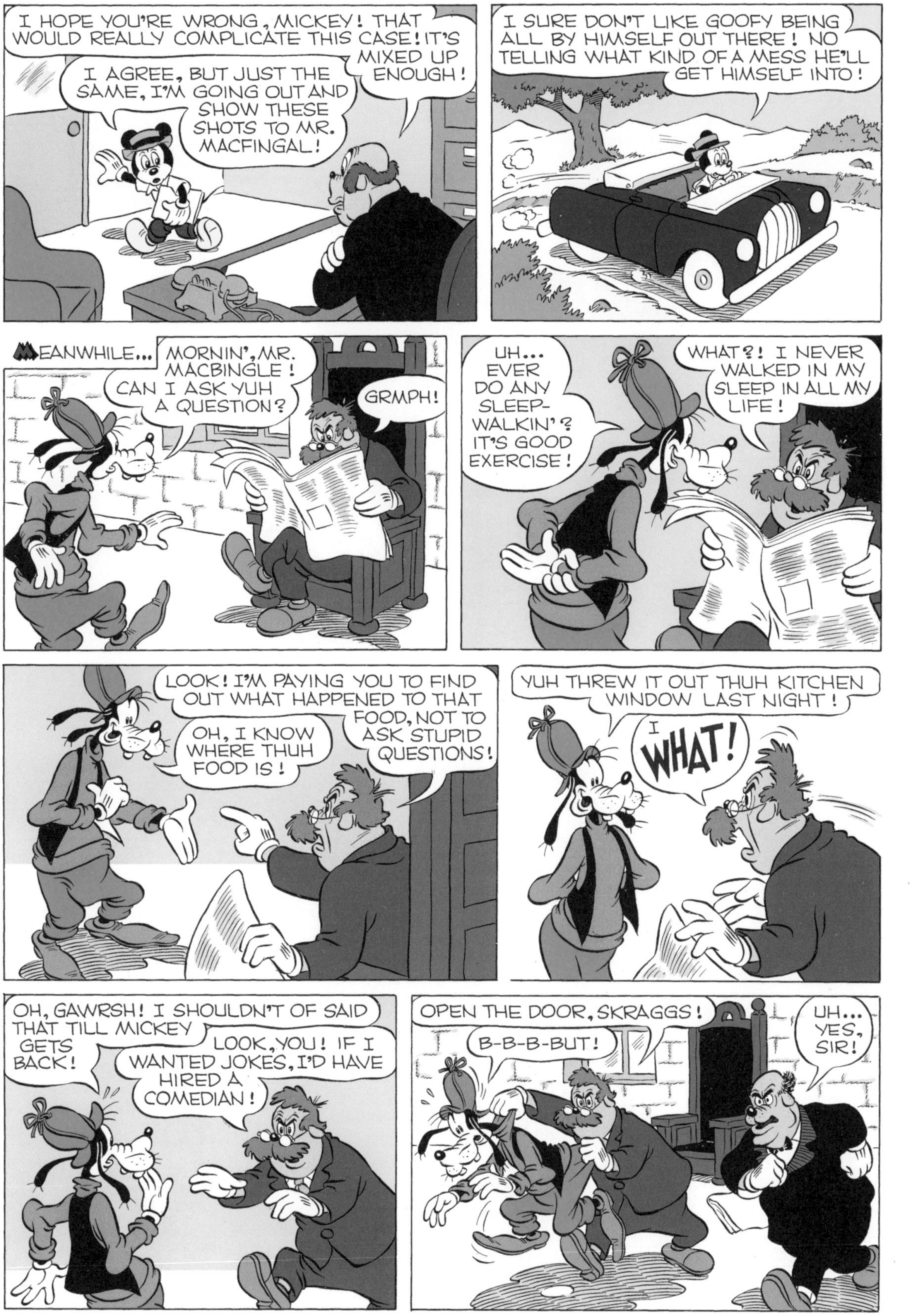
I HOPE YOU'RE WRONG, MICKEY! THAT WOULD REALLY COMPLICATE THIS CASE! IT'S MIXED UP ENOUGH!
I AGREE, BUT JUST THE SAME, I'M GOING OUT AND SHOW THESE SHOTS TO MR. MACFINGAL!
I SURE DON'T LIKE GOOFY BEING ALL BY HIMSELF OUT THERE! NO TELLING WHAT KIND OF A MESS HE'LL GET HIMSELF INTO!
MEANWHILE...
MORNIN', MR. MACBINGLE! CAN I ASK YUH A QUESTION?
GRMPH!
UH... EVER DO ANY SLEEP-WALKIN'? IT'S GOOD EXERCISE!
WHAT?! I NEVER WALKED IN MY SLEEP IN ALL MY LIFE!
LOOK! I'M PAYING YOU TO FIND OUT WHAT HAPPENED TO THAT FOOD, NOT TO ASK STUPID QUESTIONS!
OH, I KNOW WHERE THUH FOOD IS!
YUH THREW IT OUT THUH KITCHEN WINDOW LAST NIGHT!
I WHAT!
OH, GAWRSH! I SHOULDN'T OF SAID THAT TILL MICKEY GETS BACK!
LOOK, YOU! IF I WANTED JOKES, I'D HAVE HIRED A COMEDIAN!
OPEN THE DOOR, SKRAGGS!
B-B-B-BUT!
UH... YES, SIR!

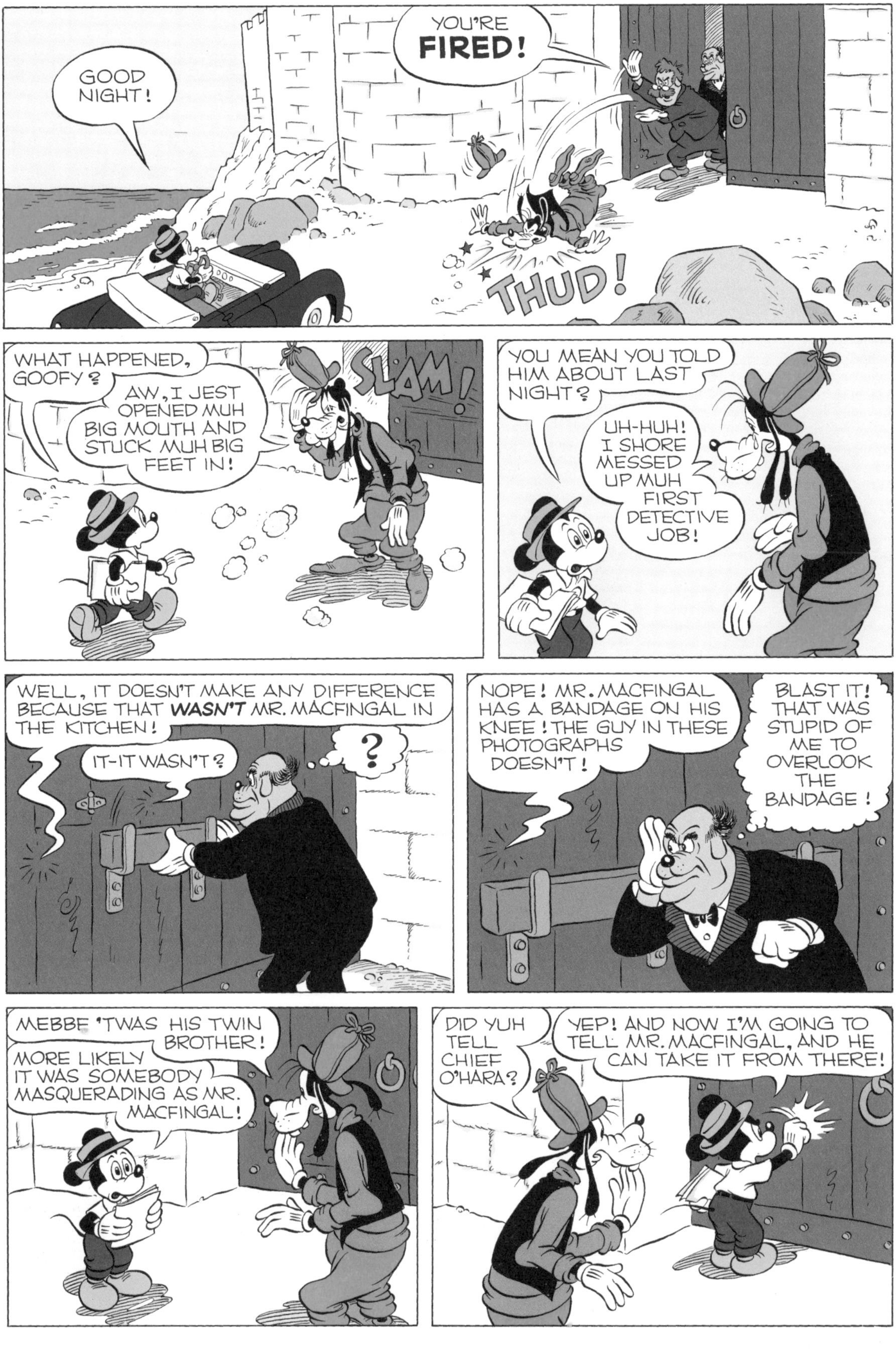
GOOD NIGHT!
YOU'RE FIRED!
THUD!
WHAT HAPPENED, GOOFY?
AW, I JEST OPENED MUH BIG MOUTH AND STUCK MUH BIG FEET IN!
SLAM!
YOU MEAN YOU TOLD HIM ABOUT LAST NIGHT?
UH-HUH! I SHORE MESSED UP MUH FIRST DETECTIVE JOB!
WELL, IT DOESN'T MAKE ANY DIFFERENCE BECAUSE THAT WASN'T MR. MACFINGAL IN THE KITCHEN!
IT-IT WASN'T?
?
NOPE! MR. MACFINGAL HAS A BANDAGE ON HIS KNEE! THE GUY IN THESE PHOTOGRAPHS DOESN'T!
BLAST IT! THAT WAS STUPID OF ME TO OVERLOOK THE BANDAGE!
MEBBE 'TWAS HIS TWIN BROTHER!
MORE LIKELY IT WAS SOMEBODY MASQUERADING AS MR. MACFINGAL!
DID YUH TELL CHIEF O'HARA?
YEP! AND NOW I'M GOING TO TELL MR. MACFINGAL, AND HE CAN TAKE IT FROM THERE!

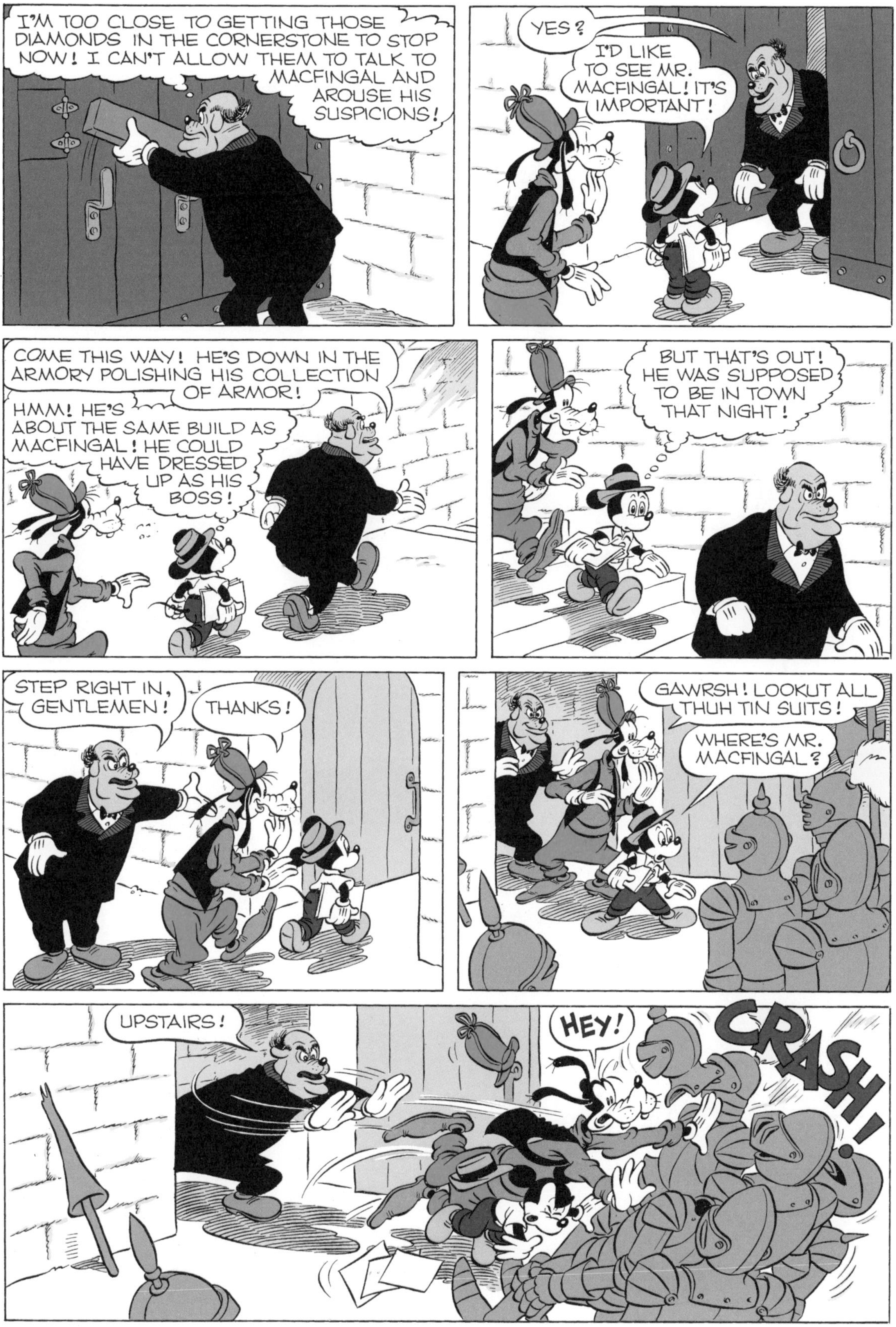
I'M TOO CLOSE TO GETTING THOSE DIAMONDS IN THE CORNERSTONE TO STOP NOW! I CAN'T ALLOW THEM TO TALK TO MACFINGAL AND AROUSE HIS SUSPICIONS!
YES?
I'D LIKE TO SEE MR. MACFINGAL! IT'S IMPORTANT!
COME THIS WAY! HE'S DOWN IN THE ARMORY POLISHING HIS COLLECTION OF ARMOR!
HMM! HE'S ABOUT THE SAME BUILD AS MACFINGAL! HE COULD HAVE DRESSED UP AS HIS BOSS!
BUT THAT'S OUT! HE WAS SUPPOSED TO BE IN TOWN THAT NIGHT!
STEP RIGHT IN, GENTLEMEN!
THANKS!
GAWRSH! LOOKUT ALL THUH TIN SUITS!
WHERE'S MR. MACFINGAL?
UPSTAIRS!
HEY!
CRASH!

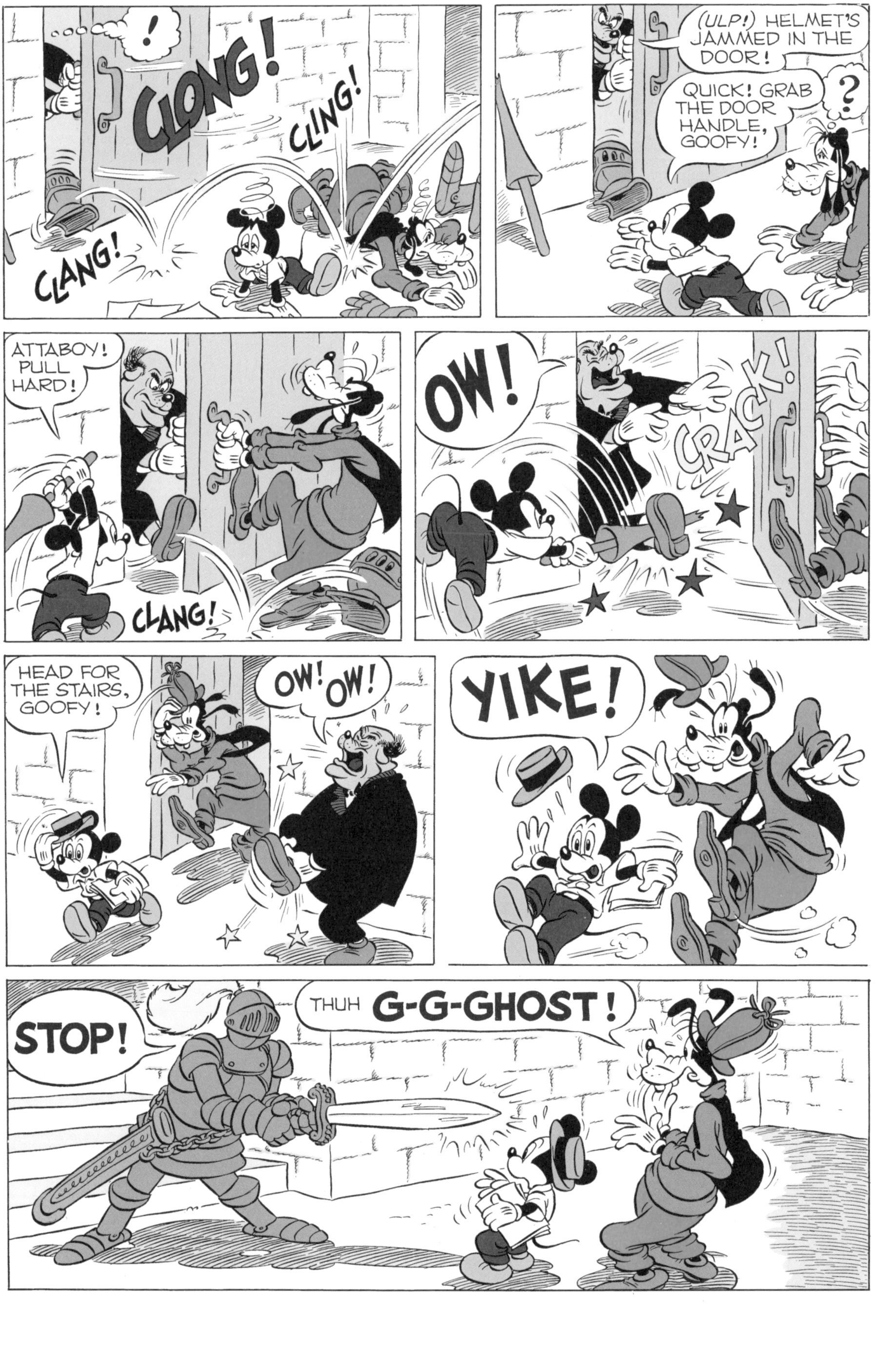
!
CLONG!
CLING!
CLANG!
(ULP!) HELMET'S JAMMED IN THE DOOR!
QUICK! GRAB THE DOOR HANDLE, GOOFY!
?
ATTABOY! PULL HARD!
CLANG!
OW!
CRACK!
HEAD FOR THE STAIRS, GOOFY!
OW! OW!
YIKE!
STOP!
THUH G-G-GHOST!

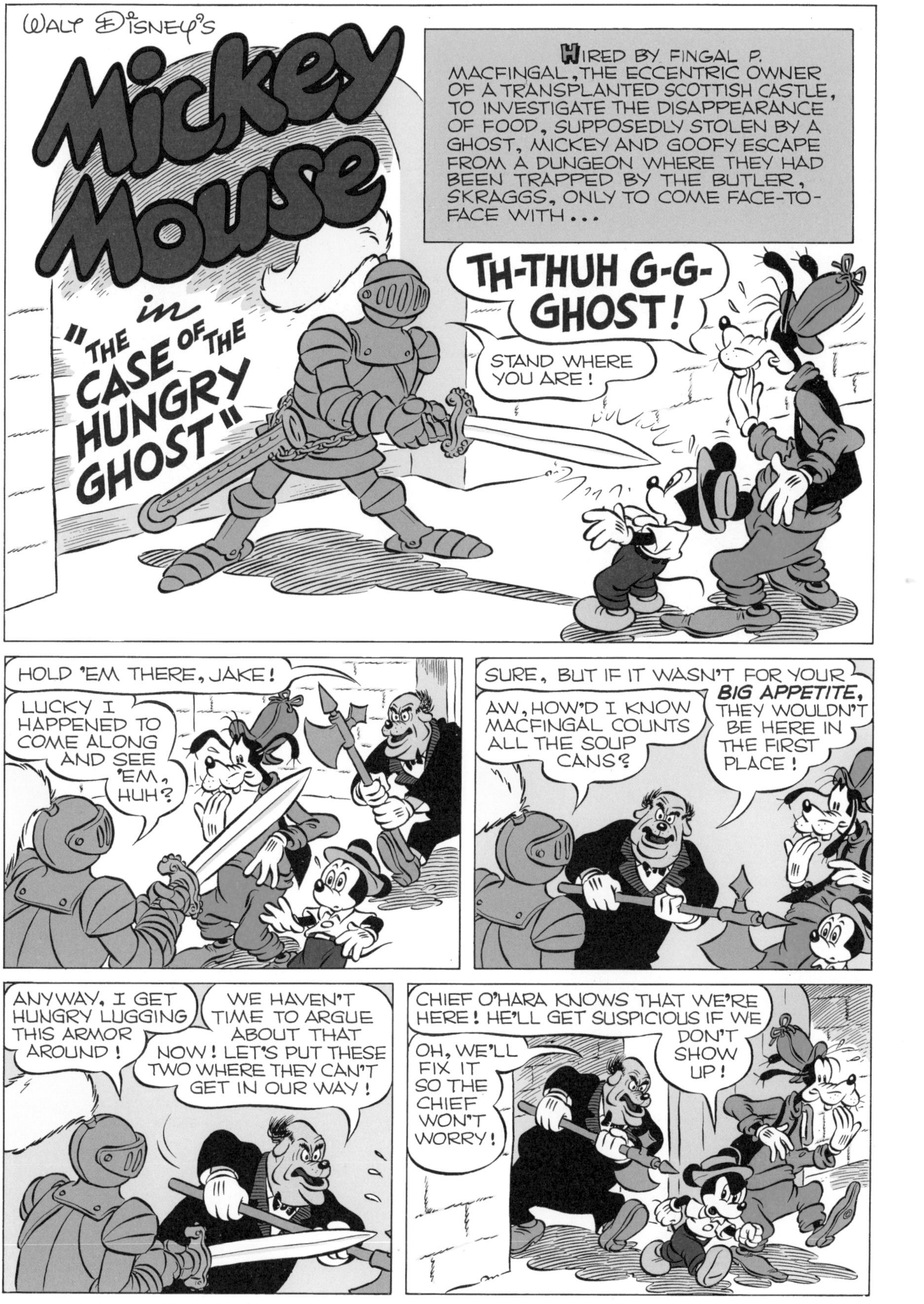

WALT DISNEY'S
Mickey Mouse
in "THE CASE OF THE HUNGRY GHOST"
HIRED BY FINGAL P. MACFINGAL, THE ECCENTRIC OWNER OF A TRANSPLANTED SCOTTISH CASTLE, TO INVESTIGATE THE DISAPPEARANCE OF FOOD, SUPPOSEDLY STOLEN BY A GHOST, MICKEY AND GOOFY ESCAPE FROM A DUNGEON WHERE THEY HAD BEEN TRAPPED BY THE BUTLER, SKRAGGS, ONLY TO COME FACE-TO-FACE WITH...
TH-THUH G-G-GHOST!
STAND WHERE YOU ARE!
HOLD 'EM THERE, JAKE!
LUCKY I HAPPENED TO COME ALONG AND SEE 'EM, HUH?
SURE, BUT IF IT WASN'T FOR YOUR BIG APPETITE, THEY WOULDN'T BE HERE IN THE FIRST PLACE!
AW, HOW'D I KNOW MACFINGAL COUNTS ALL THE SOUP CANS?
ANYWAY, I GET HUNGRY LUGGING THIS ARMOR AROUND!
WE HAVEN'T TIME TO ARGUE ABOUT THAT NOW! LET'S PUT THESE TWO WHERE THEY CAN'T GET IN OUR WAY!
CHIEF O'HARA KNOWS THAT WE'RE HERE! HE'LL GET SUSPICIOUS IF WE DON'T SHOW UP!
OH, WE'LL FIX IT SO THE CHIEF WON'T WORRY!

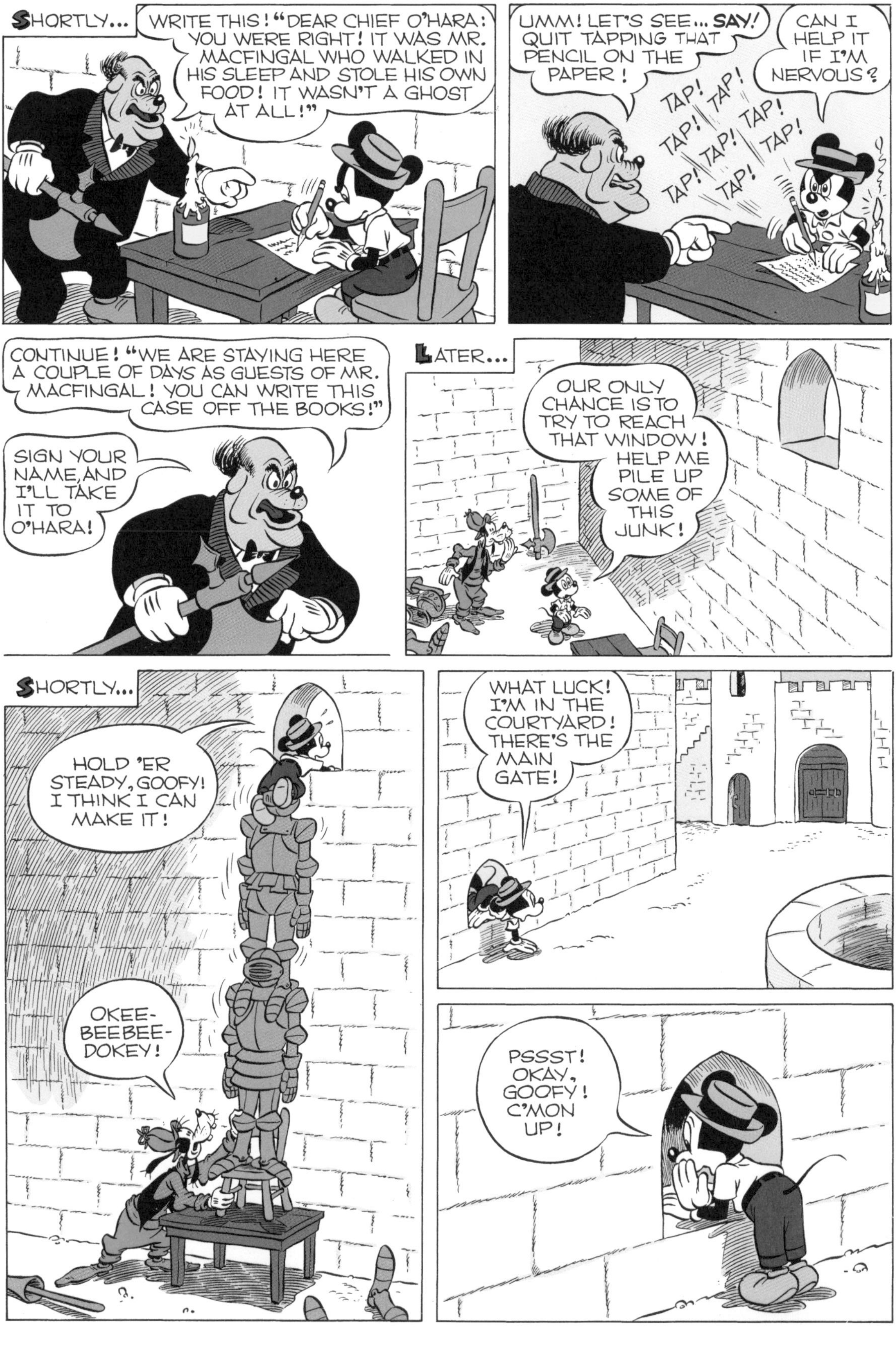
SHORTLY...
WRITE THIS! "DEAR CHIEF O'HARA: YOU WERE RIGHT! IT WAS MR. MACFINGAL WHO WALKED IN HIS SLEEP AND STOLE HIS OWN FOOD! IT WASN'T A GHOST AT ALL!"
UMM! LET'S SEE... SAY! QUIT TAPPING THAT PENCIL ON THE PAPER!
CAN I HELP IT IF I'M NERVOUS?
TAP! TAP! TAP! TAP! TAP! TAP! TAP! TAP! TAP! TAP!
CONTINUE! "WE ARE STAYING HERE A COUPLE OF DAYS AS GUESTS OF MR. MACFINGAL! YOU CAN WRITE THIS CASE OFF THE BOOKS!"
SIGN YOUR NAME, AND I'LL TAKE IT TO O'HARA!
LATER...
OUR ONLY CHANCE IS TO TRY TO REACH THAT WINDOW! HELP ME PILE UP SOME OF THIS JUNK!
SHORTLY...
HOLD 'ER STEADY, GOOFY! I THINK I CAN MAKE IT!
OKEE-BEEBEE-DOKEY!
WHAT LUCK! I'M IN THE COURTYARD! THERE'S THE MAIN GATE!
PSSST! OKAY, GOOFY! C'MON UP!

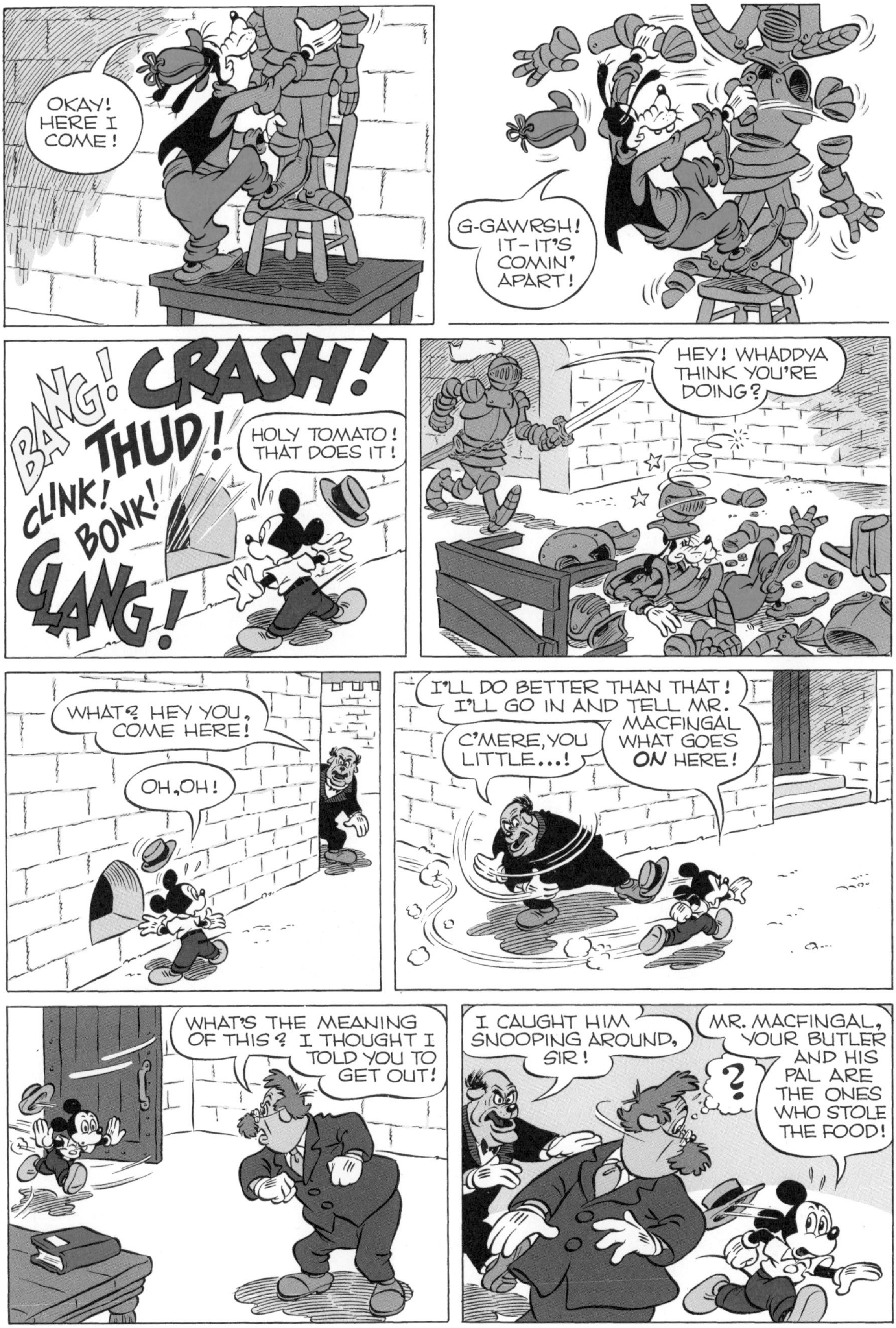

OKAY! HERE I COME!
G-GAWRSH! IT-IT'S COMIN' APART!
BANG! CRASH! THUD! CLINK! BONK! CLANG!
HOLY TOMATO! THAT DOES IT!
HEY! WHADDYA THINK YOU'RE DOING?
WHAT? HEY YOU, COME HERE!
OH, OH!
I'LL DO BETTER THAN THAT! I'LL GO IN AND TELL MR. MACFINGAL WHAT GOES ON HERE!
C'MERE, YOU LITTLE...!
WHAT'S THE MEANING OF THIS? I THOUGHT I TOLD YOU TO GET OUT!
I CAUGHT HIM SNOOPING AROUND, SIR!
MR. MACFINGAL, YOUR BUTLER AND HIS PAL ARE THE ONES WHO STOLE THE FOOD!
?

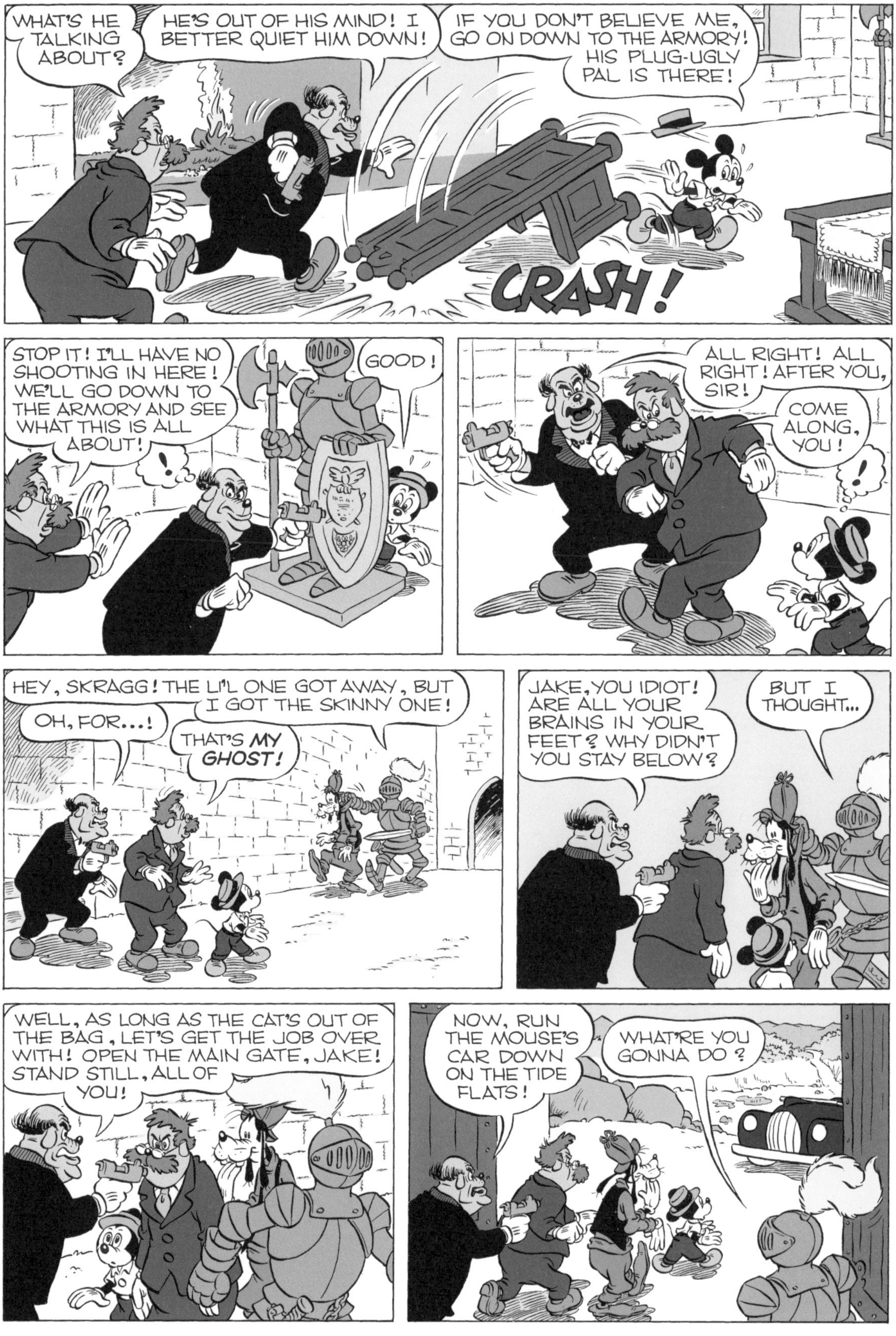
WHAT'S HE TALKING ABOUT?
HE'S OUT OF HIS MIND! I BETTER QUIET HIM DOWN!
IF YOU DON'T BELIEVE ME, GO ON DOWN TO THE ARMORY! HIS PLUG-UGLY PAL IS THERE!
CRASH!
STOP IT! I'LL HAVE NO SHOOTING IN HERE! WE'LL GO DOWN TO THE ARMORY AND SEE WHAT THIS IS ALL ABOUT!
GOOD!
!
ALL RIGHT! ALL RIGHT! AFTER YOU, SIR!
COME ALONG, YOU!
!
HEY, SKRAGG! THE LI'L ONE GOT AWAY, BUT I GOT THE SKINNY ONE!
OH, FOR...!
THAT'S MY GHOST!
JAKE, YOU IDIOT! ARE ALL YOUR BRAINS IN YOUR FEET? WHY DIDN'T YOU STAY BELOW?
BUT I THOUGHT...
WELL, AS LONG AS THE CAT'S OUT OF THE BAG, LET'S GET THE JOB OVER WITH! OPEN THE MAIN GATE, JAKE! STAND STILL, ALL OF YOU!
NOW, RUN THE MOUSE'S CAR DOWN ON THE TIDE FLATS!
WHAT'RE YOU GONNA DO?

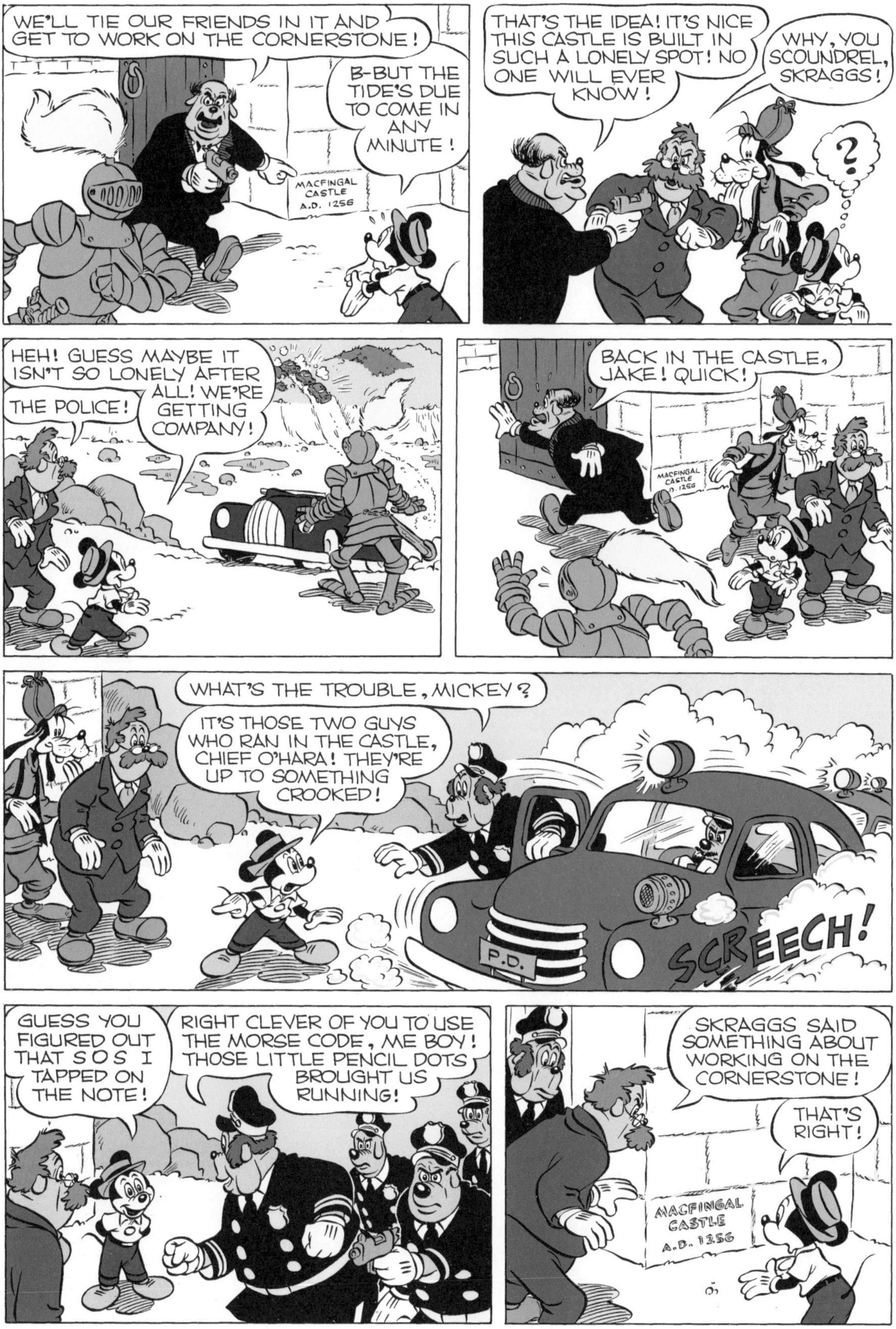
WE'LL TIE OUR FRIENDS IN IT AND GET TO WORK ON THE CORNERSTONE!
B-BUT THE TIDE'S DUE TO COME IN ANY MINUTE!
MACFINGAL CASTLE A.D. 1256
THAT'S THE IDEA! IT'S NICE THIS CASTLE IS BUILT IN SUCH A LONELY SPOT! NO ONE WILL EVER KNOW!
WHY, YOU SCOUNDREL, SKRAGGS!
?
HEH! GUESS MAYBE IT ISN'T SO LONELY AFTER ALL! WE'RE GETTING COMPANY!
THE POLICE!
BACK IN THE CASTLE, JAKE! QUICK!
MACFINGAL CASTLE A.D. 1256
WHAT'S THE TROUBLE, MICKEY?
IT'S THOSE TWO GUYS WHO RAN IN THE CASTLE, CHIEF O'HARA! THEY'RE UP TO SOMETHING CROOKED!
P.D.
SCREECH!
GUESS YOU FIGURED OUT THAT S O S I TAPPED ON THE NOTE!
RIGHT CLEVER OF YOU TO USE THE MORSE CODE, ME BOY! THOSE LITTLE PENCIL DOTS BROUGHT US RUNNING!
SKRAGGS SAID SOMETHING ABOUT WORKING ON THE CORNERSTONE!
THAT'S RIGHT!
MACFINGAL CASTLE A.D. 1256

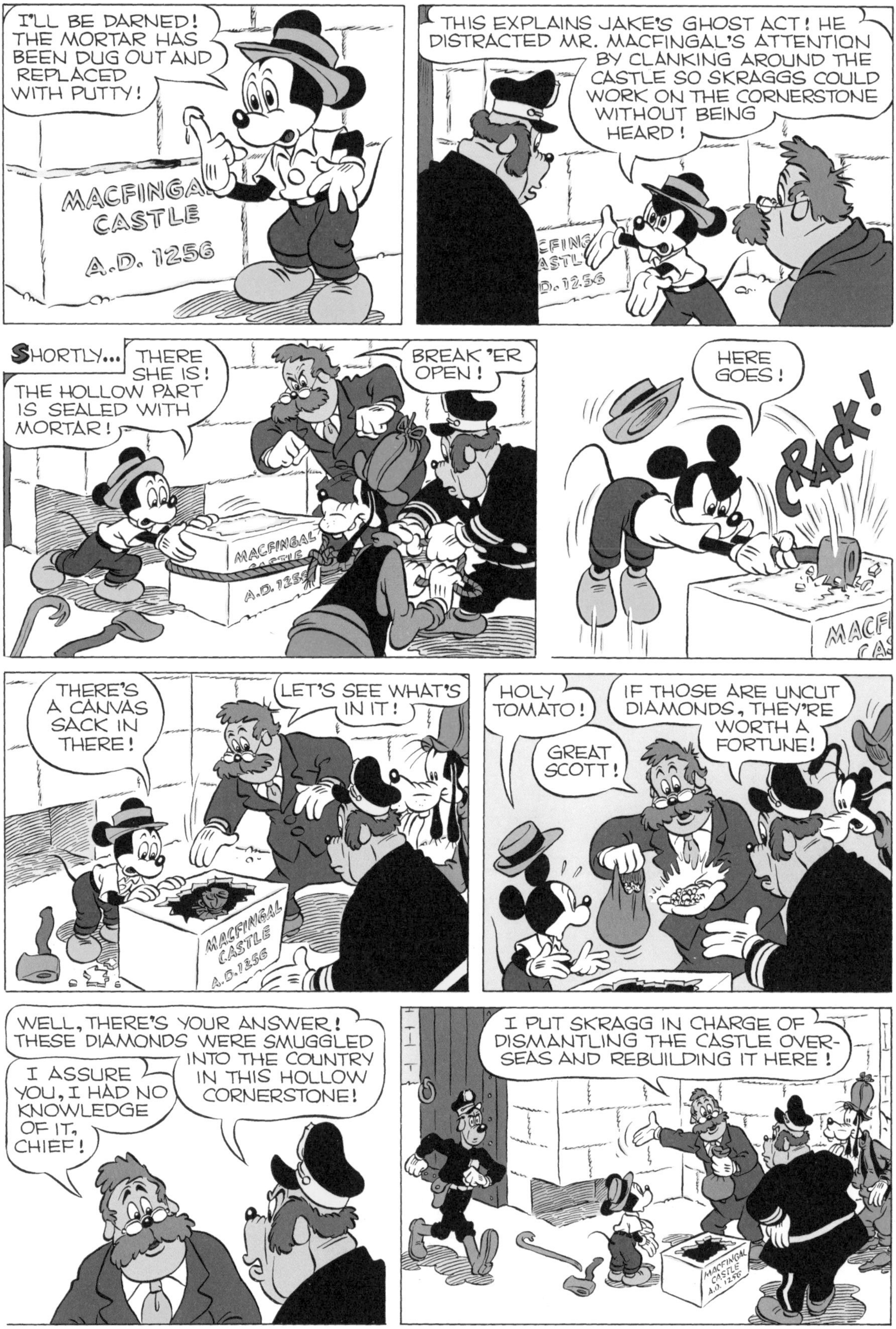
I'LL BE DARNED! THE MORTAR HAS BEEN DUG OUT AND REPLACED WITH PUTTY!
MACFINGAL CASTLE A.D. 1256
THIS EXPLAINS JAKE'S GHOST ACT! HE DISTRACTED MR. MACFINGAL'S ATTENTION BY CLANKING AROUND THE CASTLE SO SKRAGGS COULD WORK ON THE CORNERSTONE WITHOUT BEING HEARD!
SHORTLY...
THERE SHE IS! THE HOLLOW PART IS SEALED WITH MORTAR!
BREAK 'ER OPEN!
HERE GOES!
CRACK!
THERE'S A CANVAS SACK IN THERE!
LET'S SEE WHAT'S IN IT!
MACFINGAL CASTLE A.D. 1256
HOLY TOMATO!
GREAT SCOTT!
IF THOSE ARE UNCUT DIAMONDS, THEY'RE WORTH A FORTUNE!
WELL, THERE'S YOUR ANSWER! THESE DIAMONDS WERE SMUGGLED INTO THE COUNTRY IN THIS HOLLOW CORNERSTONE!
I ASSURE YOU, I HAD NO KNOWLEDGE OF IT, CHIEF!
I PUT SKRAGG IN CHARGE OF DISMANTLING THE CASTLE OVER-SEAS AND REBUILDING IT HERE!
MACFINGAL CASTLE A.D. 1256

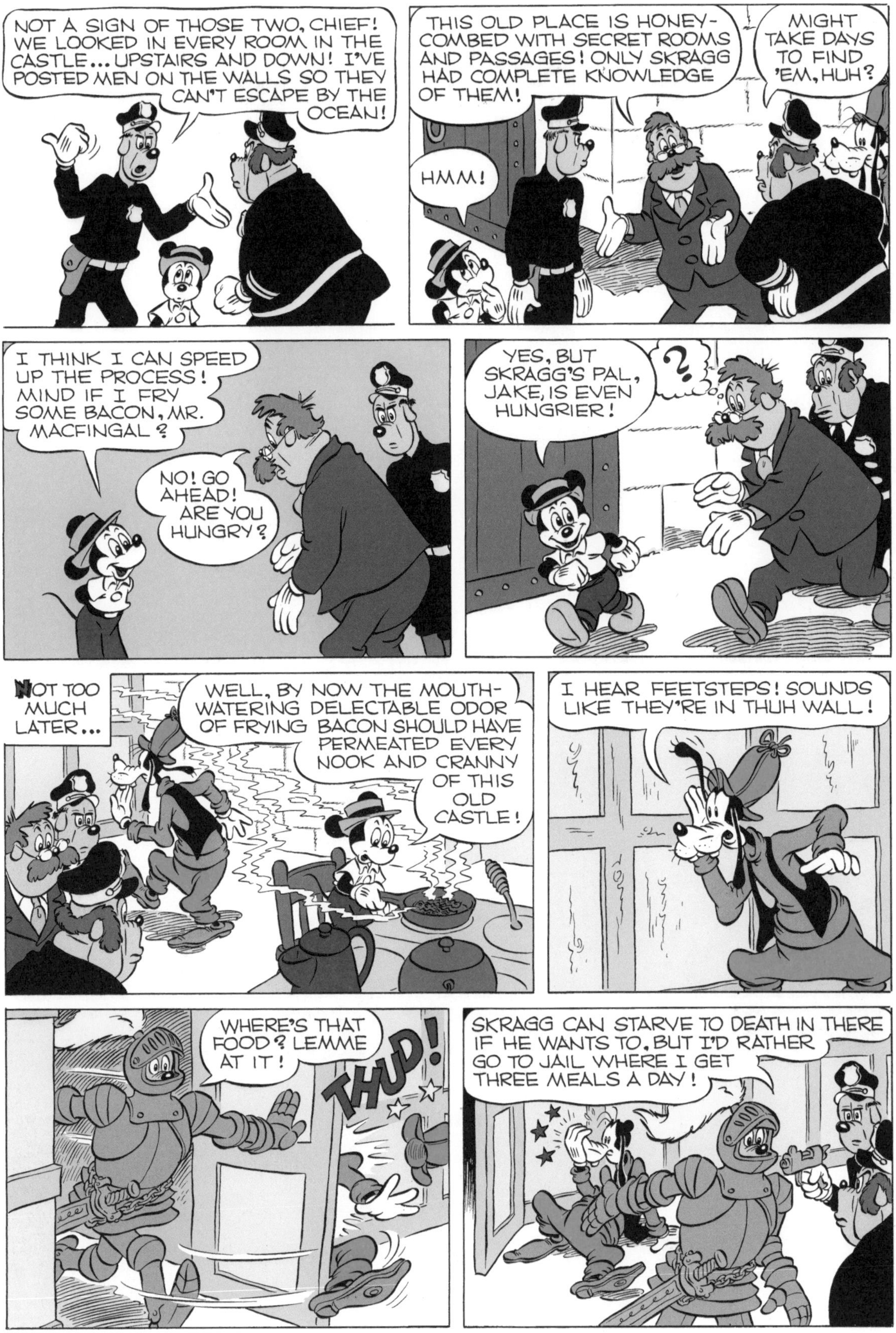
NOT A SIGN OF THOSE TWO, CHIEF! WE LOOKED IN EVERY ROOM IN THE CASTLE... UPSTAIRS AND DOWN! I'VE POSTED MEN ON THE WALLS SO THEY CAN'T ESCAPE BY THE OCEAN!
THIS OLD PLACE IS HONEY-COMBED WITH SECRET ROOMS AND PASSAGES! ONLY SKRAGG HAD COMPLETE KNOWLEDGE OF THEM!
MIGHT TAKE DAYS TO FIND 'EM, HUH?
HMM!
I THINK I CAN SPEED UP THE PROCESS! MIND IF I FRY SOME BACON, MR. MACFINGAL?
NO! GO AHEAD! ARE YOU HUNGRY?
YES, BUT SKRAGG'S PAL, JAKE, IS EVEN HUNGRIER!
?
NOT TOO MUCH LATER...
WELL, BY NOW THE MOUTH-WATERING DELECTABLE ODOR OF FRYING BACON SHOULD HAVE PERMEATED EVERY NOOK AND CRANNY OF THIS OLD CASTLE!
I HEAR FEETSTEPS! SOUNDS LIKE THEY'RE IN THUH WALL!
WHERE'S THAT FOOD? LEMME AT IT!
THUD!
SKRAGG CAN STARVE TO DEATH IN THERE IF HE WANTS TO, BUT I'D RATHER GO TO JAIL WHERE I GET THREE MEALS A DAY!

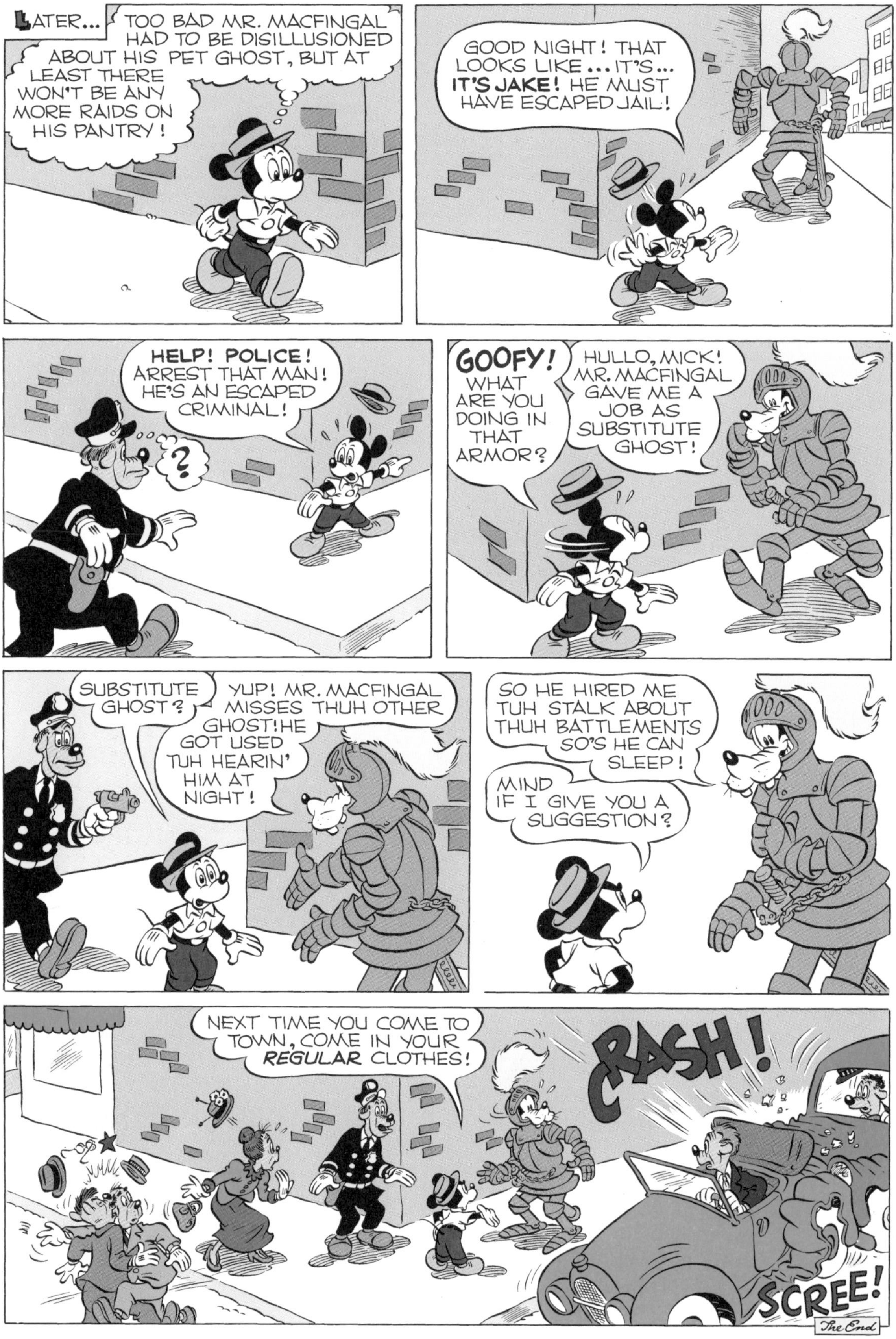
LATER...
TOO BAD MR. MACFINGAL HAD TO BE DISILLUSIONED ABOUT HIS PET GHOST, BUT AT LEAST THERE WON'T BE ANY MORE RAIDS ON HIS PANTRY!
GOOD NIGHT! THAT LOOKS LIKE... IT'S... IT'S JAKE! HE MUST HAVE ESCAPED JAIL!
HELP! POLICE! ARREST THAT MAN! HE'S AN ESCAPED CRIMINAL!
?
GOOFY! WHAT ARE YOU DOING IN THAT ARMOR?
HULLO, MICK! MR. MACFINGAL GAVE ME A JOB AS SUBSTITUTE GHOST!
SUBSTITUTE GHOST?
YUP! MR. MACFINGAL MISSES THUH OTHER GHOST! HE GOT USED TUH HEARIN' HIM AT NIGHT!
SO HE HIRED ME TUH STALK ABOUT THUH BATTLEMENTS SO'S HE CAN SLEEP!
MIND IF I GIVE YOU A SUGGESTION?
NEXT TIME YOU COME TO TOWN, COME IN YOUR REGULAR CLOTHES!
CRASH!
SCREE!
The End

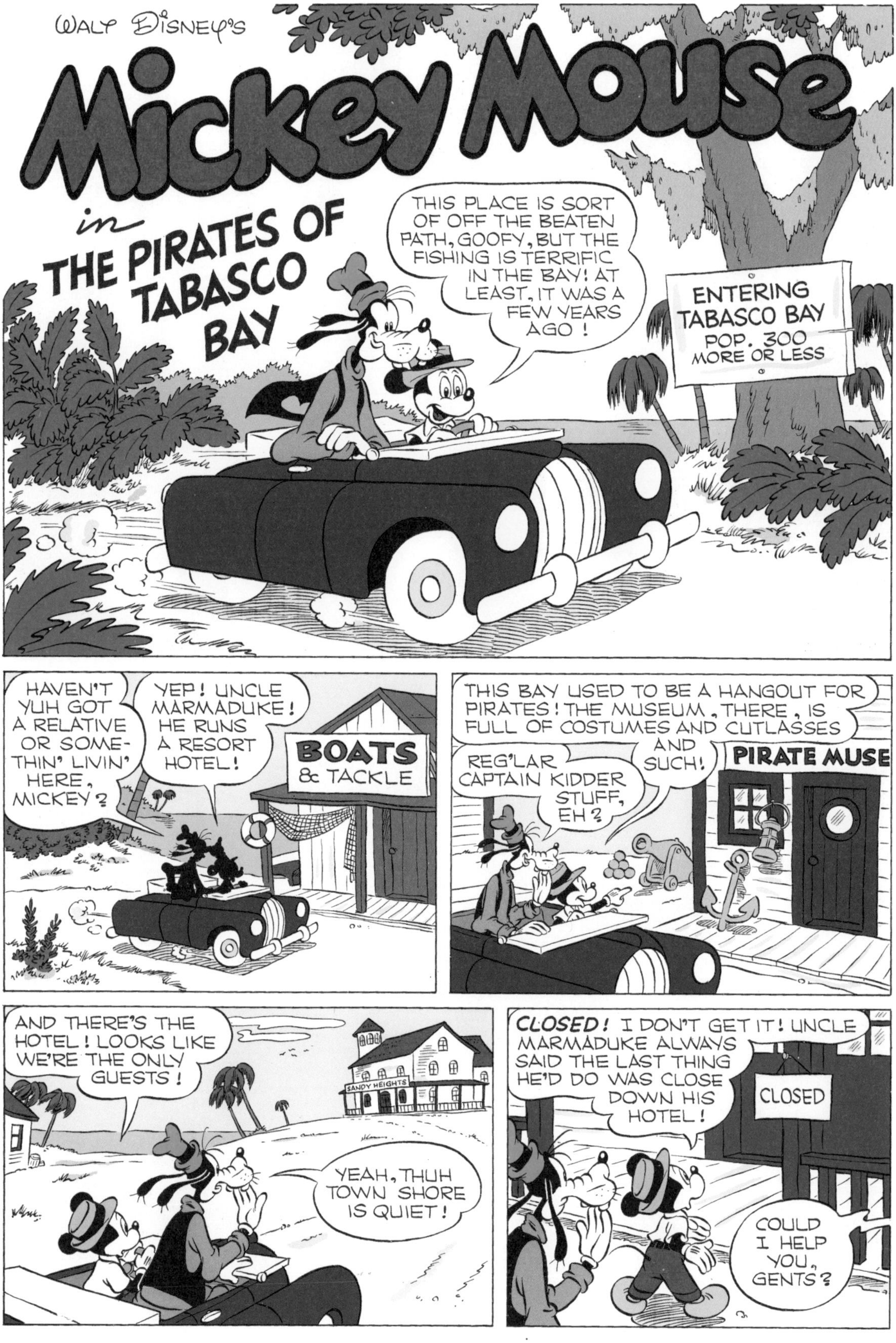

WALT DISNEY'S
Mickey Mouse
in THE PIRATES OF TABASCO BAY
THIS PLACE IS SORT OF OFF THE BEATEN PATH, GOOFY, BUT THE FISHING IS TERRIFIC IN THE BAY! AT LEAST, IT WAS A FEW YEARS AGO!
ENTERING TABASCO BAY POP. 300 MORE OR LESS
HAVEN'T YUH GOT A RELATIVE OR SOME-THIN' LIVIN' HERE, MICKEY?
YEP! UNCLE MARMADUKE! HE RUNS A RESORT HOTEL!
BOATS & TACKLE
THIS BAY USED TO BE A HANGOUT FOR PIRATES! THE MUSEUM, THERE, IS FULL OF COSTUMES AND CUTLASSES AND SUCH!
REG'LAR CAPTAIN KIDDER STUFF, EH?
PIRATE MUSE
AND THERE'S THE HOTEL! LOOKS LIKE WE'RE THE ONLY GUESTS!
SANDY HEIGHTS
YEAH, THUH TOWN SHORE IS QUIET!
CLOSED! I DON'T GET IT! UNCLE MARMADUKE ALWAYS SAID THE LAST THING HE'D DO WAS CLOSE DOWN HIS HOTEL!
CLOSED
COULD I HELP YOU, GENTS?

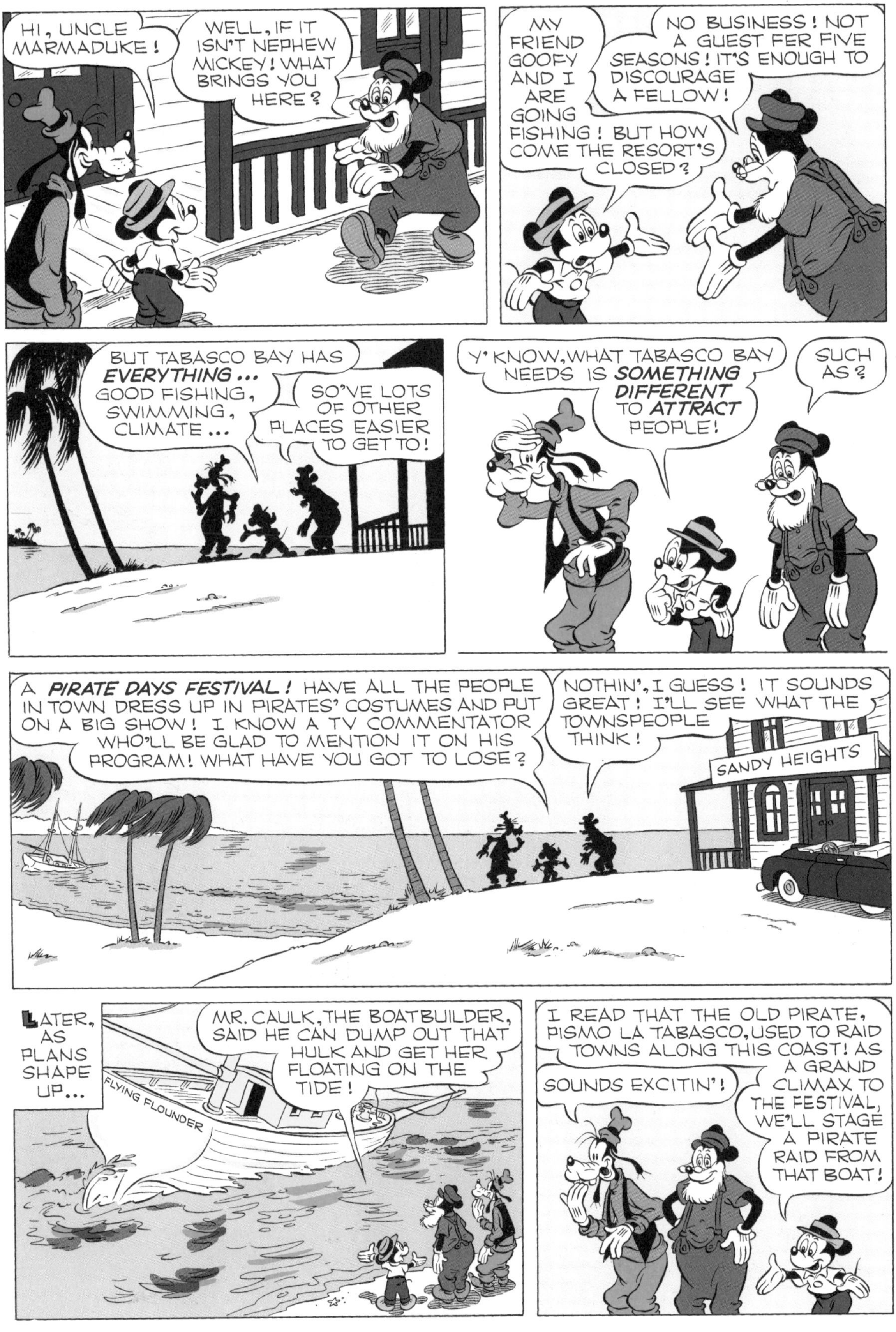
HI, UNCLE MARMADUKE!
WELL, IF IT ISN'T NEPHEW MICKEY! WHAT BRINGS YOU HERE?
MY FRIEND GOOFY AND I ARE GOING FISHING! BUT HOW COME THE RESORT'S CLOSED?
NO BUSINESS! NOT A GUEST FER FIVE SEASONS! IT'S ENOUGH TO DISCOURAGE A FELLOW!
BUT TABASCO BAY HAS EVERYTHING... GOOD FISHING, SWIMMING, CLIMATE...
SO'VE LOTS OF OTHER PLACES EASIER TO GET TO!
Y'KNOW, WHAT TABASCO BAY NEEDS IS SOMETHING DIFFERENT TO ATTRACT PEOPLE!
SUCH AS?
A PIRATE DAYS FESTIVAL! HAVE ALL THE PEOPLE IN TOWN DRESS UP IN PIRATES' COSTUMES AND PUT ON A BIG SHOW! I KNOW A TV COMMENTATOR WHO'LL BE GLAD TO MENTION IT ON HIS PROGRAM! WHAT HAVE YOU GOT TO LOSE?
NOTHIN', I GUESS! IT SOUNDS GREAT! I'LL SEE WHAT THE TOWNSPEOPLE THINK!
SANDY HEIGHTS
LATER, AS PLANS SHAPE UP...
MR. CAULK, THE BOATBUILDER, SAID HE CAN DUMP OUT THAT HULK AND GET HER FLOATING ON THE TIDE!
FLYING FLOUNDER
I READ THAT THE OLD PIRATE, PISMO LA TABASCO, USED TO RAID TOWNS ALONG THIS COAST! AS A GRAND CLIMAX TO THE FESTIVAL, WE'LL STAGE A PIRATE RAID FROM THAT BOAT!
SOUNDS EXCITIN'!

COSTUMES ARE FITTED...

I FOUND ME A COSTUME, MICK! YO HO HO AND A BOTTLE O' BILGEWATER! DO I LOOK REAL FIERCE?

YOU SURE DO!

WELL, KIND OF...

I'LL NEED ONE TAILORED TO MY SIZE! GUESS THEY DIDN'T HAVE LITTLE PIRATES IN THOSE DAYS!

PIRATE CHEST 1690

THE NEWS GETS AROUND...ON LAND...

FOR YOU PEOPLE WHO ARE LOOKING FOR A REAL OFFBEAT VACATION, TRY THE PIRATE DAYS FESTIVAL AT TABASCO BAY!

WOW TV

AND ON SEA ...

WHAT ARE YOU LISTENIN' TO THAT JABBER-MOUTH FOR, PETE?

SHUT UP! IT'S THE ONLY STATION WE GET HERE!

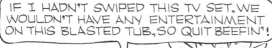

IF I HADN'T SWIPED THIS TV SET, WE WOULDN'T HAVE ANY ENTERTAINMENT ON THIS BLASTED TUB, SO QUIT BEEFIN'!

YES, SIR! THE SPANISH MAIN WILL COME TO LIFE AGAIN AT TABASCO BAY!

TABASCO BAY? THAT ISN'T FAR FROM HERE, IS IT?

TO CLIMAX PIRATE DAYS, A RAID WILL BE STAGED ON THE TOWN FROM A REAL SHIP! GREAT IDEA, EH FOLKS?

QUIET!

S'MATTER, PETE? WHY'D YOU TURN HIM OFF?

I'VE HEARD ENOUGH! SONNY BOY JUST GAVE ME A GREAT IDEA!

CLIC

YOU GUYS'VE BEEN ACHIN' FOR SOME EXCITEMENT! WELL, I'VE JUST DREAMED UP A NICE, SAFE WAY TO PICK UP SOME SPARE CASH!

TRAMP OF THE TROPICS

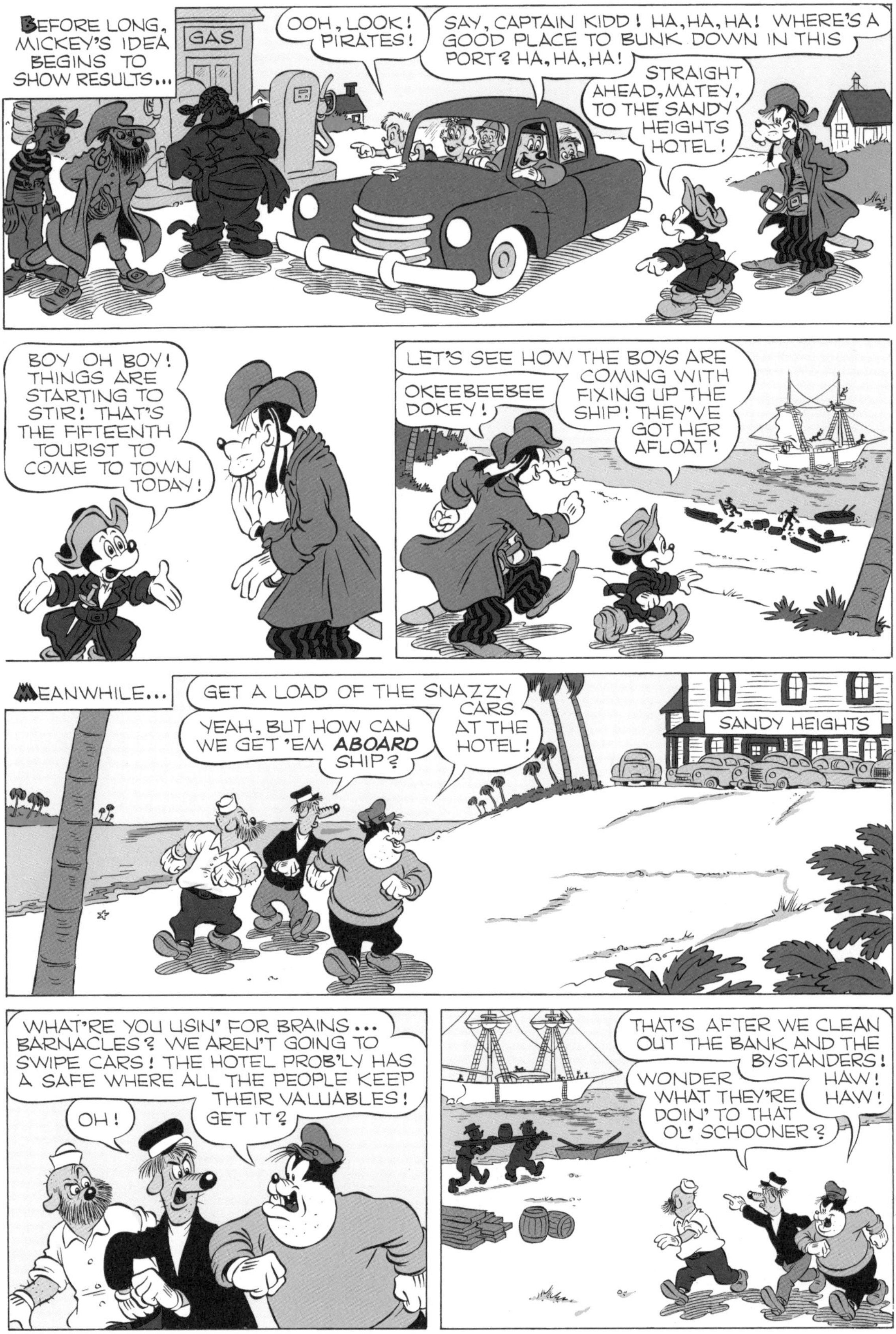
BEFORE LONG, MICKEY'S IDEA BEGINS TO SHOW RESULTS...
GAS
OOH, LOOK! PIRATES!
SAY, CAPTAIN KIDD! HA, HA, HA! WHERE'S A GOOD PLACE TO BUNK DOWN IN THIS PORT? HA, HA, HA!
STRAIGHT AHEAD, MATEY, TO THE SANDY HEIGHTS HOTEL!
BOY OH BOY! THINGS ARE STARTING TO STIR! THAT'S THE FIFTEENTH TOURIST TO COME TO TOWN TODAY!
LET'S SEE HOW THE BOYS ARE COMING WITH FIXING UP THE SHIP! THEY'VE GOT HER AFLOAT!
OKEEBEEBEE DOKEY!
MEANWHILE...
GET A LOAD OF THE SNAZZY CARS AT THE HOTEL!
YEAH, BUT HOW CAN WE GET 'EM ABOARD SHIP?
SANDY HEIGHTS
WHAT'RE YOU USIN' FOR BRAINS... BARNACLES? WE AREN'T GOING TO SWIPE CARS! THE HOTEL PROB'LY HAS A SAFE WHERE ALL THE PEOPLE KEEP THEIR VALUABLES! GET IT?
OH!
THAT'S AFTER WE CLEAN OUT THE BANK AND THE BYSTANDERS! HAW! HAW!
WONDER WHAT THEY'RE DOIN' TO THAT OL' SCHOONER?

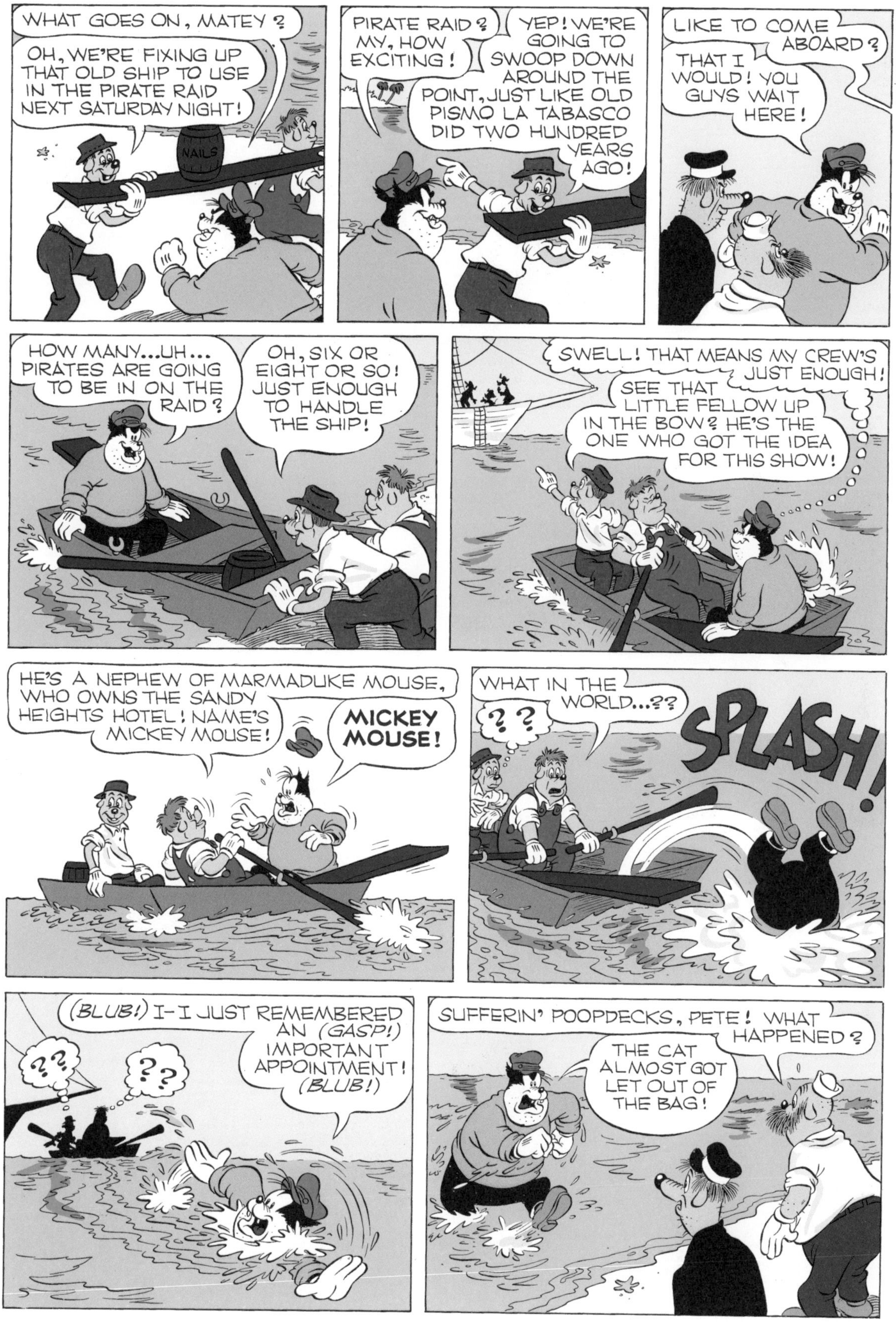
WHAT GOES ON, MATEY ?
OH, WE'RE FIXING UP THAT OLD SHIP TO USE IN THE PIRATE RAID NEXT SATURDAY NIGHT!
NAILS
PIRATE RAID ? MY, HOW EXCITING !
YEP! WE'RE GOING TO SWOOP DOWN AROUND THE POINT, JUST LIKE OLD PISMO LA TABASCO DID TWO HUNDRED YEARS AGO!
LIKE TO COME ABOARD ?
THAT I WOULD! YOU GUYS WAIT HERE!
HOW MANY...UH... PIRATES ARE GOING TO BE IN ON THE RAID ?
OH, SIX OR EIGHT OR SO! JUST ENOUGH TO HANDLE THE SHIP!
SWELL! THAT MEANS MY CREW'S JUST ENOUGH!
SEE THAT LITTLE FELLOW UP IN THE BOW? HE'S THE ONE WHO GOT THE IDEA FOR THIS SHOW!
HE'S A NEPHEW OF MARMADUKE MOUSE, WHO OWNS THE SANDY HEIGHTS HOTEL! NAME'S MICKEY MOUSE!
MICKEY MOUSE!
WHAT IN THE WORLD...??
??
SPLASH!
(BLUB!) I-I JUST REMEMBERED AN (GASP!) IMPORTANT APPOINTMENT! (BLUB!)
??
??
SUFFERIN' POOPDECKS, PETE! WHAT HAPPENED ?
THE CAT ALMOST GOT LET OUT OF THE BAG!

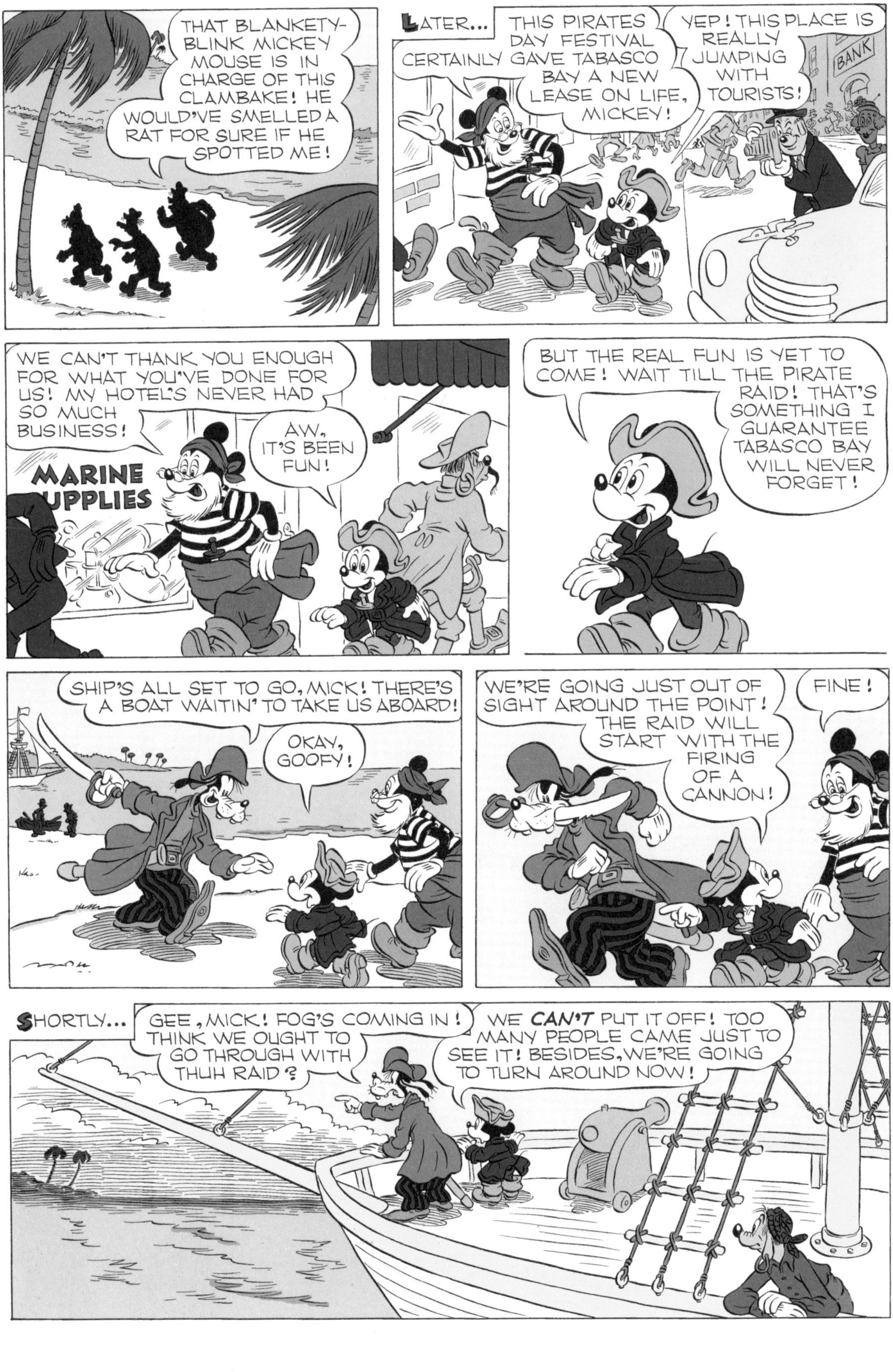
THAT BLANKETY-BLINK MICKEY MOUSE IS IN CHARGE OF THIS CLAMBAKE! HE WOULD'VE SMELLED A RAT FOR SURE IF HE SPOTTED ME!
LATER...
THIS PIRATES DAY FESTIVAL CERTAINLY GAVE TABASCO BAY A NEW LEASE ON LIFE, MICKEY!
YEP! THIS PLACE IS REALLY JUMPING WITH TOURISTS!
BANK
WE CAN'T THANK YOU ENOUGH FOR WHAT YOU'VE DONE FOR US! MY HOTEL'S NEVER HAD SO MUCH BUSINESS!
AW, IT'S BEEN FUN!
MARINE
UPPLIES
BUT THE REAL FUN IS YET TO COME! WAIT TILL THE PIRATE RAID! THAT'S SOMETHING I GUARANTEE TABASCO BAY WILL NEVER FORGET!
SHIP'S ALL SET TO GO, MICK! THERE'S A BOAT WAITIN' TO TAKE US ABOARD!
OKAY, GOOFY!
WE'RE GOING JUST OUT OF SIGHT AROUND THE POINT! THE RAID WILL START WITH THE FIRING OF A CANNON!
FINE!
SHORTLY...
GEE, MICK! FOG'S COMING IN! THINK WE OUGHT TO GO THROUGH WITH THUH RAID?
WE CAN'T PUT IT OFF! TOO MANY PEOPLE CAME JUST TO SEE IT! BESIDES, WE'RE GOING TO TURN AROUND NOW!

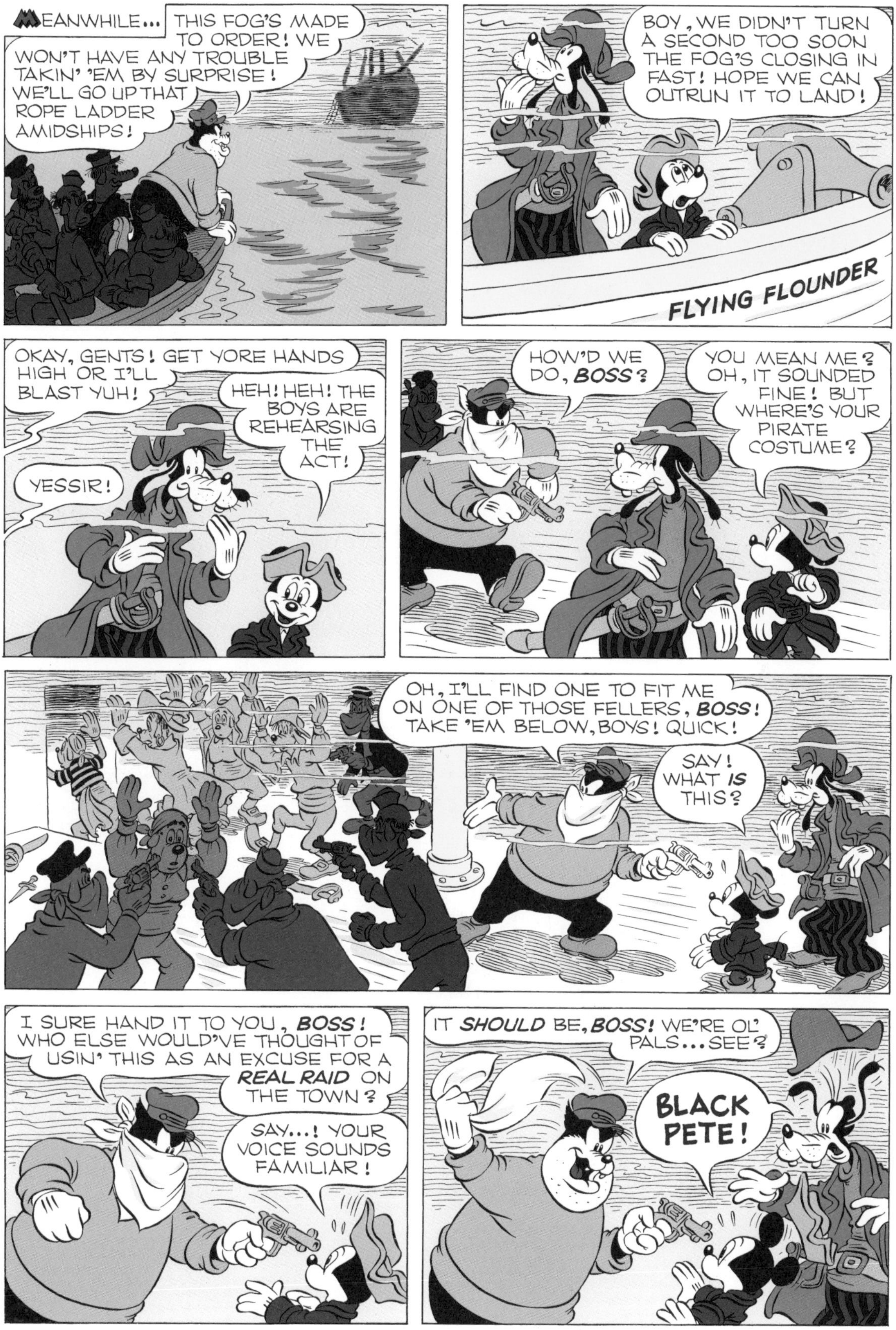
MEANWHILE...
THIS FOG'S MADE TO ORDER! WE WON'T HAVE ANY TROUBLE TAKIN' 'EM BY SURPRISE! WE'LL GO UP THAT ROPE LADDER AMIDSHIPS!
BOY, WE DIDN'T TURN A SECOND TOO SOON THE FOG'S CLOSING IN FAST! HOPE WE CAN OUTRUN IT TO LAND!
FLYING FLOUNDER
OKAY, GENTS! GET YORE HANDS HIGH OR I'LL BLAST YUH!
HEH! HEH! THE BOYS ARE REHEARSING THE ACT!
YESSIR!
HOW'D WE DO, BOSS?
YOU MEAN ME? OH, IT SOUNDED FINE! BUT WHERE'S YOUR PIRATE COSTUME?
OH, I'LL FIND ONE TO FIT ME ON ONE OF THOSE FELLERS, BOSS! TAKE 'EM BELOW, BOYS! QUICK!
SAY! WHAT IS THIS?
I SURE HAND IT TO YOU, BOSS! WHO ELSE WOULD'VE THOUGHT OF USIN' THIS AS AN EXCUSE FOR A REAL RAID ON THE TOWN?
SAY...! YOUR VOICE SOUNDS FAMILIAR!
IT SHOULD BE, BOSS! WE'RE OL' PALS...SEE?
BLACK PETE!

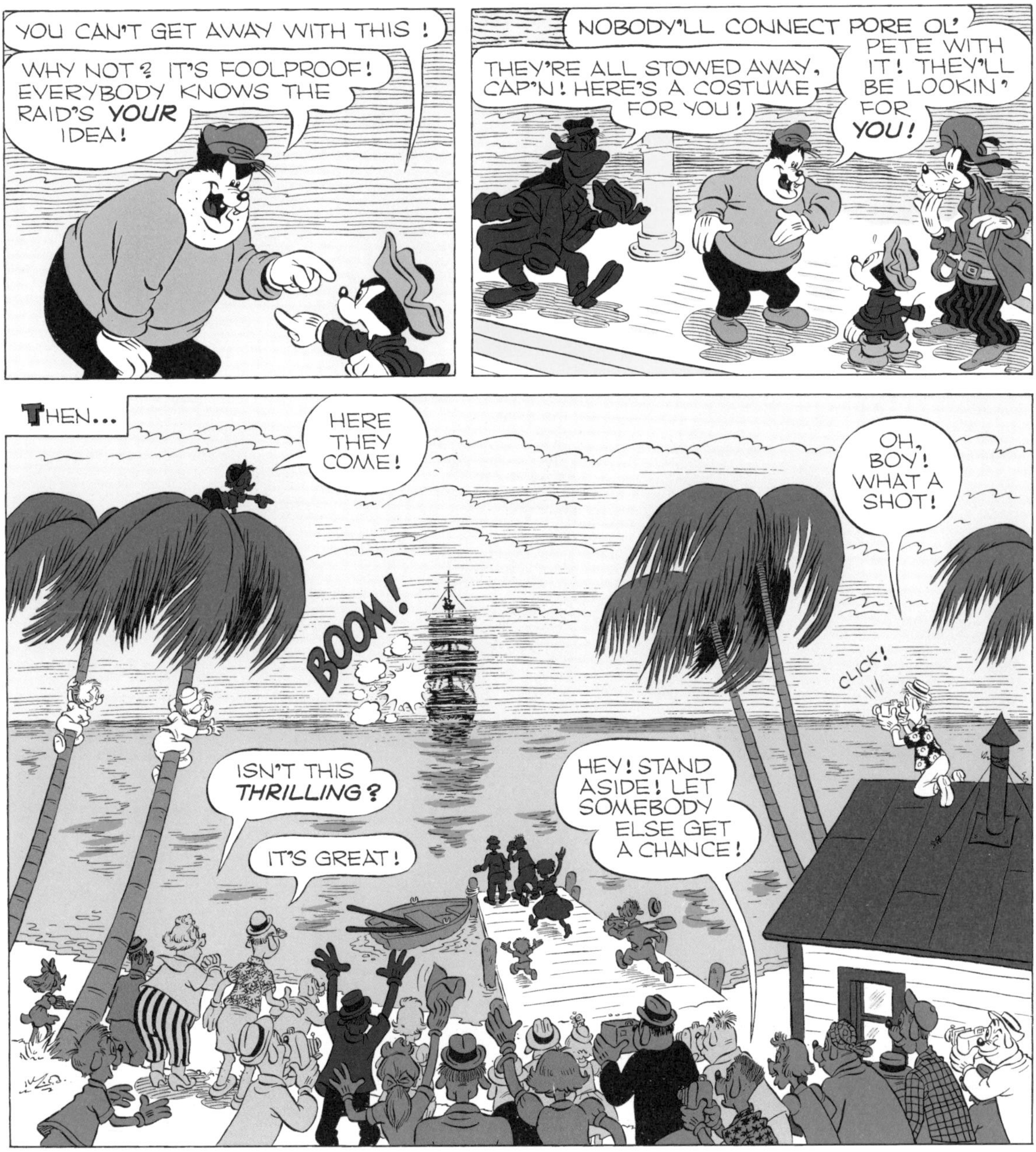
YOU CAN'T GET AWAY WITH THIS!
WHY NOT? IT'S FOOLPROOF! EVERYBODY KNOWS THE RAID'S **YOUR** IDEA!
THEY'RE ALL STOWED AWAY, CAP'N! HERE'S A COSTUME FOR YOU!
NOBODY'LL CONNECT PORE OL' PETE WITH IT! THEY'LL BE LOOKIN' FOR **YOU!**
THEN...
HERE THEY COME!
BOOM!
OH, BOY! WHAT A SHOT!
CLICK!
ISN'T THIS *THRILLING?*
IT'S GREAT!
HEY! STAND ASIDE! LET SOMEBODY ELSE GET A CHANCE!

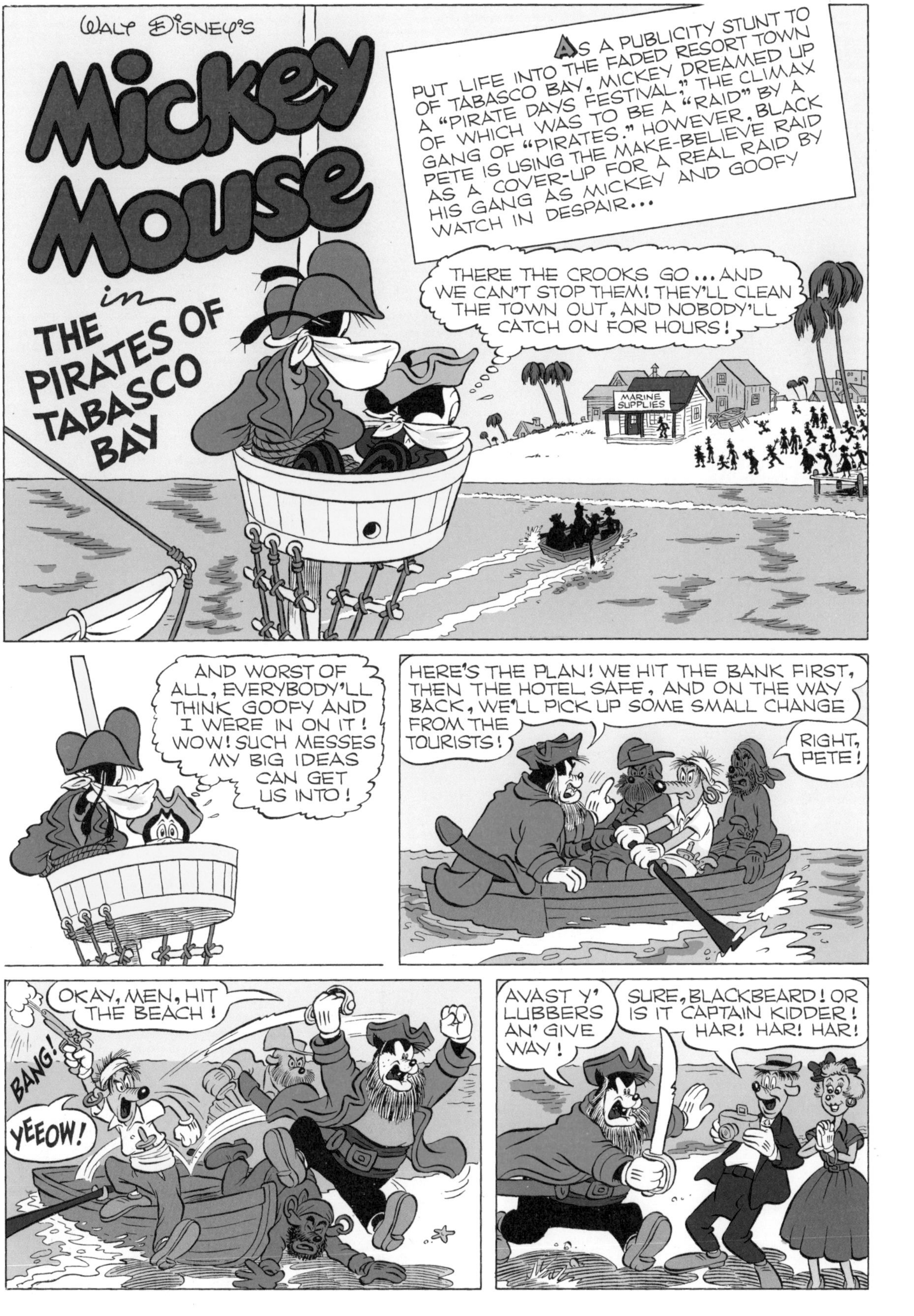
WALT DISNEY'S
Mickey Mouse
in
THE PIRATES OF TABASCO BAY
AS A PUBLICITY STUNT TO PUT LIFE INTO THE FADED RESORT TOWN OF TABASCO BAY, MICKEY DREAMED UP A "PIRATE DAYS FESTIVAL," THE CLIMAX OF WHICH WAS TO BE A "RAID" BY A GANG OF "PIRATES." HOWEVER, BLACK PETE IS USING THE MAKE-BELIEVE RAID AS A COVER-UP FOR A REAL RAID BY HIS GANG AS MICKEY AND GOOFY WATCH IN DESPAIR...
THERE THE CROOKS GO ... AND WE CAN'T STOP THEM! THEY'LL CLEAN THE TOWN OUT, AND NOBODY'LL CATCH ON FOR HOURS!
MARINE SUPPLIES
AND WORST OF ALL, EVERYBODY'LL THINK GOOFY AND I WERE IN ON IT! WOW! SUCH MESSES MY BIG IDEAS CAN GET US INTO!
HERE'S THE PLAN! WE HIT THE BANK FIRST, THEN THE HOTEL SAFE, AND ON THE WAY BACK, WE'LL PICK UP SOME SMALL CHANGE FROM THE TOURISTS!
RIGHT, PETE!
OKAY, MEN, HIT THE BEACH!
BANG!
YEEOW!
AVAST Y' LUBBERS AN' GIVE WAY!
SURE, BLACKBEARD! OR IS IT CAPTAIN KIDDER! HAR! HAR! HAR!

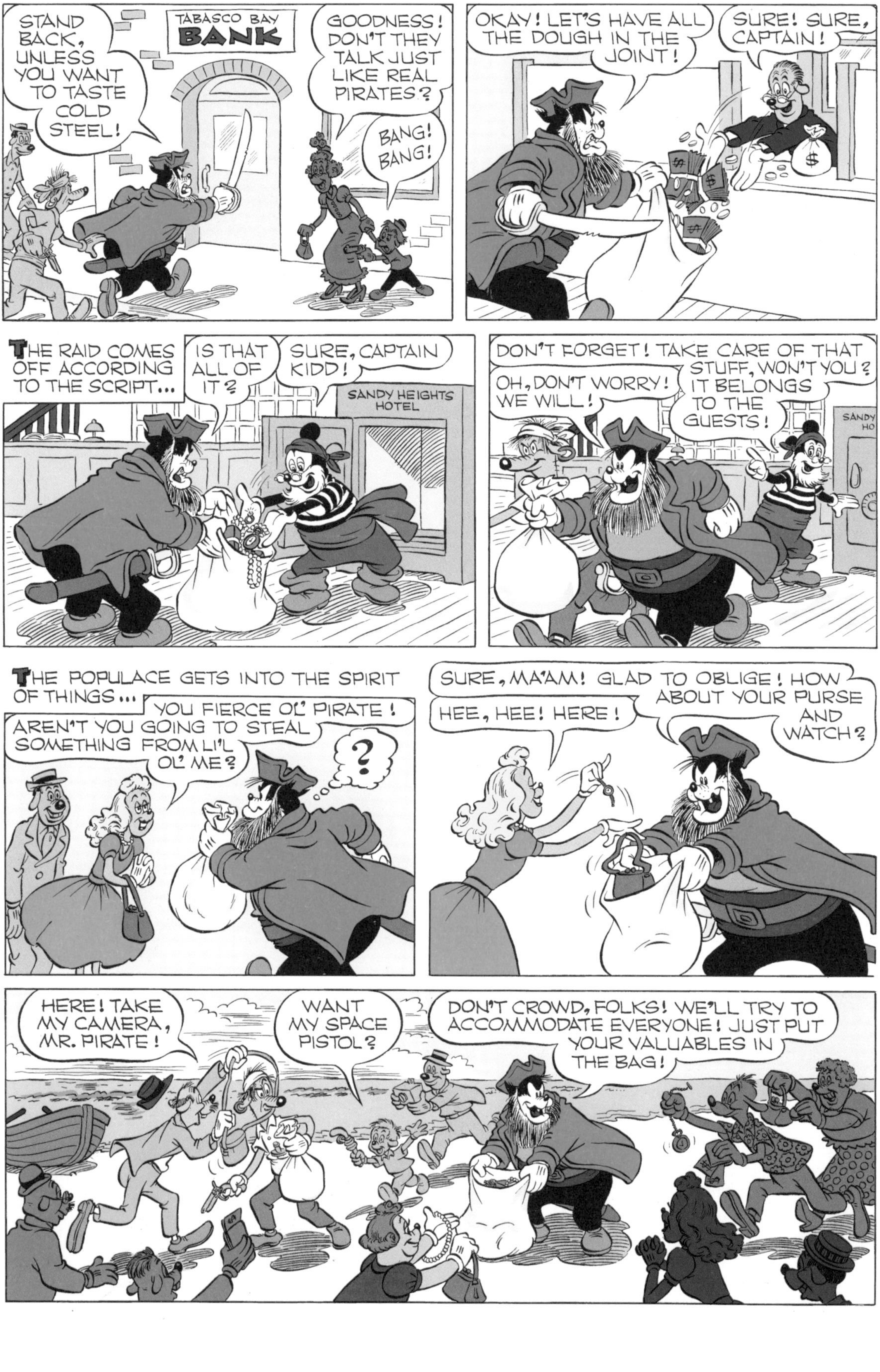

TABASCO BAY BANK
STAND BACK, UNLESS YOU WANT TO TASTE COLD STEEL!
GOODNESS! DON'T THEY TALK JUST LIKE REAL PIRATES?
BANG! BANG!
OKAY! LET'S HAVE ALL THE DOUGH IN THE JOINT!
SURE! SURE, CAPTAIN!
THE RAID COMES OFF ACCORDING TO THE SCRIPT...
IS THAT ALL OF IT?
SURE, CAPTAIN KIDD!
SANDY HEIGHTS HOTEL
DON'T FORGET! TAKE CARE OF THAT STUFF, WON'T YOU? IT BELONGS TO THE GUESTS!
OH, DON'T WORRY! WE WILL!
THE POPULACE GETS INTO THE SPIRIT OF THINGS...
YOU FIERCE OL' PIRATE! AREN'T YOU GOING TO STEAL SOMETHING FROM LI'L OL' ME?
?
HEE, HEE! HERE!
SURE, MA'AM! GLAD TO OBLIGE! HOW ABOUT YOUR PURSE AND WATCH?
HERE! TAKE MY CAMERA, MR. PIRATE!
WANT MY SPACE PISTOL?
DON'T CROWD, FOLKS! WE'LL TRY TO ACCOMMODATE EVERYONE! JUST PUT YOUR VALUABLES IN THE BAG!

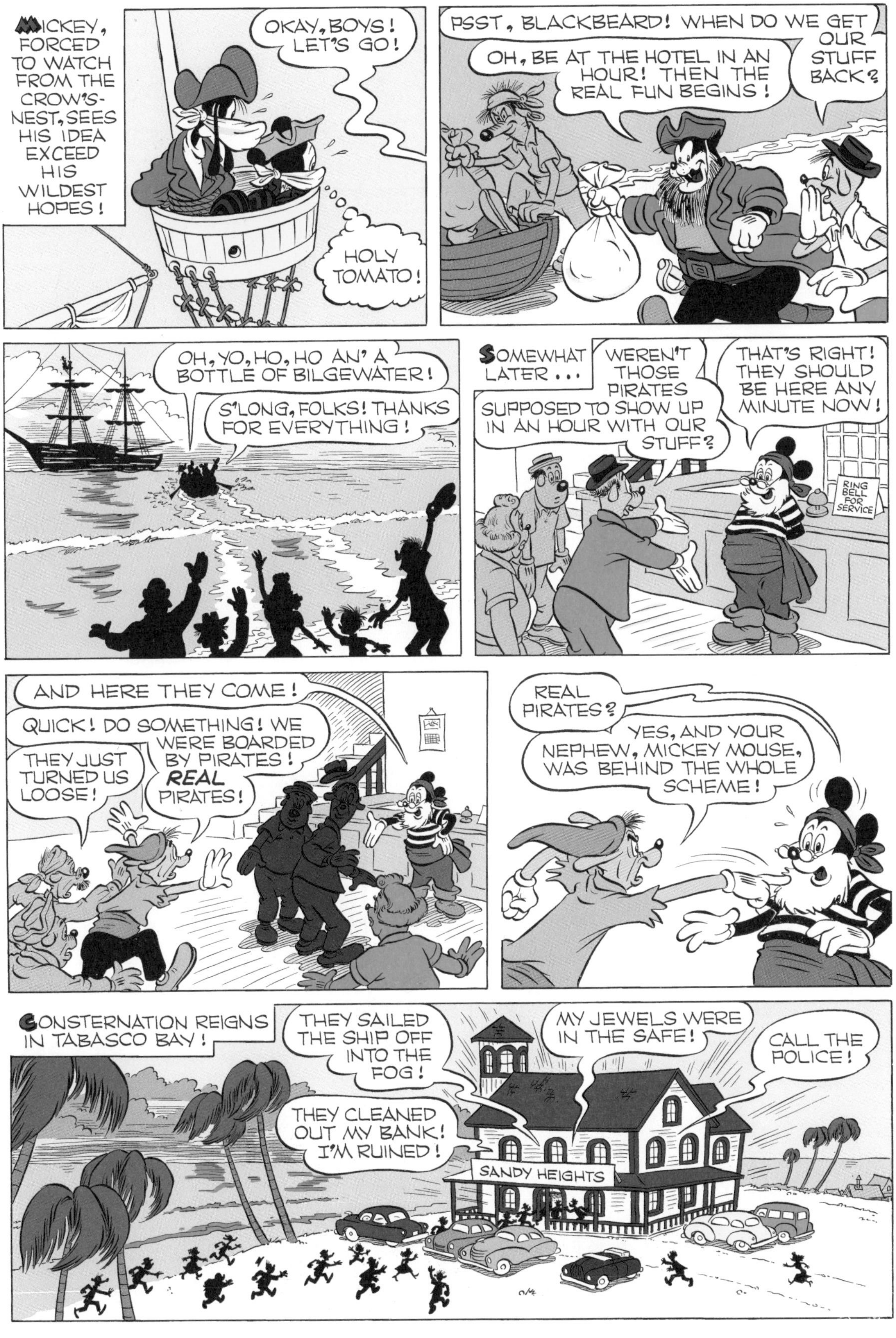
MICKEY, FORCED TO WATCH FROM THE CROW'S-NEST, SEES HIS IDEA EXCEED HIS WILDEST HOPES!
OKAY, BOYS! LET'S GO!
HOLY TOMATO!
PSST, BLACKBEARD! WHEN DO WE GET OUR STUFF BACK?
OH, BE AT THE HOTEL IN AN HOUR! THEN THE REAL FUN BEGINS!
OH, YO, HO, HO AN' A BOTTLE OF BILGEWATER!
S'LONG, FOLKS! THANKS FOR EVERYTHING!
SOMEWHAT LATER...
WEREN'T THOSE PIRATES SUPPOSED TO SHOW UP IN AN HOUR WITH OUR STUFF?
THAT'S RIGHT! THEY SHOULD BE HERE ANY MINUTE NOW!
RING BELL FOR SERVICE
AND HERE THEY COME!
QUICK! DO SOMETHING! WE WERE BOARDED BY PIRATES! REAL PIRATES!
THEY JUST TURNED US LOOSE!
REAL PIRATES?
YES, AND YOUR NEPHEW, MICKEY MOUSE, WAS BEHIND THE WHOLE SCHEME!
CONSTERNATION REIGNS IN TABASCO BAY!
THEY SAILED THE SHIP OFF INTO THE FOG!
MY JEWELS WERE IN THE SAFE!
CALL THE POLICE!
THEY CLEANED OUT MY BANK! I'M RUINED!
SANDY HEIGHTS

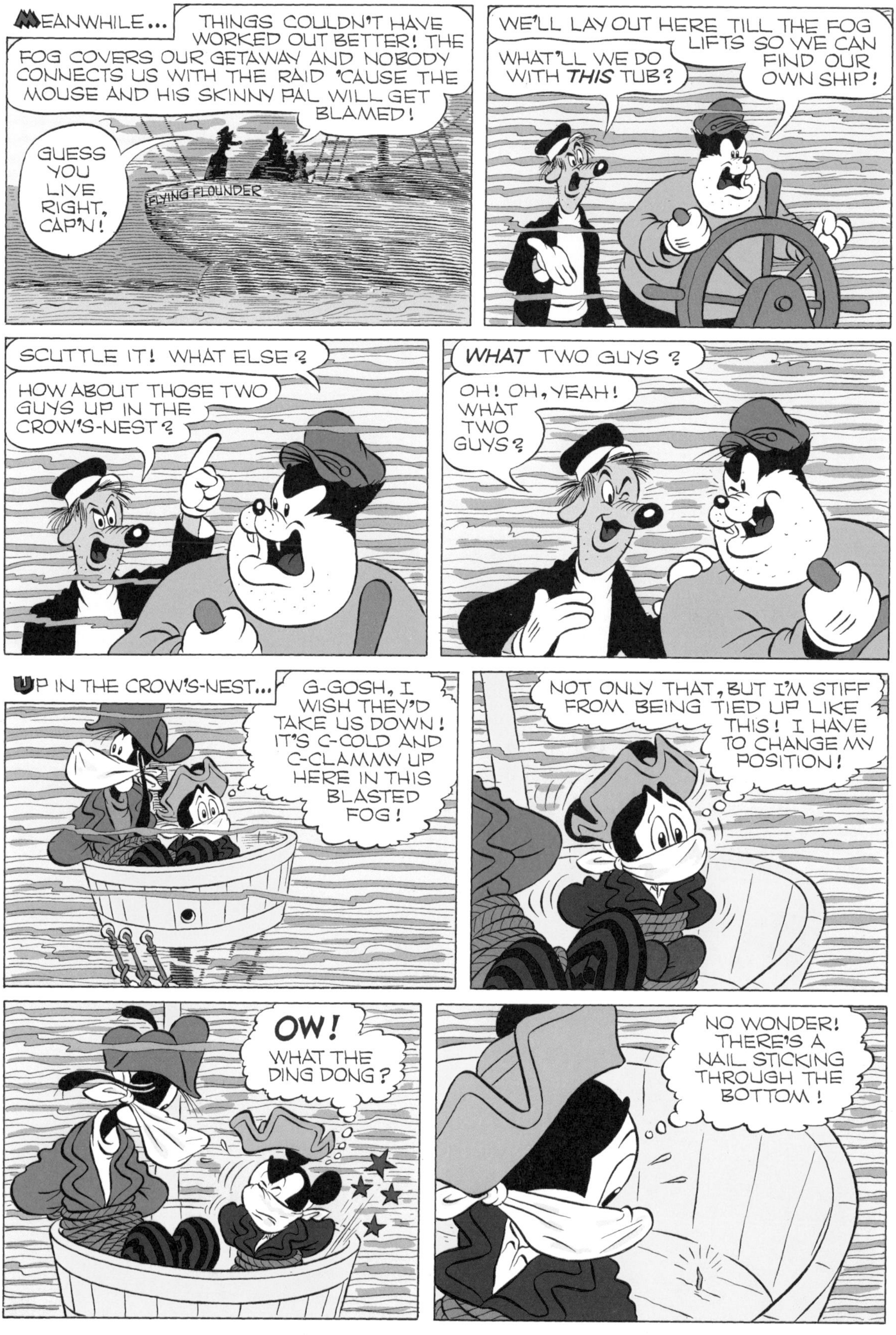
MEANWHILE...
THINGS COULDN'T HAVE WORKED OUT BETTER! THE FOG COVERS OUR GETAWAY AND NOBODY CONNECTS US WITH THE RAID 'CAUSE THE MOUSE AND HIS SKINNY PAL WILL GET BLAMED!
GUESS YOU LIVE RIGHT, CAP'N!
FLYING FLOUNDER
WE'LL LAY OUT HERE TILL THE FOG LIFTS SO WE CAN FIND OUR OWN SHIP!
WHAT'LL WE DO WITH **THIS** TUB?
SCUTTLE IT! WHAT ELSE?
HOW ABOUT THOSE TWO GUYS UP IN THE CROW'S-NEST?
WHAT TWO GUYS?
OH! OH, YEAH! WHAT TWO GUYS?
UP IN THE CROW'S-NEST...
G-GOSH, I WISH THEY'D TAKE US DOWN! IT'S C-COLD AND C-CLAMMY UP HERE IN THIS BLASTED FOG!
NOT ONLY THAT, BUT I'M STIFF FROM BEING TIED UP LIKE THIS! I HAVE TO CHANGE MY POSITION!
OW! WHAT THE DING DONG?
NO WONDER! THERE'S A NAIL STICKING THROUGH THE BOTTOM!

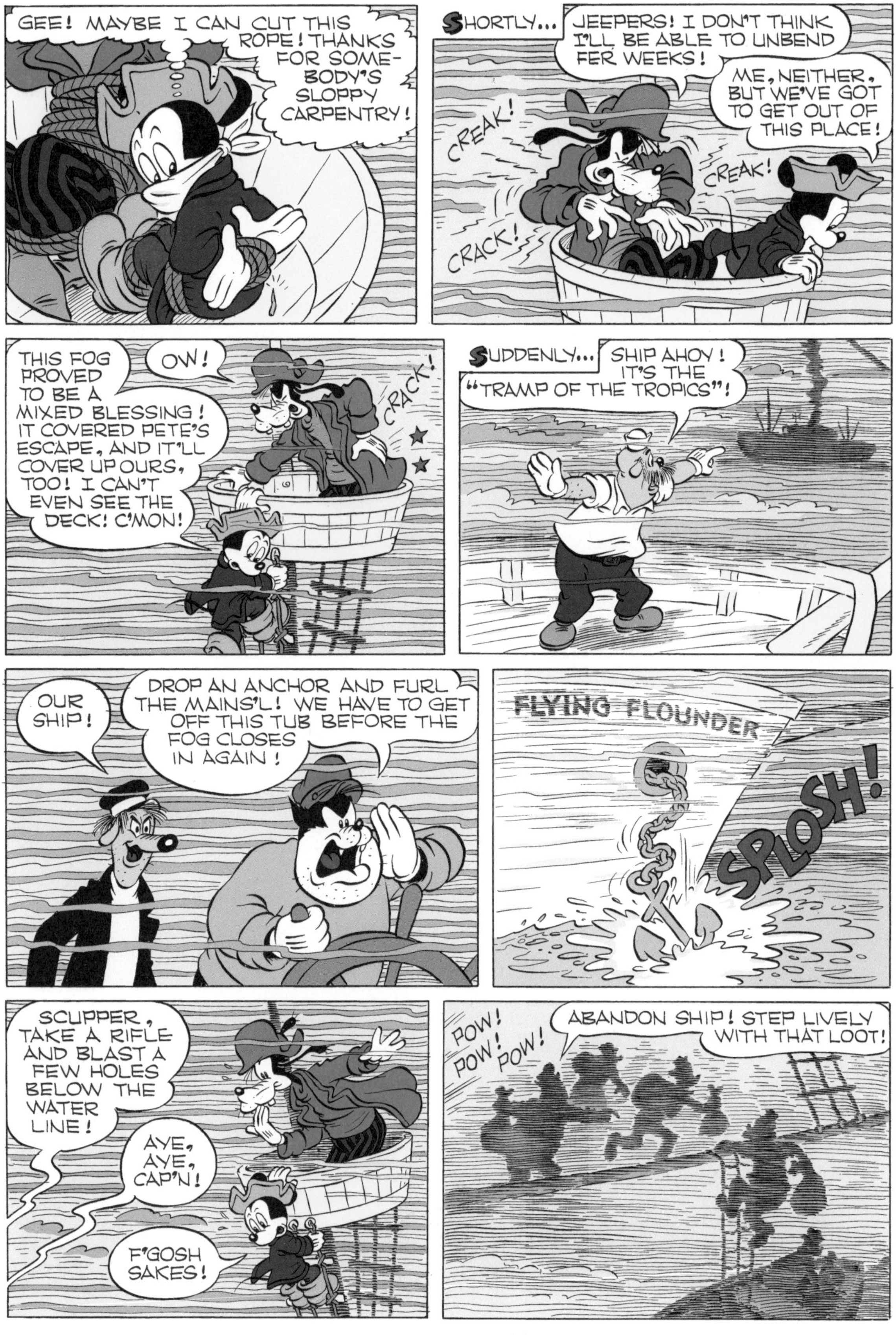
GEE! MAYBE I CAN CUT THIS ROPE! THANKS FOR SOMEBODY'S SLOPPY CARPENTRY!
SHORTLY...
JEEPERS! I DON'T THINK I'LL BE ABLE TO UNBEND FER WEEKS!
ME, NEITHER. BUT WE'VE GOT TO GET OUT OF THIS PLACE!
CREAK!
CRACK!
CREAK!
THIS FOG PROVED TO BE A MIXED BLESSING! IT COVERED PETE'S ESCAPE, AND IT'LL COVER UP OURS, TOO! I CAN'T EVEN SEE THE DECK! C'MON!
OW!
CRACK!
SUDDENLY...
SHIP AHOY! IT'S THE "TRAMP OF THE TROPICS"!
OUR SHIP!
DROP AN ANCHOR AND FURL THE MAINS'L! WE HAVE TO GET OFF THIS TUB BEFORE THE FOG CLOSES IN AGAIN!
FLYING FLOUNDER
SPLOSH!
SCUPPER, TAKE A RIFLE AND BLAST A FEW HOLES BELOW THE WATER LINE!
AYE, AYE, CAP'N!
F'GOSH SAKES!
POW! POW! POW!
ABANDON SHIP! STEP LIVELY WITH THAT LOOT!

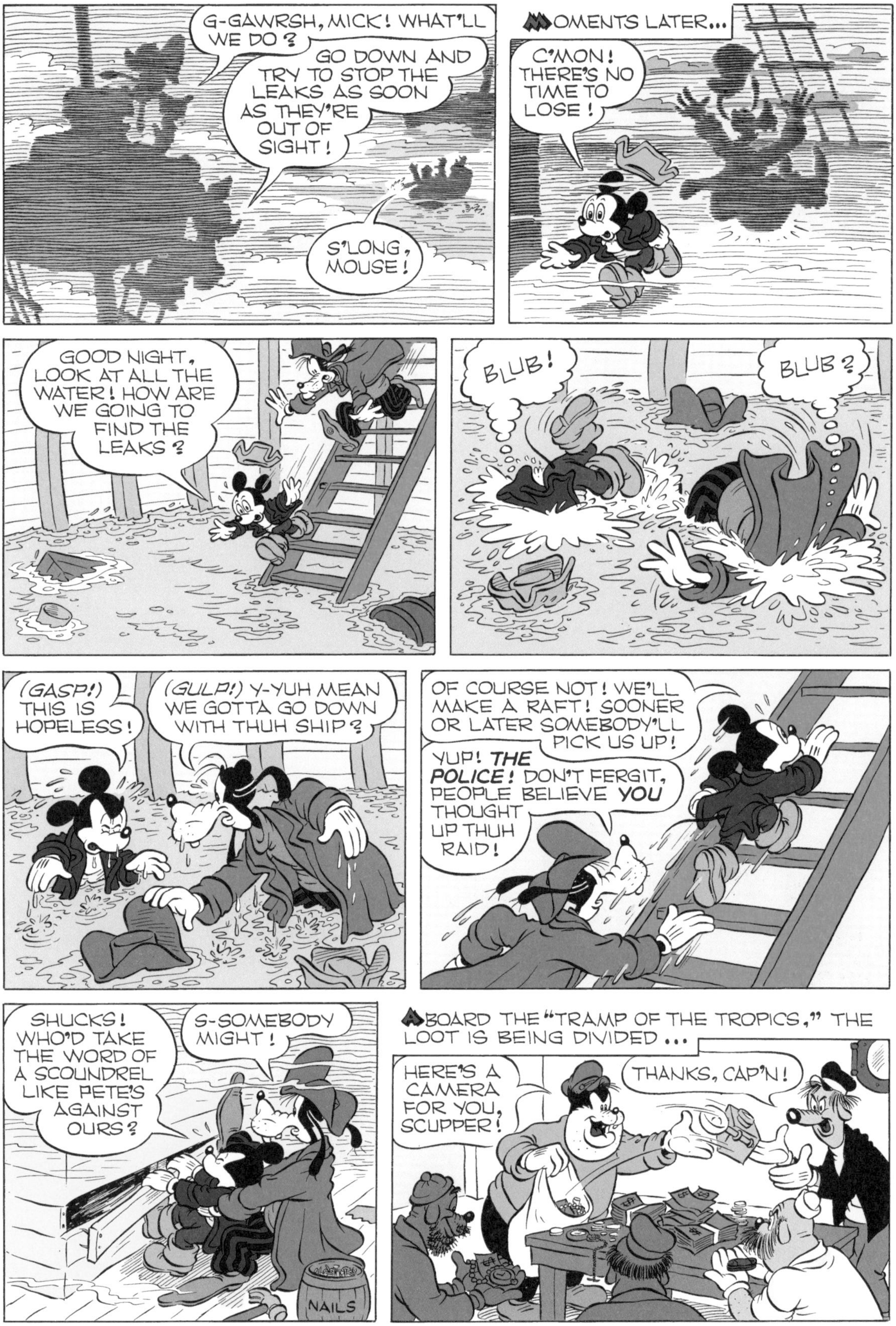
G-GAWRSH, MICK! WHAT'LL WE DO?
GO DOWN AND TRY TO STOP THE LEAKS AS SOON AS THEY'RE OUT OF SIGHT!
S'LONG, MOUSE!
MOMENTS LATER...
C'MON! THERE'S NO TIME TO LOSE!
GOOD NIGHT, LOOK AT ALL THE WATER! HOW ARE WE GOING TO FIND THE LEAKS?
BLUB!
BLUB?
(GASP!) THIS IS HOPELESS!
(GULP!) Y-YUH MEAN WE GOTTA GO DOWN WITH THUH SHIP?
OF COURSE NOT! WE'LL MAKE A RAFT! SOONER OR LATER SOMEBODY'LL PICK US UP!
YUP! THE POLICE! DON'T FERGIT, PEOPLE BELIEVE YOU THOUGHT UP THUH RAID!
SHUCKS! WHO'D TAKE THE WORD OF A SCOUNDREL LIKE PETE'S AGAINST OURS?
S-SOMEBODY MIGHT!
NAILS
ABOARD THE "TRAMP OF THE TROPICS," THE LOOT IS BEING DIVIDED...
HERE'S A CAMERA FOR YOU, SCUPPER!
THANKS, CAP'N!

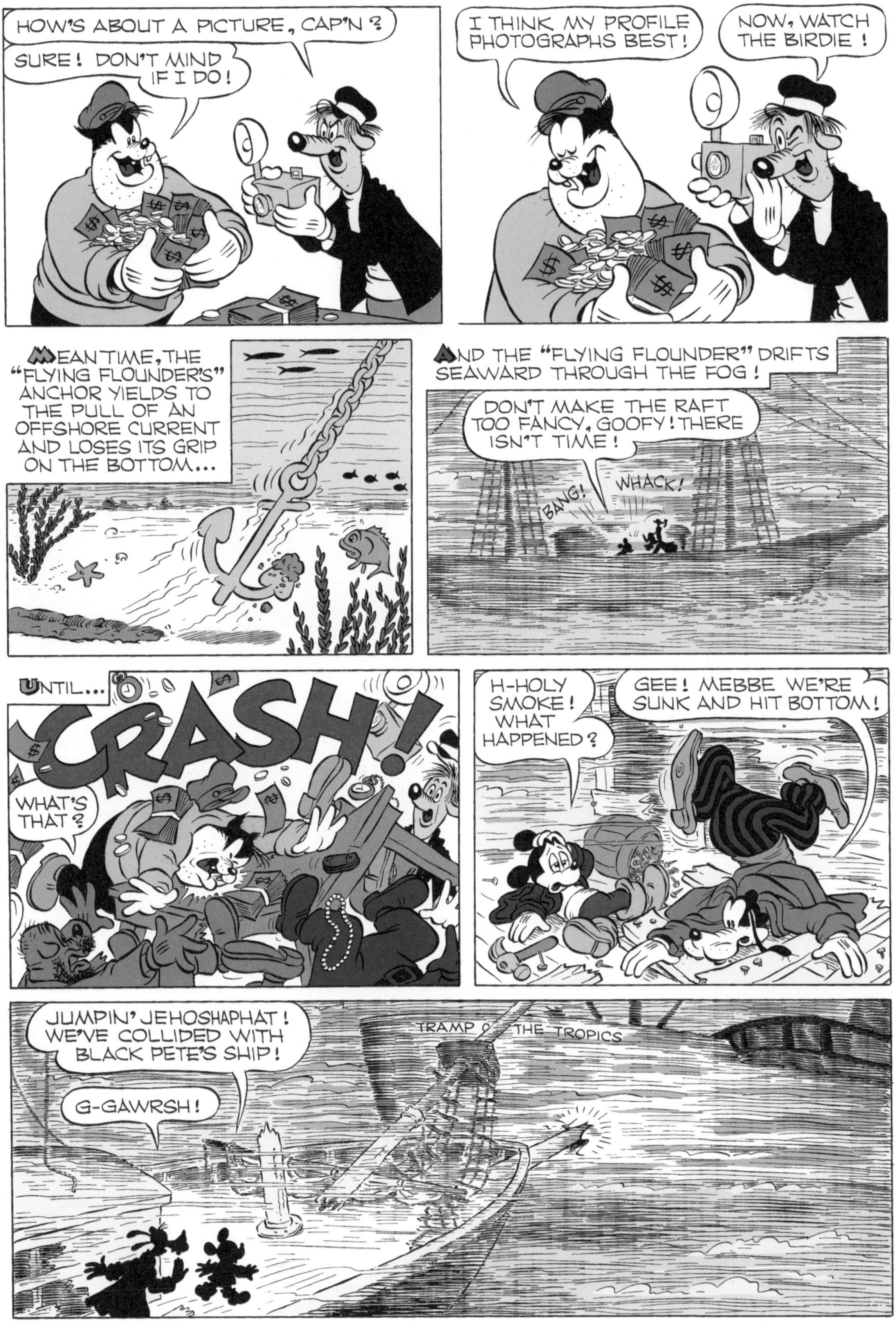

HOW'S ABOUT A PICTURE, CAP'N ?
SURE! DON'T MIND IF I DO!
I THINK MY PROFILE PHOTOGRAPHS BEST!
NOW, WATCH THE BIRDIE !
MEANTIME, THE "FLYING FLOUNDER'S" ANCHOR YIELDS TO THE PULL OF AN OFFSHORE CURRENT AND LOSES ITS GRIP ON THE BOTTOM...
AND THE "FLYING FLOUNDER" DRIFTS SEAWARD THROUGH THE FOG !
DON'T MAKE THE RAFT TOO FANCY, GOOFY! THERE ISN'T TIME!
BANG!
WHACK!
UNTIL...
CRASH!
WHAT'S THAT?
H-HOLY SMOKE! WHAT HAPPENED?
GEE! MEBBE WE'RE SUNK AND HIT BOTTOM!
JUMPIN' JEHOSHAPHAT! WE'VE COLLIDED WITH BLACK PETE'S SHIP!
G-GAWRSH!
TRAMP O THE TROPICS

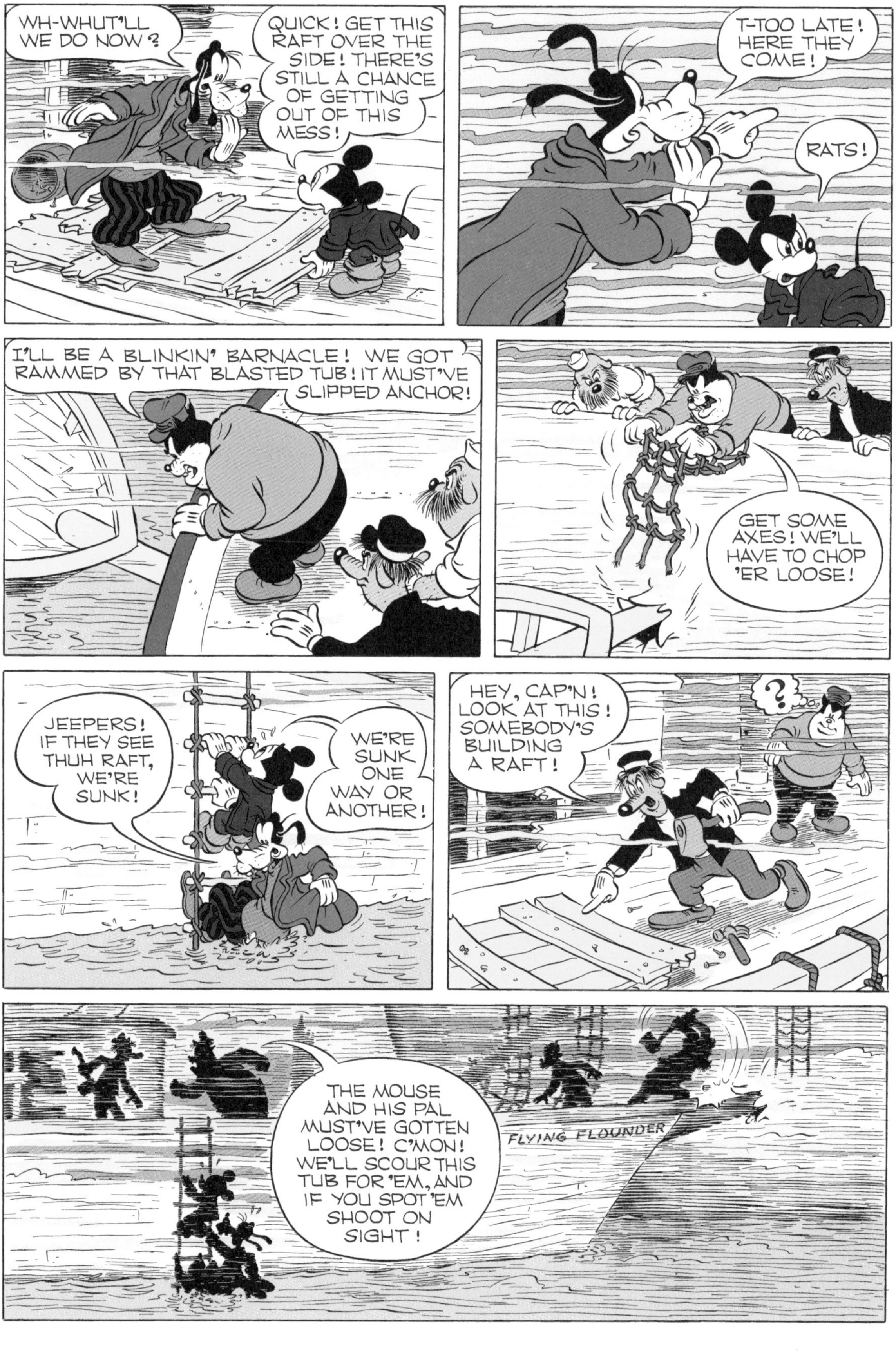
WH-WHUT'LL WE DO NOW ?
QUICK! GET THIS RAFT OVER THE SIDE! THERE'S STILL A CHANCE OF GETTING OUT OF THIS MESS!
T-TOO LATE! HERE THEY COME!
RATS!
I'LL BE A BLINKIN' BARNACLE! WE GOT RAMMED BY THAT BLASTED TUB! IT MUST'VE SLIPPED ANCHOR!
GET SOME AXES! WE'LL HAVE TO CHOP 'ER LOOSE!
JEEPERS! IF THEY SEE THUH RAFT, WE'RE SUNK!
WE'RE SUNK ONE WAY OR ANOTHER!
HEY, CAP'N! LOOK AT THIS! SOMEBODY'S BUILDING A RAFT!
?
THE MOUSE AND HIS PAL MUST'VE GOTTEN LOOSE! C'MON! WE'LL SCOUR THIS TUB FOR 'EM, AND IF YOU SPOT 'EM SHOOT ON SIGHT!
FLYING FLOUNDER

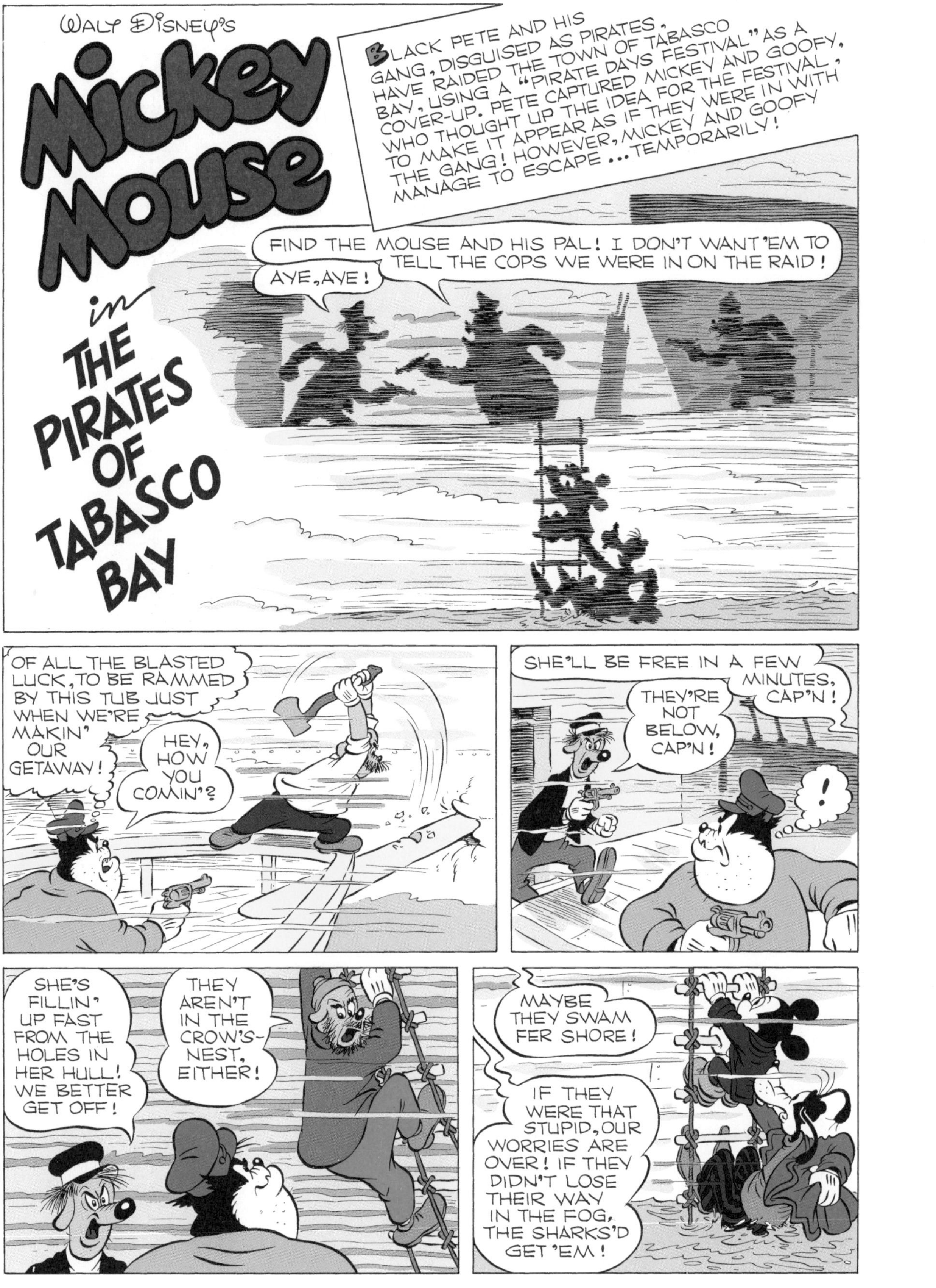
WALT DISNEY'S
Mickey Mouse
in
THE PIRATES OF TABASCO BAY
BLACK PETE AND HIS GANG, DISGUISED AS PIRATES, HAVE RAIDED THE TOWN OF TABASCO BAY, USING A "PIRATE DAYS FESTIVAL" AS A COVER-UP. PETE CAPTURED MICKEY AND GOOFY, WHO THOUGHT UP THE IDEA FOR THE FESTIVAL, TO MAKE IT APPEAR AS IF THEY WERE IN WITH THE GANG! HOWEVER, MICKEY AND GOOFY MANAGE TO ESCAPE ... TEMPORARILY!
FIND THE MOUSE AND HIS PAL! I DON'T WANT 'EM TO TELL THE COPS WE WERE IN ON THE RAID!
AYE, AYE!
OF ALL THE BLASTED LUCK, TO BE RAMMED BY THIS TUB JUST WHEN WE'RE MAKIN' OUR GETAWAY!
HEY, HOW YOU COMIN'?
SHE'LL BE FREE IN A FEW MINUTES, CAP'N!
THEY'RE NOT BELOW, CAP'N!
!
SHE'S FILLIN' UP FAST FROM THE HOLES IN HER HULL! WE BETTER GET OFF!
THEY AREN'T IN THE CROW'S-NEST, EITHER!
MAYBE THEY SWAM FER SHORE!
IF THEY WERE THAT STUPID, OUR WORRIES ARE OVER! IF THEY DIDN'T LOSE THEIR WAY IN THE FOG, THE SHARKS'D GET 'EM!

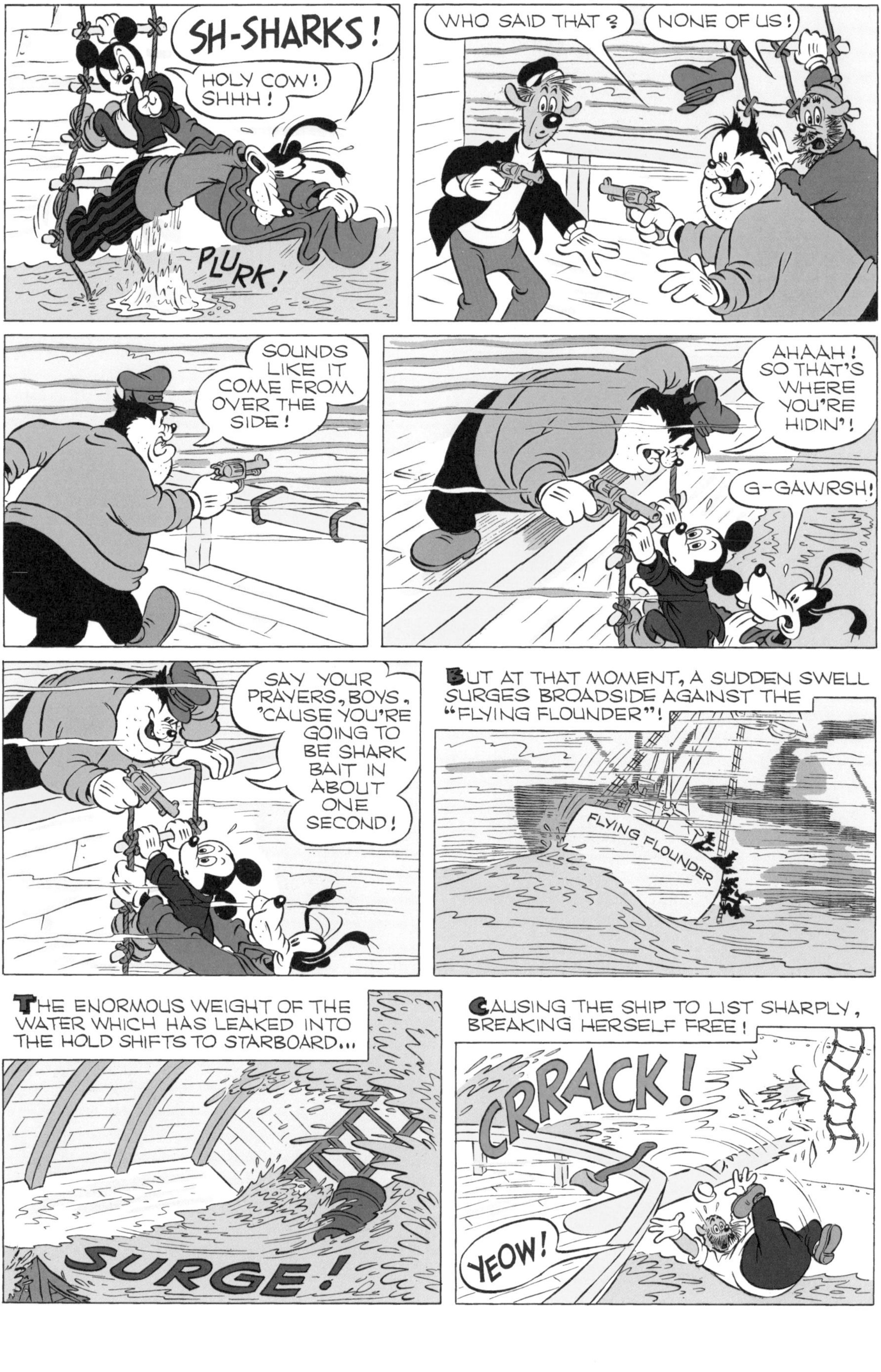
SH-SHARKS!
HOLY COW! SHHH!
PLURK!
WHO SAID THAT?
NONE OF US!
SOUNDS LIKE IT COME FROM OVER THE SIDE!
AHAAH! SO THAT'S WHERE YOU'RE HIDIN'!
G-GAWRSH!
SAY YOUR PRAYERS, BOYS. 'CAUSE YOU'RE GOING TO BE SHARK BAIT IN ABOUT ONE SECOND!
BUT AT THAT MOMENT, A SUDDEN SWELL SURGES BROADSIDE AGAINST THE "FLYING FLOUNDER"!
FLYING FLOUNDER
THE ENORMOUS WEIGHT OF THE WATER WHICH HAS LEAKED INTO THE HOLD SHIFTS TO STARBOARD...
SURGE!
CAUSING THE SHIP TO LIST SHARPLY, BREAKING HERSELF FREE!
CRRACK!
YEOW!

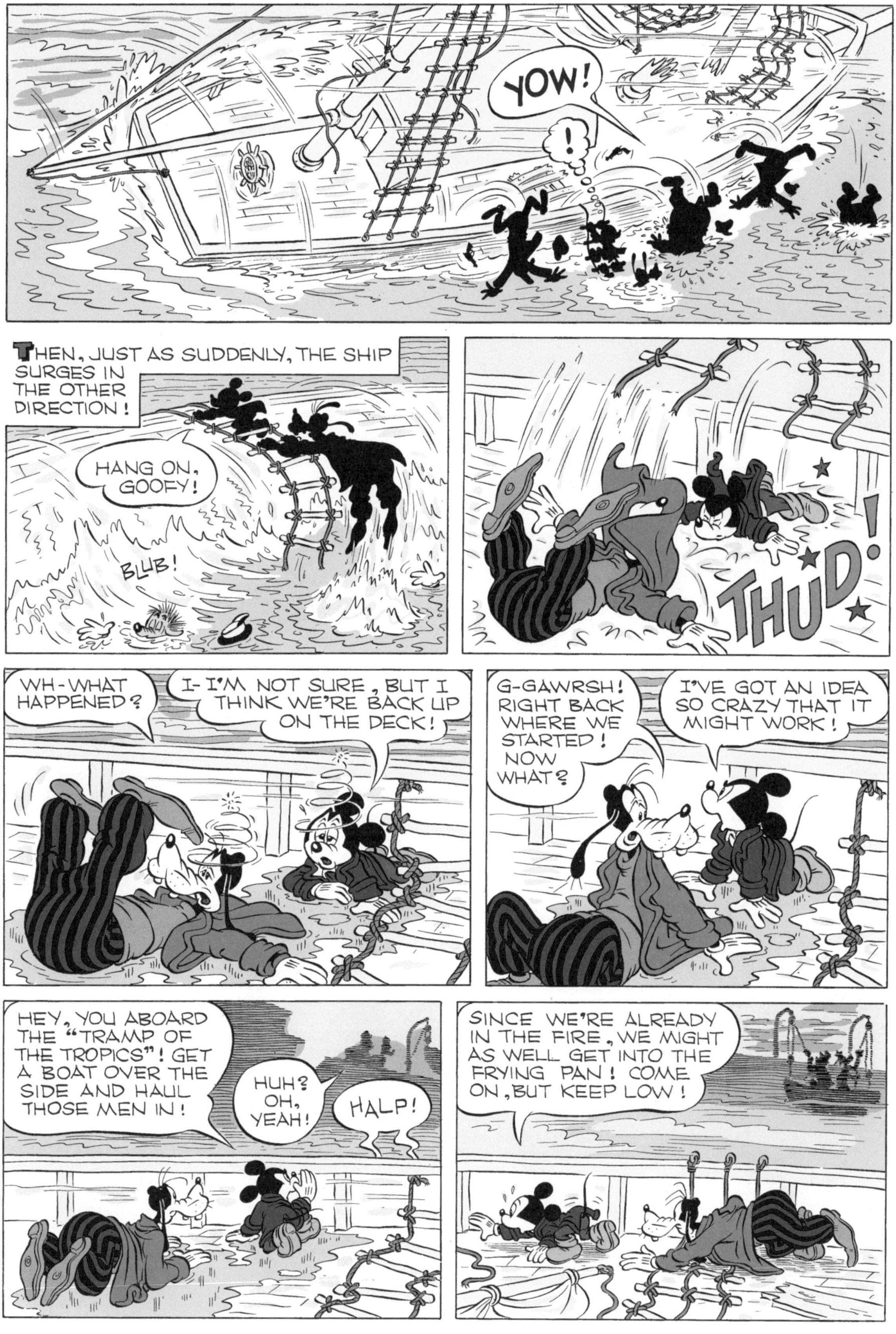
YOW!
!
THEN, JUST AS SUDDENLY, THE SHIP SURGES IN THE OTHER DIRECTION!
HANG ON, GOOFY!
BLUB!
THUD!
WH-WHAT HAPPENED?
I-I'M NOT SURE, BUT I THINK WE'RE BACK UP ON THE DECK!
G-GAWRSH! RIGHT BACK WHERE WE STARTED! NOW WHAT?
I'VE GOT AN IDEA SO CRAZY THAT IT MIGHT WORK!
HEY, YOU ABOARD THE "TRAMP OF THE TROPICS"! GET A BOAT OVER THE SIDE AND HAUL THOSE MEN IN!
HUH? OH, YEAH!
HALP!
SINCE WE'RE ALREADY IN THE FIRE, WE MIGHT AS WELL GET INTO THE FRYING PAN! COME ON, BUT KEEP LOW!

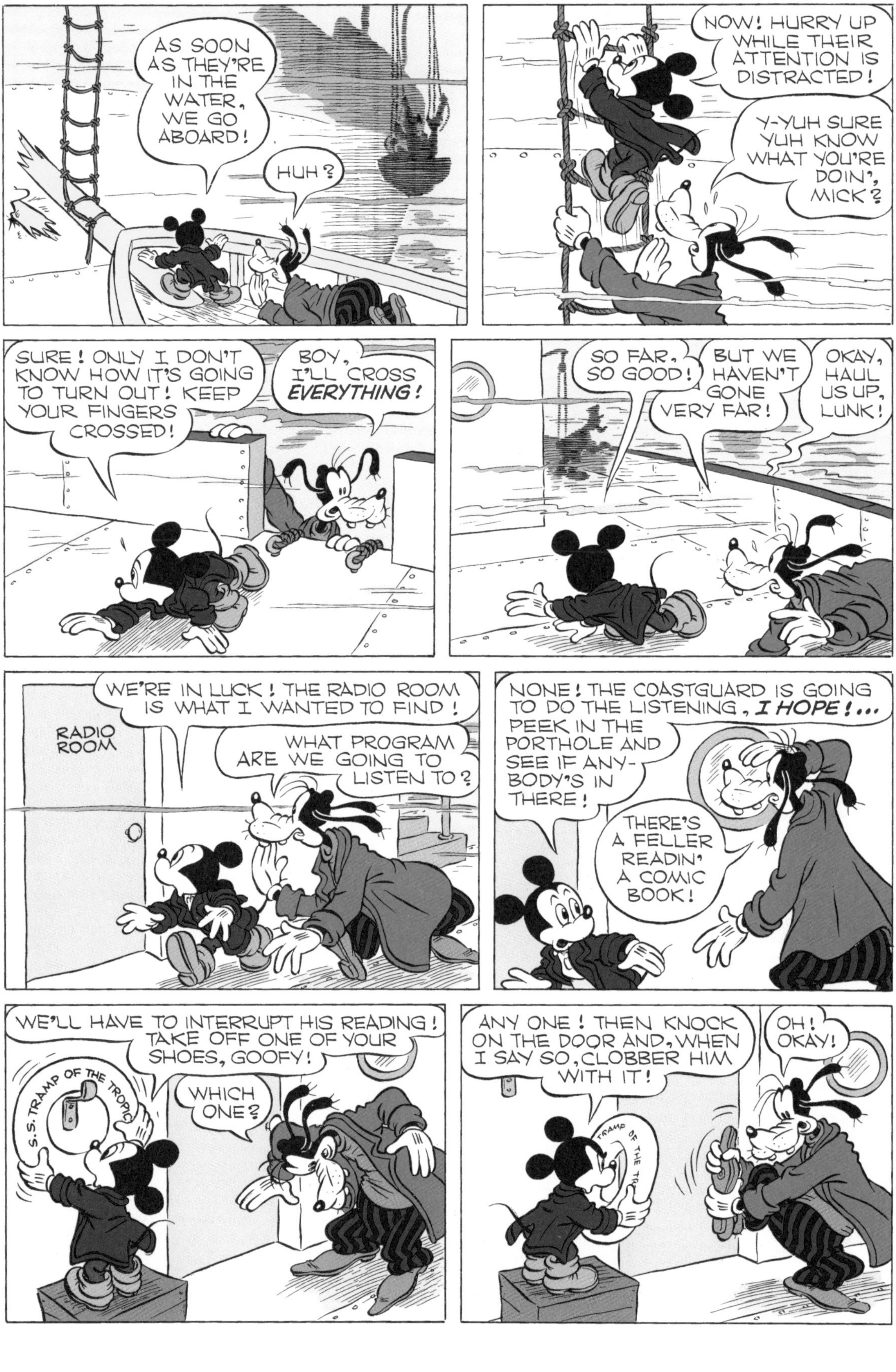
AS SOON AS THEY'RE IN THE WATER, WE GO ABOARD!
HUH?
NOW! HURRY UP WHILE THEIR ATTENTION IS DISTRACTED!
Y-YUH SURE YUH KNOW WHAT YOU'RE DOIN', MICK?
SURE! ONLY I DON'T KNOW HOW IT'S GOING TO TURN OUT! KEEP YOUR FINGERS CROSSED!
BOY, I'LL CROSS *EVERYTHING!*
SO FAR, SO GOOD!
BUT WE HAVEN'T GONE VERY FAR!
OKAY, HAUL US UP, LUNK!
WE'RE IN LUCK! THE RADIO ROOM IS WHAT I WANTED TO FIND!
RADIO ROOM
WHAT PROGRAM ARE WE GOING TO LISTEN TO?
NONE! THE COASTGUARD IS GOING TO DO THE LISTENING, *I HOPE!...* PEEK IN THE PORTHOLE AND SEE IF ANYBODY'S IN THERE!
THERE'S A FELLER READIN' A COMIC BOOK!
WE'LL HAVE TO INTERRUPT HIS READING! TAKE OFF ONE OF YOUR SHOES, GOOFY!
S.S. TRAMP OF THE TROPIC
WHICH ONE?
ANY ONE! THEN KNOCK ON THE DOOR AND, WHEN I SAY SO, CLOBBER HIM WITH IT!
OH! OKAY!

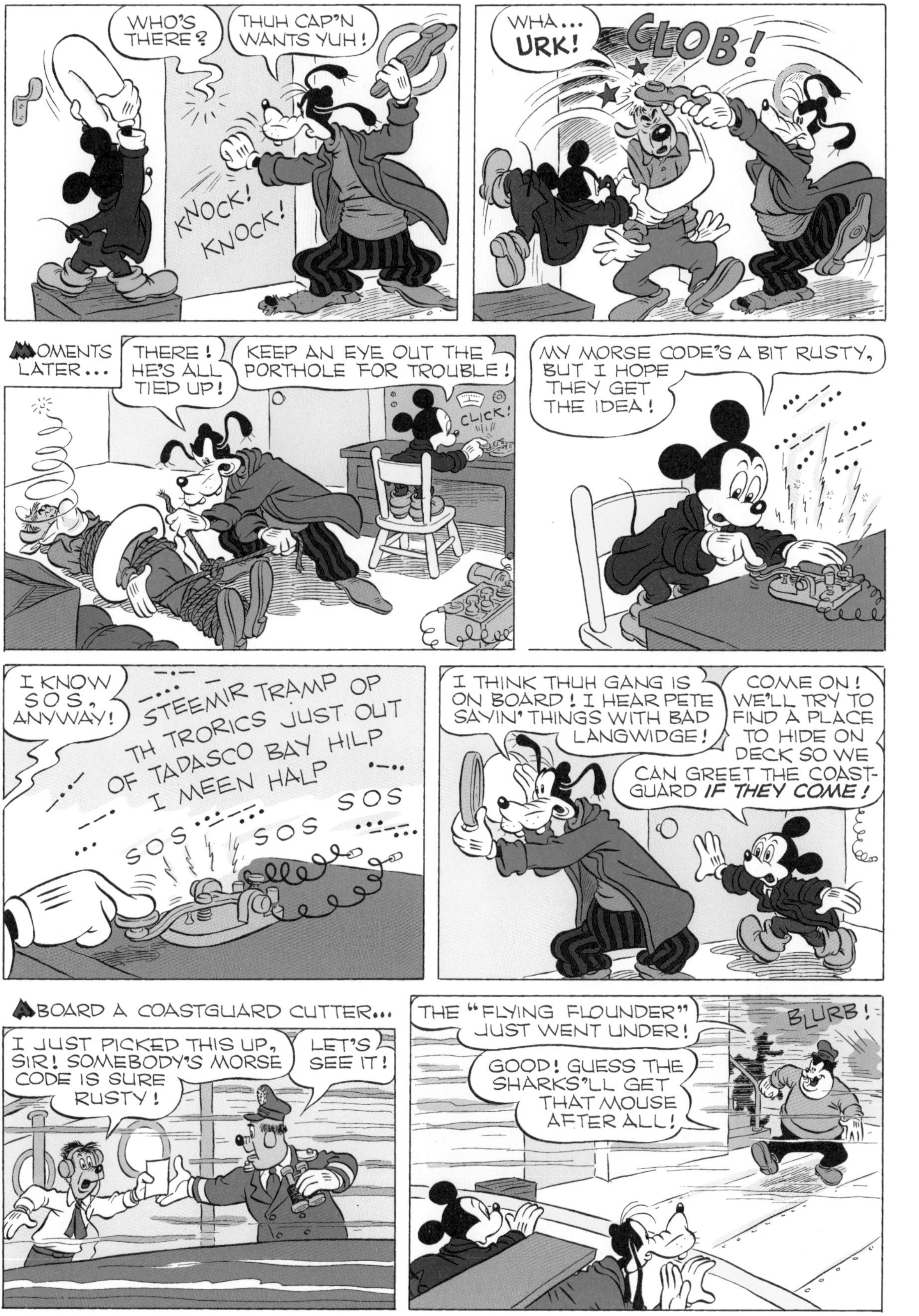
WHO'S THERE?
THUH CAP'N WANTS YUH!
KNOCK! KNOCK!
WHA... URK!
CLOB!
MOMENTS LATER...
THERE! HE'S ALL TIED UP!
KEEP AN EYE OUT THE PORTHOLE FOR TROUBLE!
CLICK!
MY MORSE CODE'S A BIT RUSTY, BUT I HOPE THEY GET THE IDEA!
I KNOW SOS, ANYWAY!
STEEMIR TRAMP OP TH TRORICS JUST OUT OF TADASCO BAY HILP I MEEN HALP
SOS SOS SOS
I THINK THUH GANG IS ON BOARD! I HEAR PETE SAYIN' THINGS WITH BAD LANGWIDGE!
COME ON! WE'LL TRY TO FIND A PLACE TO HIDE ON DECK SO WE CAN GREET THE COAST-GUARD *IF THEY COME!*
ABOARD A COASTGUARD CUTTER...
I JUST PICKED THIS UP, SIR! SOMEBODY'S MORSE CODE IS SURE RUSTY!
LET'S SEE IT!
THE "FLYING FLOUNDER" JUST WENT UNDER!
BLURB!
GOOD! GUESS THE SHARKS'LL GET THAT MOUSE AFTER ALL!

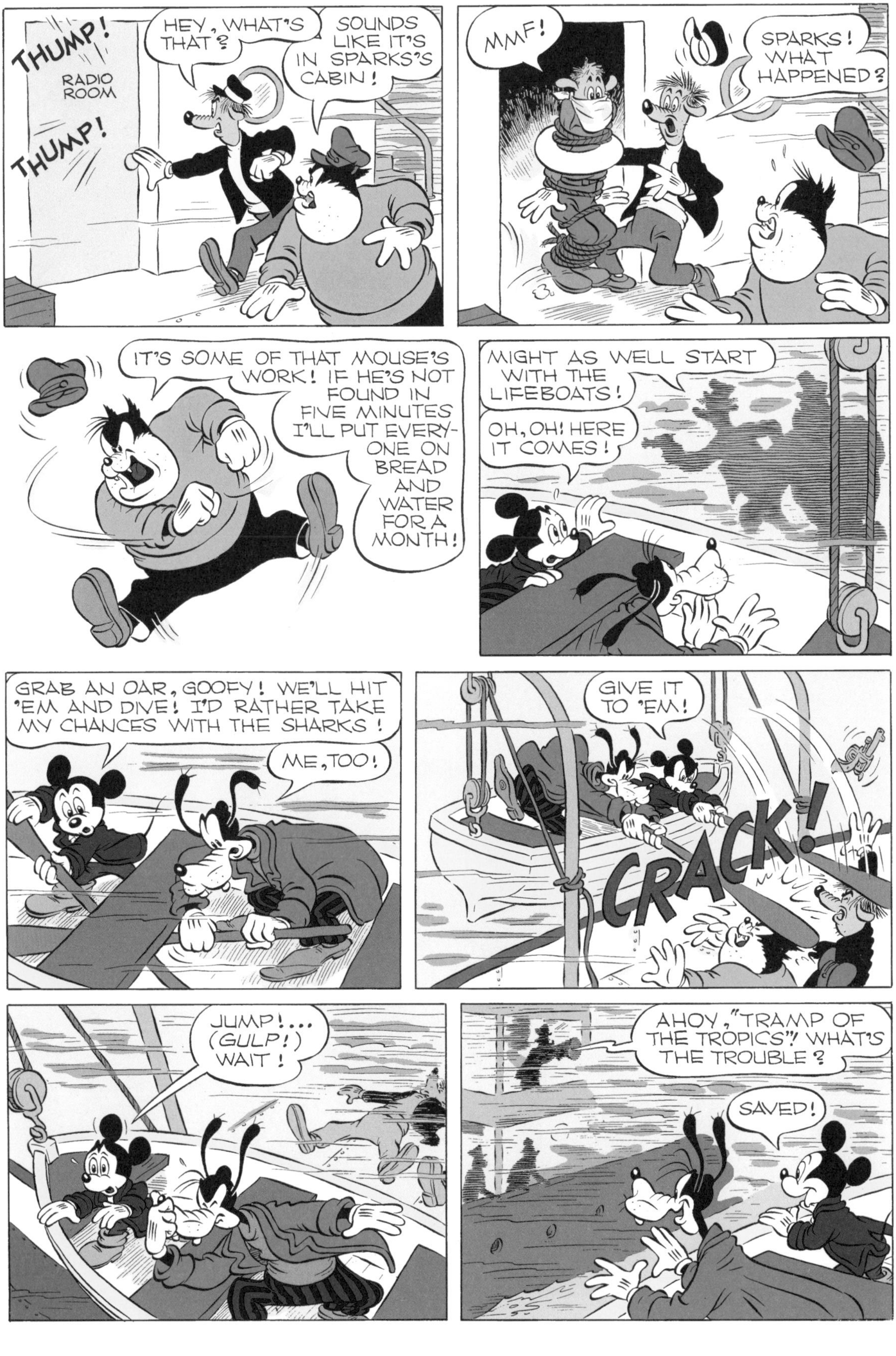
THUMP!
RADIO ROOM
THUMP!
HEY, WHAT'S THAT?
SOUNDS LIKE IT'S IN SPARKS'S CABIN!
MMF!
SPARKS! WHAT HAPPENED?
IT'S SOME OF THAT MOUSE'S WORK! IF HE'S NOT FOUND IN FIVE MINUTES I'LL PUT EVERY-ONE ON BREAD AND WATER FOR A MONTH!
MIGHT AS WELL START WITH THE LIFEBOATS!
OH, OH! HERE IT COMES!
GRAB AN OAR, GOOFY! WE'LL HIT 'EM AND DIVE! I'D RATHER TAKE MY CHANCES WITH THE SHARKS!
ME, TOO!
GIVE IT TO 'EM!
CRACK!
JUMP!... (GULP!) WAIT!
AHOY, "TRAMP OF THE TROPICS"! WHAT'S THE TROUBLE?
SAVED!

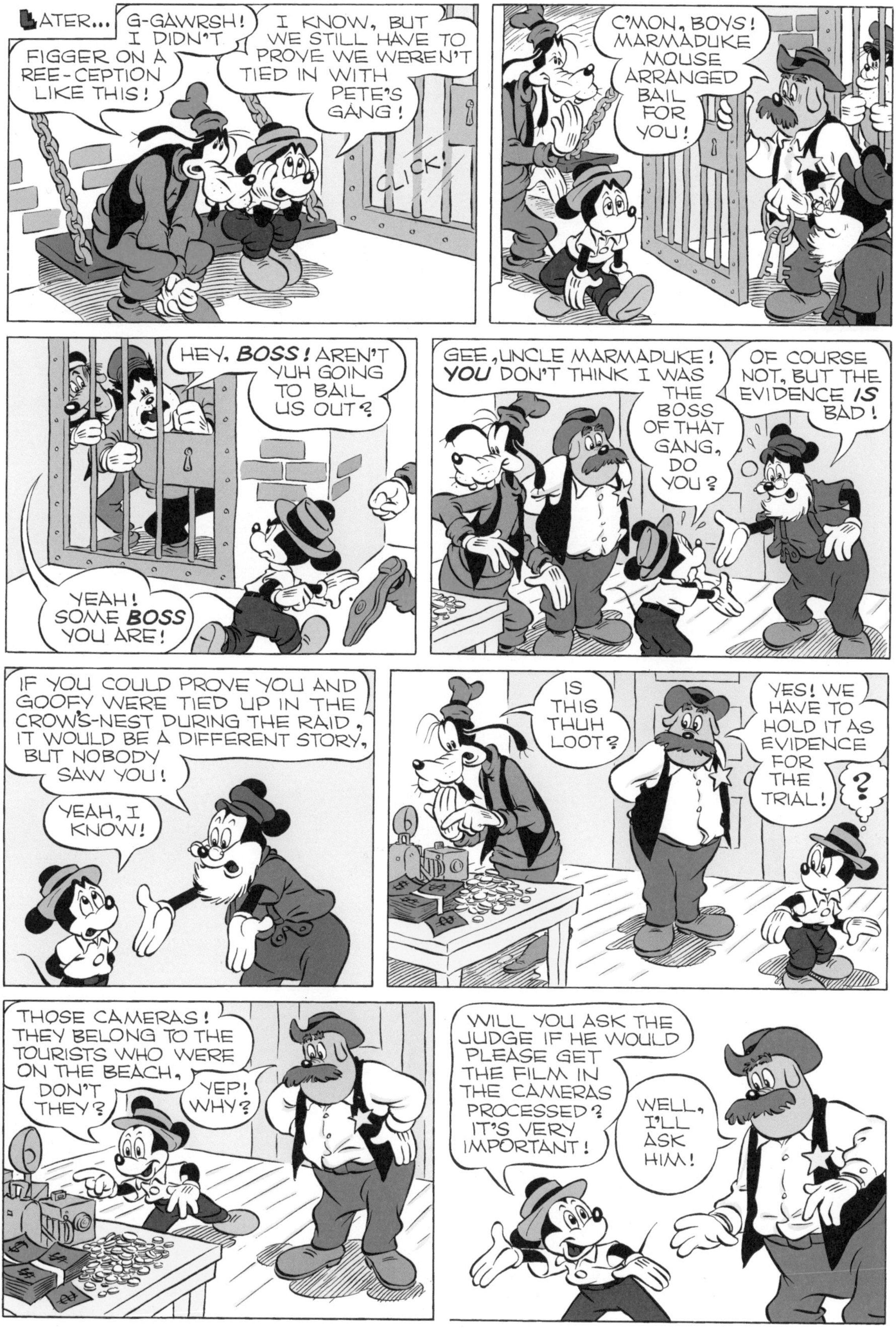
LATER...
G-GAWRSH! I DIDN'T FIGGER ON A REE-CEPTION LIKE THIS!
I KNOW, BUT WE STILL HAVE TO PROVE WE WEREN'T TIED IN WITH PETE'S GANG!
CLICK!
C'MON, BOYS! MARMADUKE MOUSE ARRANGED BAIL FOR YOU!
HEY, BOSS! AREN'T YUH GOING TO BAIL US OUT?
YEAH! SOME BOSS YOU ARE!
GEE, UNCLE MARMADUKE! YOU DON'T THINK I WAS THE BOSS OF THAT GANG, DO YOU?
OF COURSE NOT, BUT THE EVIDENCE IS BAD!
IF YOU COULD PROVE YOU AND GOOFY WERE TIED UP IN THE CROW'S-NEST DURING THE RAID, IT WOULD BE A DIFFERENT STORY, BUT NOBODY SAW YOU!
YEAH, I KNOW!
IS THIS THUH LOOT?
YES! WE HAVE TO HOLD IT AS EVIDENCE FOR THE TRIAL!
?
THOSE CAMERAS! THEY BELONG TO THE TOURISTS WHO WERE ON THE BEACH, DON'T THEY?
YEP! WHY?
WILL YOU ASK THE JUDGE IF HE WOULD PLEASE GET THE FILM IN THE CAMERAS PROCESSED? IT'S VERY IMPORTANT!
WELL, I'LL ASK HIM!

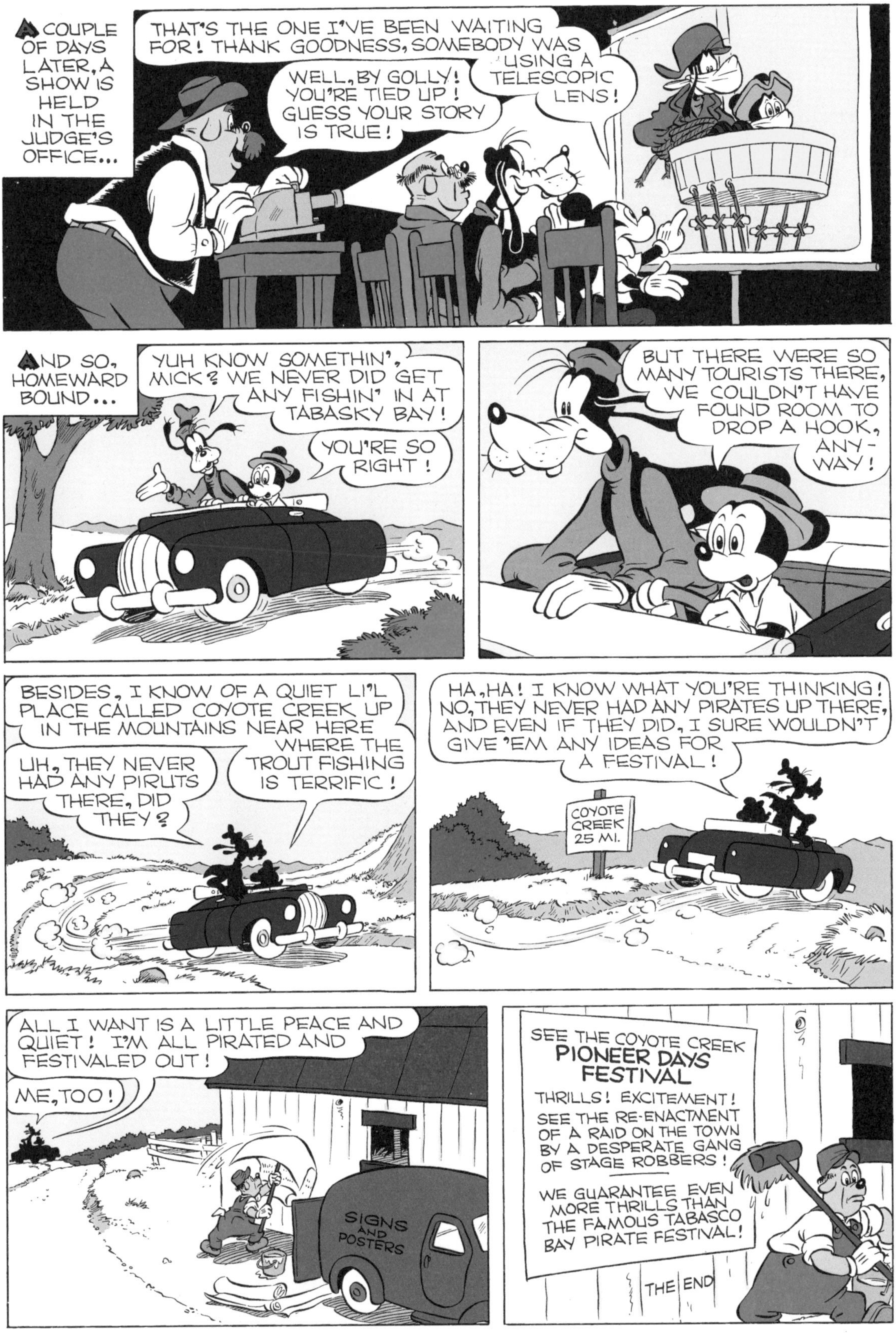
A COUPLE OF DAYS LATER, A SHOW IS HELD IN THE JUDGE'S OFFICE...
THAT'S THE ONE I'VE BEEN WAITING FOR! THANK GOODNESS, SOMEBODY WAS USING A TELESCOPIC LENS!
WELL, BY GOLLY! YOU'RE TIED UP! GUESS YOUR STORY IS TRUE!
AND SO, HOMEWARD BOUND...
YUH KNOW SOMETHIN', MICK? WE NEVER DID GET ANY FISHIN' IN AT TABASKY BAY!
YOU'RE SO RIGHT!
BUT THERE WERE SO MANY TOURISTS THERE, WE COULDN'T HAVE FOUND ROOM TO DROP A HOOK, ANY-WAY!
BESIDES, I KNOW OF A QUIET LI'L PLACE CALLED COYOTE CREEK UP IN THE MOUNTAINS NEAR HERE WHERE THE TROUT FISHING IS TERRIFIC!
UH, THEY NEVER HAD ANY PIRUTS THERE, DID THEY?
HA, HA! I KNOW WHAT YOU'RE THINKING! NO, THEY NEVER HAD ANY PIRATES UP THERE, AND EVEN IF THEY DID, I SURE WOULDN'T GIVE 'EM ANY IDEAS FOR A FESTIVAL!
COYOTE CREEK 25 MI.
ALL I WANT IS A LITTLE PEACE AND QUIET! I'M ALL PIRATED AND FESTIVALED OUT!
ME, TOO!
SIGNS AND POSTERS
SEE THE COYOTE CREEK PIONEER DAYS FESTIVAL
THRILLS! EXCITEMENT!
SEE THE RE-ENACTMENT OF A RAID ON THE TOWN BY A DESPERATE GANG OF STAGE ROBBERS!
WE GUARANTEE EVEN MORE THRILLS THAN THE FAMOUS TABASCO BAY PIRATE FESTIVAL!
THE END

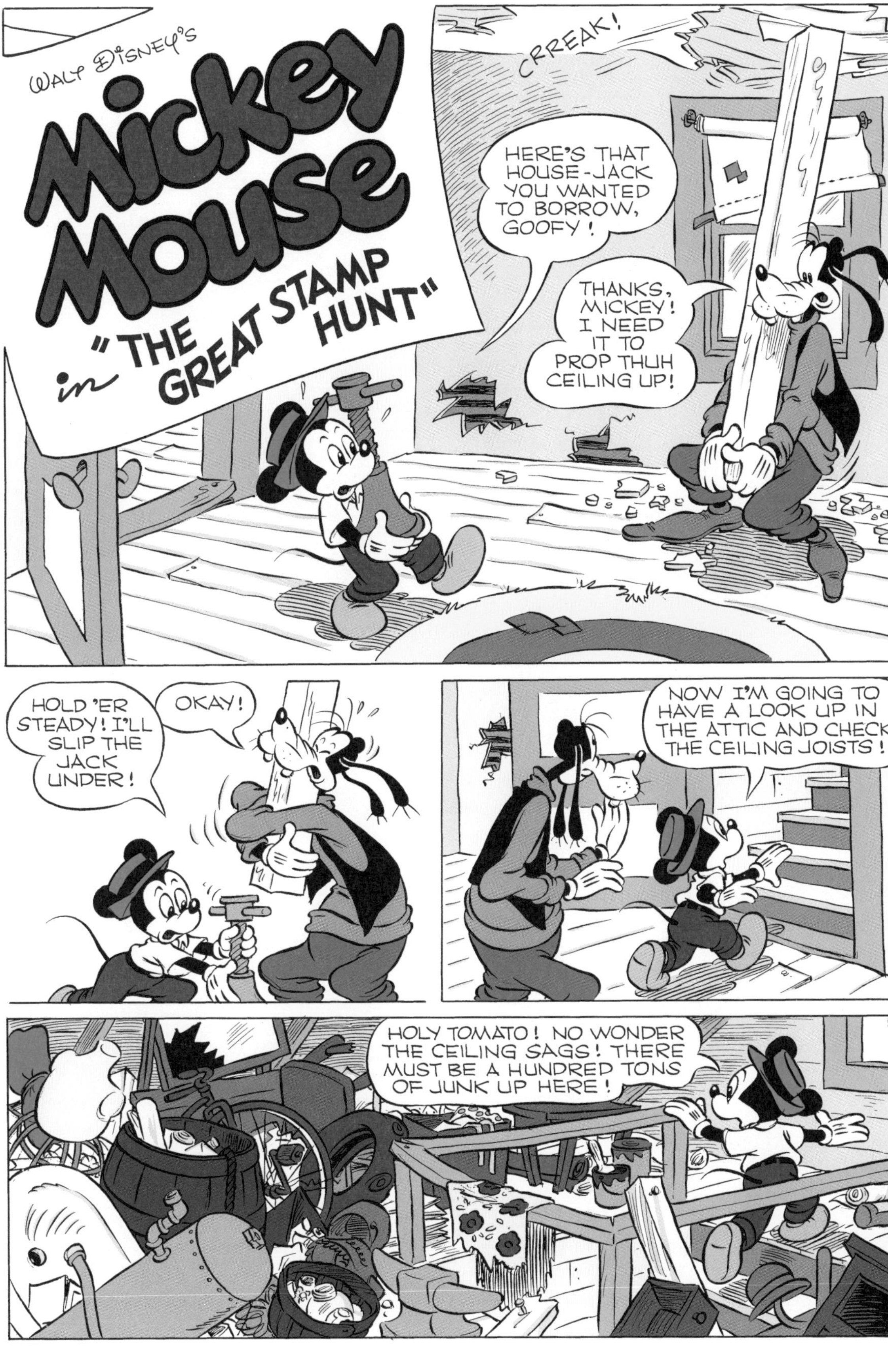
WALT DISNEY'S
Mickey Mouse
in "THE GREAT STAMP HUNT"
CRREAK!
HERE'S THAT HOUSE-JACK YOU WANTED TO BORROW, GOOFY!
THANKS, MICKEY! I NEED IT TO PROP THUH CEILING UP!
HOLD 'ER STEADY! I'LL SLIP THE JACK UNDER!
OKAY!
NOW I'M GOING TO HAVE A LOOK UP IN THE ATTIC AND CHECK THE CEILING JOISTS!
HOLY TOMATO! NO WONDER THE CEILING SAGS! THERE MUST BE A HUNDRED TONS OF JUNK UP HERE!

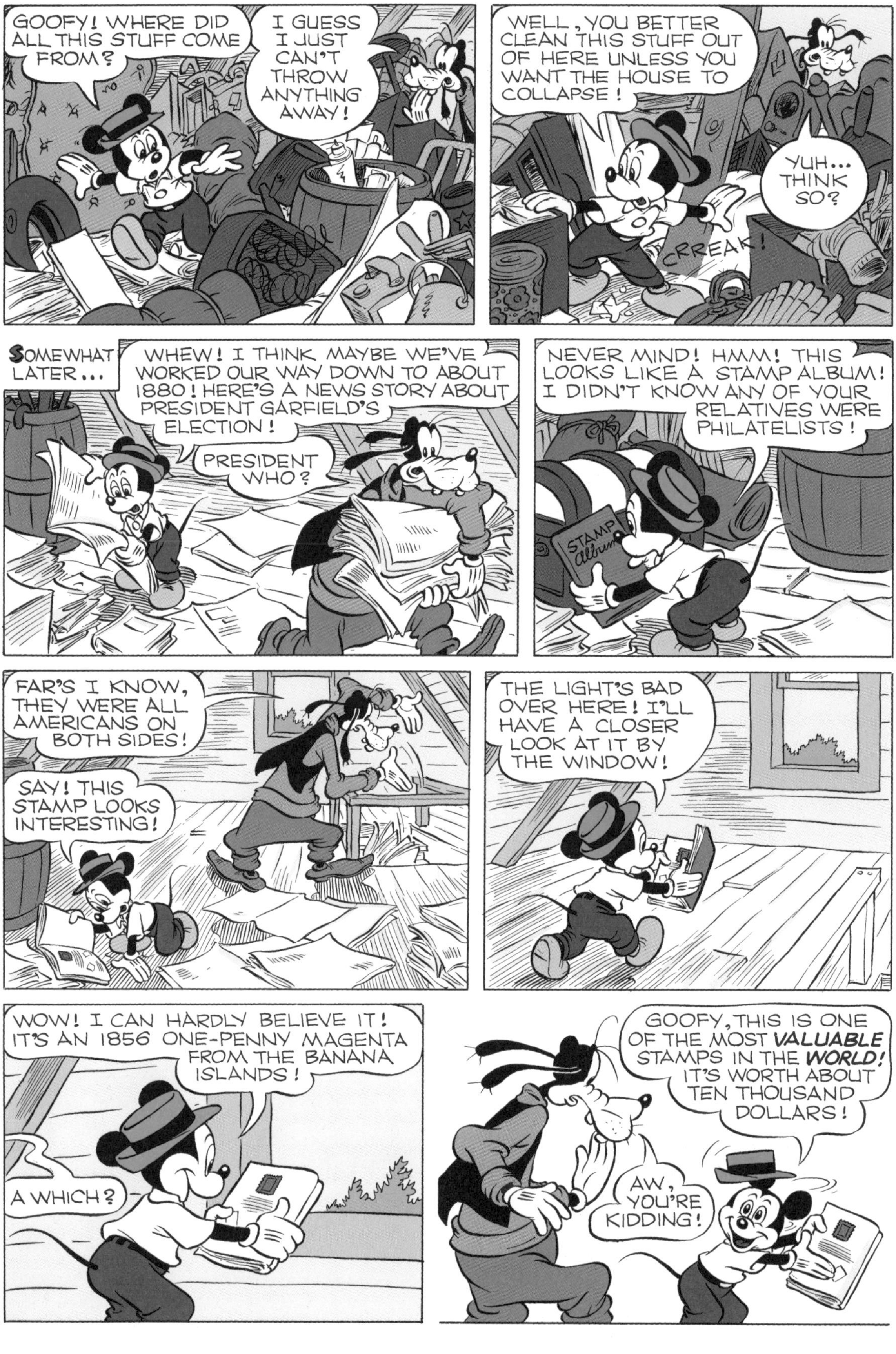
GOOFY! WHERE DID ALL THIS STUFF COME FROM?
I GUESS I JUST CAN'T THROW ANYTHING AWAY!
WELL, YOU BETTER CLEAN THIS STUFF OUT OF HERE UNLESS YOU WANT THE HOUSE TO COLLAPSE!
YUH... THINK SO?
CRREAK!
SOMEWHAT LATER...
WHEW! I THINK MAYBE WE'VE WORKED OUR WAY DOWN TO ABOUT 1880! HERE'S A NEWS STORY ABOUT PRESIDENT GARFIELD'S ELECTION!
PRESIDENT WHO?
NEVER MIND! HMM! THIS LOOKS LIKE A STAMP ALBUM! I DIDN'T KNOW ANY OF YOUR RELATIVES WERE PHILATELISTS!
STAMP Album
FAR'S I KNOW, THEY WERE ALL AMERICANS ON BOTH SIDES!
SAY! THIS STAMP LOOKS INTERESTING!
THE LIGHT'S BAD OVER HERE! I'LL HAVE A CLOSER LOOK AT IT BY THE WINDOW!
WOW! I CAN HARDLY BELIEVE IT! IT'S AN 1856 ONE-PENNY MAGENTA FROM THE BANANA ISLANDS!
A WHICH?
GOOFY, THIS IS ONE OF THE MOST VALUABLE STAMPS IN THE WORLD! IT'S WORTH ABOUT TEN THOUSAND DOLLARS!
AW, YOU'RE KIDDING!

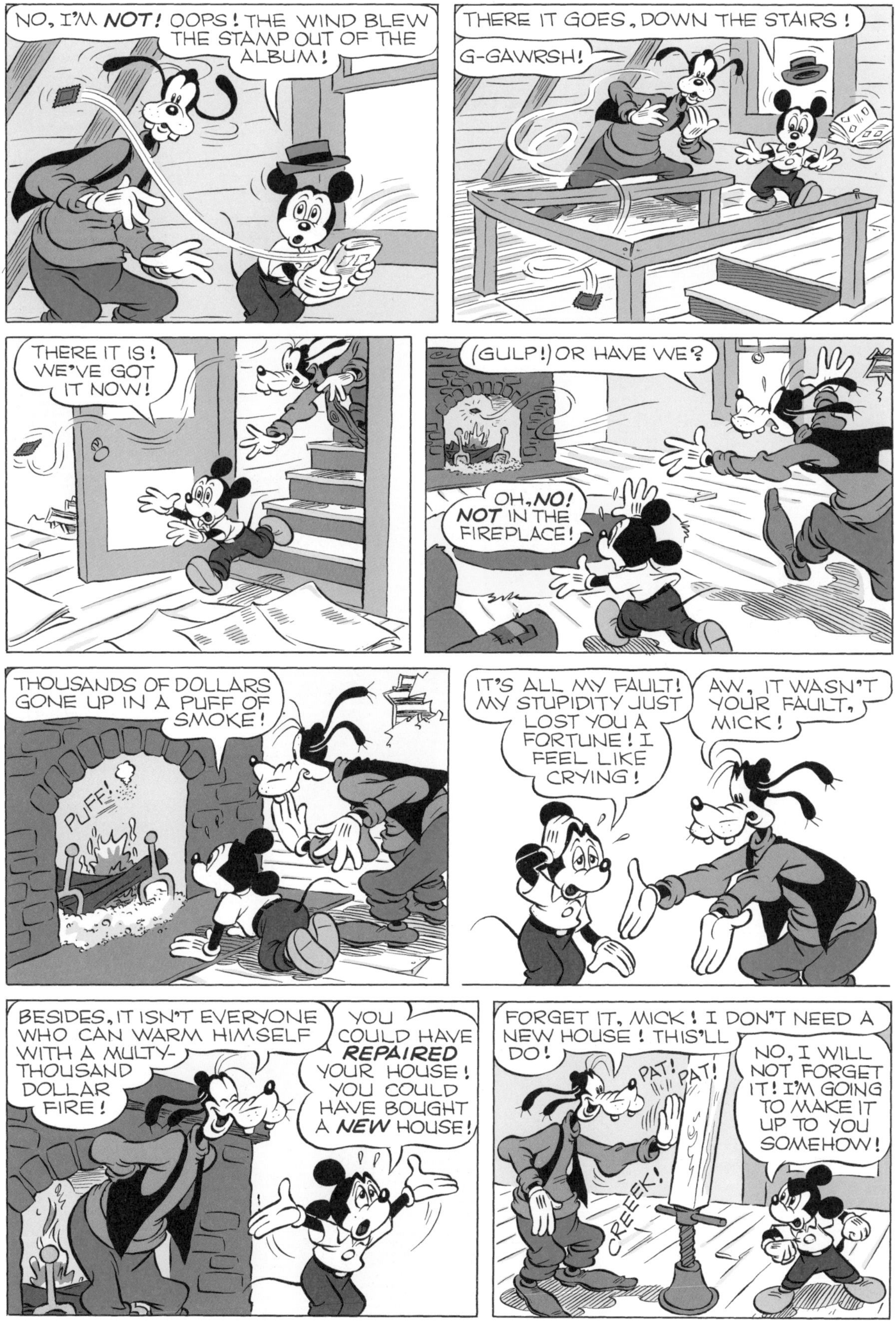

NO, I'M NOT! OOPS! THE WIND BLEW THE STAMP OUT OF THE ALBUM!
THERE IT GOES, DOWN THE STAIRS!
G-GAWRSH!
THERE IT IS! WE'VE GOT IT NOW!
(GULP!) OR HAVE WE?
OH, NO! NOT IN THE FIREPLACE!
THOUSANDS OF DOLLARS GONE UP IN A PUFF OF SMOKE!
PUFF!
IT'S ALL MY FAULT! MY STUPIDITY JUST LOST YOU A FORTUNE! I FEEL LIKE CRYING!
AW, IT WASN'T YOUR FAULT, MICK!
BESIDES, IT ISN'T EVERYONE WHO CAN WARM HIMSELF WITH A MULTY-THOUSAND DOLLAR FIRE!
YOU COULD HAVE REPAIRED YOUR HOUSE! YOU COULD HAVE BOUGHT A NEW HOUSE!
FORGET IT, MICK! I DON'T NEED A NEW HOUSE! THIS'LL DO!
PAT! PAT!
CREEEK!
NO, I WILL NOT FORGET IT! I'M GOING TO MAKE IT UP TO YOU SOMEHOW!

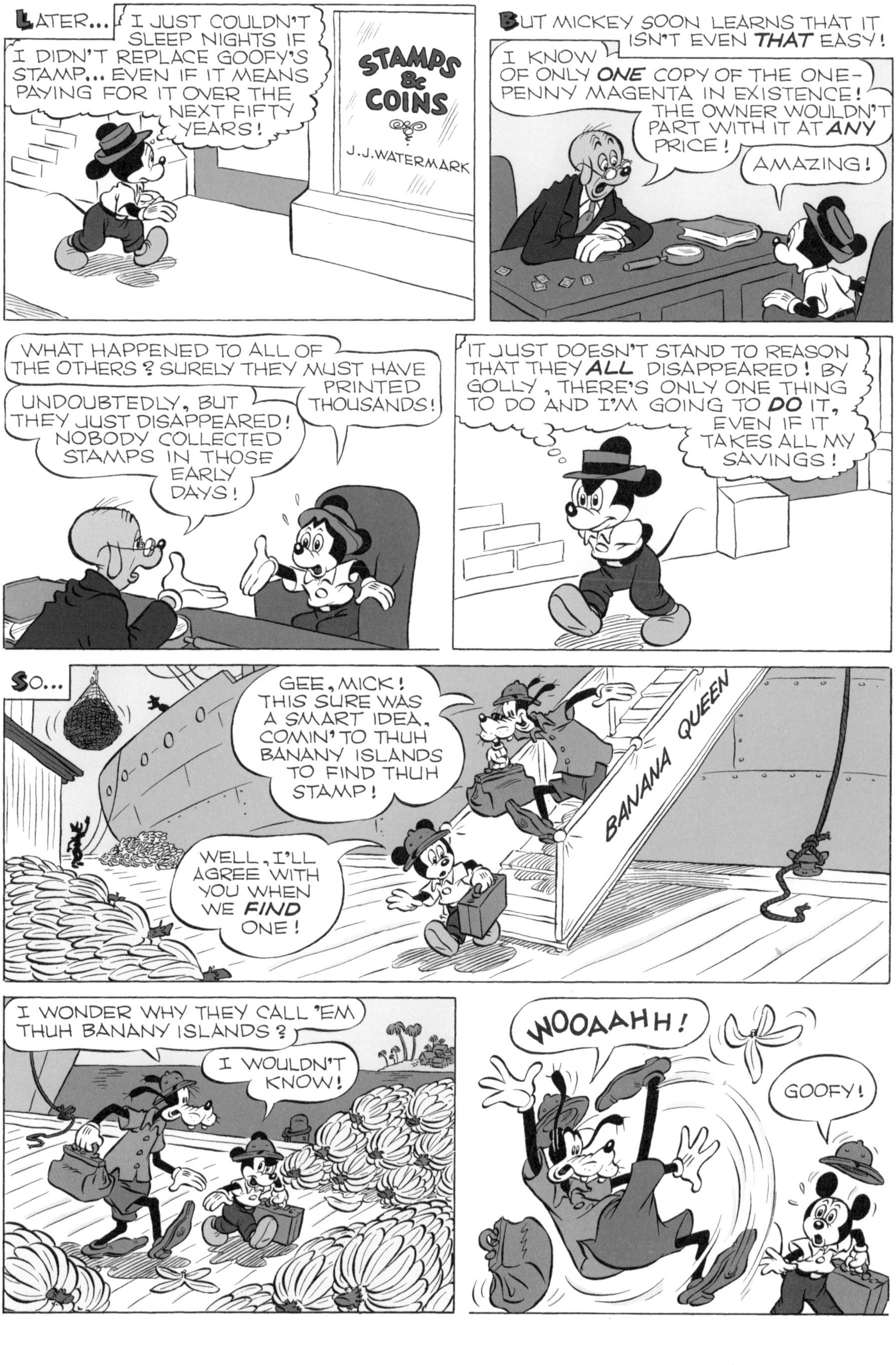
LATER...
I JUST COULDN'T SLEEP NIGHTS IF I DIDN'T REPLACE GOOFY'S STAMP... EVEN IF IT MEANS PAYING FOR IT OVER THE NEXT FIFTY YEARS!
STAMPS & COINS
J.J.WATERMARK
BUT MICKEY SOON LEARNS THAT IT ISN'T EVEN THAT EASY!
I KNOW OF ONLY ONE COPY OF THE ONE-PENNY MAGENTA IN EXISTENCE!
THE OWNER WOULDN'T PART WITH IT AT ANY PRICE!
AMAZING!
WHAT HAPPENED TO ALL OF THE OTHERS? SURELY THEY MUST HAVE PRINTED THOUSANDS!
UNDOUBTEDLY, BUT THEY JUST DISAPPEARED! NOBODY COLLECTED STAMPS IN THOSE EARLY DAYS!
IT JUST DOESN'T STAND TO REASON THAT THEY ALL DISAPPEARED! BY GOLLY, THERE'S ONLY ONE THING TO DO AND I'M GOING TO DO IT, EVEN IF IT TAKES ALL MY SAVINGS!
SO...
GEE, MICK! THIS SURE WAS A SMART IDEA, COMIN' TO THUH BANANY ISLANDS TO FIND THUH STAMP!
BANANA QUEEN
WELL, I'LL AGREE WITH YOU WHEN WE FIND ONE!
I WONDER WHY THEY CALL 'EM THUH BANANY ISLANDS?
I WOULDN'T KNOW!
WOOAAHH!
GOOFY!

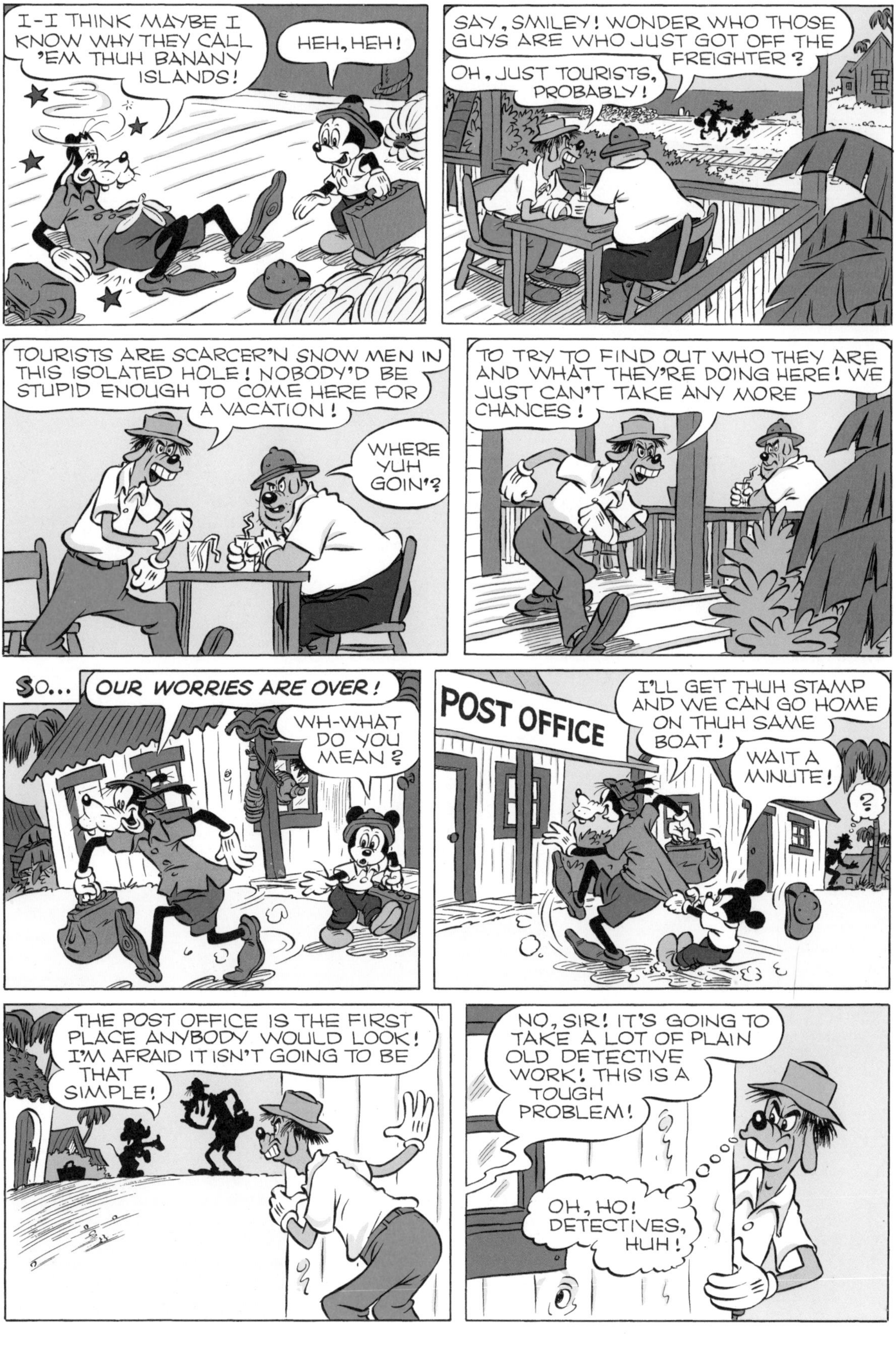

I-I THINK MAYBE I KNOW WHY THEY CALL 'EM THUH BANANY ISLANDS!
HEH, HEH!
SAY, SMILEY! WONDER WHO THOSE GUYS ARE WHO JUST GOT OFF THE FREIGHTER?
OH, JUST TOURISTS, PROBABLY!
TOURISTS ARE SCARCER'N SNOW MEN IN THIS ISOLATED HOLE! NOBODY'D BE STUPID ENOUGH TO COME HERE FOR A VACATION!
WHERE YUH GOIN'?
TO TRY TO FIND OUT WHO THEY ARE AND WHAT THEY'RE DOING HERE! WE JUST CAN'T TAKE ANY MORE CHANCES!
SO...
OUR WORRIES ARE OVER!
WH-WHAT DO YOU MEAN?
POST OFFICE
I'LL GET THUH STAMP AND WE CAN GO HOME ON THUH SAME BOAT!
WAIT A MINUTE!
?
THE POST OFFICE IS THE FIRST PLACE ANYBODY WOULD LOOK! I'M AFRAID IT ISN'T GOING TO BE THAT SIMPLE!
NO, SIR! IT'S GOING TO TAKE A LOT OF PLAIN OLD DETECTIVE WORK! THIS IS A TOUGH PROBLEM!
OH, HO! DETECTIVES, HUH!

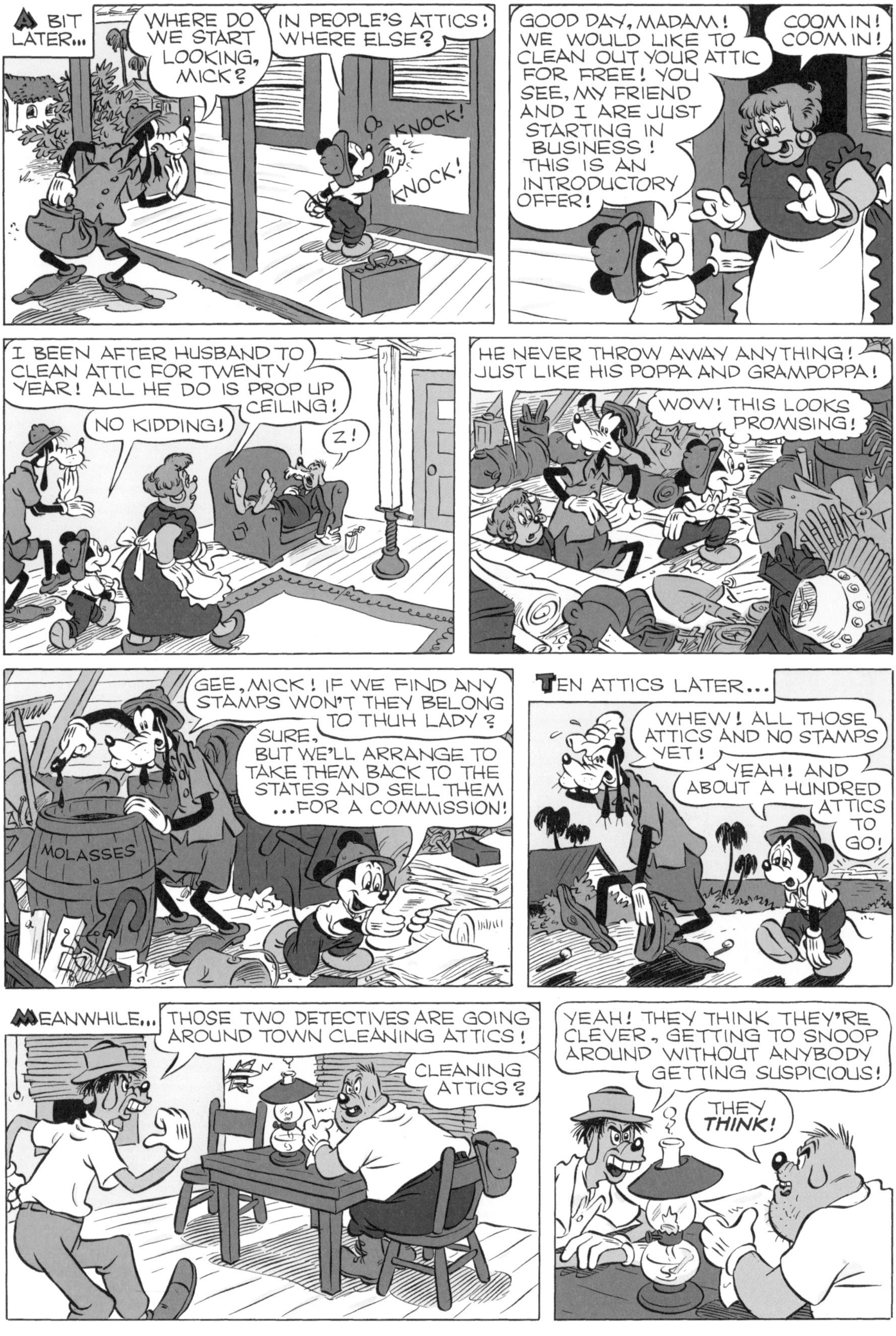
A BIT LATER...
WHERE DO WE START LOOKING, MICK?
IN PEOPLE'S ATTICS! WHERE ELSE?
KNOCK! KNOCK!
GOOD DAY, MADAM! WE WOULD LIKE TO CLEAN OUT YOUR ATTIC FOR FREE! YOU SEE, MY FRIEND AND I ARE JUST STARTING IN BUSINESS! THIS IS AN INTRODUCTORY OFFER!
COOM IN! COOM IN!
I BEEN AFTER HUSBAND TO CLEAN ATTIC FOR TWENTY YEAR! ALL HE DO IS PROP UP CEILING!
NO KIDDING!
Z!
HE NEVER THROW AWAY ANYTHING! JUST LIKE HIS POPPA AND GRAMPOPPA!
WOW! THIS LOOKS PROMSING!
GEE, MICK! IF WE FIND ANY STAMPS WON'T THEY BELONG TO THUH LADY?
SURE, BUT WE'LL ARRANGE TO TAKE THEM BACK TO THE STATES AND SELL THEM ...FOR A COMMISSION!
MOLASSES
TEN ATTICS LATER...
WHEW! ALL THOSE ATTICS AND NO STAMPS YET!
YEAH! AND ABOUT A HUNDRED ATTICS TO GO!
MEANWHILE...
THOSE TWO DETECTIVES ARE GOING AROUND TOWN CLEANING ATTICS!
CLEANING ATTICS?
YEAH! THEY THINK THEY'RE CLEVER, GETTING TO SNOOP AROUND WITHOUT ANYBODY GETTING SUSPICIOUS!
THEY *THINK*!

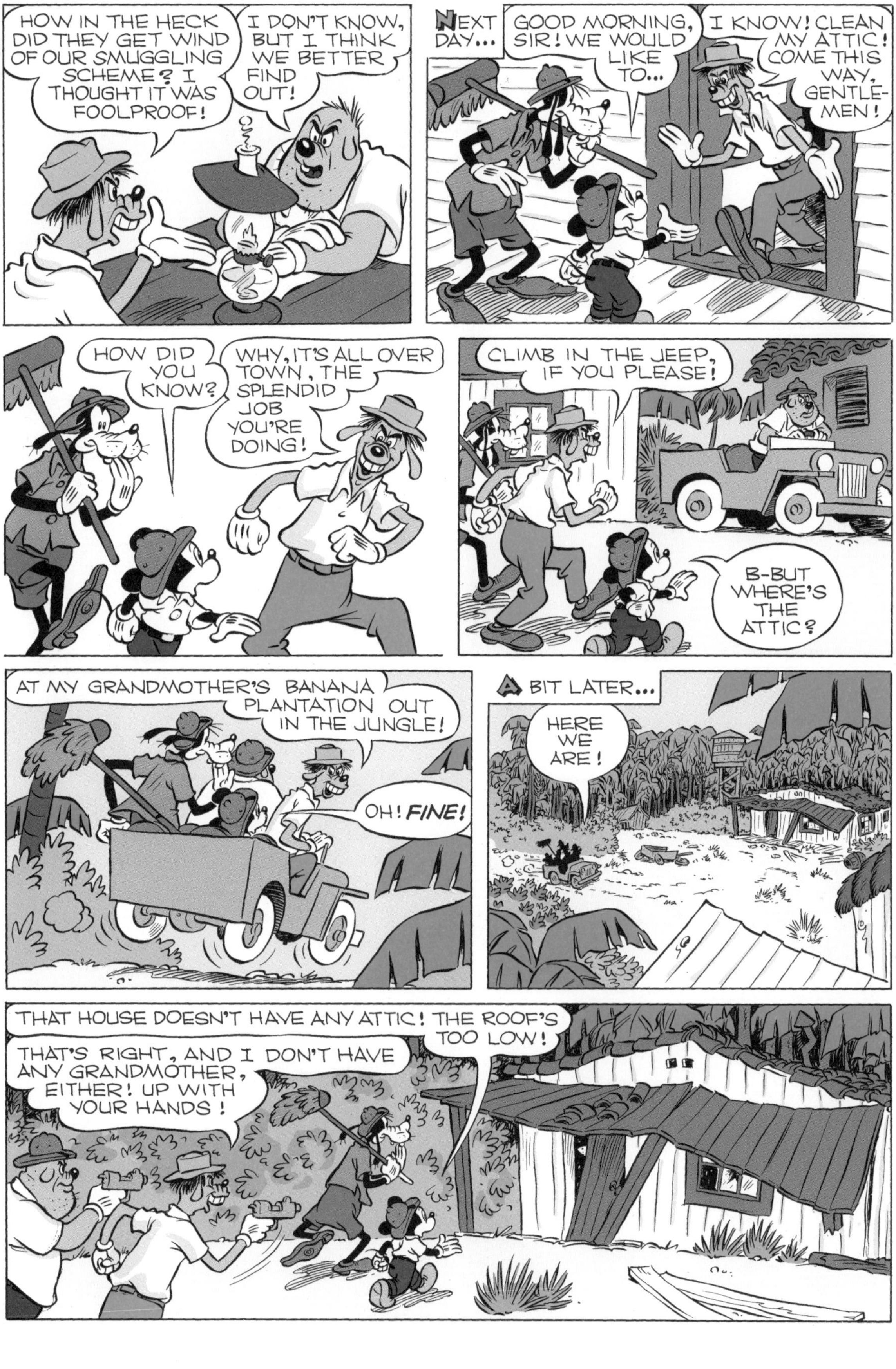
HOW IN THE HECK DID THEY GET WIND OF OUR SMUGGLING SCHEME? I THOUGHT IT WAS FOOLPROOF!
I DON'T KNOW, BUT I THINK WE BETTER FIND OUT!
NEXT DAY...
GOOD MORNING, SIR! WE WOULD LIKE TO...
I KNOW! CLEAN MY ATTIC! COME THIS WAY, GENTLEMEN!
HOW DID YOU KNOW?
WHY, IT'S ALL OVER TOWN, THE SPLENDID JOB YOU'RE DOING!
CLIMB IN THE JEEP, IF YOU PLEASE!
B-BUT WHERE'S THE ATTIC?
AT MY GRANDMOTHER'S BANANA PLANTATION OUT IN THE JUNGLE!
OH! FINE!
A BIT LATER...
HERE WE ARE!
THAT HOUSE DOESN'T HAVE ANY ATTIC! THE ROOF'S TOO LOW!
THAT'S RIGHT, AND I DON'T HAVE ANY GRANDMOTHER, EITHER! UP WITH YOUR HANDS!

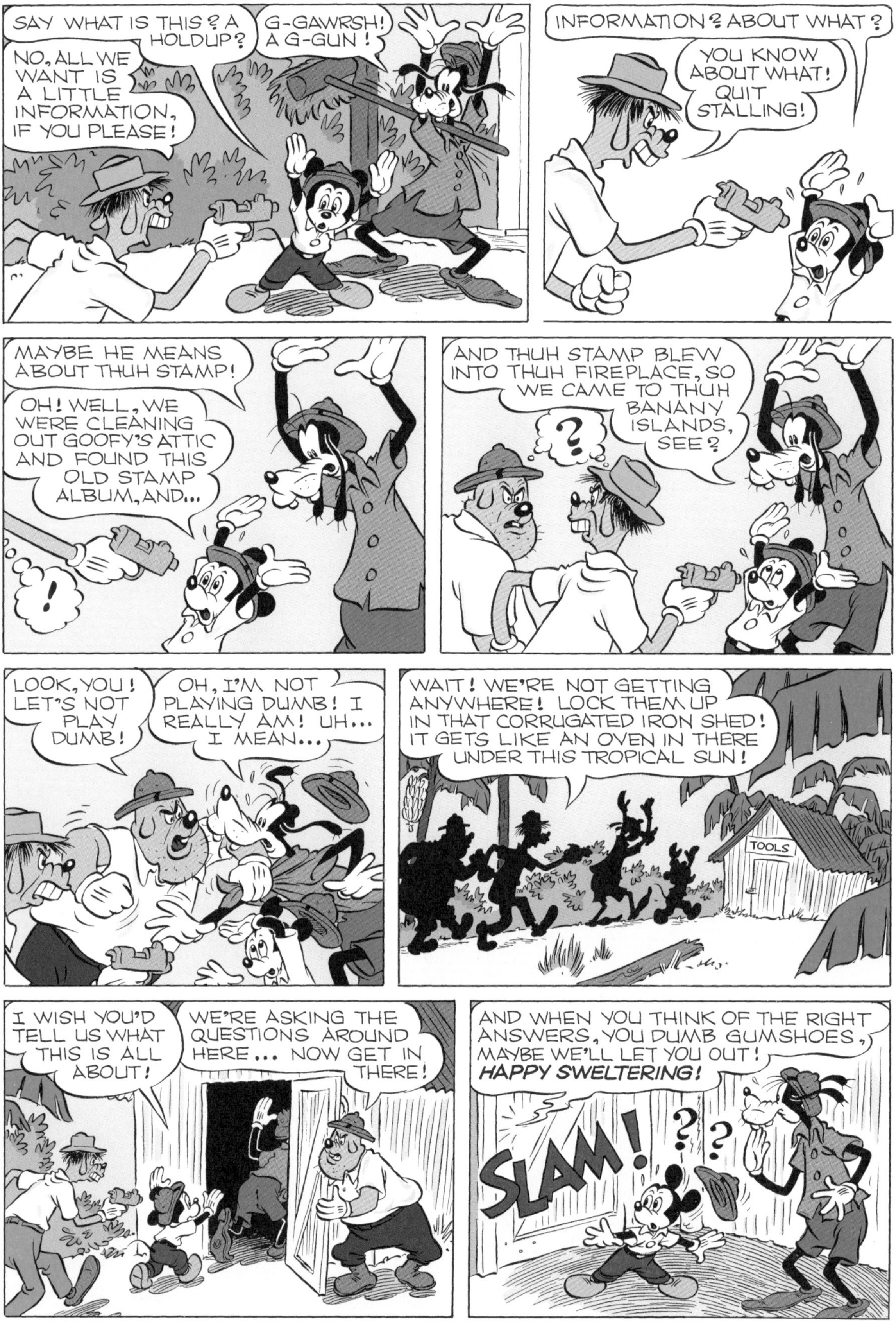
SAY WHAT IS THIS? A HOLDUP?
G-GAWRSH! A G-GUN!
NO, ALL WE WANT IS A LITTLE INFORMATION, IF YOU PLEASE!
INFORMATION? ABOUT WHAT?
YOU KNOW ABOUT WHAT! QUIT STALLING!
MAYBE HE MEANS ABOUT THUH STAMP!
OH! WELL, WE WERE CLEANING OUT GOOFY'S ATTIC AND FOUND THIS OLD STAMP ALBUM, AND...
!
AND THUH STAMP BLEW INTO THUH FIREPLACE, SO WE CAME TO THUH BANANY ISLANDS, SEE?
?
LOOK, YOU! LET'S NOT PLAY DUMB!
OH, I'M NOT PLAYING DUMB! I REALLY AM! UH... I MEAN...
WAIT! WE'RE NOT GETTING ANYWHERE! LOCK THEM UP IN THAT CORRUGATED IRON SHED! IT GETS LIKE AN OVEN IN THERE UNDER THIS TROPICAL SUN!
TOOLS
I WISH YOU'D TELL US WHAT THIS IS ALL ABOUT!
WE'RE ASKING THE QUESTIONS AROUND HERE... NOW GET IN THERE!
AND WHEN YOU THINK OF THE RIGHT ANSWERS, YOU DUMB GUMSHOES, MAYBE WE'LL LET YOU OUT! ***HAPPY SWELTERING!***
SLAM!
? ?

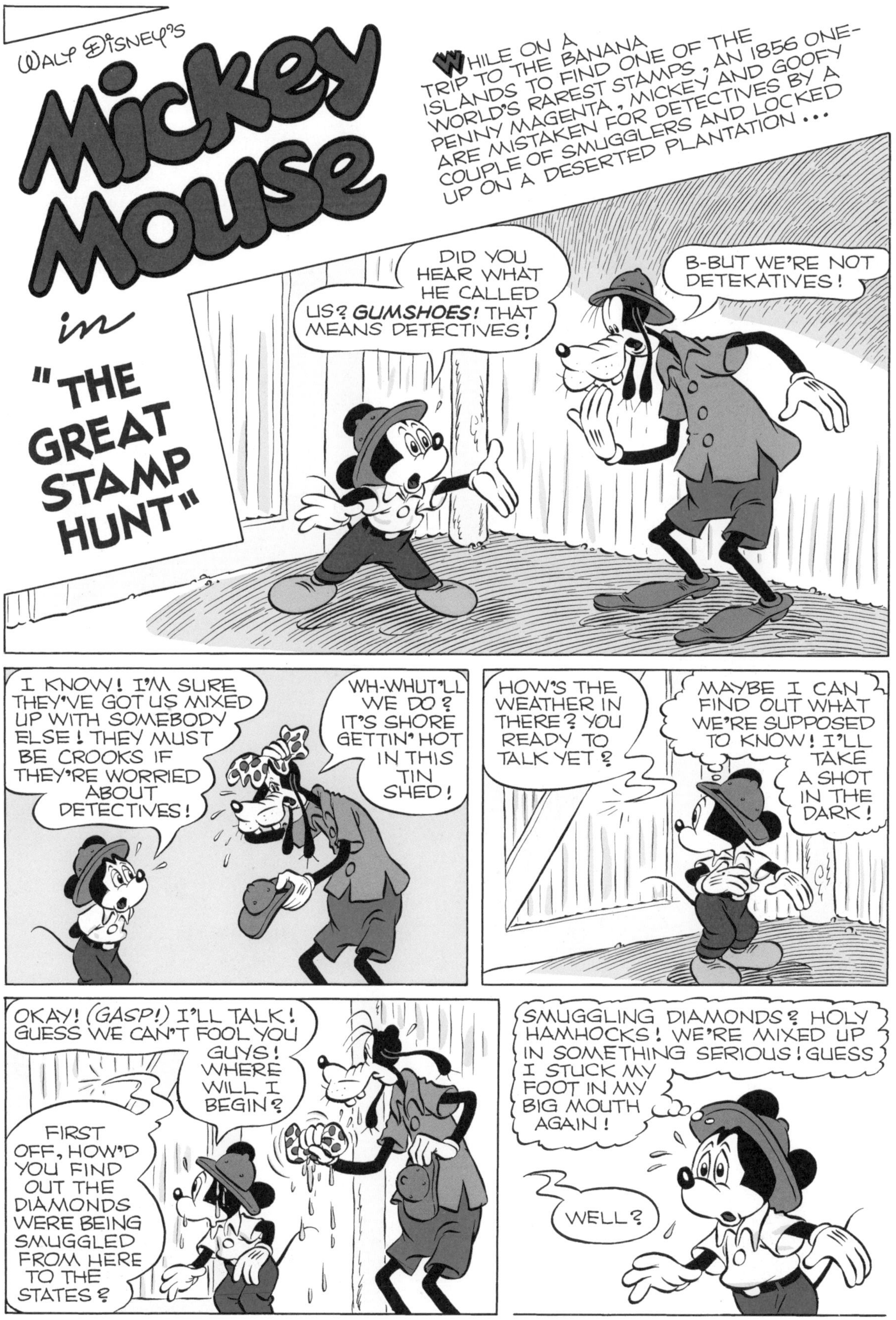

WALT DISNEY'S
Mickey Mouse
in
"THE GREAT STAMP HUNT"
WHILE ON A TRIP TO THE BANANA ISLANDS TO FIND ONE OF THE WORLD'S RAREST STAMPS, AN 1856 ONE-PENNY MAGENTA, MICKEY AND GOOFY ARE MISTAKEN FOR DETECTIVES BY A COUPLE OF SMUGGLERS AND LOCKED UP ON A DESERTED PLANTATION...
DID YOU HEAR WHAT HE CALLED US? GUMSHOES! THAT MEANS DETECTIVES!
B-BUT WE'RE NOT DETEKATIVES!
I KNOW! I'M SURE THEY'VE GOT US MIXED UP WITH SOMEBODY ELSE! THEY MUST BE CROOKS IF THEY'RE WORRIED ABOUT DETECTIVES!
WH-WHUT'LL WE DO? IT'S SHORE GETTIN' HOT IN THIS TIN SHED!
HOW'S THE WEATHER IN THERE? YOU READY TO TALK YET?
MAYBE I CAN FIND OUT WHAT WE'RE SUPPOSED TO KNOW! I'LL TAKE A SHOT IN THE DARK!
OKAY! (GASP!) I'LL TALK! GUESS WE CAN'T FOOL YOU GUYS! WHERE WILL I BEGIN?
FIRST OFF, HOW'D YOU FIND OUT THE DIAMONDS WERE BEING SMUGGLED FROM HERE TO THE STATES?
SMUGGLING DIAMONDS? HOLY HAMHOCKS! WE'RE MIXED UP IN SOMETHING SERIOUS! GUESS I STUCK MY FOOT IN MY BIG MOUTH AGAIN!
WELL?

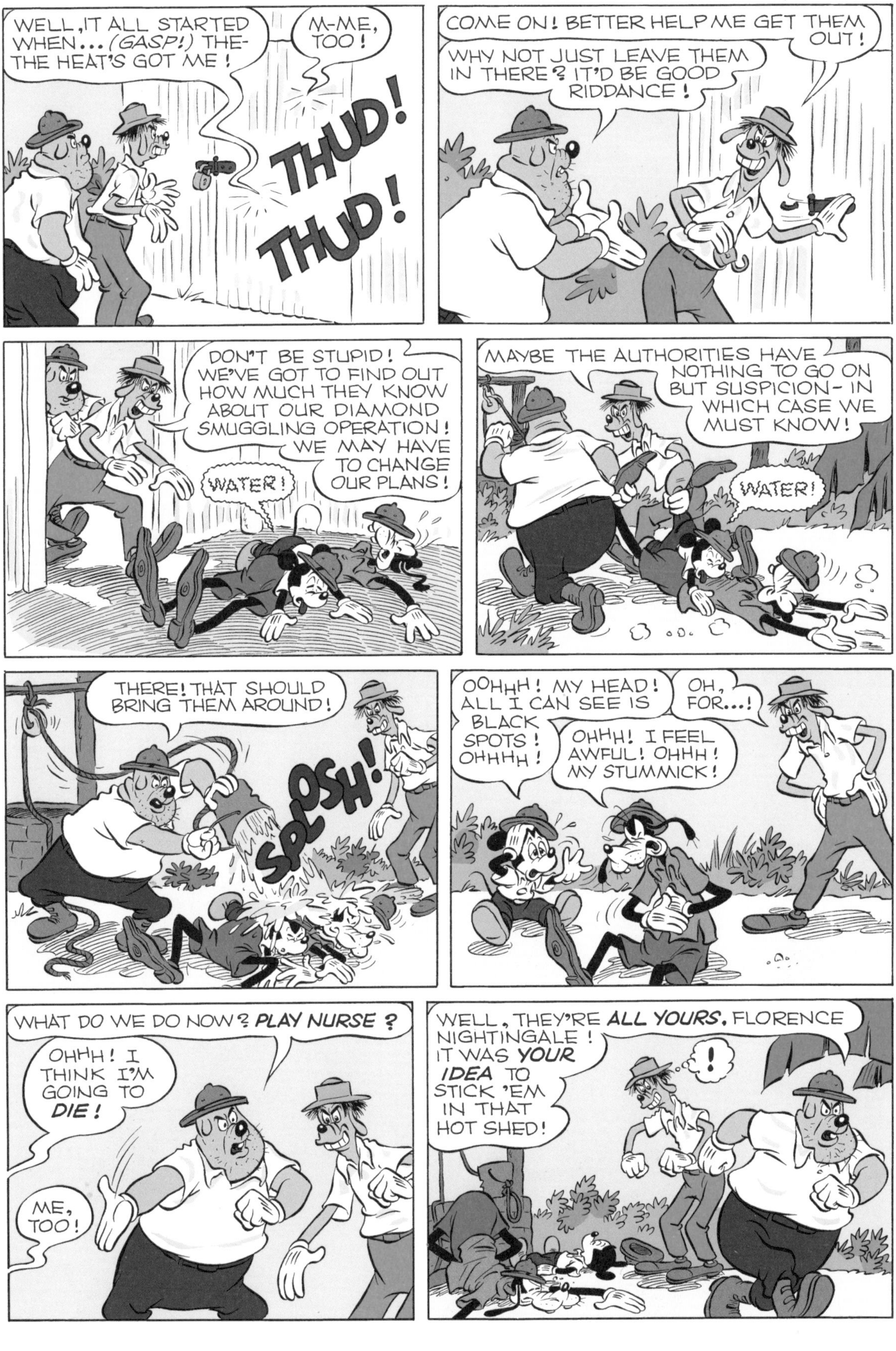
WELL, IT ALL STARTED WHEN... (GASP!) THE- THE HEAT'S GOT ME!
M-ME, TOO!
THUD! THUD!
COME ON! BETTER HELP ME GET THEM OUT!
WHY NOT JUST LEAVE THEM IN THERE? IT'D BE GOOD RIDDANCE!
DON'T BE STUPID! WE'VE GOT TO FIND OUT HOW MUCH THEY KNOW ABOUT OUR DIAMOND SMUGGLING OPERATION! WE MAY HAVE TO CHANGE OUR PLANS!
WATER!
MAYBE THE AUTHORITIES HAVE NOTHING TO GO ON BUT SUSPICION- IN WHICH CASE WE MUST KNOW!
WATER!
THERE! THAT SHOULD BRING THEM AROUND!
SPLOSH!
OOHHH! MY HEAD! ALL I CAN SEE IS BLACK SPOTS! OHHHH!
OH, FOR...!
OHHH! I FEEL AWFUL! OHHH! MY STUMMICK!
WHAT DO WE DO NOW? PLAY NURSE?
OHHH! I THINK I'M GOING TO DIE!
ME, TOO!
WELL, THEY'RE ALL YOURS, FLORENCE NIGHTINGALE! IT WAS YOUR IDEA TO STICK 'EM IN THAT HOT SHED!
!

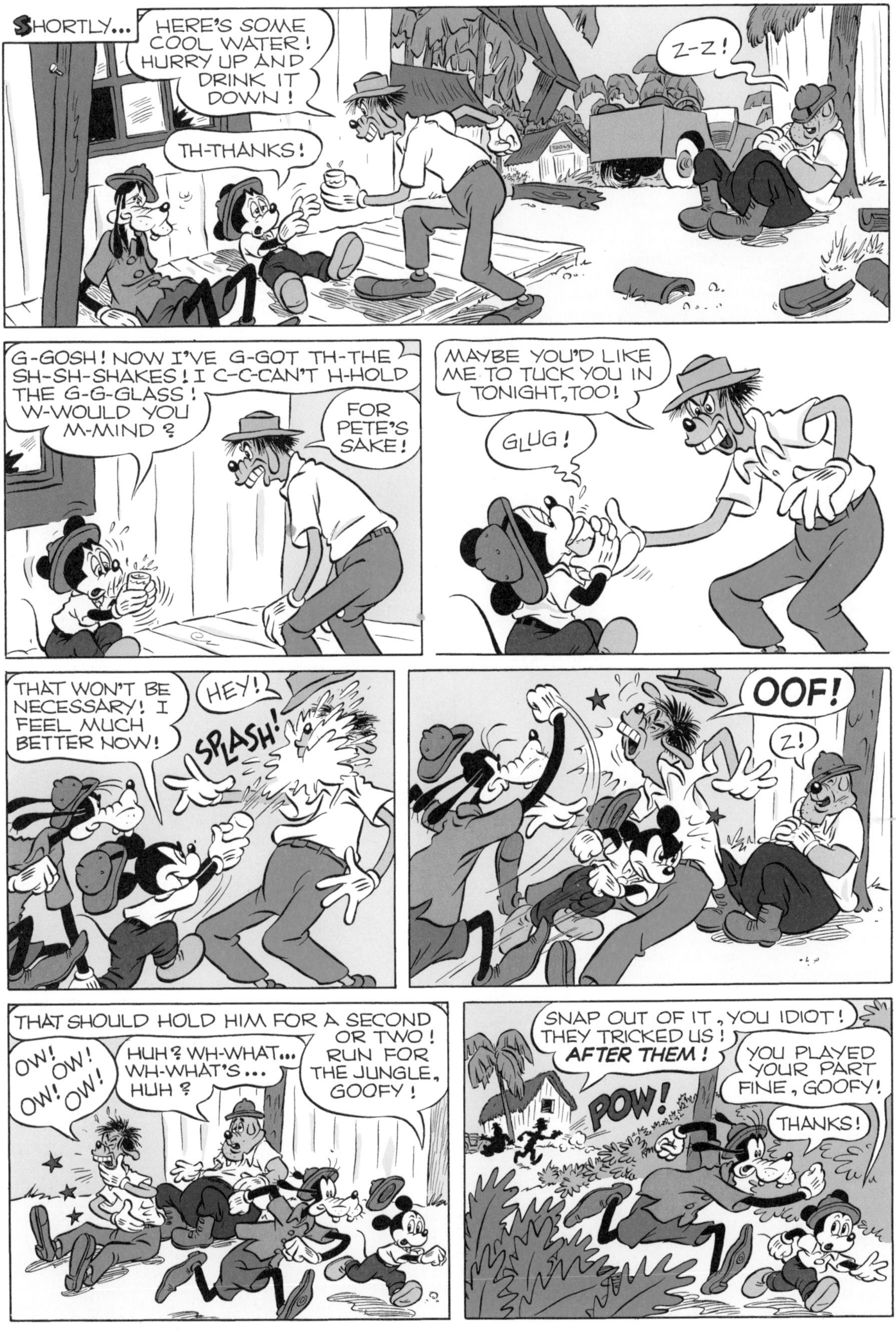
SHORTLY...
HERE'S SOME COOL WATER! HURRY UP AND DRINK IT DOWN!
Z-Z!
TH-THANKS!
TOOLS
G-GOSH! NOW I'VE G-GOT TH-THE SH-SH-SHAKES! I C-C-CAN'T H-HOLD THE G-G-GLASS! W-WOULD YOU M-MIND?
FOR PETE'S SAKE!
MAYBE YOU'D LIKE ME TO TUCK YOU IN TONIGHT, TOO!
GLUG!
THAT WON'T BE NECESSARY! I FEEL MUCH BETTER NOW!
HEY!
SPLASH!
OOF!
Z!
THAT SHOULD HOLD HIM FOR A SECOND OR TWO! RUN FOR THE JUNGLE, GOOFY!
OW! OW! OW! OW!
HUH? WH-WHAT... WH-WHAT'S... HUH?
SNAP OUT OF IT, YOU IDIOT! THEY TRICKED US! AFTER THEM!
YOU PLAYED YOUR PART FINE, GOOFY!
POW!
THANKS!

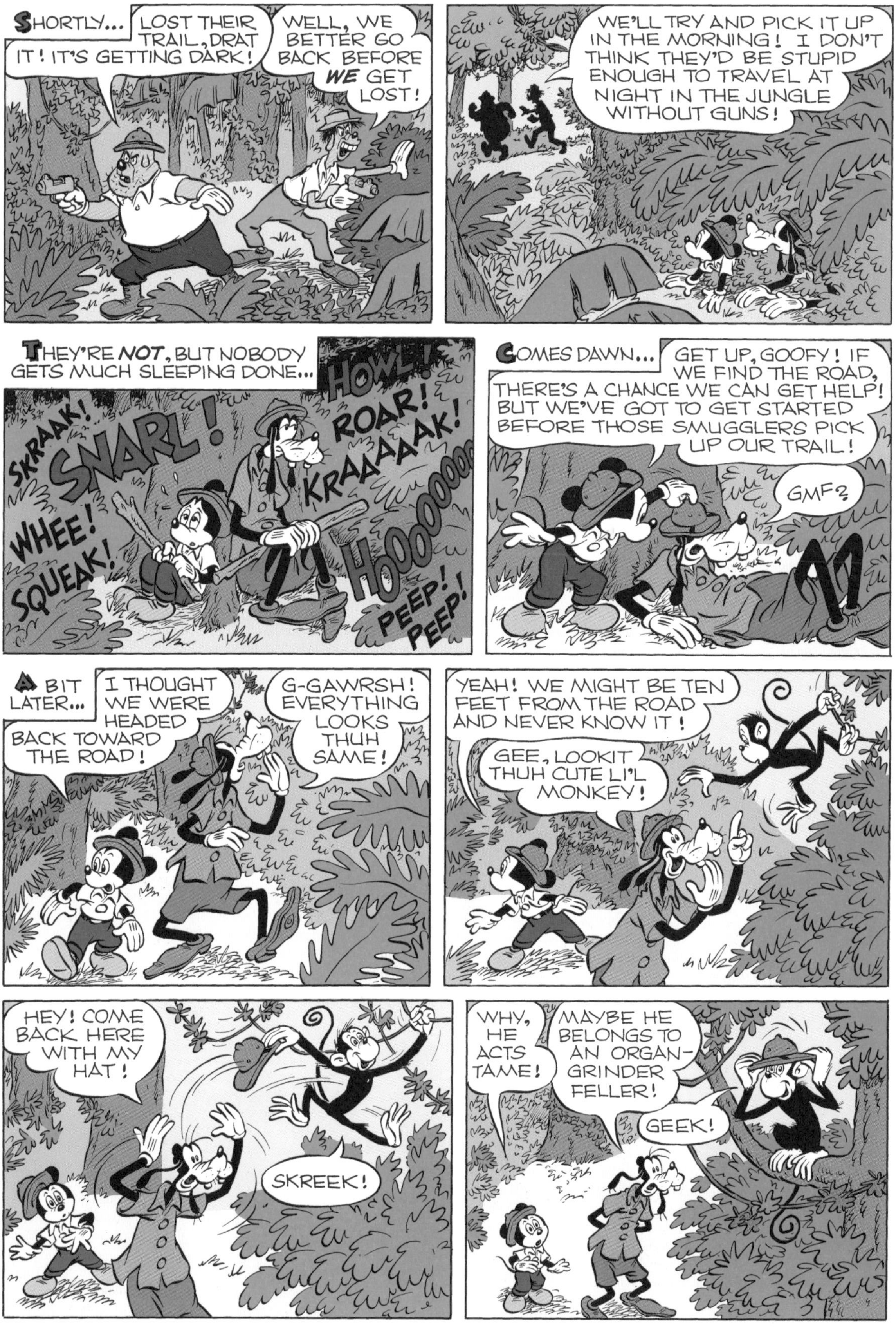
SHORTLY...
LOST THEIR TRAIL, DRAT IT! IT'S GETTING DARK!
WELL, WE BETTER GO BACK BEFORE WE GET LOST!
WE'LL TRY AND PICK IT UP IN THE MORNING! I DON'T THINK THEY'D BE STUPID ENOUGH TO TRAVEL AT NIGHT IN THE JUNGLE WITHOUT GUNS!
THEY'RE NOT, BUT NOBODY GETS MUCH SLEEPING DONE...
HOWL!
SKRAAK!
SNARL!
ROAR!
KRAAAAAK!
WHEE!
SQUEAK!
HOOOOOOOOO
PEEP! PEEP!
COMES DAWN...
GET UP, GOOFY! IF WE FIND THE ROAD, THERE'S A CHANCE WE CAN GET HELP! BUT WE'VE GOT TO GET STARTED BEFORE THOSE SMUGGLERS PICK UP OUR TRAIL!
GMF?
A BIT LATER...
I THOUGHT WE WERE HEADED BACK TOWARD THE ROAD!
G-GAWRSH! EVERYTHING LOOKS THUH SAME!
YEAH! WE MIGHT BE TEN FEET FROM THE ROAD AND NEVER KNOW IT!
GEE, LOOKIT THUH CUTE LI'L MONKEY!
HEY! COME BACK HERE WITH MY HAT!
SKREEK!
WHY, HE ACTS TAME!
MAYBE HE BELONGS TO AN ORGAN-GRINDER FELLER!
GEEK!

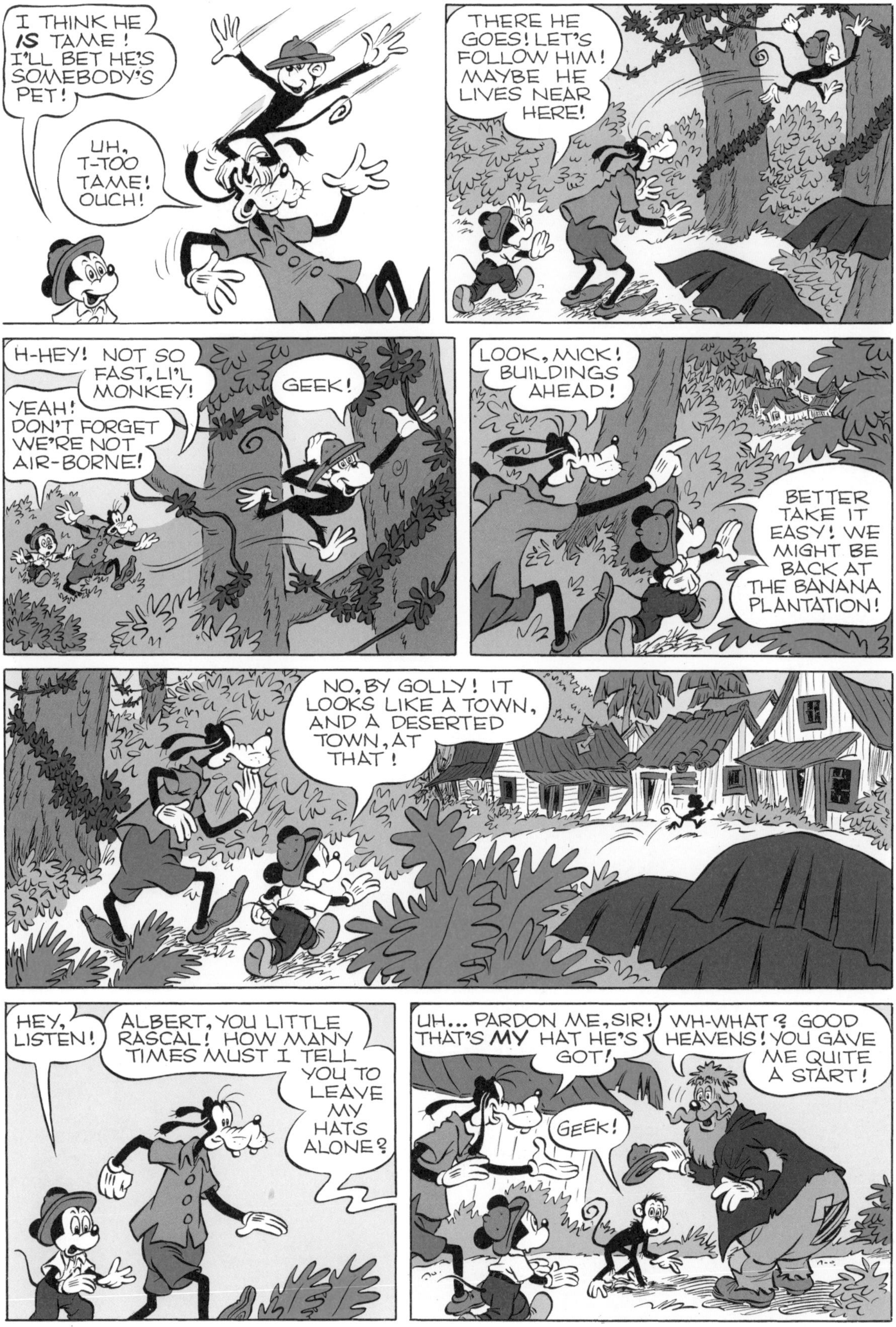

I THINK HE IS TAME! I'LL BET HE'S SOMEBODY'S PET!
UH, T-TOO TAME! OUCH!
THERE HE GOES! LET'S FOLLOW HIM! MAYBE HE LIVES NEAR HERE!
H-HEY! NOT SO FAST, LI'L MONKEY!
YEAH! DON'T FORGET WE'RE NOT AIR-BORNE!
GEEK!
LOOK, MICK! BUILDINGS AHEAD!
BETTER TAKE IT EASY! WE MIGHT BE BACK AT THE BANANA PLANTATION!
NO, BY GOLLY! IT LOOKS LIKE A TOWN, AND A DESERTED TOWN, AT THAT!
HEY, LISTEN!
ALBERT, YOU LITTLE RASCAL! HOW MANY TIMES MUST I TELL YOU TO LEAVE MY HATS ALONE?
UH... PARDON ME, SIR! THAT'S MY HAT HE'S GOT!
WH-WHAT? GOOD HEAVENS! YOU GAVE ME QUITE A START!
GEEK!

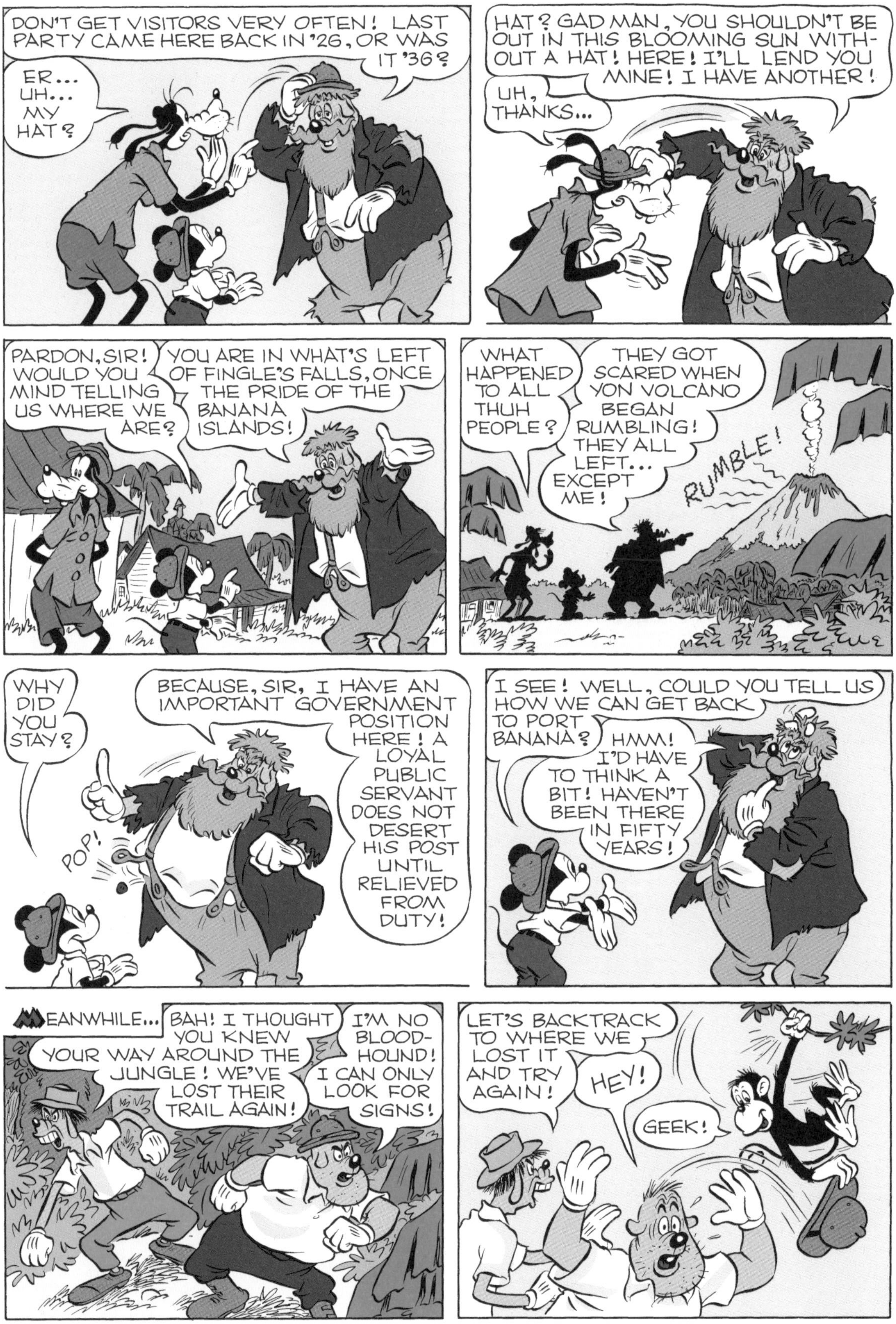
DON'T GET VISITORS VERY OFTEN! LAST PARTY CAME HERE BACK IN '26, OR WAS IT '36?
ER... UH... MY HAT?
HAT? GAD MAN, YOU SHOULDN'T BE OUT IN THIS BLOOMING SUN WITH-OUT A HAT! HERE! I'LL LEND YOU MINE! I HAVE ANOTHER!
UH, THANKS...
PARDON, SIR! WOULD YOU MIND TELLING US WHERE WE ARE?
YOU ARE IN WHAT'S LEFT OF FINGLE'S FALLS, ONCE THE PRIDE OF THE BANANA ISLANDS!
WHAT HAPPENED TO ALL THUH PEOPLE?
THEY GOT SCARED WHEN YON VOLCANO BEGAN RUMBLING! THEY ALL LEFT... EXCEPT ME!
RUMBLE!
WHY DID YOU STAY?
BECAUSE, SIR, I HAVE AN IMPORTANT GOVERNMENT POSITION HERE! A LOYAL PUBLIC SERVANT DOES NOT DESERT HIS POST UNTIL RELIEVED FROM DUTY!
POP!
I SEE! WELL, COULD YOU TELL US HOW WE CAN GET BACK TO PORT BANANA?
HMM! I'D HAVE TO THINK A BIT! HAVEN'T BEEN THERE IN FIFTY YEARS!
MEANWHILE...
BAH! I THOUGHT YOU KNEW YOUR WAY AROUND THE JUNGLE! WE'VE LOST THEIR TRAIL AGAIN!
I'M NO BLOOD-HOUND! I CAN ONLY LOOK FOR SIGNS!
LET'S BACKTRACK TO WHERE WE LOST IT AND TRY AGAIN!
HEY!
GEEK!

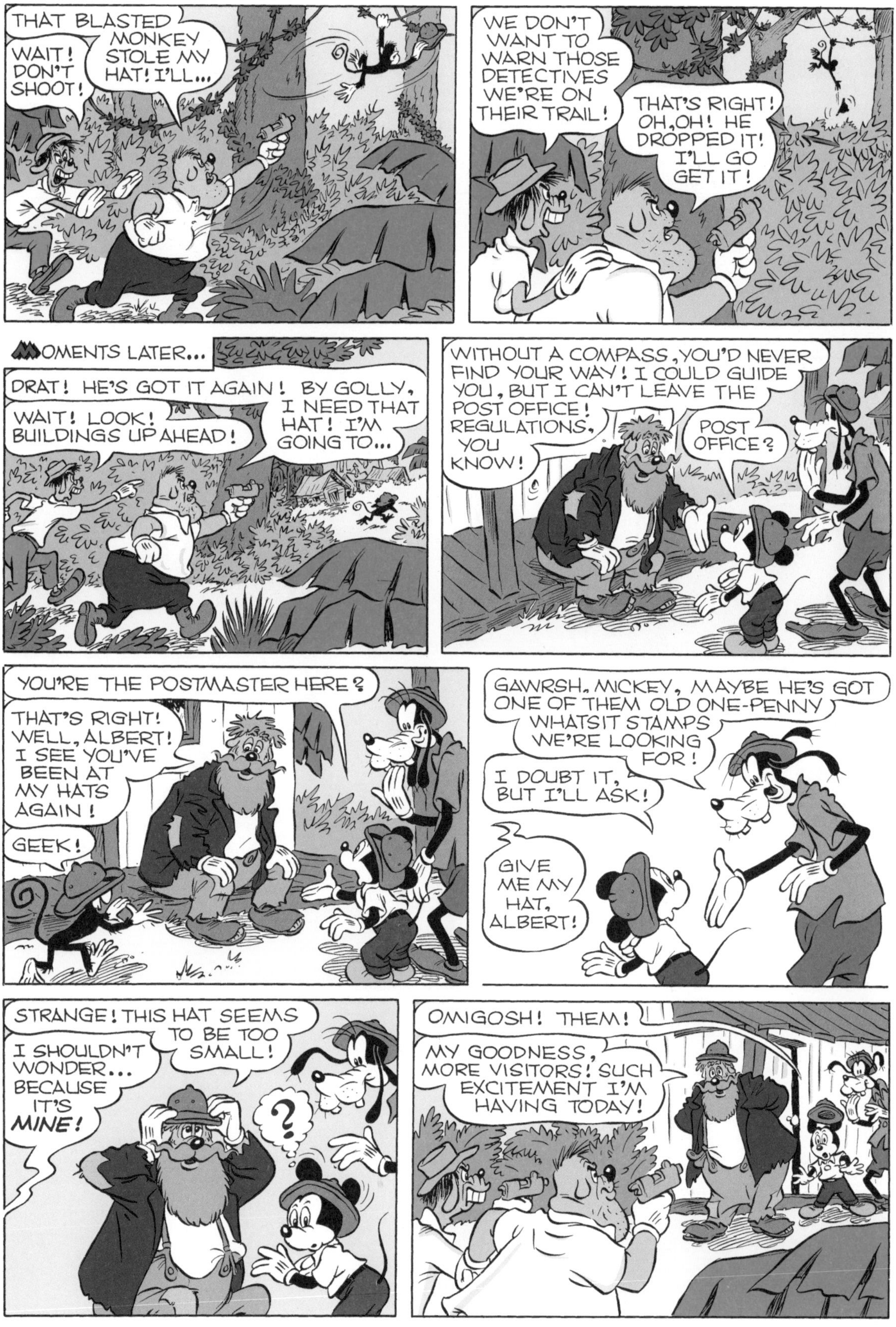
THAT BLASTED MONKEY STOLE MY HAT! I'LL...
WAIT! DON'T SHOOT!
WE DON'T WANT TO WARN THOSE DETECTIVES WE'RE ON THEIR TRAIL!
THAT'S RIGHT! OH, OH! HE DROPPED IT! I'LL GO GET IT!
MOMENTS LATER...
DRAT! HE'S GOT IT AGAIN! BY GOLLY, I NEED THAT HAT! I'M GOING TO...
WAIT! LOOK! BUILDINGS UP AHEAD!
WITHOUT A COMPASS, YOU'D NEVER FIND YOUR WAY! I COULD GUIDE YOU, BUT I CAN'T LEAVE THE POST OFFICE! REGULATIONS, YOU KNOW!
POST OFFICE?
YOU'RE THE POSTMASTER HERE?
THAT'S RIGHT! WELL, ALBERT! I SEE YOU'VE BEEN AT MY HATS AGAIN!
GEEK!
GAWRSH, MICKEY, MAYBE HE'S GOT ONE OF THEM OLD ONE-PENNY WHATSIT STAMPS WE'RE LOOKING FOR!
I DOUBT IT, BUT I'LL ASK!
GIVE ME MY HAT, ALBERT!
STRANGE! THIS HAT SEEMS TO BE TOO SMALL!
I SHOULDN'T WONDER... BECAUSE IT'S *MINE!*
?
OMIGOSH! THEM!
MY GOODNESS, MORE VISITORS! SUCH EXCITEMENT I'M HAVING TODAY!

MOMENTS LATER...
YOU'VE GOT TEN SECONDS TO TELL US HOW YOU FOUND OUT ABOUT OUR SMUGGLING!
YOU GUYS WOULDN'T WANT ANYTHING TO HAPPEN TO AN INNOCENT POSTMASTER, WOULD YOU?
RUMBLE!
HEY! WHAT'S THAT?
OH, JUST THE VOLCANO, I DARE SAY!
MY, MY! IT LOOKS AS THOUGH IT'S REALLY ABOUT TO BLOW ITS TOP *THIS* TIME!
BAROOOOOOOOOOOM

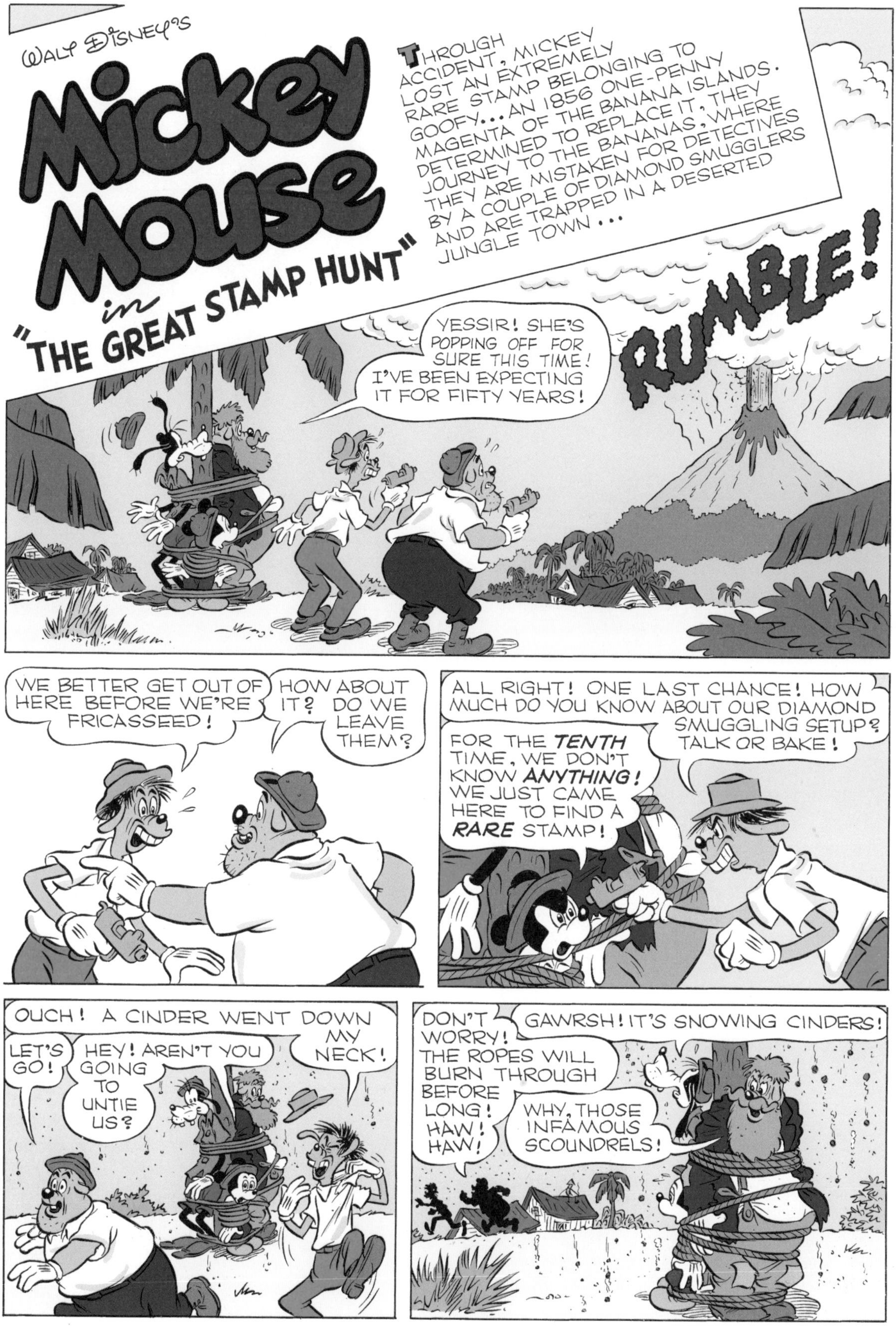

WALT DISNEY'S
Mickey Mouse
in
"THE GREAT STAMP HUNT"
THROUGH ACCIDENT, MICKEY LOST AN EXTREMELY RARE STAMP BELONGING TO GOOFY... AN 1856 ONE-PENNY MAGENTA OF THE BANANA ISLANDS. DETERMINED TO REPLACE IT, THEY JOURNEY TO THE BANANAS, WHERE THEY ARE MISTAKEN FOR DETECTIVES BY A COUPLE OF DIAMOND SMUGGLERS AND ARE TRAPPED IN A DESERTED JUNGLE TOWN...
YESSIR! SHE'S POPPING OFF FOR SURE THIS TIME! I'VE BEEN EXPECTING IT FOR FIFTY YEARS!
RUMBLE!
WE BETTER GET OUT OF HERE BEFORE WE'RE FRICASSEED!
HOW ABOUT IT? DO WE LEAVE THEM?
ALL RIGHT! ONE LAST CHANCE! HOW MUCH DO YOU KNOW ABOUT OUR DIAMOND SMUGGLING SETUP? TALK OR BAKE!
FOR THE TENTH TIME, WE DON'T KNOW ANYTHING! WE JUST CAME HERE TO FIND A RARE STAMP!
OUCH! A CINDER WENT DOWN MY NECK!
LET'S GO!
HEY! AREN'T YOU GOING TO UNTIE US?
DON'T WORRY! THE ROPES WILL BURN THROUGH BEFORE LONG! HAW! HAW!
GAWRSH! IT'S SNOWING CINDERS!
WHY, THOSE INFAMOUS SCOUNDRELS!

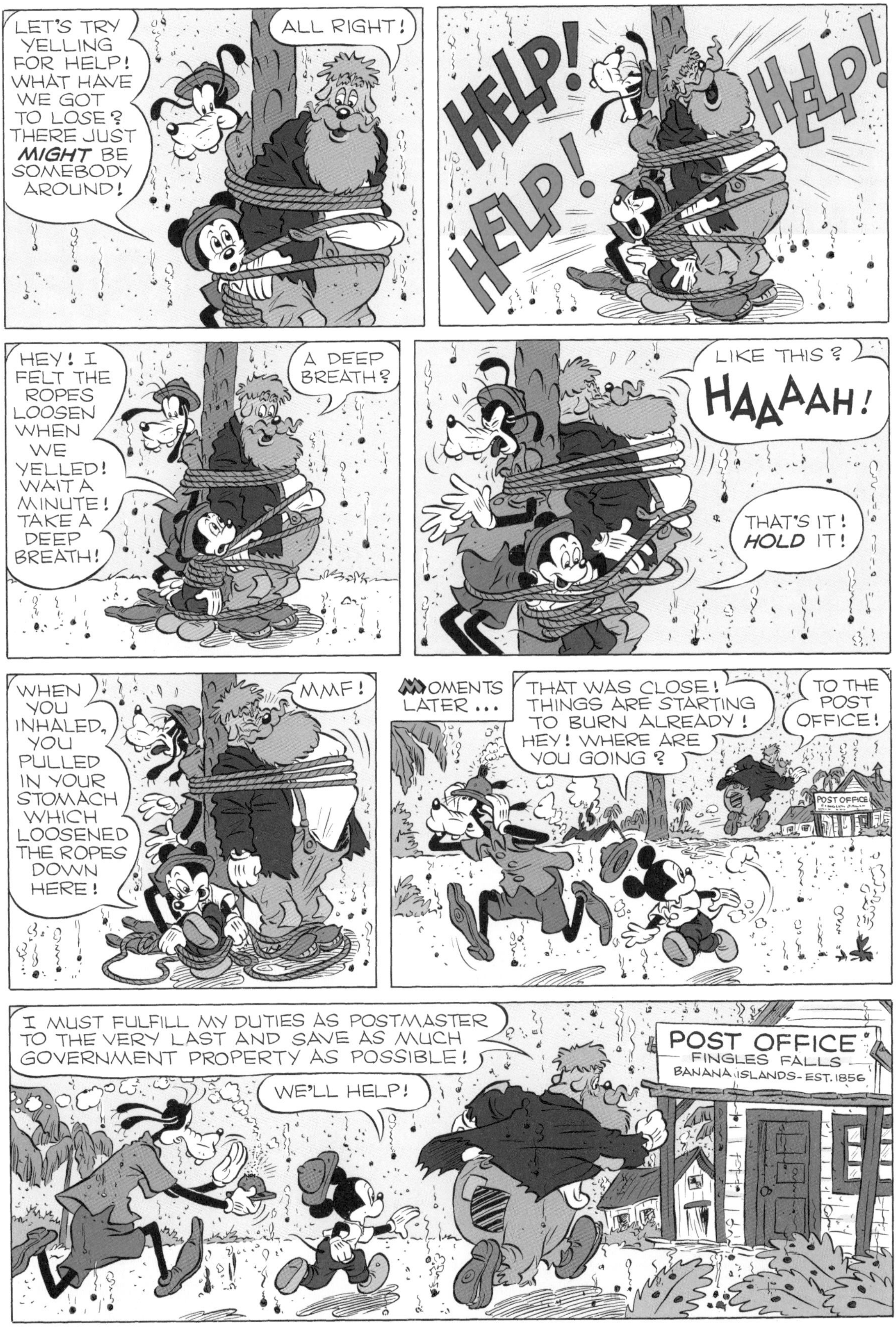
LET'S TRY YELLING FOR HELP! WHAT HAVE WE GOT TO LOSE? THERE JUST *MIGHT* BE SOMEBODY AROUND!
ALL RIGHT!
HELP!
HELP!
HELP!
HEY! I FELT THE ROPES LOOSEN WHEN WE YELLED! WAIT A MINUTE! TAKE A DEEP BREATH!
A DEEP BREATH?
LIKE THIS? HAAAAH!
THAT'S IT! *HOLD* IT!
WHEN YOU INHALED, YOU PULLED IN YOUR STOMACH WHICH LOOSENED THE ROPES DOWN HERE!
MMF!
MOMENTS LATER...
THAT WAS CLOSE! THINGS ARE STARTING TO BURN ALREADY! HEY! WHERE ARE YOU GOING?
TO THE POST OFFICE!
POST OFFICE
I MUST FULFILL MY DUTIES AS POSTMASTER TO THE VERY LAST AND SAVE AS MUCH GOVERNMENT PROPERTY AS POSSIBLE!
WE'LL HELP!
POST OFFICE
FINGLES FALLS
BANANA ISLANDS-EST. 1856

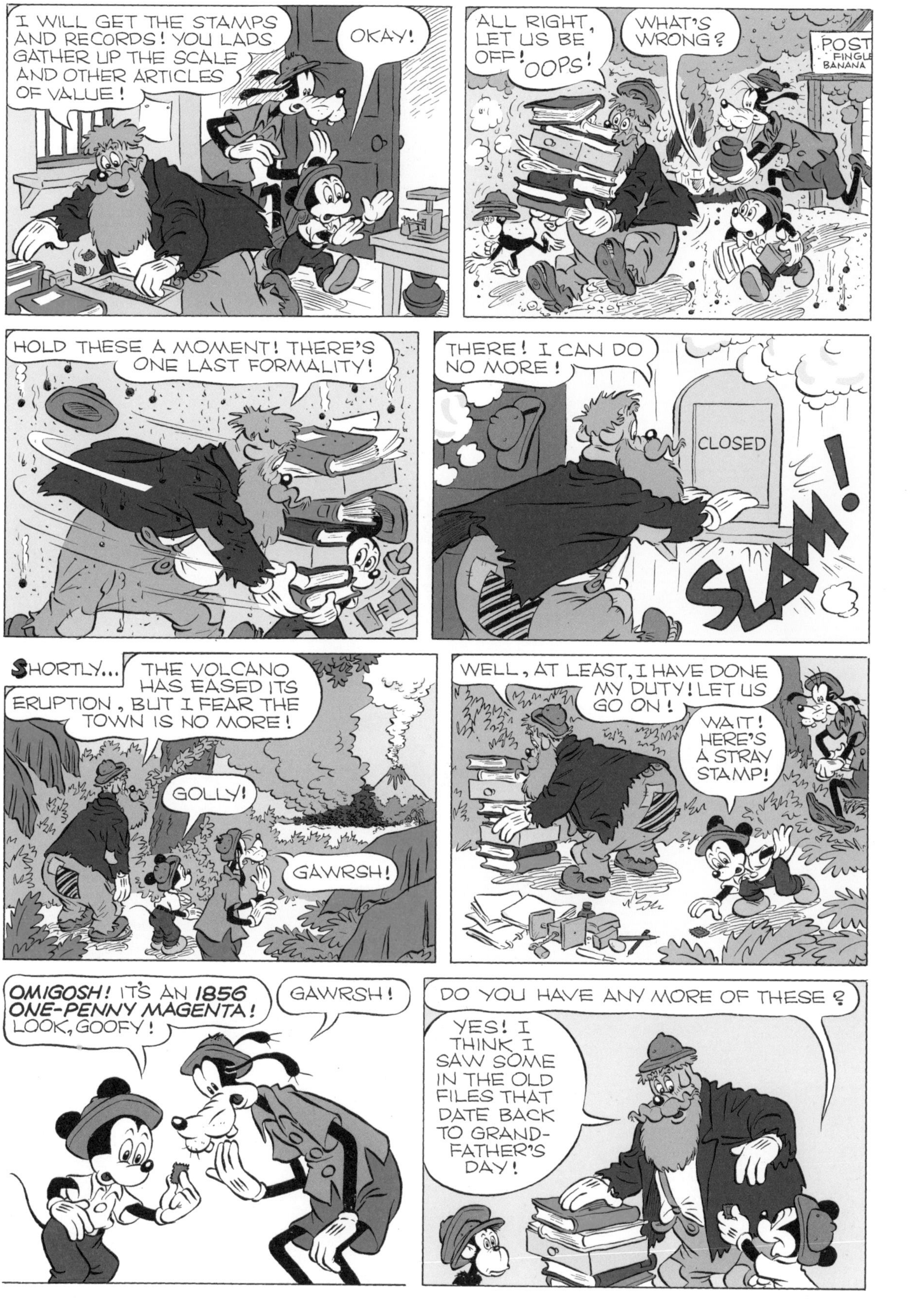

I WILL GET THE STAMPS AND RECORDS! YOU LADS GATHER UP THE SCALE AND OTHER ARTICLES OF VALUE!
OKAY!
ALL RIGHT, LET US BE OFF!
OOPS!
WHAT'S WRONG?
POST
FINGLE
BANANA
HOLD THESE A MOMENT! THERE'S ONE LAST FORMALITY!
THERE! I CAN DO NO MORE!
CLOSED
SLAM!
SHORTLY...
THE VOLCANO HAS EASED ITS ERUPTION, BUT I FEAR THE TOWN IS NO MORE!
GOLLY!
GAWRSH!
WELL, AT LEAST, I HAVE DONE MY DUTY! LET US GO ON!
WAIT! HERE'S A STRAY STAMP!
OMIGOSH! IT'S AN 1856 ONE-PENNY MAGENTA! LOOK, GOOFY!
GAWRSH!
DO YOU HAVE ANY MORE OF THESE?
YES! I THINK I SAW SOME IN THE OLD FILES THAT DATE BACK TO GRAND-FATHER'S DAY!

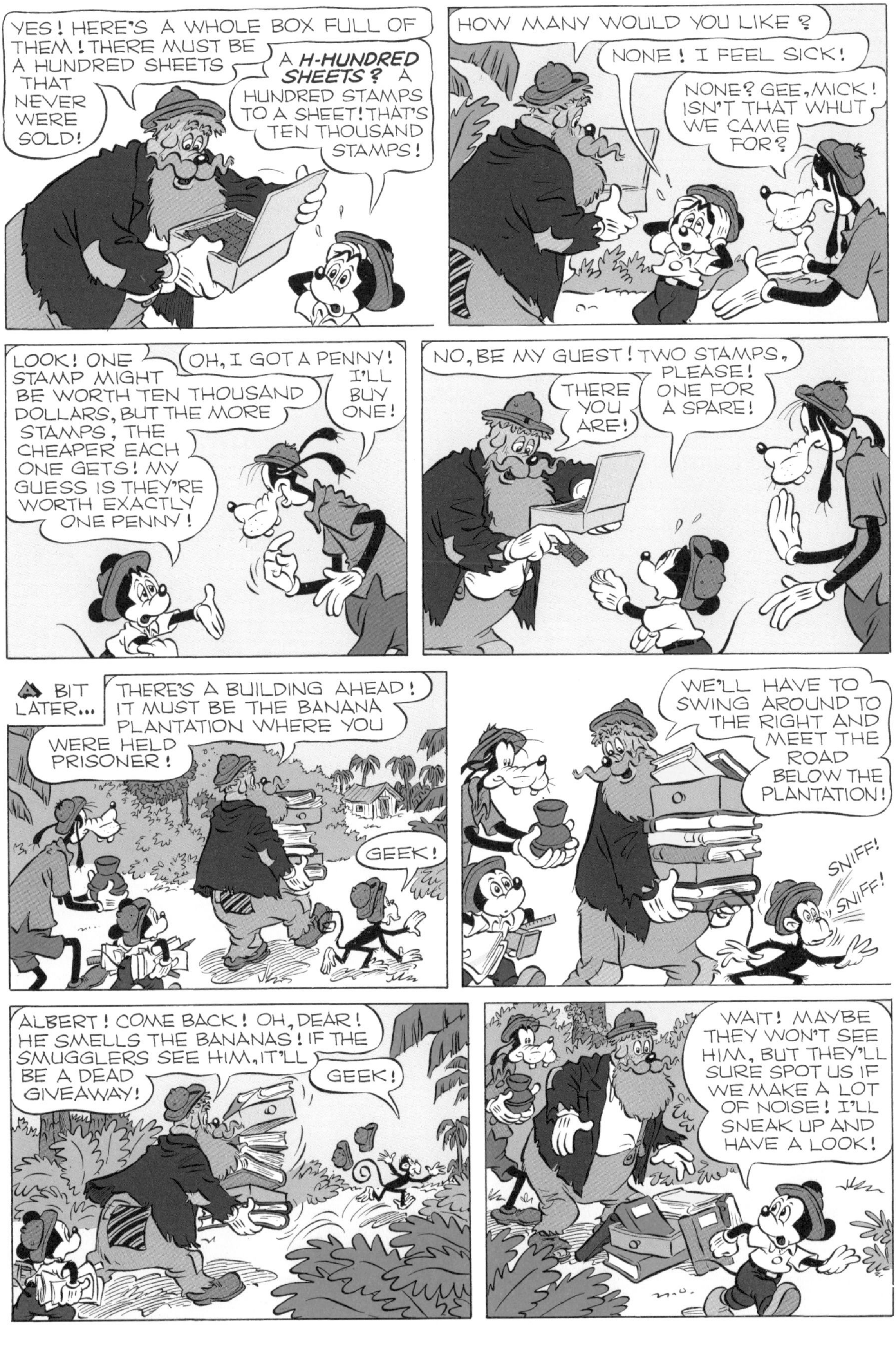
YES! HERE'S A WHOLE BOX FULL OF THEM! THERE MUST BE A HUNDRED SHEETS THAT NEVER WERE SOLD!
A H-HUNDRED SHEETS? A HUNDRED STAMPS TO A SHEET! THAT'S TEN THOUSAND STAMPS!
HOW MANY WOULD YOU LIKE?
NONE! I FEEL SICK!
NONE? GEE, MICK! ISN'T THAT WHUT WE CAME FOR?
LOOK! ONE STAMP MIGHT BE WORTH TEN THOUSAND DOLLARS, BUT THE MORE STAMPS, THE CHEAPER EACH ONE GETS! MY GUESS IS THEY'RE WORTH EXACTLY ONE PENNY!
OH, I GOT A PENNY! I'LL BUY ONE!
NO, BE MY GUEST!
TWO STAMPS, PLEASE! ONE FOR A SPARE!
THERE YOU ARE!
A BIT LATER...
THERE'S A BUILDING AHEAD! IT MUST BE THE BANANA PLANTATION WHERE YOU WERE HELD PRISONER!
GEEK!
WE'LL HAVE TO SWING AROUND TO THE RIGHT AND MEET THE ROAD BELOW THE PLANTATION!
SNIFF!
SNIFF!
ALBERT! COME BACK! OH, DEAR! HE SMELLS THE BANANAS! IF THE SMUGGLERS SEE HIM, IT'LL BE A DEAD GIVEAWAY!
GEEK!
WAIT! MAYBE THEY WON'T SEE HIM, BUT THEY'LL SURE SPOT US IF WE MAKE A LOT OF NOISE! I'LL SNEAK UP AND HAVE A LOOK!

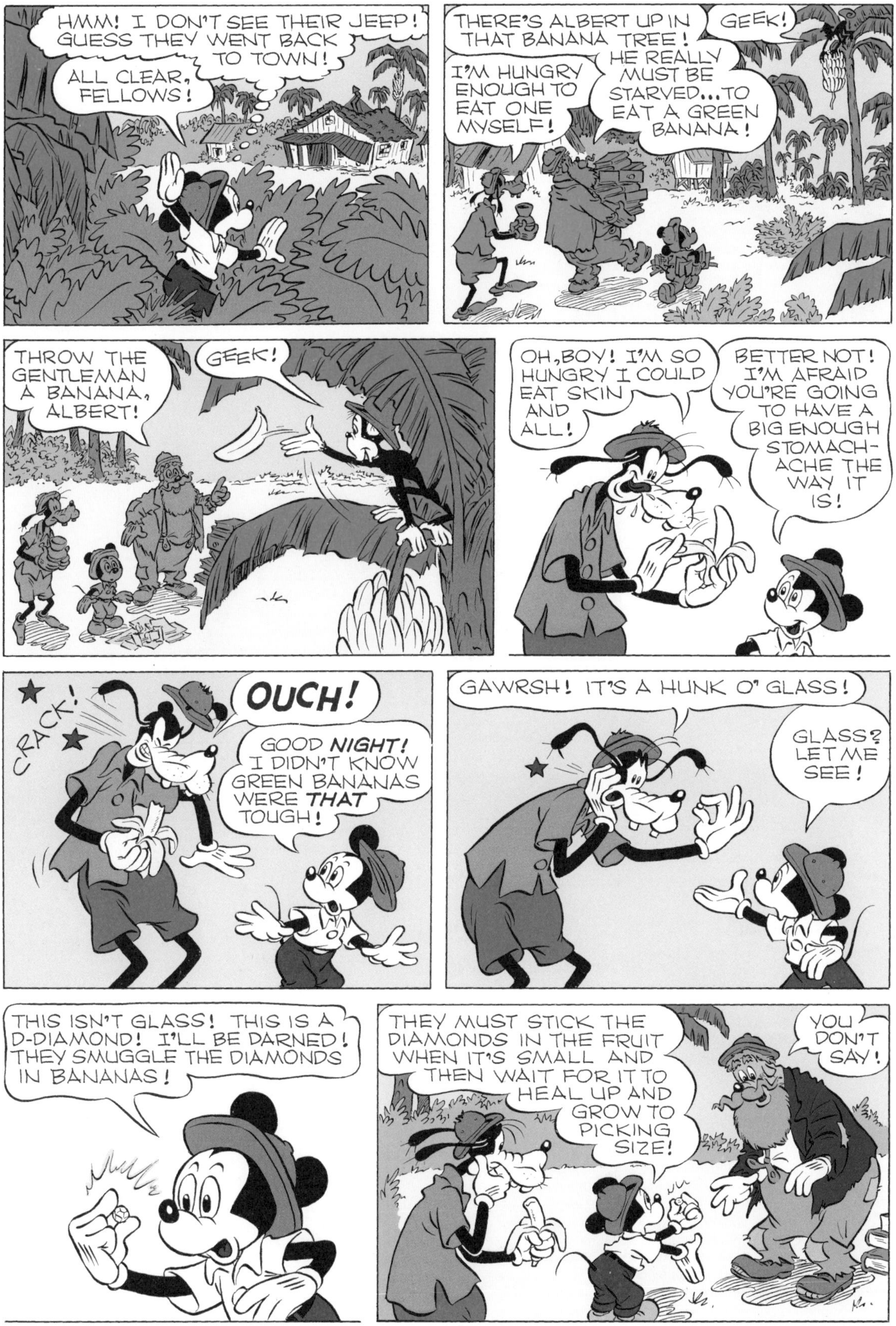

HMM! I DON'T SEE THEIR JEEP! GUESS THEY WENT BACK TO TOWN!
ALL CLEAR, FELLOWS!
THERE'S ALBERT UP IN THAT BANANA TREE!
GEEK!
I'M HUNGRY ENOUGH TO EAT ONE MYSELF!
HE REALLY MUST BE STARVED...TO EAT A GREEN BANANA!
THROW THE GENTLEMAN A BANANA, ALBERT!
GEEK!
OH, BOY! I'M SO HUNGRY I COULD EAT SKIN AND ALL!
BETTER NOT! I'M AFRAID YOU'RE GOING TO HAVE A BIG ENOUGH STOMACH-ACHE THE WAY IT IS!
CRACK!
OUCH!
GOOD NIGHT! I DIDN'T KNOW GREEN BANANAS WERE THAT TOUGH!
GAWRSH! IT'S A HUNK O' GLASS!
GLASS? LET ME SEE!
THIS ISN'T GLASS! THIS IS A D-DIAMOND! I'LL BE DARNED! THEY SMUGGLE THE DIAMONDS IN BANANAS!
THEY MUST STICK THE DIAMONDS IN THE FRUIT WHEN IT'S SMALL AND THEN WAIT FOR IT TO HEAL UP AND GROW TO PICKING SIZE!
YOU DON'T SAY!

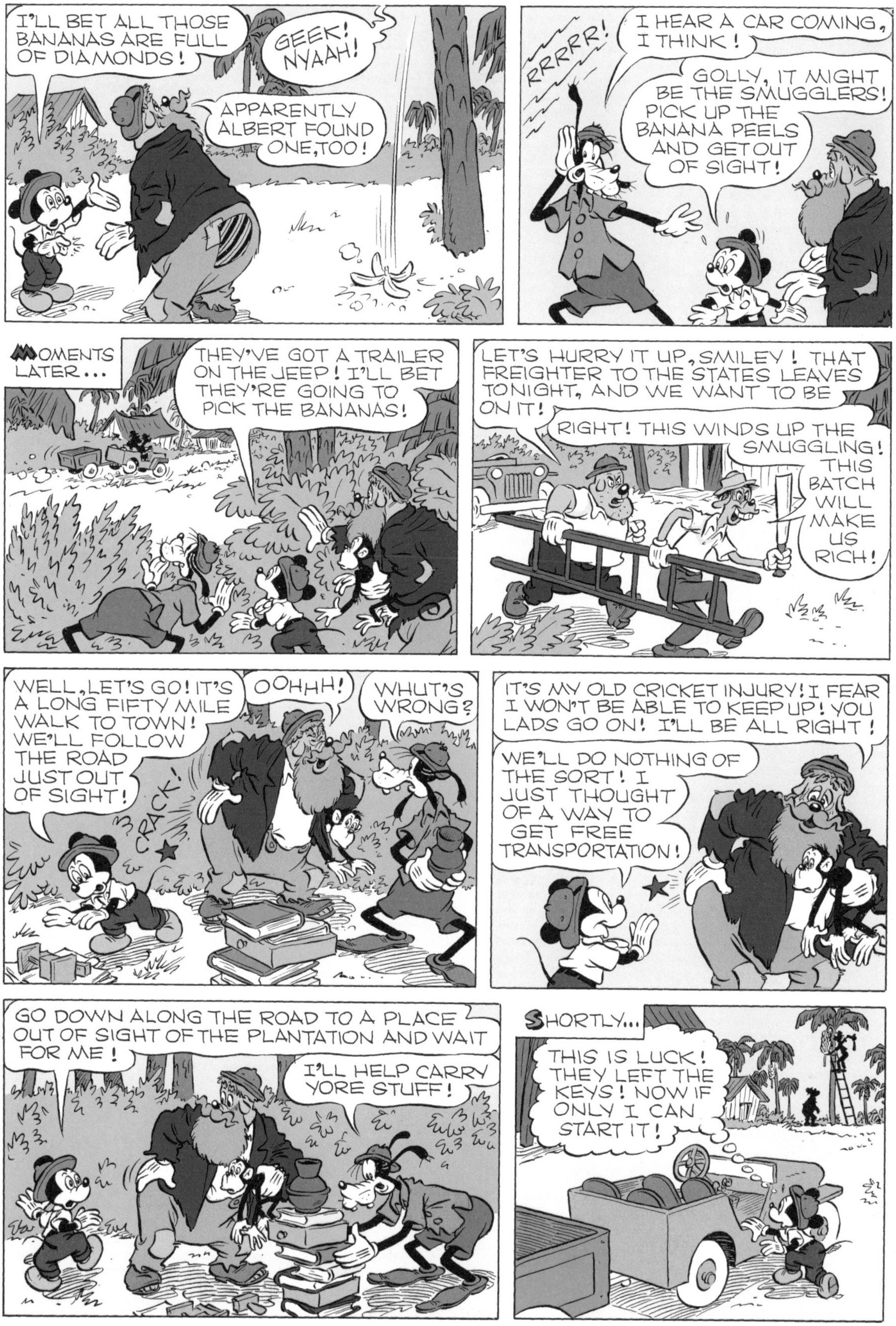
I'LL BET ALL THOSE BANANAS ARE FULL OF DIAMONDS!
GEEK! NYAAH!
APPARENTLY ALBERT FOUND ONE, TOO!
RRRRR!
I HEAR A CAR COMING, I THINK!
GOLLY, IT MIGHT BE THE SMUGGLERS! PICK UP THE BANANA PEELS AND GET OUT OF SIGHT!
MOMENTS LATER...
THEY'VE GOT A TRAILER ON THE JEEP! I'LL BET THEY'RE GOING TO PICK THE BANANAS!
LET'S HURRY IT UP, SMILEY! THAT FREIGHTER TO THE STATES LEAVES TONIGHT, AND WE WANT TO BE ON IT!
RIGHT! THIS WINDS UP THE SMUGGLING! THIS BATCH WILL MAKE US RICH!
WELL, LET'S GO! IT'S A LONG FIFTY MILE WALK TO TOWN! WE'LL FOLLOW THE ROAD JUST OUT OF SIGHT!
OOHHH!
WHUT'S WRONG?
CRACK!
IT'S MY OLD CRICKET INJURY! I FEAR I WON'T BE ABLE TO KEEP UP! YOU LADS GO ON! I'LL BE ALL RIGHT!
WE'LL DO NOTHING OF THE SORT! I JUST THOUGHT OF A WAY TO GET FREE TRANSPORTATION!
GO DOWN ALONG THE ROAD TO A PLACE OUT OF SIGHT OF THE PLANTATION AND WAIT FOR ME!
I'LL HELP CARRY YORE STUFF!
SHORTLY...
THIS IS LUCK! THEY LEFT THE KEYS! NOW IF ONLY I CAN START IT!

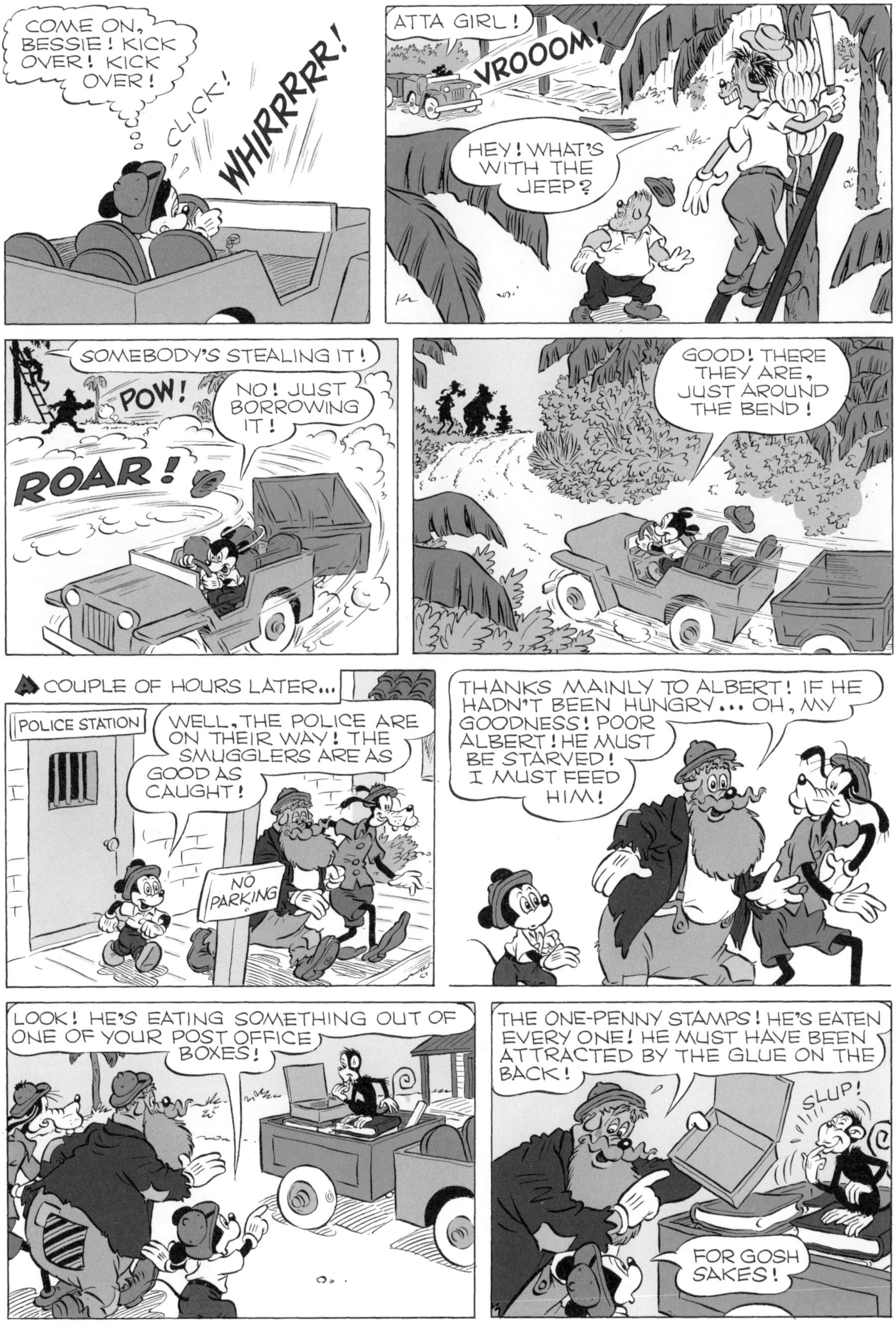

COME ON, BESSIE! KICK OVER! KICK OVER!
CLICK!
WHIRRRRR!
ATTA GIRL!
VROOOM!
HEY! WHAT'S WITH THE JEEP?
SOMEBODY'S STEALING IT!
POW!
NO! JUST BORROWING IT!
ROAR!
GOOD! THERE THEY ARE, JUST AROUND THE BEND!
A COUPLE OF HOURS LATER...
POLICE STATION
WELL, THE POLICE ARE ON THEIR WAY! THE SMUGGLERS ARE AS GOOD AS CAUGHT!
NO PARKING
THANKS MAINLY TO ALBERT! IF HE HADN'T BEEN HUNGRY... OH, MY GOODNESS! POOR ALBERT! HE MUST BE STARVED! I MUST FEED HIM!
LOOK! HE'S EATING SOMETHING OUT OF ONE OF YOUR POST OFFICE BOXES!
THE ONE-PENNY STAMPS! HE'S EATEN EVERY ONE! HE MUST HAVE BEEN ATTRACTED BY THE GLUE ON THE BACK!
SLUP!
FOR GOSH SAKES!

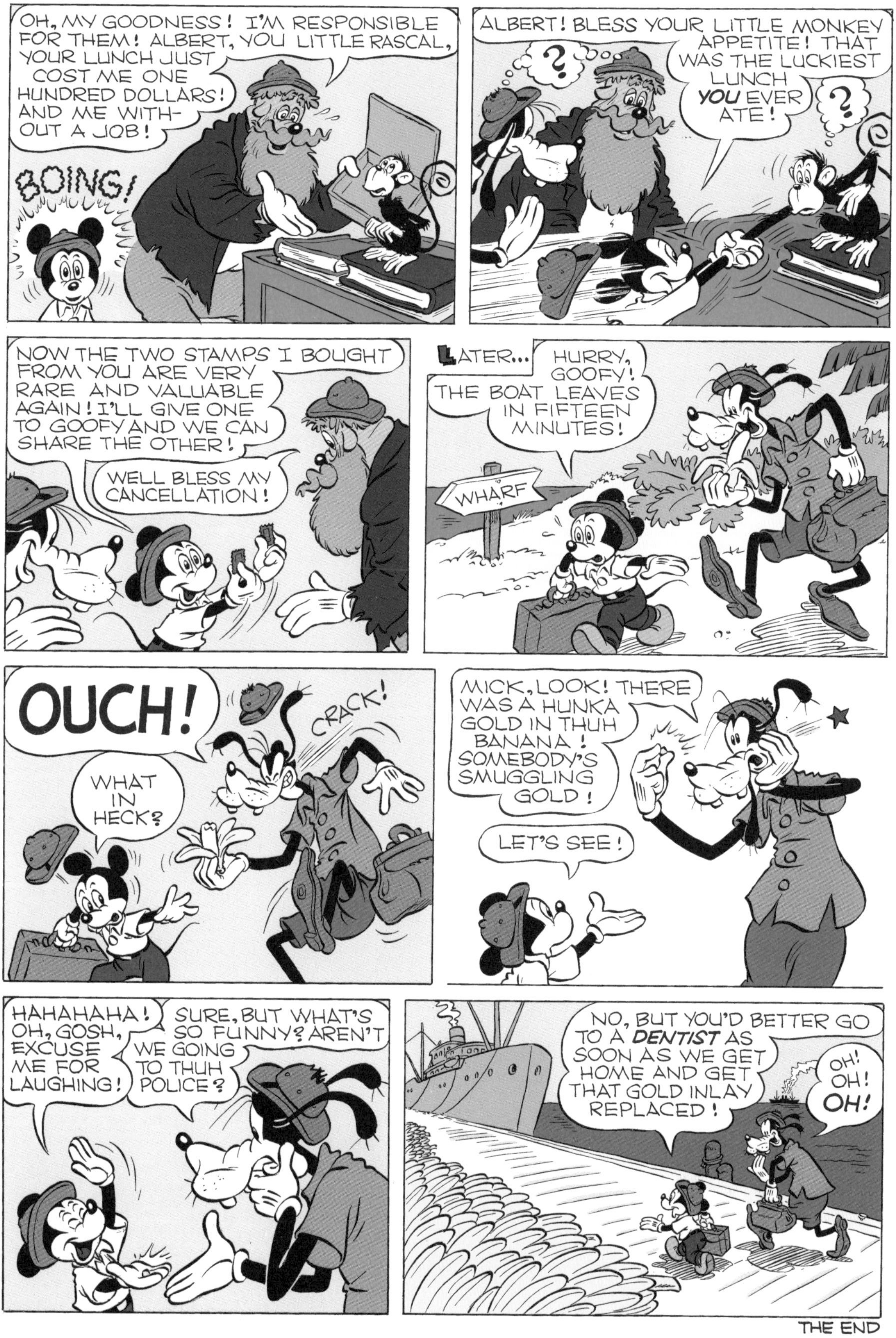
OH, MY GOODNESS! I'M RESPONSIBLE FOR THEM! ALBERT, YOU LITTLE RASCAL, YOUR LUNCH JUST COST ME ONE HUNDRED DOLLARS! AND ME WITH-OUT A JOB!
BOING!
ALBERT! BLESS YOUR LITTLE MONKEY APPETITE! THAT WAS THE LUCKIEST LUNCH YOU EVER ATE!
?
?
NOW THE TWO STAMPS I BOUGHT FROM YOU ARE VERY RARE AND VALUABLE AGAIN! I'LL GIVE ONE TO GOOFY AND WE CAN SHARE THE OTHER!
WELL BLESS MY CANCELLATION!
LATER...
HURRY, GOOFY! THE BOAT LEAVES IN FIFTEEN MINUTES!
WHARF
OUCH!
CRACK!
WHAT IN HECK?
MICK, LOOK! THERE WAS A HUNKA GOLD IN THUH BANANA! SOMEBODY'S SMUGGLING GOLD!
LET'S SEE!
HAHAHAHA! OH, GOSH, EXCUSE ME FOR LAUGHING!
SURE, BUT WHAT'S SO FUNNY? AREN'T WE GOING TO THUH POLICE?
NO, BUT YOU'D BETTER GO TO A DENTIST AS SOON AS WE GET HOME AND GET THAT GOLD INLAY REPLACED!
OH! OH! OH!

THE END

Paul Murry

by GERMUND VON WOWERN

IT WAS A cold winter's evening in the new year of 1938. Heavy snow covered northwest Missouri and the city of St. Joseph. Paul Murry, a 26-year-old artist and employee of the Artcrafts Engraving Co., suddenly found himself stranded in the city when his bus home was cancelled.

Unaware that he was making a life-changing decision, Murry walked over to the old Missouri Theater to see a new animated feature film, *Snow White and the Seven Dwarfs*. In an interview three decades later with comics scholar Donald Ault, Murry briefly recalled that long-ago evening: "I didn't realize when I was looking at [*Snow White and the Seven Dwarfs*], that five months later I would be in Hollywood."

At the time of Ault's interview, Murry could look back at thousands of penciled and inked comic book pages — his Mickey Mouse stories had been printed in hundreds of millions of newsstand comic books, and his Disney artwork had captivated children around the globe.

That snowy evening in 1938, little in Paul Murry's life foretold such a successful career. Born November 25, 1911, he was raised in Stanberry, 45 miles north of St. Joseph, and spent his young years on a farm, living with his grandparents and devoting himself to farm chores. His mother's fate is unknown; she disappears from records not long after his birth. His father remarried in 1917, just days after Paul's sixth birthday. Murry's unpretentious countryside childhood shaped him for life. The image of Murry that emerges from interviews, family members, and acquaintances is that of a highly pragmatic person. His granddaughter Shannon Murry captured his spirit perhaps better than anyone: "Paul liked things simple. He seemed to be a lonely man, yet preferred it that way. He always poked fun at everything, almost as if he saw life in a cartoon manner."

Paul Murry in 1951. Photo © and courtesy Richard Huemer.

Yet he did not interact much with other professional artists, with whom he felt he had little in common. He loved the outdoors and playing the harmonica, and he often rose early to play before sitting down at his drawing table.

It was likely Murry's unyielding nature — combined with his interest in drawing — that landed him his employment at the engraving company, despite his lack of formal art education. According to Murry's own account, he entered a puzzle contest in 1937 and decorated his entry with drawings, which caught the eye of the organizers. Not only did he win first prize — a piano — but he was offered a position at the engraving company doing what he later described as "commercial advertising" art. With that work experience — and *Snow White* fresh in mind — he answered an ad from the Disney studio and was given a trainee position. His grandmother then sold the piano, which paid for his trip across the country.

Thus, on June 6, 1938, Murry walked through the doors of the Disney Studio for the first time. Less than four months later, on September 26, he was officially hired and placed in the training department. Murry's employment as inbetweener and assistant animator at the studio taught him a lot. He soon found himself assisting Fred Moore, the studio's principal Mickey man, whose animation work Murry admired immensely. Murry's years with Moore, which included work on *Fantasia* (1940), formed his view of what "Disney art" should look like. Moore's major lesson for Murry — which Murry carried with him to the comics — was that any Disney character drawn correctly had to lend itself to animation. Murry never mimicked popular artists whose styles relied on improvising from panel to panel, imprecise ink lines, stiff poses, tweaking of

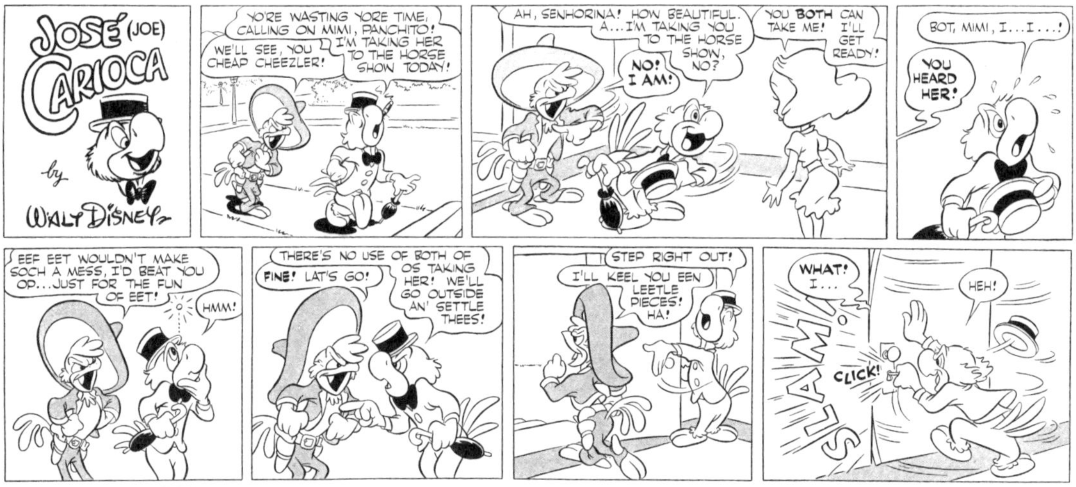
JOSÉ (JOE) CARIOCA
by WALT DISNEY
YO'RE WASTING YORE TIME, CALLING ON MIMI, PANCHITO!
WE'LL SEE, YOU CHEAP CHEEZLER!
I'M TAKING HER TO THE HORSE SHOW TODAY!
AH, SENHORINA! HOW BEAUTIFUL. A...I'M TAKING YOU TO THE HORSE SHOW, NO?
NO! I AM!
YOU BOTH CAN TAKE ME! I'LL GET READY!
BOT, MIMI, I...I...!
YOU HEARD HER!
EEF EET WOULDN'T MAKE SOCH A MESS, I'D BEAT YOU OP...JUST FOR THE FUN OF EET!
HMM!
THERE'S NO USE OF BOTH OF OS TAKING HER! WE'LL GO OUTSIDE AN' SETTLE THEES!
FINE! LAT'S GO!
STEP RIGHT OUT!
I'LL KEEL YOU EEN LEETLE PIECES! HA!
WHAT! I...
HEH!
SLAM!
CLICK!

Murry's first comics work with Disney characters were *Silly Symphonies* strips starring the eternally lovestruck José Carioca and his temperamental caballero friend, Panchito. *Silly Symphonies*, Sunday, May 28, 1944. Image courtesy Disney Publishing Worldwide.

perspectives, or breaking of the fourth wall. Instead, Murry's fairly thick ink lines, drawn with a seemingly determined and steady hand, gave his comics artwork a distinct and easily recognizable quality.

Murry was a fast learner in the Disney animation department. After *Fantasia*, he went on to work on *Dumbo* (1941), *Saludos Amigos* (1942), and *Song of the South* (1946). Gradually, however, he got more involved with the comic strip department — and with its manager, *Mickey Mouse* daily strip artist Floyd Gottfredson, who assigned Murry an increasing number of important jobs. His first comic art task was to pencil the José Carioca *Silly Symphonies* Sunday strips in early 1943, replacing artist Bob Grant, who had been drafted. The work suited Murry well. José was supplanted as the lead character in *Silly Symphonies* by Panchito, from the film *The Three Caballeros*, in 1944; then the *Symphonies* strip itself was replaced by *Uncle Remus and His Tales of Brer Rabbit* beginning October 14, 1945.

In a glimpse of what the future held for him, Murry also occasionally ghosted the *Mickey Mouse* daily strip between 1944 and 1946, when Gottfredson needed help to catch up on his deadlines. Seen from today's vantage point, these strips showcase Murry's eventual *Mickey Mouse* comic book style. But always the critic — not least of his own work — Murry did not hold his early *Mickey* newspaper strips in high regard when later asked about them.

Upon Murry's arrival in California, he had initially rented a studio apartment within walking distance of the Disney studio. But in 1939, he married and moved in with Gladys Bennett, already the mother of seven children. Their son together, John, was born in 1941, followed by their daughter Peggy in 1944. In 1946, with a total of nine children to support, they decided that Murry should leave his job with Disney and pursue a freelance career.

In the summer of 1946 they bought a piece of land in Wendling, Oregon, a lumber town in which the sawmill had closed a few months earlier and property was cheap. Murry got a job picking ferns, but he also produced a large number of gag cartoons. Murry had sold such gags to various magazines as early as 1943, while still working at Disney, but he seems to have ramped up to at least one inked cartoon per day from 1947 to 1949. Most of his cartoon work, though innocent by today's standards, was published in the risqué magazines of the time. For some, he teamed with gag writer George A. Posner, resulting in numerous cartoons signed "Posner Murry."

It was the Brer Rabbit characters that pulled Murry back to the Disney properties and the resumption of his comics career. His first stories for comic books were drawn for Western Publishing and appeared in Dell Publishing's *Four Color* #129, December 1946, a Brer Rabbit issue. (Western, which held the license to create Disney comic books, arranged financing and distribution through Dell, hired writers and artists, and then printed the comics on its own presses to Dell's order. Dell's logo appeared on the covers, so the comics Western produced and printed were referred to as "Dell Comics." In 1962, Western ended its deal with Dell and continued on its own as Gold Key Comics.)

In between work on gag cartoons, Murry also drew several Brer Rabbit and Li'l Bad Wolf stories in 1947 for Western's flagship title, *Walt Disney's Comics and Stories*, thus keeping his hand in the comic book business.

In 1949, the Murrys returned to California. After another brief stint as a Disney in-betweener, Murry partnered with former Disney and Max Fleischer talent Dick Huemer to draw a humorous cowboy newspaper comic strip called *Buck O'Rue*. Huemer had created the character as early as 1948, but two years later the project was still in a holding pattern. With Murry's bouncy graphic characterization added to the mix, however, the strip was picked up for syndication and debuted in January 1951. Set in Mesa Trubil — a Wild West town "so rotten it got booted out of the U.S. of A." — *Buck O'Rue* combined its Western landscapes with a wild and cartoony rogues' gallery, possessed of all the ingredients for soap opera and intrigue.

Unfortunately, while it is obvious from the artwork that Murry enjoyed *Buck O'Rue*, the strip ran for less than two years in a very limited number of newspapers. On the upside, the demise of *Buck O'Rue* coincided with an early 1950s sales boom in Western/Dell/Disney comics, and Murry was suddenly in the right place at the right time. Murry's first three Mickey Mouse stories were long ones: "The Monster Whale" (24 pages, *Walt Disney's Vacation Parade* #1, July 1950), "The Mystery of the Double-Cross Ranch" (32 pages, *Four Color* #313, February 1951), and "The Ruby Eye of Homar Guy-Am" (16 pages, *Four Color* #343, August-September 1951). But it was only the start.

Mickey serials had been a regular feature in *Walt Disney's Comics and Stories* from the beginning, but they were just reformatted newspaper strip adventures, drawn primarily by Gottfredson. Now Western wanted to produce original Mickey comic book stories,

so, in 1949, it began inviting artists to illustrate new adventures. Having already drawn the three *Four Color* stories, Murry fit the bill, and his chance came in 1953. Magic occurred instantly when Murry's artwork was paired with the skills of writer Carl Fallberg, who was also a cartoonist and a devoted railroad enthusiast. "The Last Resort," featured in Volume 3 of this series, was the first of their *Walt Disney's Comics and Stories* Mickey Mouse serials.

The comic book Mickey Mouse, as he had graphically evolved by that time, was a serious-minded and relatively inexpressive figure, so Murry instead relied on Goofy to bring graphic comedy and humor to the panels — sometimes he featured the Goof in action sequences that seem almost animated. It was Murry who introduced the classic comics pose of Goofy holding his hand in front of his mouth, all the better to make him look constantly dumbfounded.

Another integral part of the Fallberg/Murry stories' appeal was their settings: wild woods, rugged mountains, mysterious swamps, or deep underwater. Murry excelled in his intricate renderings of weather elements such as rain, fog, snow, wind, and storms, and Fallberg soon began supplying him with scripts designed specifically to capture that aspect of his imagination.

Thus, like his Disney comics contemporary, Carl Barks, Murry found a stable income — and began his work on the stories he is most associated with — shortly after turning 40 years old. Like Barks, Murry had already experienced years

Murry's Goofy emphasized his befuddlement by holding his hand in front of his face, as in these examples from stories in this volume. How many can you find?

SEE THOSE MARKS IN THE GRAVEL? JUST LIKE SOMEBODY DRAGGED A BOAT UP!
THINK SO?
CRUNCH!
C'MON! WE'LL SOON FIND OUT!
SLOSH!
SLOSH!

Paul Murry's special sense of atmosphere is exemplified by his depictions of stormy weather in this volume's "Mickey Mouse and The Marvelous Magnet."

of hard work and struggle to support himself and his family. Like Barks, Murry used his life experience to create compelling stories well worth reading ell worth reading more than six decades later. The background elements of the Mickey Mouse stories inspired Murry to create graphically spectacular pages, while the use of the Disney characters allowed him to show off the storytelling skills he had first learned during his years in animation.

Carl Fallberg left the Mickey Mouse serials in 1962, and, with only a few exceptions, Murry continued to draw them until 1973. But they were not his sole output. With the exception of occasional gag pages, Murry never wrote his own stories — Western frequently called on him to draw scripts with a wide variety of other characters, including Donald Duck and Pluto, and he was even assigned a handful of non-Disney Woody Woodpecker stories.

That versatility made Murry a prominent artist in the mid-1960s transformation of American Disney comics. Declining sales and competition for readers drove the editors at Western to target the Disney stories at a younger audience. They also introduced new characters and combined heroes from previously separate universes within single stories: Goofy could team up with Mowgli, Donald Duck with Captain Hook. The mix suited Murry well, and he became the main artist of novel comic book titles — such as *Super Goof* and *The Phantom Blot* — which featured those crossover stories.

That peak in productivity was short-lived. In the 1970s, Murry's assignments turned him almost exclusively into a Mickey Mouse artist again, including, in 1971, a pivotal series of Mouse model sheets for Walt Disney Publications. As time wore on, Murry became less than enthusiastic about the comic books to which he contributed, gradually drawing fewer pages. His last regular Mickey Mouse story appeared in 1984 in *Walt Disney's Comics and Stories* #510, the final Western Publishing issue. Three more were later published posthumously. (Western had dropped its Gold Key brand in 1980 but continued publishing comics under its Whitman imprint until 1984, when it got out of the comics business altogether.)

Paul Murry spent his retirement years with his wife in their desert home just outside of Palmdale, California, taking wildlife and nature photographs, gardening their five acres, and playing his beloved harmonica. Comics became a very distant part of his life, and he likely preferred it that way. He died August 4, 1989, at age 77. But his delightful work lives on, and fans around the world continue to enjoy it.

Numerous scholars have generously shared information with me about Paul Murry's life and work. There is not room here to thank each one, but I would like to acknowledge three of them for their contributions: Donald Ault, for his devoted work preserving the history of many Disney comics artists, including taping a long interview with Paul Murry; Klaus Spillman, who interviewed Murry in letter form in the early 1980s; and last — but certainly not least — Murry's granddaughter Shannon Murry, who shared her insightful thoughts and knowledge about Murry's life and career.